HOSPITAL COST ANALYSIS

Developments in Health Economics and Public Policy

VOLUME 3

Series Editors
Peter Zweifel, *University of Zürich, Switzerland*
H.E. Frech III, *University of California, Santa Barbara, U.S.A.*

HOSPITAL COST ANALYSIS

by

J. R. G. Butler

Department of Economics,
The University of Newcastle, Australia

KLUWER ACADEMIC PUBLISHERS
DORDRECHT / BOSTON / LONDON

338.433621
B 98h

Library of Congress Cataloging-in-Publication Data

```
Butler, J.R.G. (James Robert Gerard), 1952-
    Hospital cost analysis / by J.R.G. Butler.
        p.   cm. -- (Developments in health economics and public policy
   ; v. 3)
    Includes bibliographical references and index.
    ISBN 0-7923-3247-4
    1. Hospitals--Cost of operation--Econometric models.
    2. Hospitals--Australia--Cost of operation--Case studies.
    I. Title.  II. Series.
    RA971.3.B875  1995
    338.4'336211--dc20                                         94-41366
```

ISBN 0-7923-3247-4

Published by Kluwer Academic Publishers,
P.O. Box 17, 3300 AA Dordrecht, The Netherlands.

Kluwer Academic Publishers incorporates
the publishing programmes of
D. Reidel, Martinus Nijhoff, Dr W. Junk and MTP Press.

Sold and distributed in the U.S.A. and Canada
by Kluwer Academic Publishers,
101 Philip Drive, Norwell, MA 02061, U.S.A.

In all other countries, sold and distributed
by Kluwer Academic Publishers Group,
P.O. Box 322, 3300 AH Dordrecht, The Netherlands.

Printed on acid-free paper

Printed in the Netherlands

In memory of my Father

James Butler

Born: 27 August, 1909
Died: 31 August, 1966

TABLE OF CONTENTS

PART B — EMPIRICAL RESULTS

PART C — HOSPITAL COST ANALYSIS AND
HOSPITAL PAYMENT SCHEMES

List of Figures

LIST OF TABLES

PREFACE

The central theme of this book is that economists interested in the empirical estimation of hospital cost functions face a dilemma. Theoretical developments in the analysis of production and costs for multiproduct firms over the last thirty years have deepened our understanding of the complexities involved in specifying and estimating cost functions for such firms. Along with these developments, a number of flexible functional forms have been proposed for investigating characteristics such as jointness, input/output separability and economies of scale (both overall and product-specific) in multiproduct firms.

However, flexible functional forms entail an exponential increase in the number of parameters to be estimated as the number of output categories increases. For hospitals, the number of output categories required to approximate within-group homogeneity of output is quite large. Consequently, economists seeking to estimate hospital cost functions are confronted with a dilemma. Adoption of a flexible functional form capable of incorporating a number of potentially important characteristics of multiproduct cost functions as testable hypotheses requires aggregation of hospital outputs into a relatively small number of categories in order to achieve parameter parsimony. The alternative is to adopt a more restricted functional form which incorporates these characteristics as maintained hypotheses but allows the use of a more disaggregated taxonomy of hospital outputs.

In short, economists working in this area face a trade-off between flexibility in functional form and homogeneity within hospital output categories.

The book seeks to provide an overview and clarification of the theoretical developments in the analysis of production and costs for multiproduct firms, and to illustrate the difficulties in estimating hospital cost functions by reference to an empirical analysis of hospital costs in two States of Australia. It also provides a discussion of hospital cost functions in the context of hospital payment schemes, including the scheme based upon Diagnosis Related Groups (DRGs). In so doing, it draws together the relevant literature from microeconomic theory and health economics, providing a synthesis which is presently unavailable in any other single source.

The book should be of interest to both students of health economics and researchers interested in the estimation of hospital cost functions. It should also be of some use to health policy advisers interested in, for example, an overview of the effects of public/private ownership on hospital costs or a discussion of multiproduct cost functions and the DRG hospital payment scheme. Only an elementary understanding of calculus is required to digest the arguments in those sections where mathematical notation has been employed.

This book has grown out of my PhD thesis submitted to the Department of Economics at the University of Queensland and I am indebted to my supervisor, Ron Lane, for his comments and guidance during my candidature. Sam Strong, also from that Department, provided helpful comments on several chapters.

The Commonwealth Department of Health in Australia provided financial assistance for this work by way of Health Services Research and Development Grants, while the Planning and Development Unit in the Queensland Department of Health allowed access to the data on Queensland hospitals and assisted with the data processing. While several members of this Unit were helpful in various ways, I am particularly indebted to Bill Stomfai who was tireless and unstinting in his provision of computing assistance. The New South Wales Department of Health kindly made available the data on New South Wales public hospitals. Without the assistance of these individuals and organisations, the empirical work presented in this book could not have been undertaken.

I am also indebted to The Australian National University (where I spent several enjoyable years as a Senior Research Fellow in the National Centre for Epidemiology and Population Health) for its financial assistance in bringing this book to fruition.

My wife, Colleen, and children, Stacey, Jimmy and Erica, have borne the usual external costs associated with these endeavours. To them, I can now say unambiguously, "Yes, the book is finished—for the moment".

1

INTRODUCTION

Health economics is a relatively recent addition to the economics domain—twenty years ago it was described as being "as yet only in its adolescence" (Cooper and Culyer 1973, p.7). Since then, however, it has grown quickly, with the first journal devoted solely to this branch of economics—the *Journal of Health Economics*—being launched in 1982, and another—*Health Economics*—in 1992.

Within the health economics sphere, hospitals have received considerable attention. This is not surprising given the central role they play in the health care system. Described by Feldstein (1993, p.214) as "the most important institutional setting to be analyzed", hospitals account for a considerable proportion of total expenditures on health care. For example, in 1989 in the United States (US), expenditures on hospitals amounted to 46% of all total health care expenditures. This compares with Australia (48%), Canada (49%), the United Kingdom (56%) and New Zealand (57%) (Organisation for Economic Co-operation and Development (OECD) 1993).[1] The attention given to hospitals by economists and others is then commensurate with their role in the health care system.

---

[1]   The figure for the United Kingdom is for 1988.

The central concern of this book is indicated by its title—the analysis of hospital cost behaviour. It has three major objectives which are addressed in the three major parts of which it is comprised. First, it seeks to provide an overview and clarification of the economic theory of production and cost in the multiproduct firm paying particular attention to the conceptual, measurement and classification problems involved in dealing with hospital output. Using this theoretical basis, the second main objective is to undertake an empirical analysis of hospital costs specifically incorporating the multiproduct nature of hospital output. Third, it seeks to demonstrate the relevance of hospital cost analysis to hospital payment schemes.

As with the analysis of costs of any industry, two major issues must be addressed. First, a specific functional form for the cost/output relationship must be selected. Second, the problems of conceptualising, measuring and classifying the output of firms in the industry have to be considered. These two issues are considered in Part A, in Chapters 2 and 3 respectively.

In discussing the question of functional form, Chapter 2 provides an overview of the economic theory of production and costs in the multiproduct firm. The last few decades have witnessed significant advances in the theoretical and empirical analysis of multiproduct firms. Arguably one of the most notable contributions in this area of late is the work of Baumol, Panzar and Willig (1982) who, in rigorously investigating the concept of a contestable market in the economics of industrial organisation, have explicitly incorporated the multiproduct firm into the analysis. In surveying these developments, it is argued in this chapter that there is an inconsistency in some results which have been obtained concerning non-jointness, overall returns to scale and product-specific returns to scale. This inconsistency is clarified, but the main purpose of the chapter is to highlight the point that complex functional forms which incorporate, as testable hypotheses, all of the major possible cost characteristics of a multiproduct firm, do so at the expense of parameter parsimony. The trade-off becomes increasingly acute as the number of possible output categories increases.

Chapter 3 then addresses the second of the two major issues mentioned above—the concept, measurement and classification of output—with respect to hospitals. It is argued here that the 'health status' conception of hospital output, which views hospitals as producing improvements in the health of patients, can be rejected on both conceptual and pragmatic grounds. A 'treatment' conception of output is defended, a proximate measure of which is the number of episodes of hospitalisation, or cases discharged. The 'day' is rejected as a unit of output on the grounds that it is an input-related concept. Classifying cases so as to take account of the different outputs (treatments) produced by a hospital results in a potentially large number of output categories, and so the trade-off discussed in Chapter 2 becomes particularly acute. Hospital cost analysts then face a dilemma—adopting sophisticated functional forms for the cost/output relationship requires a relatively small number of output categories be used with a consequent increase in the heterogeneity of case types within any output category. Alternatively, a larger number of output categories can be employed using a more restricted functional form.

Part B of the book (Chapters 4-9) presents empirical results based upon data from hospitals in the States of Queensland and New South Wales, Australia. Following an overview in Chapter 4 of the public hospital system in Queensland (to which most of the results pertain), Chapters 5 and 6 examine the effects of output mix, or case mix, scale, utilisation and input prices on hospital costs. Chapters 7-9 each involve a comparison of two groups of hospitals. The general objective in these chapters is to document the differences in cost, case mix, scale and utilisation which exist between the two groups and ascertain whether any cost differences between them are explicable by differences in output composition, scale and utilisation. In Chapter 7, the two groups of hospitals are formed on the basis of whether they are teaching or non-teaching hospitals. Chapter 8 uses a public/private dichotomy while Chapter 9 undertakes a comparison of hospital costs in two States of Australia.

The empirical analysis presented in Part B of the book works with a restricted functional form which enables a larger number of hospital output categories to be employed as compared with a flexible functional form containing the same number of parameters. Case mix is found to be an important determinant of interhospital variation in average cost per case but the individual case mix category parameter estimates have incorrect signs and large variances (Chapter 5). The evidence suggests this problem arises because of multicollinearity and several alternatives are explored which may alleviate the problem. The *ad hoc* data reduction technique of principal components analysis is employed but this does not solve the problem. Increasing the sample size by pooling Queensland and New South Wales data also does not produce sensible estimates. The information theory scalar case mix index, whose complexity weights are also relative cost weights, did result in a set of plausible estimates being obtained.

With regard to the effects of scale and utilisation on hospital costs, only weak evidence of any scale effects is found, but utilisation of capacity is found to exert an important influence on average cost per case in every year and in every specification (Chapter 6). Increasing the case flow rate, whether by increasing occupancy or reducing average length of stay, reduces average cost per case.

Differences in costs and other factors between various groups of hospitals are also examined. Hospital groups are formed on the basis of being either teaching or non-teaching (Chapter 7), public or private (Chapter 8), and located in Queensland or New South Wales (Chapter 9). There is only limited evidence of any independent influence of teaching on hospital costs. Some evidence is found that private hospitals have a lower average cost per case than predicted on the basis of their case mix, scale and utilisation, suggesting a superior cost performance as compared with public hospitals. This conclusion, however, is tentative because of the meagre private hospital cost data available. For the interstate comparisons, Queensland's superior cost performance is found to remain even after adjustment for case mix, scale and utilisation, supporting the argument that organisational factors as manifested in that State's high degree of centralised control over its hospitals may be responsible for its relatively low average cost per case.

The empirical work in each of these chapters reflects the stance taken on various theoretical matters in Part A of the book. Two points in particular characterise this work. First, the functional form adopted reflects the trade-off which has been made favouring the use of a more finely disaggregated output classification scheme at the expense of working with a restricted specification of the cost function. Second, in view of the conceptual position adopted in Chapter 3 that the 'case' rather than the 'day' is the unit of hospital output, the average cost functions used in Part B all employ average cost per case as the relevant cost concept.

Part C of the book deals with a particular policy problem to which hospital cost analysis is relevant, *viz.* hospital payment schemes. The relevance of hospital cost analysis to hospital payment schemes is demonstrated in two ways. First, a possible performance appraisal and payment scheme is outlined using estimated cost equations, but it is concluded that the effects of multicollinearity on individual parameter estimates and on future prediction impart fundamental flaws to such a scheme. Second, the Diagnosis Related Group (DRG) payment scheme currently employed in the US and elsewhere is examined. It is argued that the scheme implies a restricted form of the multiproduct cost function precluding jointness in production, and overall and product-specific economies or diseconomies of scale. As a result it is concluded that, if these restrictions are not fulfilled and the volume and composition of hospital output are exogenous, the stochastic nature of hospital case mix will be reflected in the financial performance of hospitals. In this context some evidence is produced which suggests that hospital case mix does fluctuate through time and that, in Australia, small cell size may be a problem with the use of DRGs.

The main conclusions are summarised in Chapter 12.

PART A

THEORETICAL CONSIDERATIONS

2

THE ECONOMIC THEORY OF PRODUCTION

AND COST IN THE MULTIPRODUCT FIRM

2.1 Introduction

Although the single product firm often dominates theoretical treatises and textbooks on the economics of the firm, the importance of the multiproduct firm has long been recognised by economists. The first treatment of a firm producing more than one output appeared in John Stuart Mill's *Principles of Political Economy* (1st edn 1848). This presentation was in terms of joint production in fixed proportions, i.e. where the production of one commodity generates output of another commodity in a fixed proportion. Mill cited as examples coke and coal-gas; beef, hides and tallow; and chickens and eggs, amongst others. When production occurs in fixed proportions, the cost of producing a particular commodity bundle is a joint cost—"the outlay is incurred for the sake of both together, not part for one and part for the other. The same outlay would have to be incurred for either of the two, if the other were not wanted or used at all" (Mill 1909, p.570). It was argued that, in such cases, the price of each commodity will be such as to equate the demand for and supply of each, subject to the condition that the prices of the commodities are sufficient "to repay the expenses of their production, with the ordinary profit" (Mill 1909, p.570).

That Mill considered such cases to be unusual is evidenced by his relegation of the topic to a chapter entitled "Some Peculiar Cases of Value". The primary sense in which Mill considered joint production to be "peculiar" was that it afforded an example of the exchange value of commodities being determined by the law of supply and demand rather than by the cost of production, i.e. it was a case where the labour theory of value was inapplicable.[1] It can be inferred, however, that Mill did not consider such cases to be prevalent, since his treatment of this topic occupies less than three pages.

The above discussion indicates that the first appearance of the multiproduct firm in economics was in the context of joint production in fixed proportions. An extension of this analysis was provided by Marshall in his *Principles of Economics* (1st edn 1890) and later in his *Industry and Trade* (1st edn 1919). Marshall argued that "in practice ... there are few, if any, cases of joint products the cost of production of both of which together is exactly the same as that of them alone" (Marshall 1923, p.192). In so doing, he introduced the case of variable proportions.

The years since these authors' writings have seen significant theoretical and empirical developments in the analysis of the multiproduct firm. This chapter attempts to provide an overview of some concepts relevant to an empirical study of production and costs in such a firm. More particularly, the concept of jointness in production is investigated in more detail, along with input/output separability and returns to scale. Section 2.2 examines these concepts in terms of the multiproduct production function, while Section 2.3 presents the corresponding results which have been obtained for cost functions through duality theory. Section 2.4 relates the foregoing sections to the concepts of joint and common costs. Some specific functional forms for the estimation of multiproduct cost functions are discussed in Section 2.5 where it is shown that functional forms capable of testing for the existence of the characteristics mentioned above have a relatively large number of parameters to be estimated. This implies that the number of output categories which can be employed is less than in a more rigid functional form. Selected empirical examples are summarised in Section 2.6, and a summary and conclusions are presented in Section 2.7.

---

[1]   In discussing this chapter of Mill's, Blaug says "The case of joint costs presents a new qualification to the labor theory of value. Even in a one-factor economy, the relative prices of joint products—say, venison and deer skins—are determined by demand as well as supply" (Blaug 1968, p.198).

2.2   **Multiproduct Production Functions**

2.2.1   Jointness

In discussing the concept of jointness in production, it is convenient to begin
with a simple presentation of fixed and variable output proportions in terms
of the production possibility frontier. Consider a firm producing two
products y_1 and y_2 with given quantities of inputs. If the proportions in
which these outputs can be produced are completely variable, the firm will
face a production possibility frontier or transformation frontier such as *AB* in
Figure 2.1. A zero quantity of either output can be produced and the
proportions in which the two can be produced are freely variable between
these extremes.

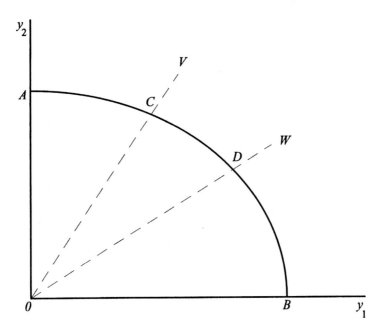

Figure 2.1. Production Possibility Frontier—Fixed and Variable Proportions

If output proportions are variable only within certain bounds, then only a
portion of the frontier *AB* will be relevant. For example, the proportions
indicated by the rays *0V* and *0W* in Figure 2.1 may be the limits within

which proportions can be varied, in which case the transformation frontier becomes *CD*, demonstrating limited variability in proportions.[2]

If the two products must be produced in fixed proportions, the ratio in which they must be produced will be indicated by a ray through the origin such as *0V* in Figure 2.1. The given quantity of resources enables production only at point C in this case. In terms of an analysis of production and costs, the fixed proportions case is relatively uninteresting because, apart from any separable costs incurred in bringing the products to a saleable state, the fixity in proportions renders the concepts of marginal and average cost of any one of the products meaningless. For the most part, this chapter concentrates on the case of freely variable proportions. Fixed proportions will be discussed again in Section 2.4 with regard to joint and common costs.

Suppose then that a firm is observed producing non-zero quantities of y_1 and y_2 along the frontier *AB* in Figure 2.1. Can this be described as joint production? The answer to this question is 'not necessarily', and derives from a clarification of the meaning of the term 'joint production' by Samuelson (1966). Consider Figure 2.2 which reproduces the frontier *AB*, and suppose the firm is at point *C*. The production process is characterised by joint production if the production possibility frontier arising from the production of the two commodities in separate production processes lies inside the frontier which arises when they are produced together in a single production process, given a particular resource endowment. That is, the production of the two commodities together results in a higher frontier being attained than if they were produced separately. This is illustrated in Figure 2.2 where the production possibility frontier under separate production of y_1 and y_2 is given by *ADB*. Conversely, if production of the two commodities together does not result in the attainment of a higher production possibility frontier then the production process is characterised by non-joint production.[3]

---

[2]   For a discussion of this case see Hibdon (1969). An advanced mathematical treatment is given by Shephard (1970, Ch.9). An example might be the limited variability in the proportions of various cuts of beef which could be obtained by selective cross-breeding.

[3]   A test proposed by Samuelson is to construct "pseudo-industry" production functions for each commodity by successively substituting a value of zero for all but one of the outputs in the industry production function. From this set of pseudo functions, a transformation frontier can be derived for comparison with the frontier arising from production of all commodities together. Samuelson's results have been extended to obtain sufficient as well as necessary conditions for non-joint production by Hirota and Kuga (1971), and to the treatment of mixed cases where specific subsets of commodities or industries may involve joint production by Burmeister and Turnovsky (1971).

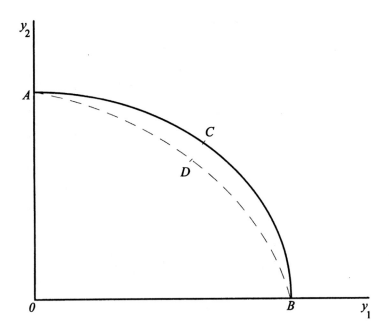

Figure 2.2. Production Possibility Frontier—Joint and Non-Joint Production

More formally, consider the following general specification of a production technology in implicit form:

$$t(y_1, y_2, x_1, x_2) = 0 \qquad \text{... (2.1)}$$

where x_1 and x_2 are the quantities of two inputs used in production. If the technology is characterised by non-joint production, then this multiproduct firm can be regarded as a collection of two single product firms each of which has a separate production function for one of the outputs, as follows:

$$y_1 = f^1(x_1^1, x_2^1)$$
$$\qquad \text{... (2.2)}$$
$$y_2 = f^2(x_1^2, x_2^2)$$

where x_i^j is the amount of input i used in product j. The output of each commodity depends only on the quantities of inputs devoted to its production. Because of the absence of any economies of jointness, the output of the multiproduct firm will simply be the sum of the outputs of y_1 and y_2 obtained from the separate production functions in equation (2.2). Hall (1973, p.880) states this as follows: "A technology expressed by a transformation function is said to be joint if there is no way to portray it in terms of separate production functions, and non-joint if it can be so portrayed."[4]

The presence or absence of joint production is then an empirical matter, and the imposition of non-jointness on the production function amounts to a restriction on the specification of this function. This can be seen by considering the following explicit form of the production technology given in equation (2.1):[5]

$$y_1 = h(y_2, x_1, x_2) \qquad\qquad \text{... (2.3)}$$

The output of y_1 is dependent on the output of y_2 in addition to the quantities of factors available, a more general formulation than the production function for y_1 given in equation (2.2). Mundlak and Razin (1971) have proposed estimating the following modified version of equation (2.2) to test for non-jointness:

$$y_1 = f^1(x_1^1, x_2^1, y_2)$$
$$\qquad\qquad \text{... (2.4)}$$
$$y_2 = f^2(x_1^2, x_2^2, y_1)$$

"If the empirical test shows that [2.4] does not reduce to [2.2], it is evident that there is joint production" (Mundlak and Razin 1971, p.493—our

---

4   Laitinen (1980) uses the term "output independence" to describe non-jointness for the following reason: "When three or more outputs are produced, this term [non-joint] becomes ambiguous because it is possible for two or more groups of outputs to be produced with no economies or diseconomies of jointness among the groups. Thus, production can be simultaneously nonjoint among the groups and joint within the groups. Use of the term "output independence" when all goods are produced nonjointly permits the term "block independence" to be used for the case of nonjoint groups" (p.63, n.6).

5   The explicit formulation is used by Samuelson (1966).

equation numbers inserted). However, this test requires data on factor allocations to products, a requirement which is seldom fulfilled.[6]

2.2.2   Input/Output Separability

Another restriction on the multiproduct production function suggested by Mundlak (1963) is input/output separability. In economic terms, separability of a function implies that a group of variables in the function can be separated from the remaining variables so that "the marginal rates of substitution between variables in that group are independent of the values of variables outside the group" (Blackorby, Primont and Russell 1978, p.1). In terms of the production technology in equation (2.1), input/output separability involves the grouping of inputs and outputs into separate functions as follows:

$$t(y_1, y_2, x_1, x_2) = -g(y_1, y_2) + f(x_1, x_2) \qquad \qquad \text{... (2.5)}$$

This then gives

$$g(y_1, y_2) = f(x_1, x_2) \qquad \qquad \text{... (2.6)}$$

Under this restriction, there is no interaction between individual inputs and outputs. The output function $g(\cdot)$ is an aggregator function, the value of which can remain unchanged for a range of values of y_1 and y_2, and similarly for the input function $f(\cdot)$. "With this kind of production the firm can choose its allocation of outputs independently of its allocation of inputs" (Laitinen 1980, p.6). The marginal rate of transformation between any pair of outputs is independent of input levels and the marginal rate of technical substitution between any pair of inputs is independent of output

---

6   Strictly, the concept of non-jointness elaborated here is that of a technology which is non-joint in inputs. Lau (1972) has defined a technology to be non-joint in outputs if there exist "individual factor requirements functions" (p.287) such that one input is 'broken down' into a number of outputs (e.g. crude oil used as an input into petrol and kerosene). Under output non-jointness there is a separate production possibility frontier for each input. Kohli (1983) has extended the concept of non-jointness to distinguish between non-jointness in input *quantities* and non-jointness in input *prices*, and between non-jointness in output quantities and output prices. These refinements will not be discussed further here. For an elaboration, see Chambers (1988, Ch.7).

levels or "distinct output trade-offs are available for a given set of aggregate inputs" (Just, Zilberman and Hochman 1983, p.771).[7]

When combined with non-jointness, input/output separability severely constrains the functional form of the production function and (as will be seen in Section 2.3) the cost function. It does, however, have an attractive feature from the standpoint of empirical estimation—it does not require information on factor allocations to products. Total quantities of inputs and outputs are all that are needed.

2.2.3   Returns to Scale

A third aspect of the multiproduct production technology which is often of importance is returns to scale or homogeneity. Following Hanoch (1970), a production frontier is defined to be homogeneous of degree h if, when all inputs are increased by a factor k, all outputs increase by k^h. In terms of the production technology given in equation (2.1), homogeneity implies

$$t\left(k^h y_1, k^h y_2, kx_1, kx_2\right) = 0 \qquad \qquad \text{... (2.7)}$$

Returns to scale are then increasing, constant or decreasing according to whether h is greater than, equal to or less than unity respectively. This accords with the definition of constant returns to scale adopted by Hall (1973, p.882).

A difficulty arises here, however, in that, for a multiproduct production technology, an equal proportionate change in all inputs will not necessarily give rise to a uniform proportionate change in all outputs. For example, if $k=2$, output y_1 may increase by k^2 while output y_2 increases by y^3. While both outputs have more than doubled following a doubling of all inputs, both outputs have not increased in the same proportion. Hence, this does not satisfy the strict definition of increasing returns to scale in terms of equation (2.7).

Lau (1972, pp.282-3) proposes a weaker definition based upon the concept of an "almost homogeneous" transformation function. For applied work, however, these complications can be avoided by dealing with the corresponding cost or profit functions. "Although one can surely spell out

---

[7]   An empirical study using a multiple output production function of this type is that by Klein (1953, pp.226-36) of US railroads. For a critical appraisal of this study, see Nerlove (1965, Ch.4) who points out that Klein's output function results in a concave transformation frontier. See also Hasenkamp (1976a, 1976b).

relatively plausible definitions of increasing or decreasing returns to scale, the economic phenomena underlying much of the applied interest in scale economies seem best addressed in terms of cost or profit functions rather than [the production possibilities set]" (Chambers 1988, p.258).

2.3   Multiproduct Cost Functions

The fundamental relationship which exists between the firm's production technology and its cost function has been demonstrated by duality theory. This theory has shown that, for a wide range of maximisation (minimisation) problems, a corresponding minimisation (maximisation) problem can be formulated. This corresponding problem is described as the dual of the original problem.[8] In terms of production and costs, the problem of maximising output subject to given input constraints has as its dual the problem of minimising costs subject to a given output level. This duality between production and costs has been explored intensively by Shephard (1970) and shows that the production technology "may be equivalently represented by a production function, satisfying certain regularity conditions, or a cost function, satisfying certain regularity conditions" (Diewert 1971, p.482). Several versions of this duality theorem have been developed, each differing according to the regularity conditions which are imposed on the production function (see Diewert 1974, 1982).

2.3.1   Jointness

Of particular interest in this Section are the results obtained by Hall (1973) who used duality theory to examine the implications of non-jointness, input/output separability and constant returns to scale in the production function for the specification of the cost function. The following cost function corresponds to the production technology given in equation (2.1):

$$C = C(y_1, y_2, w_1, w_2) \qquad \qquad ...(2.8)$$

where C is total cost and w_1 and w_2 are the per unit prices of inputs x_1 and x_2 respectively. Total cost is then a function of output levels and input prices.

---

8   A relatively simple exposition of duality theory can be found in Baumol (1977). For a more intensive treatment with applications to a range of economic problems, see Cornes (1992).

If the production process is characterised by non-jointness, the cost function in equation (2.8) can then be written as

$$C(y_1,y_2,w_1,w_2) = C^{(1)}(y_1,w_1,w_2) + C^{(2)}(y_2,w_1,w_2) \qquad \text{... (2.9)}$$

That is, each product *i* has a separate cost function $C^{(i)}$ with total cost being equal to the sum of the costs of producing each output separately. This corresponds to the production technology under non-jointness being the sum of the separate production functions given by equation (2.2). Again, the multiproduct firm can be regarded simply as a collection of single product firms with the cost of producing each product being independent of whether the products are produced together or separately.

The absence of economies of jointness is also evident in this result, for total costs remain the same whether the products are produced together or not. In terms of the cost function, joint production arises if the total cost of producing the two output levels together is less than the cost of producing them separately. The cost implications of joint production have been stated clearly by Carlson (1956, p.81): " ... the total cost of the joint output of the two products is less than the sum of the total costs would be if the two products were produced separately. There would be no inducement for joint production were this not true."

It is also evident from equation (2.9) that non-jointness implies that the marginal cost of producing each product is independent of the output level of any other product. Such products have been described by Carlson as being technically independent—"an increase in the output of one of the products will ... leave unchanged the marginal cost of the other product" (Carlson 1956, p.83).[9] As will be seen shortly however, the converse of this proposition is not true—technical independence does not imply non-jointness.

The concept of jointness in the cost function is closely related to the concept of economies of scope elaborated by Baumol, Panzar and Willig (1982): " ... cost savings may result from simultaneous production of several different outputs in a single enterprise, as contrasted with their production in isolation, each by its own specialized firm. That is, there may exist economies resulting from the *scope* of the firm's operations" (p.71—emphasis in original). For two products, economies of scope (or economies of jointness) arise if

---

9   In mathematical terms, this is reflected in the fact that the second cross-partial derivative between C, y_1 and y_2 is zero, i.e.$(\partial^2 C / \partial y_1 y_2) = 0$.

$$C(y_1,y_2) < C(y_1,0)+C(0,y_2) \qquad \ldots (2.10)$$

If this inequality does not hold, then the equation becomes identical to equation (2.9) (allowing for the dependence of the cost function on input prices) and exhibits non-jointness or an absence of economies of scope.[10]

Baumol, *et al.* have also shown that a sufficient condition for the existence of economies of scope is the presence of cost complementarities—the marginal cost of a product falls as the output of another product increases.[11] This is identical to two products being technically complementary in Carlson's terminology. It should be noted, however, that the converse is not true—the existence of economies of scope does not imply the presence of cost complementarities. This can be seen in the following example of a multiproduct cost function:

$$C(y_1,y_2) = F + y_1 + y_2 \qquad \ldots (2.11)$$

where F is a fixed cost independent of output levels or output mix. This cost function exhibits economies of scope because

$$C(y_1,0) = F + y_1$$

$$C(0,y_2) = F + y_2$$

$$C(y_1,0) + C(0,y_2) = 2F + y_1 + y_2 > C(y_1,y_2)$$

Production of each commodity separately entails a duplication of the fixed costs F and is hence more costly than their production together. There is, however, no cost complementarity—the marginal cost of each output is independent of the output level of the other.

It is pertinent to ask whether the cost function given by equation (2.11) involves joint production. Fuss and Waverman (1981) state that "economies

---

10   The concept of economies of scope is a restricted form of subadditivity in that the latter requires the inequality (2.10) to hold for *all* possible subdivisions of the output levels y_1 and y_2 among two or more firms, and not just for that subdivision which produces specialised firms. For an example of a cost function which exhibits economies of scope but not subadditivity, see Sharkey (1982, pp.68-9).

11   Mathematically, the second cross-partial derivative between C, y_1 and y_2 is negative, i.e. $(\partial^2 C / \partial y_1 y_2) < 0$.

of scope exist if and only if production is joint" (p.279) and that jointness in production "is known in the industrial organization literature as economies of scope" (p.283). In a comment on this paper, Braeutigam (1981) rejected this position, using a cost function of the form given in equation (2.11) to argue that economies of scope can exist even though production is non-joint. Using Fuss and Waverman's definition of a joint production process as one in which each input cannot be uniquely attributed to the production of a particular output, Braeutigam asserts that a cost function of the form (2.11) is non-joint even though all costs cannot be attributed to individual outputs. This argument, however, is a non sequitur. The fixed cost component F arises from the use of fixed factors which do not vary as output levels and output mix change. It is impossible to allocate those fixed factors uniquely to particular products. Jointness in production *will* arise in these circumstances because, if each output were produced separately, a set of fixed factors would have to be employed in each of the separate production processes. This is, of course, exactly what is reflected by the presence of economies of scope, as demonstrated.

What have been termed here fixed factors in relation to equation (2.11) have been treated by Baumol, *et al.* (1982) as "public inputs in the sense that, once they are acquired for use in producing one good, they are available costlessly for use in the production of others" (p.76).[12] These authors demonstrate that such public inputs give rise to economies of scope and, under stronger conditions, to cost complementarities. It should be noted again, however, that while cost complementarities are a sufficient condition for the existence of economies of scope, they are not a necessary condition. Economies of scope, and hence jointness in production, can arise in the absence of any cost complementarities, as in equation (2.11). Braeutigam's argument that this cost function is non-joint may have been based on the absence of any cost complementarities.

It is, of course, possible to *define* jointness in terms of cost complementarities, but this would lead to the conclusion that an absence of such complementarities means an absence of jointness, even though the costs of producing the outputs together may be less than the sum of the costs of producing them separately. It seems preferable, therefore, to adopt the Samuelson (1966) concept of jointness and the associated cost concept of economies of scope.

Before proceeding, it is worth summarising the relationships between jointness, economies of scope and cost complementarities. Jointness in

---

12   See also Panzar and Willig (1981).

production is manifested in a cost function if it is less costly to produce two or more outputs together than it is to produce them separately. This corresponds to the concept of economies of scope. Jointness, or economies of scope, can exist in the absence of cost complementarities, as in equation (2.11), but the presence of cost complementarities implies jointness or economies of scope.

The existence of jointness in the production technology gives rise to joint or common costs, a matter which will be taken up in Section 2.4. We proceed next to summarise the implications for the cost function of input/output separability in the production function.

2.3.2   Input/Output Separability

Hall (1973) has shown that if the production function is restricted to be input/output separable as in equations (2.5) and (2.6), then the cost function takes the following general form:

$$C(y_1, y_2, w_1, w_2) = C(g(y), w_1, w_2) \qquad \qquad ...(2.12)$$

Recall that under input/output separability, inputs and outputs are grouped so that there is no specific interaction between individual inputs and outputs. The value of the output aggregator function then becomes a function of outputs, with the marginal rate of transformation between any pair of outputs being independent of input levels. These results are reflected in the corresponding cost function (2.12). Costs are now a function of the value of the output aggregator function and input prices, with relative marginal costs being independent of input prices.

2.3.3   Returns to Scale

With reference to the multiproduct cost function, it can be shown that if the production technology is homogeneous of degree h then the cost function is homogeneous of degree $1/h$, (see Baumol, *et al.* 1982, pp.52-7), that is,

$$C(ky_1, ky_2, w_1, w_2) = k^{1/h} C(y_1, y_2, w_1, w_2) \qquad \qquad ...(2.13)$$

This is a generalisation of the corresponding result for a single product firm.

This concept of returns to scale is a concept based upon an equal proportionate change in all outputs. Baumol, *et al.* (1982) have employed this concept in defining scale economies in the multiproduct firm in terms of "ray average cost". With fixed output proportions, output changes cause a movement along a ray through the origin in output space. Ray average cost is the average cost of an output bundle at some particular point along a ray. The behaviour of ray average cost as all outputs expand proportionately forms the basis of the definition of multiproduct scale economies. Ray average cost (*RAC*) is defined as follows:

$$RAC = \frac{C(y)}{t} \qquad\qquad \dots (2.14)$$

where $C(y)$ is the total cost of the output vector y containing n distinct products $(y_1, y_2,..., y_n)$ and t is the proportion by which all outputs in y have been changed from the unit bundle of outputs y^0, so that $y = ty^0$. The degree of scale economies for the product set N at the output vector y is given by

$$S_N = \frac{C(y)}{\displaystyle\sum_{i=1}^{n} y_i C_i(y)} \qquad\qquad \dots (2.15)$$

where

$$C_i(y) = \frac{\partial C(y)}{\partial y_i}$$

The ratio S_N will be greater than, equal to, or less than unity as returns to scale are increasing, constant or decreasing respectively, and is the ratio of ray average cost to marginal cost of the composite commodity y.[13]

_____

[13]   The marginal cost of y is $dC(y)/dty^0$ where $y = ty^0$. Expanding this gives

$$MC(y) = \frac{\partial C(y)}{\partial ty_1^0}\frac{\partial ty_1^0}{\partial ty^0} + \frac{\partial C(y)}{\partial ty_2^0}\frac{\partial ty_2^0}{\partial ty^0} + \dots\dots + \frac{\partial C(y)}{\partial ty_n^0}\frac{\partial ty_n^0}{\partial ty^0}$$

$$= \frac{\partial C(y)}{\partial y_1}y_1^0 + \frac{\partial C(y)}{\partial y_2}y_2^0 + \dots\dots + \frac{\partial C(y)}{\partial y_n}y_n^0$$

$$= \sum_{i=1}^{n} y_i^0 C_i(y) \text{ where } C_i(y) = \frac{\partial C(y)}{\partial y_i}$$

(continued over page)

The above concept of returns to scale must be distinguished from product-specific returns to scale, the latter being based upon the behaviour of a firm's cost as the output of one product is varied while the outputs of all other products are held constant. Baumol, *et al.* (1982) have defined the degree of scale economies specific to a product *i* at output vector *y* as

$$S_i = \frac{IC_i(y)}{y_i C_i(y)} = \frac{AIC_i}{MC_i} \qquad \text{... (2.16)}$$

where $IC_i(y)$ is the total incremental cost of product i,[14] AIC_i is the average incremental cost of product i, and MC_i is the marginal cost of product i, given by $C_i(y)$ as defined above.[15] Again, this ratio will be greater than, equal to, or less than unity as product-specific returns to scale are increasing, constant or decreasing respectively.

The above definition of product-specific returns to scale can be expanded to encompass subsets of two or more of a firm's products. The degree of scale economies specific to such a subset *T* is given by

$$S_T = \frac{IC_T(y)}{\sum_{i=1}^{j} y_i C_i(y)} \qquad \text{... (2.17)}$$

$$= \frac{1}{t} \sum_{i=1}^{n} y_i C_i(y) \text{ since } y_i = t y_i^0.$$

Now $RAC(y) = \dfrac{C(y)}{t}$

So $\dfrac{RAC(y)}{MC(y)} = \dfrac{C(y)}{\sum_{i=1}^{n} y_i C_i(y)}$

which is the measure of the degree of scale economies given in equation (2.15).

[14] Total incremental cost is the cost of the firm's operations at output vector *y* less the cost of the firm's operations if product *i* were deleted from the product line, all other outputs constant. Total incremental cost includes any product-specific fixed costs.

[15] Note that the marginal cost of the composite commodity, defined in footnote 12, is actually a weighted sum of the marginal costs of producing each product with the weights equal to the output levels in the unit bundle y^0.

where there are *j* products in the subset. Again, this can be shown to be a ratio of 'average cost/marginal cost' with 'average cost' this time being the average incremental cost of the product set *T* and 'marginal cost' being an output-weighted sum of marginal costs.[16] Further, returns to scale are increasing, constant or decreasing as S_T is greater than, equal to, or less than unity respectively.

The degree of scale economies for a subset of products S_T given by equation (2.17) is 'consistent' with the degree of scale economies for the full set of products S_N given by (2.15) and with the product-specific degree of scale economies given by (2.16). If the number of products in the subset *T* is equal to the number of products in the full product set *N*, i.e. if *j* = *n*, then equation (2.17) becomes identical to (2.15), while if the subset is restricted to one product, i.e. *j* = 1, then equation (2.17) becomes identical to (2.16).

2.3.4   Non-Jointness and Input/Output Separability

Suppose that the multiproduct cost function is constrained to exhibit *both* non-jointness and input/output separability. Hall (1973) has shown that such a cost function (for two outputs and two inputs) has the form

$$C(y_1, y_2, w_1, w_2) = \left[g^{(1)}(y_1) + g^{(2)}(y_2) \right] \cdot c(w_1, w_2) \qquad \text{... (2.18)}$$

where $c(w_1, w_2)$ is the cost per unit of aggregated output.

It might seem unusual that the production function can possess both these characteristics simultaneously since input/output separability does not allow for any interaction between specific outputs and inputs while non-jointness requires separate production functions for each output. The above cost function does, however, allow for both restrictions. The individual cost function for product 1 is

$$g^{(1)}(y_1) c(w_1, w_2)$$

and similarly for y_2, reflecting non-jointness. At the same time, the influence of output on total cost depends only on the *value* of the output aggregator function

---

[16]   The derivation parallels that given in footnote 12. The concept of average incremental cost for a subset of products is analogous to ray average cost for the complete product set. See Baumol, *et al.* (1982, pp.68-70).

$$\left[g^{(1)}(y_1) + g^{(2)}(y_2) \right]$$

and not its *composition*—a given value of the output aggregator function determines a given value for total cost regardless of the individual values of y_1 and y_2 which underlie the aggregated value.[17]

The coexistence of both input/output separability and non-jointness imposes severe limitations on the separate functions for each commodity. In particular, Green (1964, Ch.6) has shown that the expansion paths for each production process must be parallel straight lines passing through the origin, implying that the isoquants for each separate production process are identical except for the output levels which attach to them. Hall (1973) expresses this by saying that "the separate production functions are identical except for pure scale effects" (p.891).[18]

---

[17]   Consider the following numerical example of a separable, non-joint cost function:

$$g^{(1)}(y_1) = y_1^2$$

$$g^{(2)}(y_2) = y_2^3$$

$$c(w_1, w_2) = \$10.$$

Then $C(y, w) = 10(y_1^2 + y_2^3)$

Now let $y_1 = y_2 = 2$. Total cost is then \$120 and will remain so as long as the value of the output aggregator function is 12. Hence any solution to the equation

$$y_1^2 + y_2^3 = 12$$

has the same total cost. The individual cost functions for y_1 and y_2 are $10y_1^2$ and $10y_2^3$ respectively, with marginal costs being given by

$$MC(y_1) = 20y_1$$

$$MC(y_2) = 30y_2^2$$

Relative marginal costs are then given as $(2y_1/3y_2^2)$ This ratio is independent of input prices, a characteristic of input/output separability. Any change in input prices will give rise to the same proportionate change in the marginal cost of each commodity.

[18]   In the words of Denny and Pinto (1978, p.252), for a non-joint production technology, "the production function is never separable unless the isoquants for each

2.3.5   Input/Output Separability and Overall Constant Returns to Scale

If the production technology is input/output separable and also exhibits overall constant returns to scale, then the joint cost function given in equation (2.12) becomes multiplicatively separable as follows (Hall 1973, p.882-3):

$$C(y_1, y_2, w_1, w_2) = g(y) \cdot h(w) \qquad \qquad \text{... (2.19)}$$

Total cost is now the product of the values of an output aggregator function $g(y)$ and an input price aggregator function $h(w)$. In contrast with equation (2.12), a change in relative input prices will now affect total cost only if it affects the value of the input price aggregator function.

2.3.6   Non-Jointness and Overall Constant Returns to Scale

Under these conditions Hall (1973, pp.884-5) purports to prove that the total cost function has the form

$$C(y, w) = y_1 \phi^{(1)}(w) + \dots y_n \phi^{(n)}(w) \qquad \qquad \text{... (2.20)}$$

where $\phi^{(i)}(w)$ is the cost of producing a unit of the ith output. This cost function certainly exhibits non-jointness (the total cost function is the sum of separate cost functions) and overall constant returns to scale (an equal proportionate change in all outputs will give rise to the same proportionate change in total cost), but it also exhibits product-specific constant returns to scale for all products. This is so because the cost per unit of the ith product —$\phi^{(i)}(w)$—is independent of the output of the ith product. In fact, Hall's proof is based on showing "that if the *whole* technology has constant returns to scale, then the *individual* cost function for a typical output, say the first, has the form of constant returns to scale ... " (Hall 1973, pp.884-5, emphasis added). That is, if the technology has overall constant returns to scale then, in the presence of non-jointness, each separate cost function will exhibit constant returns to scale.

---

technology ... are identical up to a renumbering of the isoquants." See also Lau (1978, pp.186-7).

This conclusion appears to contradict a result obtained by Baumol, *et al.* (1982, Ch.4). In examining the relationship between jointness, overall and product-specific returns to scale, these authors derived a formula which expresses the overall degree of scale economies S_N in terms of product-specific scale economies and the degree of economies of scope (or jointness). The degree of economies of scope at output vector y for the subset of products contained in set T is defined as

$$SC_T = \frac{\left[C(y_T) + C(y_{N-T}) - C(y)\right]}{C(y)} \qquad \ldots (2.21)$$

That is, it is the difference in costs between producing product sets T and $(N-T)$ separately as compared with producing them together, divided by the cost of producing them together. If there are economies of scope, i.e. if there is jointness, then the sum of separate costs will exceed the cost of producing the product sets together and SC_T will exceed zero. Similarly, if SC_T is less than zero there are diseconomies of scope (non-jointness) while if SC_T equals zero, production separately or together has no impact on total cost (also non-jointness).

The overall degree of scale economies as defined in equation (2.15) is related to product-specific scale economies and economies of scope as follows:

$$S_N = \frac{\alpha_T S_T + (1 - \alpha_T) S_{N-T}}{1 - SC_T} \qquad \ldots (2.22)$$

where α_T is the ratio of the output-weighted sum of marginal costs in product set T to the equivalent sum in product set N.[19]

Non-jointness under Hall's definition is equivalent to setting $SC_T = 0$ with the result that the overall degree of scale economies S_N "is a simple

---

[19] That is,

$$\alpha_T = \frac{\sum_{i=1}^{j} y_i C_i(y)}{\sum_{i=1}^{n} y_i C_i(y)}$$

where there are j products in set T and n products in set N with T a subset of N (see Baumol, *et al.* 1982, p.70).

weighted sum of its component product-specific scale economies" (Baumol, *et al.* 1982, p.74). Overall constant returns to scale (S_N = 1) combined with non-jointness (SC_T = 0) does *not* imply constant returns to scale in each product set (S_T = S_N= 1). For a given value of α_T (say α_T = 0·5), overall constant returns to scale could arise with increasing returns to scale in product set T (S_T = 1·5) and decreasing returns to scale in product set N-T (S_{N-T} = 0·5). Of these two conflicting results, it seems that Hall's is erroneous. Hall's proof is as follows. Since the cost function $C(y,w)$ exhibits overall constant returns to scale, $C(\lambda y,w) = \lambda C(y,w)$. Setting y_i = 0 for all products but one, and given that $C(y,w)$ is additively separable because of non-jointness, then

$$C^{(1)}(\lambda y_1, w) + C^{(2)}(0,w) + ... + C^{(n)}(0,w)$$

$$= \lambda C^{(1)}(y_1, w) + C^{(2)}(0,w) + C^{(n)}(0,w)$$

Taking $\lambda = 0$, $C^{(i)}(0,w) = 0$ for all i since the costs of any product cannot be negative. Finally, setting $\lambda = 1/y_i$ gives

$$C^{(1)}(1,w) = \frac{1}{y_1} C^{(1)}(y_1, w)$$

or $$C^{(1)}(y_1, w) = y_1 C^{(1)}(1,w) = y_1 \phi^{(1)}(w).$$

The problem with this proof is that it demonstrates that if there are overall constant returns to scale, and all outputs but one are set equal to zero, then the cost function for that output must exhibit constant returns to scale. This is intuitively plausible and does not contradict the conclusion of Baumol, *et al.*, but it does not prove that *all* of the cost functions of the remaining products must *simultaneously* exhibit constant returns to scale.

An alternative approach to the relationship between overall and product-specific returns to scale under non-jointness is to constrain the cost functions to be homogeneous and show that homogeneity of degree one in overall costs is consistent with homogeneity of degrees other than one in the separate cost functions. This is more restrictive than the proof by Baumol, *et.al.* which does not require homogeneity, but it parallel's more closely the proof given by Hall.

Suppose two outputs y_1 and y_2 are each increased by a factor λ. Under non-jointness the cost function can be written as:

$$C(\lambda y_1, \lambda y_2, w) = C^{(1)}(\lambda y_1, w) + C^{(2)}(\lambda y_2, w)$$

With overall linear homogeneity or constant returns to scale,

$$C(\lambda y_1, \lambda y_2, w) = \lambda C(y_1, y_2, w)$$

With homogeneity in each of the separate cost functions, overall constant returns to scale will be consistent with product-specific economies or diseconomies of scale if

$$\lambda C(y_1, y_2, w) = \lambda^a C^{(1)}(y_1, w) + \lambda^b C^{(2)}(y_2, w) \qquad \text{... (2.23)}$$

does not require $a = b = 1$ (or linear homogeneity in the individual cost functions). It can be shown[20] that the relationship between a and b consistent with the requirement expressed by equation (2.23) is

$$a = \frac{log\left[\left(\lambda(k+1) - \lambda^b\right)/k\right]}{log\,\lambda} \qquad \text{... (2.24)}$$

It can be seen from this equation that if $b = 1$ (i.e. if one product exhibits constant returns to scale) then $a = 1$ also (i.e. the other product must also exhibit constant returns to scale) if there are to be overall constant returns to scale. Now as b increases above unity (one product exhibits decreasing returns to scale), the term λ^b increases thus reducing the value of the numerator and hence of a, so that the value of a would fall below unity (the other product must exhibit increasing returns to scale). It is then possible for the separate cost functions to be characterised by product-specific economies and diseconomies of scale while overall there are constant returns to scale.

2.3.7   Non-Jointness, Input/Output Separability and Overall Constant Returns to Scale

Recall from Section 2.3.5 that input/output separability combined with overall constant returns to scale produced a joint cost function that was multiplicatively separable, being the product of an output aggregator

---

[20]   The derivation is contained in Appendix 2.I.

function and an input price aggregator function. Adding to this the constraint of non-jointness results in the output aggregator function becoming a linear weighted sum of the individual outputs. The cost function (for two outputs and two inputs) can then be written as

$$C(y_1, y_2, w_1, w_2) = (a_1 y_1 + a_2 y_2) \cdot c(w_1, w_2) \qquad \qquad \ldots (2.25)$$

The marginal costs of y_1 and y_2 are $a_1 c(\cdot)$ and $a_2 c(\cdot)$ respectively. For given input prices, the marginal and average costs of each product are equal and constant, and independent of the output level of any commodity, i.e. each product exhibits product-specific constant returns to scale. Relative marginal costs are given by the ratio (a_1/a_2) and are again independent of input prices.

It is evident from equation (2.25) that, for given input prices, total cost is a linear function of the output level of each product. Hence, while it embodies severe restrictions on the underlying multiproduct production technology, *viz.* input/output separability, non-jointness and constant returns to scale, it is relatively simple to estimate empirically. Further, the number of parameters to be estimated is equal to the number of products so that, for firms producing many outputs, it is relatively parsimonious in parameters. These points, however, anticipate later discussion and will be taken up again in Section 2.5 in the context of specific functional forms.

2.4   Joint and Common Costs

Joint and common costs arise from the presence of jointness in production. Recall that if production is non-joint, the multiproduct firm can be broken up into as many single product firms as there are products with no change in total cost. All costs are capable of being assigned to the product responsible for their incurrence, i.e. all costs are fully allocable to particular products on the basis of the production function, as evidenced in the general forms of the non-joint cost functions given by equations (2.9), (2.20) and (2.25). If production is subject to jointness as defined previously, then either joint or common costs will arise.

The distinction between joint and common costs is summarised neatly in the following definition by Kolsen (1968, p.50):

> There are joint costs when two or more products are produced
> jointly in technically necessary proportions and where the

> alternative to producing any one of them is either not to produce
> the joint bundle at all or to treat it as waste. There are common
> costs when two or more products are produced jointly and where
> an alternative to producing more or less of any one of them is
> producing less or more of the other(s).

Joint costs are then a result of products being produced in fixed proportions, while common costs arise if output proportions are variable and production is joint.

In terms of cost analysis, the case of joint production in fixed proportions is relatively straightforward. If *all* costs are joint, the general cost function given by equation (2.8) can be written as

$$C = C(y, w_1, w_2) \qquad \qquad \text{... (2.26)}$$

where y is a weighted sum of the outputs with the weights reflecting the fixed proportions of the outputs. In effect, the firm becomes a single product firm for the purposes of cost analysis.[21] In the words of Carlson (1956, p.75, our emphasis):

> *As far as the technical and cost relations are concerned,* there is,
> therefore, no difference between an analysis of joint production
> with fixed proportions and an analysis of simple production. In
> both cases the different relations may be expressed simply as
> functions of a single homogeneous output quantity.[22]

It should be noted that this conclusion relates to the implications of fixed output proportions for cost analysis. In an analysis of pricing, the presence of joint costs and the distinction between joint and common costs is of paramount importance, as will be seen shortly.

More realistically, in the fixed proportions case, it is unlikely that *all* costs will be joint. Typically, there will be costs associated with the preparation of each product for sale, such costs being specifically assignable to each particular product. These costs have been termed "prime

---

[21] It is interesting to note that the fixed proportions case results in an input/output separable cost function (compare equations (2.26) and (2.12)) with the output aggregator function being defined as a linear weighted sum.

[22] Henderson and Quandt (1958) make the same point: "The production of joint products does not require an extended analysis unless they can be produced in varying proportions" (p.67, see footnote 1).

costs" by Marshall (1923), but are more commonly referred to as separate or separable costs (Harbeson 1953; Wiles 1961; Kolsen 1966, 1968). The cost function (2.26) then becomes

$$C = C(y,w) + C^{(1)}(y_1,w) + C^{(2)}(y_2,w) \qquad \text{... (2.27)}$$

with $C^{(1)}(\cdot)$ and $C^{(2)}(\cdot)$ being the total separable costs of producing y_1 and y_2 respectively and w being a vector of input prices.

With joint production in fixed proportions, the average and marginal cost of any particular product is undefined. It is, however, possible to calculate the average and marginal separable cost of each product in the presence of separable costs. From equation (2.27) the average separable cost of y_1 is given by $C^{(1)}(\cdot)/y_1$ while marginal separable cost is given by $(\partial C^{(1)}(\cdot)/\partial y_1)$ and analogously for y_2.

In the variable output proportions case, costs which cannot be specifically assigned to the products responsible for their incurrence are termed common costs—costs incurred in common in the production of the various products. An important distinction between this and the fixed proportions case is that the marginal cost of any individual product is now defined, with the ratio of the marginal costs of any pair of commodities being equal to the slope of the transformation frontier or the marginal rate of transformation. This is so even though the common costs cannot be meaningfully assigned to the various products and the *average* cost of any product is undefined.[23]

As in the fixed proportions case, individual products may have separate costs directly attributable to them, extending the cost function (2.8) to

$$C = C(y_1,y_2,w) + C^{(1)}(y_1,w) + C^{(2)}(y_2,w) \qquad \text{... (2.28)}$$

The average cost of any particular product is still undefined since the common costs cannot be meaningfully assigned to individual products. Average *separable* cost, however, is defined in this situation.

The distinction between joint and common costs has important implications for pricing. With joint costs, marginal cost is undefined and the

---

[23] Recent research on the problem of allocating common costs has focussed on the achievement of 'fair' or 'just' solutions primarily through the application of game-theoretic methods. See Young (1985) for a collection of theoretical and applied papers on this subject.

relative prices of joint products are determined solely by demand, subject to the revenue from the sale of any product at least covering its separable costs. With common costs, marginal cost is defined and the relative prices of the joint products under perfect competition will equal relative marginal costs. This fundamental difference in outcomes lay at the heart of the celebrated Pigou/Taussig controversy over railway rates.[24] In this debate, Taussig took the position that the costs involved in transporting different commodities on a particular directional leg of a journey were predominantly joint and therefore justified differential prices. Pigou on the other hand contended that such costs were primarily common costs and that, under competition, a uniform rate would evolve for all classes of freight. While Pigou was correct in his argument that the costs were common, his argument that a uniform freight rate would emerge would only apply if the marginal costs of transporting different commodities were equal. This point was clarified in an often neglected contribution by Barone (1955).

The discussion in this chapter so far has outlined the concepts of jointness, input/output separability and returns to scale and examined the implications of these for the general functional form of multiproduct production and cost functions. The concepts of joint and common costs have now been integrated into this discussion. It remains to examine some specific functional forms which have been suggested for investigating the presence of jointness and input/output separability, and to illustrate these with some empirical examples.

2.5   Specific Functional Forms

In order to breathe empirical life into the concepts elaborated so far, the general functional forms for cost functions with which we have been dealing must be given specific, testable forms. If jointness, input/output separability and constant returns to scale are to be empirically investigated, then a functional form which allows the presence of these characteristics to be tested must be adopted. Alternatively one might, for reasons to be discussed shortly, adopt a functional form which includes one or more of these characteristics as maintained hypotheses, i.e. "hypotheses which are not themselves tested as part of the analysis, but are assumed true" (Fuss, McFadden and Mundlak 1978, p.222).

---

24   For an overview of this debate and references to the literature, see Ekelund and Hulett (1973).

An important development which has facilitated the empirical investigation of these characteristics is the concept of a flexible functional form. This has been described by Blackorby, Primont and Russell (1978, p.291) as follows:

> ... a functional form is flexible if the parameters of the functional form can be chosen to make the values of its first- and second-order derivatives (and, trivially, the function image itself) equal to the first- and second-order derivatives (and the level) of the function being approximated at any point (of approximation) in the domain.[25]

In other words, a flexible functional form can be made to approximate any function at a point by an appropriate selection of values for the parameters.

2.5.1   The Generalised Linear-Generalised Leontief Cost Function

A flexible functional form capable of testing the restrictions of input/output separability and non-jointness is the following Generalised Linear-Generalised Leontief Joint Cost Function proposed by Hall (1973):

$$C(y,w) = \sum_{i=1}^{n} \sum_{j=1}^{n} \sum_{k=1}^{m} \sum_{l=1}^{m} a_{ijkl} (y_k y_l)^{\frac{1}{2}} (w_i w_j)^{\frac{1}{2}} \qquad \text{... (2.29)}$$

For input/output separability, the estimated parameters a_{ijkl} must satisfy $a_{ijkl} = r_{ij} s_{kl}$ allowing equation (2.29) to be written as

$$C(y,w) = \left[\sum_{k=1}^{m} \sum_{l=1}^{m} s_{kl} (y_k y_l)^{\frac{1}{2}} \right] \left[\sum_{k=1}^{n} \sum_{j=1}^{n} r_{ij} (w_i w_j)^{\frac{1}{2}} \right] \qquad \text{... (2.30)}$$

This is a specific form of the general input/output separable cost function given in equation (2.19) with total cost being equal to the product of the value of the output aggregator function (given in the first set of square brackets) and the input price aggregator function. For non-jointness, all

---

[25]   This concept of flexibility is due to Diewert (1973), and is described by Blackorby, Primont and Russell as being "a fairly weak notion of approximation". They go on to derive a stronger approximation property which is beyond our concern here.

output interaction terms must vanish, giving $a_{ijkl} = 0$ for all $k \neq 1$. This is easily seen by taking two outputs with input prices constant, in which case equation (2.29) can be written as[26]

$$C(y,w) = b_1 y_1 + b_2 y_2 + b_3 (y_1 y_2)^{\frac{1}{2}} \qquad \qquad ...(2.31)$$

If the parameter b_3 attaching to the output interaction term is not significantly different from zero, this cost function exhibits non-jointness or an absence of economies of scope.[27]

While this cost function enables the presence of jointness and input/output separability to be empirically tested, it incorporates overall constant returns to scale as a maintained hypothesis. If all outputs are increased by some given proportion, total cost increases by the same proportion. Hence, even this functional form is not capable of incorporating all three of these characteristics as testable hypotheses.

A further important point to be noted about this cost function is the number of parameters to be estimated. With m outputs and n inputs, equation (2.29) contains $[m\,(m+1)\,n\,(n+1)\,/\,4]$ parameters. For example, two outputs and three inputs give rise to 18 parameters. If input prices are taken as constant so that (2.29) contains terms in outputs only (as in equation (2.31)), the cost function will contain $[m\,(m+1)\,/\,2]$ parameters. For two outputs this gives three parameters (as in (2.31)), with three outputs giving six parameters. While this is not an excessive number of parameters for small numbers of products, the number of parameters increases at an increasing rate as the number of products increases. For five outputs there would be 15 parameters while ten outputs give rise to 55 parameters. This arises because each additional output gives rise to one additional parameter in its own right plus a series of additional parameters attaching to the interactive terms between this and all other outputs. This illustrates an important limitation of flexible functional forms, *viz.* that they are not generally parsimonious in parameters.

---

[26]   The full expansion for the two output/two input case is given in Hall (1973, p.887). The b's in our expression can be written as functions of the a_{ijkl}, w_i and w_j, e.g.

$b_1 = a_{1111}w_1 + a_{2211}w_2 + 2a_{1211}(w_1 w_2)^{\frac{1}{2}}$

[27]   Diseconomies of scope would be indicated by $b_3 > 0$.

2.5.2   The Translog Cost Function

Another flexible functional form which has received considerable attention is the transcendental logarithmic, or translog, cost function.[28] If input prices are constant, this can be written as

$$\log C = a_0 + \sum_j a_{ij} \log y_i + \sum_i \sum_j a_{ij} \log y_i \log y_j \qquad \ldots (2.32)$$

Again, for m outputs, there are $[m\,(m+1)\,/\,2]$ parameters.[29] The translog cost function allows jointness, input/output separability and constant returns to scale to be treated as testable hypotheses or incorporated as maintained hypotheses with appropriate parametric restrictions (see Burgess 1974, 1975; Denny and Pinto 1978). A drawback, however, is that zero output values for any product are inadmissible (log zero is undefined) so that all firms in a sample must produce positive amounts of all outputs. This limitation of the translog cost function has been overcome by Caves, Christensen and Tretheway (1980), who have generalised this function by transforming the output measures so that a zero output level does not give a zero value of the transformed measure.[30]

2.5.3   The Linear Total Cost Function

It is evident from the above discussion that flexibility in functional form, necessary to test the hypotheses of non-jointness, input/output separability and constant returns to scale, is bought at the expense of parameter parsimony. Conversely, if one or more of these characteristics is incorporated as a maintained hypothesis, the number of parameters to be estimated can be reduced. Indeed, as has already been shown, if the cost function is constrained to exhibit non-jointness, input/output separability

---

[28]   The function is transcendental, or non-algebraic, because the parameters to be estimated attach to logs. If the function could be expressed in exponential form, the parameters to be estimated would then appear in the exponents.

[29]   A specification of the translog cost function including input prices is given by Brown, Caves and Christensen (1979, pp.258-9), who point out that for m outputs and n inputs the function contains $[(m+n)\,(m+n+1)\,/\,2]$ parameters.

[30]   Baumol, *et al.* (1982, pp.450-3) also provide a discussion of this amended version of the translog cost function.

and constant returns to scale, then for given input prices the total cost function becomes a simple linear function of the output levels of each product,

$$C = \sum_i a_i y_i \qquad \qquad ...(2.33)$$

This function, as was pointed out in the discussion of its counterpart (2.25) earlier, imposes non-jointness on the production process with the marginal and average cost of each product being constant and independent of the output level of any product. Further, input/output separability implies that relative marginal costs (a_i / a_j for $i \neq j$) are independent of input prices. The acceptance of these restrictions, however, gives in return a functional form which is easy to estimate and which is relatively parsimonious in parameters. There is now one parameter for each output type, so that 20 outputs result in 20 parameters as compared with 210 parameters in the Generalised Linear-Generalised Leontief cost function (2.29) with input prices constant, or the same number in the translog formulation (2.32).

In analysing costs for firms which produce a large range of outputs, decisions need to be made concerning the level of aggregation which is to be adopted and the degree of flexibility in the functional form. The higher the level of disaggregation and the more flexible the functional form, the lower will be the degrees of freedom for a given sample size. With regard to hospitals, it will be argued in the next chapter that the number of output types produced is very large, and that aggregation into a small number of categories would produce output categories that are not very meaningful. Consequently, the trade-off between flexibility in functional form and disaggregation of output types is a trade-off which must be confronted in hospital cost analysis (Breyer 1987).

The discussion so far has been theoretical in nature and devoid of empirical content. Before concluding this chapter, therefore, the concepts and issues which have been raised will be exemplified with reference to some selected empirical studies undertaken in this area.

2.6   Selected Empirical Examples

Perhaps the earliest attempt to empirically estimate a cost function for a multiproduct firm was that by Crum (1926). Using data on US railroads for six separate time periods between 1911 and 1923, six cost functions of the form

$$E = a_0 + a_1 F + a_2 P \qquad\qquad\qquad \text{... (2.34)}$$

were estimated, where E = expenses per mile of line, F = freight ton-miles per mile of line, and P = passenger miles per mile of line. This equation has the same form as that given in equation (2.11), with a_0 representing joint fixed costs, and jointness or economies of scope being embodied as a maintained hypothesis.[31] The values for a_1 fell into the range 0·33 to 0·80 cents while for a_2 the range was 1·8 to 3·3 cents, indicating a substantially higher marginal cost for passenger services.

An important study of hospital costs undertaken by Feldstein (1967) was the first to take account of the multiproduct nature of these institutions in cost analysis. This was done by classifying the case load of each of 177 National Health Service hospitals in Britain into eight mutually exclusive specialty groups (general medicine, paediatrics, gynaecology, etc.) and one miscellaneous group.[32] A relationship of the form (2.33) was estimated, showing that variations in the composition of cases explained 27.5 per cent of the variation in average cost per case between hospitals in the sample, after adjusting for degrees of freedom. Input prices were not included as a possible source of interhospital cost variation as they were virtually constant across the country.

The two studies just discussed both employed rather inflexible functional forms and consequently embody certain possible characteristics of multiproduct production processes already discussed as maintained hypotheses. The development of the flexible functional form has led to its increased use in more recent times. One of the first studies to employ the Generalised Linear-Generalised Leontief function proposed by Hall (1973) (see equation (2.29)) was that by Burgess (1976). Using two output categories (durables and non-durables as one category regarded as tradeable goods, and non-government services and structures as the other, regarded as non-tradeables) and three input categories (capital services, labour services and imported materials), Burgess adopted this functional form in addressing the problem of the income distribution effects of tariffs in the United States.

---

[31]   In a discussion of Crum's work, Lorenz (1926) points out that the constant term a_0 "seems to indicate" the costs which are unallocable to the particular products, but states that Crum "tells me that this constant is not in any way identifiable with the unallocated expenses" (p.26). Lorenz's interpretation is, however, correct since $a_1 F$ is then equal to the total separable cost of F and analogously for $a_2 P$, with the sum of these and the joint costs a_0 giving the total cost.

[32]   The thorny problems associated with the concept and measurement of hospital output are discussed in the next chapter.

"The manner by which higher tariffs affect factor rewards depends critically upon whether the technology is separable or nonjoint" (Burgess 1976, p.17). Under input/output separability, the effect of an increase in import prices on the prices of labour and capital depends on the relative magnitudes of the partial elasticities of substitution of capital and labour for imported materials, as if a single good were provided. For example, if capital and imported goods are complementary inputs, higher tariffs will increase import prices, reduce the demand for both imported goods and capital, and increase the demand for labour with a consequent increase in wage rates.

Under non-jointness, the effect of higher import prices on capital and labour prices depends on the capital and labour intensities, and the imported materials cost share for each output. For example, suppose the services and structures sector is labour intensive and has a lower imported materials cost share. Higher tariffs will initially tend to raise costs more in the capital intensive sector (durables and non-durables) with the larger imported materials cost share. Taking output prices as given, a rise in wage rates and a reduction in rental rates will be necessary to restore unit costs and equivalent profitability for each output.

The evidence produced by Burgess strongly rejected input/output separability as an appropriate specification, but also rejected non-jointness, with the consequence that no inference can be drawn about the distributional impact of higher tariffs from a knowledge of elasticities of substitution or factor intensities and import cost shares. If, however, either of these restrictions is adopted *a priori*, then both indicate "that higher tariffs redistribute real income from capital to labour for the postwar US economy" (Burgess 1976, p.42). This conclusion, though, is very sensitive to any special restrictions, e.g. zero input substitutability, imposed on the non-joint specification.

An example of the use of a multiproduct translog cost function is provided in a study of US railroads by Brown, Caves and Christensen (1979). Using two outputs (freight and passenger services) and three inputs (capital, labour and fuel), an unrestricted (except for linear homogeneity in factor prices) translog cost function together with four restricted versions—incorporating constant returns to scale or linear homogeneity in outputs; input/output separability; homogeneity plus separability; and a separable form with Cobb-Douglas aggregator functions for inputs and outputs—were estimated. All four restricted versions were decisively rejected, leading the authors to conclude that "the full generality of the unconstrained translog form is required to adequately represent the structure of production" (Brown, *et al.* 1979, p.261).

Although non-jointness was not tested as a parametric restriction in this study, evidence on the curvature of the transformation frontier for freight and passenger services was produced. At the observed level of costs and prices for every railroad, this frontier demonstrated convexity. In particular, an economic incentive to specialise in freight services at the particular relative prices was indicated.

Two more recent studies on hospital costs, both of which employed translog cost functions, are those by Conrad and Strauss (1983) and Cowing and Holtmann (1983). In the former, data on 114 North Carolina hospitals were used in a specification comprising three outputs (non-Medicare, Medicare, and child inpatient days) and four inputs (general services, nursing services, ancillary services, and capital). As in the railroad study just considered, a number of restricted versions of the function were tested, in this case three—linear homogeneity in outputs; input/output separability; and homogeneity plus separability. Constant returns to scale could not be rejected but the remaining two restrictions were both statistically unacceptable. Nursing and ancillary services were found to be complementary to capital while general services and capital were found to be substitutes. The marginal cost of child inpatient days was substantially greater than the marginal cost of patient days in the other two output categories. The authors conclude that complementarity between capital and nursing and ancillary services may provide an explanation of rapidly increasing hospital costs, since the technology of treatment has become increasingly capital-intensive.

In the study by Cowing and Holtmann (1983), five outputs were employed, *viz.* patient days per year in each of five diagnostic categories— medical-surgical, maternity, paediatrics, other inpatient care, and emergency room care. Six input price variables were included, along with the book value of buildings and equipment as a measure of capital, the number of admitting physicians, and dummy variables to identify ownership type and teaching status. The results generated from the sample of 138 hospitals indicate economies of scope or jointness with respect to the production of some but not all output groupings, suggesting that indiscriminate merging of hospitals may not give rise to cost savings. The short run elasticities of substitution between labour inputs suggest that a relatively high degree of substitutability is possible amongst these input types.

Grannemann, Brown and Pauly (1986) used a "hybrid functional form which incorporates desirable features both of some *ad hoc* cost functions and of commonly used forms for structural cost functions" (p.111) in estimating a hospital cost function based on data from 867 US Hospitals. In contrast to the 'pure' structural cost functions which incorporate only output quantities and input prices (as used in the Conrad-Strauss and Cowing-Holtmann studies), the hybrid form also includes potentially relevant variables on an *ad hoc* basis while allowing economies of scope and scale to be incorporated as testable hypotheses. While the large sample size in this study eased the trade-off between flexibility in functional form and parameter parsimony, the use of interactive terms between a range of output categories still resulted in a relatively high degree of output aggregation, e.g. inpatient discharges were classified as being acute, intensive care, or subacute and other, and five categories were used to differentiate the case mix of specialist admissions, *viz.* paediatrics, surgery, psychiatry, obstetrics and gynaecology, and other. In total, 63 regressors were included in the estimated equation.

These hospital cost studies in particular, and the other studies using flexible functional forms, bear witness to the argument of the previous section that adoption of such a form involves a trade-off in the level of disaggregation which can be adopted. As will be argued in the next chapter, five output categories is a relatively small number of output types for a hospital, representing a high degree of aggregation for these institutions.

2.7 Summary and Conclusions

This chapter has presented an overview of the concepts of jointness, input/output separability and returns to scale in the context of production and cost functions for multiproduct firms. Economies of jointness, or economies of scope, arise when the cost of producing any given output levels of two or more products is less if the products are produced together rather than separately. This gives rise to joint costs if the outputs are produced in fixed proportions, and common costs if the outputs are produced in variable proportions. In either case, some costs may be product-specific and allocable to that product. If production is non-joint then the multiproduct production function is simply the sum of the separate production functions for each product and the corresponding dual cost function is additively separable. Total cost in this case is then the sum of the costs of producing each product separately, and all costs are separable in the sense that they are fully allocable to individual products. Joint or common costs do not arise in this case.

If the multiproduct production function is input/output separable, it can be separated into an output aggregator function the value of which is determined by the value of an input aggregator function. The marginal rate of transformation between any pair of outputs is then independent of specific input levels, and there can be no interaction between any particular inputs and outputs. The cost function becomes a function of the output aggregator function and input prices with relative marginal costs being independent of input prices.

The production technology exhibits constant returns to scale if a given proportionate increase in inputs gives rise to an equal proportionate increase in all outputs. For the cost function, a given proportionate increase in all outputs causes an equal proportionate increase in total costs. Defined in this way, the existence of constant returns to scale is consistent with the existence of product-specific economies or diseconomies of scale.

If non-jointness and input/output separability are both imposed as constraints on the multiproduct cost function, the function takes a multiplicative form between an output and an input price aggregator function. The output aggregator function is a sum of the separate output functions each of which depends only on the output of one particular product. If input/output separability and constant returns to scale are both imposed, the cost function is again multiplicatively separable between the output and input price aggregator functions, but the form of the output aggregator function is not constrained. If non-jointness and overall constant returns to scale are both imposed, the cost function becomes a linear weighted sum of each output level where the weights are the marginal costs of producing each product. The marginal cost of each product may, however, vary with the output level of that particular product—product-specific economies and diseconomies of scale may still be present. If, however, overall constant returns to scale is imposed along with non-jointness and input/output separability, the cost function is again a linear weighted sum of outputs but the marginal cost of producing each product is constant—product-specific economies and diseconomies of scale are inadmissible.

The development of flexible functional forms for production and cost functions has enabled these characteristics to be treated as testable rather than maintained hypotheses, i.e. their existence can be investigated with statistical tests on the parameters of the function rather than adopting a functional form which presumes certain characteristics exist. Such functions, however, gain this flexibility at the expense of parameter parsimony, and this trade-off becomes more pronounced as the number of output and input categories increases. The trade-off becomes particularly acute in hospital cost analysis.

Appendix 2.I

Non-Jointness, Overall and Product-Specific Returns to Scale

For two outputs under non-jointness,

$$C(y_1, y_2, w) = C^{(1)}(y_1, w) + C^{(2)}(y_2, w)$$

Let y_1, y_2 be increased by a factor λ. Then

$$C(\lambda y_1, \lambda y_2, w) = C^{(1)}(\lambda y_1, w) + C^{(2)}(\lambda y_2, w)$$

With overall constant returns to scale,

$$C(\lambda y_1, \lambda y_2, w) = \lambda C(y_1, y_2, w).$$

We wish to show that this does *not* imply that

$$C^{(1)}(\lambda y, w) = \lambda C^{(1)}(y_1, w)$$

and $C^{(2)}(\lambda y_2, w) = \lambda C^{(2)}(y_2, w)$

i.e., it does not imply that each product's cost function exhibits constant returns to scale.

Let the individual cost functions for y_1 and y_2 be homogeneous of degree a and b respectively in output, i.e.

let $C^{(1)}(\lambda y_1, w) = \lambda^a \, C^{(1)}(y_1, w)$

$$C^{(2)}(\lambda y_2, w) = \lambda^b C^{(2)}(y_2, w)$$

We require

$$\lambda^a C^{(1)}(y_1, w) + \lambda^b C^{(2)}(y_2, w) = \lambda C(y_1, y_2, w)$$

This allows for non-constant returns to scale in the individual cost functions for y_1 and y_2 but requires overall constant returns to scale.

Dividing by λ we obtain

$$\lambda^{a-1} C^{(1)}(y_1, w) + \lambda^{b-1} C^{(2)}(y_2, w) = C(y_1, y_2, w)$$

$$= C^{(1)}(y_1, w) + C^{(2)}(y_2, w)$$

Rearranging this gives

$$C^{(1)}(y_1, w)\left(\lambda^{a-1} - 1\right) = C^{(2)}(y_2, w)\left(1 - \lambda^{b-1}\right)$$

Letting $k = \dfrac{C^{(1)}(y_1, w)}{C^{(2)}(y_2, w)}$ we have

$$k = \frac{1 - \lambda^{b-1}}{\lambda^{a-1} - 1} = \frac{\lambda - \lambda^b}{\lambda^a - \lambda}$$

$$\therefore \quad \lambda^a = \frac{\left(\lambda - \lambda^b\right)}{k} + \lambda$$

$$a = \frac{\log\left[\left(\lambda(k+1) - \lambda^b\right)/k\right]}{\log \lambda}$$

3

THE CONCEPT, MEASUREMENT AND
CLASSIFICATION OF HOSPITAL OUTPUT

3.1   Introduction

The empirical analysis of cost behaviour in any industry must confront the
problem of defining output, and such an analysis of hospitals is no
exception. While this problem can be a difficult one to resolve for any
industry, it is particularly acute for studies of service industries which, by
their nature, produce intangible outputs.

In terms of the traditional trichotomous distinction between primary,
secondary and tertiary industries in the economy, the service sector is
usually embodied in the tertiary sector. Although the discipline of
economics has made substantial progress since the time of Adam Smith, the
analysis of the tertiary sector has tended to lag far behind that of the other
two sectors. In terms of this time horizon, 1940 is relatively recent, yet in
that year, in what one author has described as a "prophetic" book (Fuchs
1969, p.1), Colin Clark made the following observation: "The economics of
tertiary industry remains to be written. Many as yet feel uncomfortable
about even admitting their existence" (Clark 1940, p.341). Some possible

explanations for this have been offered by Fuchs (1969, p.1, emphasis added).

> Reasons for this neglect in the past are not difficult to find. They include the greater importance of primary and secondary employment at lower levels of real income per capita; the belief of some economists, notably Adam Smith, that only the primary and secondary sectors were "productive"; *the difficulty of measuring service output*; the difficulty of obtaining data because of the heterogeneity of activities and the small size of most firms in the service sector; and the large role of nonprofit organizations in the service sector and the difficulty of analyzing their behaviour.

What follows in this chapter will bear witness to the emphasised phrase in this passage.[1]

The title of this chapter indicates the three major sections of which it is comprised. Conceptual issues involved in defining hospital output are addressed in section 3.2 while section 3.3 confronts the problem of adopting a unit of output measurement. Section 3.4 considers the multiproduct nature of hospital output, being concerned with the classification of output. A summary and the conclusions are presented in the final section.

3.2   Conceptual Issues

3.2.1   What is a Hospital?

At the outset, it is necessary to clarify briefly what is meant by a 'hospital'. One dictionary definition of the term is "an institution in which sick or injured persons are given medical or surgical treatment" (*The Random House College Dictionary*, Revised Edition, 1982, p.640). Such a definition raises a number of questions. Does the treatment have to be provided on an inpatient basis, i.e. does the patient have to be lodged and fed as well as treated? Does it matter whether the illness is acute (brief and severe) or chronic (recurring or of long duration)? Is treatment narrowly defined to include only curative care or does it also include observation of patients and preventive health measures not aimed at curing a specific condition?

---

[1]   An overview of various aspects of the economic analysis of the service sector can be found in Tucker (1977).

In economic terms, what is required is a delineation of the hospital industry. What are the essential characteristics of a firm which would lead to its inclusion as part of the hospital industry?[2] In answering this question, consider the following four broad categories of hospital output:

- inpatient treatment—the treatment of patients who are admitted to stay in hospital while being treated;

- outpatient treatment—the treatment of patients without admission to hospital;

- teaching—the provision of doctor and/or nurse education; and

- research—systematic inquiry aimed at expanding the stock of knowledge in medicine.

It will be argued here that, in terms of this categorisation of hospital outputs, the defining characteristic of a hospital is the provision of inpatient treatment. The reason for this is that the remaining types of output can each be produced in institutions other than hospitals. Outpatient treatment can be provided in an outpatient clinic or a doctor's surgery. Doctor and/or nurse education can be provided in teaching institutions,[3] and research can be undertaken in specialised research facilities. This is not to say, of course, that the production of two or more of these broad output types is subject to non-joint production in the sense defined in the previous chapter. However, for an institution to be classified as a hospital, it must provide inpatient treatment.

This should not be taken to imply that all health care institutions which admit inpatients are hospitals. In this context, the meaning of the term 'treatment' requires amplification. This will be discussed in more detail later in this chapter, but in general terms, treatment is medical care aimed at curing illness or alleviating its symptoms, and not all health care institutions which admit inpatients provide treatment. Nursing homes admit patients for 'care' rather than 'cure', providing long-term care for chronically ill patients

---

2   On the general problems associated with defining markets and industries, see Needham (1978, Ch.5) and references cited therein. For a more specific discussion of the problems of defining market structure in the hospital industry, see McGuire (1985a).

3   The transfer of nurse education from hospitals to universities in Australia is an example of this.

who require nursing support. This contrasts with the acute, short-term care provided by hospitals in the treatment of a specified condition. In practice, the distinction between these two types of institutions is not always clear cut, as some nursing home patients may be cared for in hospitals. This problem will be addressed again later.

3.2.2   The Concept of Output

For the remainder of this chapter, attention will be focused on the inpatient treatment category of hospital output. Problems associated with conceptualising teaching and research output will be addressed in Chapter 7 where the impact of teaching on hospital costs is explicitly addressed.

An important conceptual issue with regard to inpatient treatment is whether the output of a hospital is the actual provision of the medical treatment itself or the resulting improvement in the health status of the patient (if any). Supporters of the latter conception argue that "output measures should reflect what is believed to be the ultimate objective of the health (and hospital) system—the improvement of health levels" (Tatchell 1983, p.871). In the words of Barer (1982, p.54): "From a social valuation perspective, the most obvious expected output of a hospital is a positive increment in patient health status".

Proponents of the health status conception of output maintain that, from the point of view of consumers, hospital treatment is purchased in anticipation of a resulting improvement in health or alleviation of suffering. "Thus, from the patient's perspective, hospital output should be defined as health, illness remission or symptom relief" (Hornbrook 1982a, p.13). According to this argument, the treatment provided by a hospital is an input into the production of health. "In this formulation, the consumer does not purchase, say, two office visits, five days of hospital care, three X-rays, and sixteen tablets of antibiotics, but rather the expectation that his level of health will be improved" (Berki 1972, p.32).

This concept of output underlies the work by some economists on health status indexes. Beginning with the premise that "health services exist ... to effect the maximum increase in the health status of the client population" (Culyer 1978, p.10), this work attempts to characterise different health states in terms of, for example, pain and restriction of activity (Culyer, Lavers and Williams 1972). Another example in relation to care of the elderly is to specify health status in terms of ability to get in and out of bed, ability to negotiate a level surface, and ability to climb stairs, among other things (Wright 1978). The output of health services is then the change in these characteristics which results from their provision.

The notion of specifying various characteristics of health states lends itself to analysis in terms of the characteristics theory of consumer behaviour as developed by Lancaster (1966a, 1966b) and Ironmonger (1972). This analysis is based on the premise that consumers' preferences are defined in terms of the characteristics of goods rather than the goods themselves. "That is, a person who buys, say, a blanket is doing so not because he or she wishes to own a blanket, but because of the desire to obtain the warmth, beauty, protection, and so forth that the blanket provides" (Nicholson 1985, p.160). In the same way, consumers have preferences not for health care *per se* but for the improvement in the attributes of their health status which this care provides, such as alleviation of pain, improved ability to climb stairs, and so on. This connection between the characteristics theory of consumer behaviour and health care has been established by Doessel and Marshall (1982, 1985). These authors have employed the characteristics framework to provide an economic interpretation of the 'health outcome' concept of quality of care in medicine.[4]

An alternative approach to this conceptual problem of defining hospital output and the approach which underlies the empirical work presented in this book, is to define the output of a hospital in terms of the treatment it provides rather than the resulting change in the health status of the patient. The genealogy of this concept goes back to the work of A.A. Scitovsky on the construction of a medical care price index based on the costs of treatment of selected illnesses (see Scitovsky 1964, 1967). Although not explicitly concerned with the conceptual issues involved in defining the output of the health care system, Scitovsky's work clearly embodies the essential elements of the treatment conception of output. With regard to her proposed index, she argues: "This is an index which would show changes, not in the costs of such items of medical care as drugs, physicians' visits, and hospital rooms, but in the average costs of the complete treatment of individual illnesses such as, for example, pneumonia, appendicitis, or measles" (Scitovsky 1964, p.133). Subsequently, in her 1967 paper, she produced empirical results for five selected illnesses[5] and has more recently reported further findings based on this approach (Scitovsky 1985).

Supporters of the treatment conception of output often argue in favour of the concept because of the practical difficulties associated with the health

---

4   The 'outcome' concept of quality of care refers to the outcome of medical care in terms of its impact on the patient's health status. See Donabedian (1969).

5   These were: acute appendicitis; maternity care; otitis media in children; fracture of the forearm (also in children only); and cancer of the breast.

status conception. It is pointed out that, in addition to health care, there is a wide range of factors which influence a person's health—hygiene, nutrition and motor vehicle safety regulations to name just a few.[6] If the output of the hospital is viewed as a change in health status, then it is necessary to isolate the influence of each of these factors to arrive at "the hospital's marginal contribution to the patient's health, all other things held constant" (Hornbrook 1982a, p.13). Empirically this is a daunting task.[7] "Therefore, as a proximate solution to this dilemma, we usually concentrate on medical treatments as the output of the health services industry" (Hadley 1974, p.146).[8]

It is undoubtedly the case that the health status conception of hospital output is practically difficult to implement, but this does not deny its conceptual validity. The arguments just espoused could be summarised as saying that the health status conception is conceptually fertile but empirically sterile. In the words of Richardson and Wallace (1983, pp.128-9): "A ... conceptually more satisfactory measure of output is 'health outcome' ... Despite its conceptual appeal, there are serious practical problems with the use of the measure ... ".

It can be argued, however, that the health status concept of hospital output is conceptually invalid, rather than being conceptually valid but empirically problematic. Such a position involves a direct rejection of the notion that 'hospitals produce health', as exemplified in the following statement by Mann and Yett (1968, p.197): "We reject this definition of hospital output for the same reason that we do not regard the output of a beauty salon as beauty". In the same way as beauty salons produce treatment which may or may not result in an increase in beauty, hospitals produce treatment which may or may not result in an improvement in health status.

---

[6]   For a more detailed discussion of the various determinants of health status other than health services, see Lerner (1977).

[7]   Fuchs (1972, p.12) succinctly summarises the problems as follows: "Any attempt to analyze the relationship between health services and health runs headlong into two very difficult problems. The first concerns the definition and measurement of levels of health, or at least changes in levels. The second involves an attempt to estimate what portion of changes in health can be attributed to health services, as distinct from the genetic and environmental factors that also affect health".

[8]   This empirical compromise is also advocated by Hornbrook (1982a, p.13): "Instead of measuring this actual change in health status, we assess the degree to which the hospital provides the inputs that can be expected to lead to the desired change in health. In return for achieving a feasible measure, we must accept some uncertainty".

In support of this view it can be argued that an implication of the health status conception of hospital output is that where there is no change in health status, no output has been produced. Thus, a hospital which treats a person with a terminal illness may, under this conception, produce nothing if the person's life span is not increased or some other dimension of health status is not improved. This difficulty is recognised by Culyer (1978, p.10) who claims that the health status conception can be adjusted to incorporate this problem, but to date this has not been achieved.

Further support for this view emerges from a consideration of what is actually traded in medical care markets. Are consumers purchasing treatment or an improvement in health status? If it is argued that they are purchasing an improvement in health status, then it is this for which they should be required to pay, and they should not be required to pay anything if such an improvement does not eventuate. In fact, this is not very often the case, as Reder (1969, p.110) has pointed out: "While the idea of relating the size of the doctor's fee to the success of the treatment is not unthinkable, it is surely uncommon and not likely to gain favor in the near future." Certainly in many societies the impact of treatment on health status has not formed the basis of payment. Further, litigation concerning malpractice tends to be defended on the grounds that 'appropriate' treatment was provided. "It is rarely an issue at law as to whether medical care is effective—only that prevailing wisdom about "good practice" has been properly and competently applied" (Doessel and Marshall 1982, p.5).

Even if consumers were required to pay only for health status improvements rather than for all treatment, it could be argued that they are, in this case, actually purchasing two outputs rather than one. This argument is based upon the uncertainty surrounding the impact of medical treatments on health status even in the absence of any negligence on the part of suppliers.[9] In the presence of uncertainty, risk-bearing becomes a commodity. Individuals who face a risk of financial loss on the occurrence of a particular uncertain event may be prepared to pay to shift that risk to another party. This particular method of shifting risks is known as insurance. Some other ways in which risks may be shifted are by means of common stocks and cost-plus contracts.[10]

---

9   Note that this uncertainty applies to a person who is already ill, and is separate and distinct from the uncertainty of becoming ill in the first place. To quote Arrow (1963, p.959), "there are two kinds of risks involved in medical care: the risk of becoming ill, and the risk of total or incomplete or delayed recovery". It is this second kind of risk which is under discussion here.

10   For a discussion of mechanisms for shifting risks see Arrow (1974, pp.134-43).

Patients receiving treatment face some degree of uncertainty about the effect of that treatment on their health. If patients pay for treatment regardless of its impact on their health then they are bearing the risks associated with this uncertainty. If no improvement in health status arises from the treatment, then they suffer a financial loss (the cost of the treatment) and gain nothing.[11] This is then an event against which individuals may wish to take out insurance so that they pay for treatment only if it improves their health status.[12] Indeed, if such insurance is not available, there may well be a net social loss, as argued by Arrow (1963, p.961):

> Suppose ... that, given that a person is ill, the expected value of medical care is greater than its cost ... However, the recovery, though on the average beneficial, is uncertain; in the absence of insurance a risk-averter may well prefer not to take a chance on further impoverishment by buying medical care. A suitable insurance policy would, however, mean that he would pay nothing if he doesn't benefit; since the expected value is greater than the cost, there would be a net social gain.

Such insurance could be provided by a third party who pays for the treatment in the event of its being unsuccessful. However, it could also be provided by the hospital or the medical practitioner if they agreed to accept full payment only if the treatment improved health status. Under these circumstances, the risk of the financial loss following unsuccessful treatment is shifted to the supplier of the treatment. The supplier can now be thought of as producing not one but *two* outputs—the treatment itself, and insurance against the financial loss which may arise because of the uncertain impact of that treatment on health status.

If a pricing system were in operation, these two outputs could be priced separately, with a premium being paid for the insurance cover and a separate price being paid for the treatment, if successful. For example, suppose the treatment of a particular illness costs $2,000 and that the probability of this treatment having no impact on a patient's health status is 0.1. Assuming risk neutrality on the part of insurers and zero administrative costs, the actuarially fair premium for cover against the cost of treatment in the event

---

[11] The financial loss may also include loss of income because of reduced earning ability arising from the prolongation of the illness.

[12] In this context Arrow (1963, p.961) points out that "It is a popular belief that the Chinese, at one time, paid their physicians when well but not when sick".

of its being unsuccessful is \$200.[13] Prior to receiving this treatment, patients could pay this premium and receive cover or agree to pay the cost of treatment regardless of its impact on their health status. If no explicit premium is paid and patients are not required to pay for unsuccessful treatment, then the price of successful treatments will be loaded to cover the costs of unsuccessful treatments. This system would then involve cross-subsidisation in favour of those who have unsuccessful treatment.[14]

As with other types of insurance, the problem of moral hazard may arise with the provision of this type of cover. The term 'moral hazard' refers to the effect of insurance on incentives, and arises when the insured can influence the probability of occurrence of the insured event.[15] "The insurance policy might itself change incentives and therefore the probabilities upon which the insurance company has relied" (Arrow 1974, p.142).[16] In the present context, the existence of insurance against the costs of unsuccessful treatment may reduce the incentive for patients to comply with the advice of medical staff, and could encourage patients to make spurious claims about their actual state of health following the treatment.

In summary, the treatment conception of hospital output views the hospital as producing treatment of illness which, due to the inherent uncertainty surrounding the effect of that treatment, may or may not improve a patient's health status. Given the presence of this uncertainty, risk-bearing becomes a commodity—patients may desire to purchase insurance which indemnifies them against the costs of unsuccessful treatment. It may be that the hospital and/or the doctor are prepared to carry these risks, in which case they would not be paid for unsuccessful treatment. However, they may have an aversion to bearing such risks, in which case

---

13   An actuarially fair premium is one which is such that, "if the costs of medical care are a random variable with mean m, the company will charge a premium m, and agree to indemnify the individual for all medical costs" (Arrow 1963, p.960).

14   This example has implicitly assumed that the treatment will either have no impact on health status or lead to full recovery. In reality, partial recovery or, as has been argued forcefully by some (e.g. Illich 1975), a deterioration in health status are also possible. While in practice this would complicate any insurance arrangements, it does not affect the essence of the argument being presented here.

15   On the economics of moral hazard see Pauly (1968, 1983) and references cited therein. See also Gravelle and Rees (1992).

16   Common examples are the effects of fire insurance on incentives to guard against fire and the associated possibility of arson, and the effect of insurance against theft on the care taken to guard against burglaries.

"there is room for insurance carriers to pool the risks, either by contract with physicians or by contract with the potential patients" (Arrow 1963, pp.964-5). In either case, the hospital produces treatment. If it also assumes the risks associated with the uncertain effects of this treatment, then it can be argued that, in addition to such treatment, it is also producing a second output, *viz.* insurance.

An interesting parallel can be drawn here with legal services. Suppose that a person is going to court, either as a plaintiff or a defendant, and engages the services of a lawyer to prosecute or defend the case. What is the output of the lawyer? Is it legal representation or a successful prosecution or defence? Again there is inherent uncertainty about the outcome regardless of which party is actually 'innocent' or 'guilty'. If the lawyer is paid regardless of the outcome of the case, then the risks associated with this uncertainty are fully borne by the client, unless a third party has provided insurance cover. If, however, the remuneration of the lawyer depends on the outcome of the case then again it can be argued that the lawyer is providing insurance cover in addition to providing legal representation. In this context, it is interesting to note the comment by Reder (1969, p.110) that, at least in the US, "fees contingent on awards are very common in damage suits" so that the fees paid are directly dependent on the damages awarded. In such a situation the lawyer is sharing the risks arising from the uncertain outcome of the case.[17]

This argument should not be taken to imply that the impact of the treatment on health status is irrelevant. Most patients having medical treatment would be doing so in the hope that it would improve their health status in some way or another. Consequently, the impact of treatment on health status can be used as a basis for assessing the quality of the treatment where quality is viewed in terms of the extent to which a good or service purchased satisfies the end use to which it is put by the consumer. This view that treatment is the output while the impact on health status is an indication of the quality of that treatment is concisely stated in the following quotation from a comment by Klarman (1969, p.134) on the paper by Reder (1969).

> It is important, I believe, that a position be taken on what constitutes output in the health services industry. Is it the services rendered by physicians and other personnel or is it the change effected in the health status of persons? In Reder's scheme the former is output in the first instance, while the latter

---

17   The attitude to contingent fees in Australia is apparently quite different. According to Carey (1985, p.4), "A bargain for a share in the proceeds or an interest in the subject matter of the litigation (a contingent fee) is still seen as maintenance in this country and is regarded as against the public interest".

> qualifies as an adjustment in quality. I agree with this decision, because I can see no way of devising a proportionate relationship over time between health services and health status.

Clearly, Klarman's agreement with this position is on pragmatic grounds.

The treatment conception of hospital output also accords with the view of hospital output as an intermediate product used as an input into the production function for health. This view is neatly summarised by Berki (1972, p.42): "If we consider that the final product of the medical care process is the provision of the highest attainable level of health, given the state of the arts, it is clear that the output of the hospital is more precisely an intermediate input into this process." A useful analogy can be drawn here with motor vehicles. The output of a motor vehicle manufacturing plant is motor vehicles which are then combined with other inputs (fuel, roads, labour) into the production function for transport services. In the same way, the outputs of the health services industry in general, and hospitals in particular, are combined with other inputs (nutrition, sanitation, housing, environmental factors and so on) into the production of health. As such, it is legitimate to speak of the marginal product of hospital treatment as an input into the production function for health, but this is not the production function confronting hospitals.

Whatever position one adopts on these conceptual issues, empirical reality is such that the treatment conception of output forms the basis of most applied work on hospital cost analysis. However, as has been argued in this section, the treatment conception can be supported in its own right and not simply on the basis of a pragmatic argument that the health status conception is difficult to implement in practice. On this note, the discussion now turns to a consideration of the unit of measurement to be employed in empirical applications based on the treatment conception.

3.3   The Unit of Measurement

3.3.1   The Treatment Conception and Empirical Measurement

The problem to be addressed here is the definition of a unit of measurement which corresponds to the abstract concept of 'a treatment', i.e. the problem of defining a unit of output. At the outset, then, it is necessary to discuss more fully what is meant by 'a treatment'.

Generally, patients are admitted to hospital because they are ill or are suspected of being so.[18] The hospital then combines various inputs—diagnostic tests, nursing services, drugs, meals and so on—in producing a treatment of the patient's condition. A treatment is then defined as the service arising from the combination of these inputs to provide a diagnosis of an illness or suspected illness together with an attempt to cure that illness and/or alleviate its symptoms if its presence is confirmed. The term 'treatment' is used broadly here to include the outputs produced for those patients who are found not to be ill, e.g. patients who are admitted for observation and, after diagnostic tests, are found to be healthy.

The foregoing definition can be compared with that given by Hornbrook (1982a, p.14): "By the concept of "treatment", we mean provision of appropriate services to correct the underlying cause of the illness and/or alleviate its manifestations". While the two definitions are similar, the former is broader in that it allows for patients who may be admitted for observation and subsequently discharged without any illness being detected.[19]

For practical applications, some authors have suggested that the appropriate unit of output is a treatment of an episode of illness. This stems from the previously cited work of Scitovsky (1964, 1967) on a medical care price index based on changes in the costs of treatment of particular illnesses, in which she argues that "it is the illness ... rather than the individual item of service which seems the more appropriate unit of account for a medical care price index" (Scitovsky 1964, p.137). It should be noted, however, that this unit of measurement as employed in a medical care price index includes not only inpatient treatment but also outpatient treatment. Consequently it encompasses the complete treatment provided by the health care system and not just the hospital component of that treatment.

This is, of course, entirely appropriate when the concern is with the cost of treating a particular illness by the health care system as a whole and not with a subset of institutions within that system. The costs of treating an illness can be significantly affected by a change in the institutional arrangements for treating that illness, so that concentration on a subset of institutions could give quite a misleading impression of changes in such costs. For example, Scitovsky (1967) found that, over the period 1951-52 to 1964-65, the cost of treating forearm fractures requiring a general

---

[18]   An exception to this statement is organ donors.

[19]   The papers by Hornbrook (1982a, 1982b) provide an excellent review of the problems of conceptualising, measuring and classifying hospital output.

anaesthetic increased by 315 per cent. Of this increase, about half was accounted for by the fact that "in the earlier period, physicians still quite frequently administered a general anesthetic in their office when setting a fracture whereas now this is always done in the hospital" (Scitovsky 1967, p.1186). In this context, Berki (1972, p.40) points out that "the hospital's output would comprise a set of specific intermediate inputs into the treatment process. While from some points of view this may not be acceptable, from the standpoint of efficiency of resource allocation and economic welfare it is both relevant and stimulating".[20]

Ro and Auster (1969) propose a reimbursement scheme for hospitals under which "Hospital product is defined as the number and categories of episodes of illness given adequate treatment" (p.178). Berki (1972) has criticised this definition because the term 'adequate' was left undefined. However, the meaning of this term has since been discussed more fully in a paper by Auster and Gordon (1978) which employs the same definition of output.

Klarman (1969, p.135) cites five objections to treating an episode of illness as the measure of output.

- With the possible exception of some surgery, most illness cannot be divided over time into distinct episodes.

- Indeed, even for a given diagnostic condition episodes of illness are variously accompanied by complications and multiple diseases, which may outlast the episode.

- Certain health services are completely divorced from episodes of illness. A medical examination not prompted by symptoms is the most obvious example.

---

20 It should be noted that Scitovsky's approach is concerned with the *cost of treatment* of particular illnesses and not with the overall *social cost* of an episode of illness. The latter may also include such costs as the loss of production occasioned by the person being unable to work, and the reduced earning capacity of the person if the disease has impaired such capacity. Examples of studies which are concerned with the overall cost of illness are that by Klarman (1965) on syphilis control programs, Hartunian, Smart and Thompson (1981) on the costs of cancer, motor vehicle injuries, coronary heart disease and stroke, and Oster, Colditz and Kelly (1984) on the costs of smoking and the benefits of quitting with respect to three major smoking related diseases (lung cancer, coronary heart disease and chronic obstructive pulmonary disease).

- Certain health services are preventive in nature. Their purpose is to prevent the occurrence of illness. Vaccinations are an obvious example.

- The management of chronic diseases cannot be divided into episodes.

With regard to the second point listed above, it can also be added that the presence of multiple diseases can make the identification of the primary diagnosis a difficult if not impossible task. Klarman further points out that "health services are not commonly paid for in terms of treatment for an episode of illness" (p.135), an argument employed in section 3.2 of this chapter against the health status conception of hospital output. Taken together then, these objections render this unit of output virtually unworkable.

A unit of measurement which is more easily identified is an episode of hospitalisation which begins when the patient is admitted and ends when the patient is discharged. On this basis, the production of a unit of output is complete each time a patient is discharged, giving rise to a treated case as the unit of measurement. The volume of output produced over any given time period is then given by the number of patients discharged over that time period, or the number of cases treated.[21] The unit of output is no longer a treatment of a complete episode of illness but rather that treatment provided within an episode of hospitalisation. This will not correspond to the full treatment provided for an episode of illness if the full treatment is provided over several different episodes of hospitalisation.

While an episode of hospitalisation provides an operational unit of account for output measurement and overcomes some of the problems mentioned above, it may not be a homogeneous unit across hospitals. Even for the treatment of identical patients with identical illnesses, admission/discharge policies may differ between hospitals. For example, some hospitals may have a policy of discharging patients on a Friday and readmitting them on a Monday where this can be done without adversely affecting the patient's health.[22] Consequently, an episode of hospitalisation for this hospital would be different from one for another hospital which does not pursue such a policy. Hence, quite apart from any complications arising

---

[21]   The problem of classifying discharges to take account of the multiproduct nature of the hospital will be addressed in the next section.

[22]   Reder (1965) suggests that failure to pursue this policy may be a cause of overuse of hospital facilities.

from factors such as differing severities of illness between patients in different hospitals, heterogeneity may exist between hospitals with respect to an episode of hospitalisation. A similar point can be made, however, about treatments of episodes of illness. These also may not be homogeneous units of output across hospitals because of differences in the extent to which hospitals treat patients on an outpatient basis.

As is often the case in applied economics, a trade-off exists between theoretical and conceptual rigour on the one hand and empirical practicality on the other. Whatever unit of measurement is adopted, limitations arise which must be borne in mind in interpreting any empirical results which are obtained. An episode of hospitalisation, or a treated case, does however provide a measure which is readily implemented and, it can be argued, gives rise to fewer limitations than the alternative.

3.3.2   Cases vs. Days

A unit of output measurement commonly adopted in studies of hospital costs is the patient day, with total output over a given time period then being taken as the total number of patient days provided over that time period.[23] This is often considered as an alternative to measuring output by the number of cases treated. For example, Feldstein (1967, p.24) states that "we must choose between two basic units of output: the case and the patient week". Lave and Lave (1970a) employ the patient day as the unit of output measurement, arguing that although "A more relevant measure is the number of cases treated ... The question of whether patients or patient-days is the better measure cannot be settled *a priori*" (p.380).

The argument of the preceding sub-section made no reference to the patient day as a potential unit of output measurement, arguing that an episode of hospitalisation, or a treated case, provides a close and workable correspondence with its conceptual counterpart. If the argument of Lave and Lave (1970a) is correct, however, there is no *a priori* basis for choosing between the treated case and the patient day as the unit of measurement.

It will now be argued that, with respect to acute medical care provided in hospitals, the treated case is *a priori* a more defensible unit of output measurement than the patient day. Indeed, the latter is more in the nature of an input measure relating to the time dimension of the production of a treated case. The number of patient days which a hospital uses to produce a

---

[23] For a review of some earlier studies, see Mann and Yett (1968) and Hefty (1969). Lave and Lave (1979) and Long, *et al.* (1985) provide an overview of some more recent studies.

treated case indicates the time period over which production of one unit of output takes place—it does not measure the output itself.[24]

Consider the following analogy. A builder decides to produce twelve houses over the next year. The production function for the particular type of house indicates the quantities of inputs required which, together with input prices, determines the total cost of the houses. The builder now has to decide whether to complete one house at a time or to construct the twelve simultaneously. Construction time may be one month each in the former case and twelve months each in the latter. The construction time does not measure output (which is twelve houses per year in either case) but rather indicates the time span over which the inputs are used in the construction of a particular house.

In the same way, the number of days over which a treated case is produced, or the length of stay, indicates the time period over which treatment takes place. Hospitals may decide to treat cases more intensively over a shorter time span or less intensively over a longer time span. In either situation, the same quantity of output may be produced.

This relationship can be clarified by expressing it in terms of total cost (TC_i), average cost per case (ACC_i), average cost per day (ACD_i), the total number of cases treated (n_i), and the total number of patient days (d_i) for the ith hospital. These magnitudes are related as follows:

$$TC_i = ACC_i \times n_i = ACD_i \times d_i \qquad \qquad ...(3.1)$$

Total cost can be expressed as the product of the average cost per unit of output (ACC) and the total number of units of output produced (n), or as the product of the average cost of inputs used per day (ACD) and the total number of patient days provided (d).[25] Rearranging (3.1) gives

---

24   The notion of the patient day as an input into treatment is contained in the following statement by Feldstein (1969, p.145) in a comment on the paper by Reder (1969): "The dividing line between inputs and outputs is unclear. For me, the distinguishing characteristic is the possibility of substitution. Although Reder classifies a hospital bed-day as an input, I would treat it as a form of output because it can be produced with different combinations of inputs. I would not deny, of course, that a bed-day is also an input in producing the output, "a treated case". But a treated case is also an input in producing an improvement in the community's health level".

25   In terms of the house-building analogy, TC_i would represent the total cost of the twelve houses, ACC_i would represent the average cost per house, n_i would be the number of houses built ($n_i = 12$), ACD_i would be the average cost of inputs used per day of construction, and d_i would represent the total number of days taken to construct the twelve houses.

$$ACC_i = ACD_i \times ALS_i \qquad\qquad ... (3.2)$$

where ALS_i is the average length of stay in the ith hospital, given by (d_i / n_i).

It is evident from equation (3.2) that any given average cost per case can be obtained by a range of combinations of average cost per day and average length of stay. This is illustrated in Figure 3.1 which contains two contours for two particular values of average cost per case (ACC_1 and ACC_2) showing the relationship given in equation (3.2). These contours are rectangular hyperbolas—along any given contour, the product of ACD and ALS is a constant.

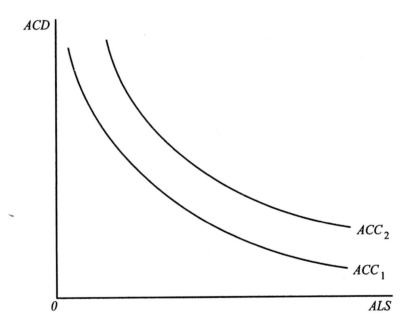

Figure 3.1. Average Cost Per Day, Average Length of Stay and Constant Average Cost Per Case Contours (not to scale)

Define the elasticity of average length of stay with respect to average cost per day (E), or the duration/intensity elasticity, as follows:

$$E = \frac{\Delta ALS / ALS}{\Delta ACD / ACD} \qquad\qquad \text{... (3.3)}$$

Then along any given contour in Figure 3.1, $E = -1$ since the proportionate changes in *ALS* and *ACD* are equal (in absolute terms). The cost-reducing (cost-increasing) effects of a reduction (increase) in average length of stay are just offset by the cost-increasing (cost-reducing) effects of higher (lower) resource usage per day of stay, or average cost per day.

In fact, a hospital may not be able to move along a given *ACC* contour. It may be the case that the cost-reducing effects of a reduction in average length of stay will be less than offset by the cost-increasing effects of increased average cost per day, so that average cost per case actually falls. The duration/intensity elasticity would be greater than unity (in absolute value) in this case, i.e. $E < -1$. It is, of course, also possible that this elasticity could be less than unity (in absolute value).

Figure 3.2 depicts one possible adjustment path which might face a particular hospital. Suppose the hospital is at point *B*. A reduction in average length of stay from ALS_1 to ALS_2 is accompanied by an increase in average cost per day from ACD_1 to ACD_2.[26] As a result, the hospital moves onto a lower average cost per case contour (point *C* on ACC_3), reducing average cost per unit of output. The duration/intensity elasticity exceeds unity (in absolute value) over this range. The same is true for the move from *C* to *D*, but for reductions in average length of stay below ALS_3, the duration/intensity elasticity is less than unity and average cost per case increases (as in the move from *D* to *E*). For the given quality of care and volume and composition of cases treated by this hospital, average cost per case is minimised at point *D* on the contour ACC_2 with the duration/intensity combination ALS_3 and ACD_3.

The adjustment path depicted in Figure 3.2 has been drawn so as to provide an interior solution for this constrained cost-minimisation problem. This presumes that this path is negatively sloped and of sufficient convexity to provide such a solution. Support for both of these properties is provided by considering what is called a 'patient cost profile'—a diagram showing the cost incurred on each day of stay for the duration of a patient's stay in hospital.

---

[26]   It is assumed that both quality of care and the volume and composition of cases treated by the hospital remain constant.

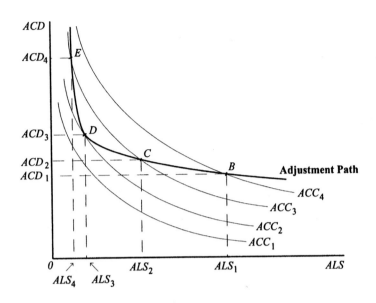

Figure 3.2. Constant Average Cost Per Case Contours and an Adjustment Path
(not to scale)

Figure 3.3 illustrates what is considered to be the general shape of such a profile (Cullis and West 1979, p.148). This diagram breaks costs down into three broad categories—the fixed costs of admission and discharge (A), hotel costs (B) and treatment costs (C). The fixed costs of admission and discharge (A) are incurred on the first and last days of the stay, while hotel costs (B) are likely to be the same on each day of stay. It can be seen that the peaking of costs relatively early in the stay is due to the pattern of treatment costs (C).

> These are hypothesised to rise to a peak relatively early in the patient's stay and then decline. Such a pattern is highly plausible for the simple surgical case, where surgery is followed by recuperation, initially with extensive supervision or intensive care but falling to only nominal supervision as the patient's health recovers. Obviously, the profile will differ for different types of illness. But even for cases that do not require surgery (unless they are long-stay cases, such as the mentally ill or the old), therapeutic activity is likely to reach a peak early in the

treatment and to decline towards the end (Cullis and West 1979, pp.147-8).

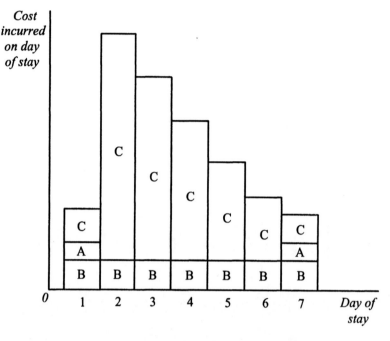

Figure 3.3. Hypothetical Patient Cost Profile

The cost of treating the patient whose profile is shown in Figure 3.3 is the sum of the costs incurred on each day of stay. Mathematically, for the jth patient in the ith hospital who has a length of stay of s days ($s = 7$ in Figure 3.3), the total cost of treating the case is given by

$$TC_{ij} = \sum_{k=1}^{s} \left(A_{ijk} + B_{ijk} + C_{ijk} \right)$$

... (3.4)

Average cost per day for this patient is then obtained by dividing this amount by the length of stay s.[27]

---

[27] Empirical evidence supporting the behaviour of the patient cost profile as depicted in Figure 3.3 has been produced by Babson (1973, esp. pp.20-28) for the treatment of inguinal hernias and appendicitis, and Kaufman and Shepard (1982) in a study of neonatal intensive care.

Suppose that the length of stay is now reduced by one day. Given the patient cost profile in Figure 3.3, and assuming initially that the costs incurred on each of the first six days of stay remain unchanged,[28] the average cost per day for this patient must rise since the marginal cost of the seventh day is less than the average cost per day of the seven day stay. If an increase in costs incurred on the remaining days of stay is then allowed for, this would increase average cost per day even further. In either case, then, the slope of the adjustment path in Figure 3.2 is negative.

The degree of convexity of the adjustment path can be related to the extent to which it is possible to reduce length of stay without increasing the costs incurred on the remaining days of stay. It can be argued that this is less likely to occur the shorter is the length of stay. Before considering this, though, it should be noted that, if the costs incurred on each remaining day of stay are unchanged, then average cost per case will fall with a reduction in length of stay. Eliminating a day of stay without incurring any further costs on the remaining days of stay must reduce the total cost of treating a case and so must reduce the average cost of treating all cases.

When length of stay is reduced, it can be argued that costs incurred on each remaining day of stay are more likely to remain unchanged the longer the length of stay. The longer a patient stays in hospital, the less important is treatment likely to become, with hotel costs eventually dominating the costs incurred on each day of stay. Further, the treatment being given each day may well be in the form of 'check ups' which can be eliminated without affecting the quality of care being delivered. Consequently, eliminating one of these days of stay seems least likely to push up costs on any of the remaining days of stay.

As length of stay shortens, however, this will become progressively more difficult to achieve. Treatment scheduled for the day to be eliminated may have to be brought forward, causing average cost per day to rise more quickly than it would when this is not the case. This may well lead to average cost per case increasing as length of stay is reduced.

The foregoing argument leads to an adjustment path the general shape of which is depicted in Figure 3.2. When length of stay is relatively long, a reduction in length of stay is less likely to increase costs incurred on the remaining days of stay so that average cost per case will fall (as in the move from *B* to *C*). As length of stay is further reduced, however, it becomes

---

28   Strictly speaking, in terms of the profile given in Figure 3.3, this is impossible since the fixed costs of discharge (A) would now have to be added on to the costs incurred on the sixth day of stay.

increasingly likely that costs incurred earlier in the stay will rise and, at some point, cause average cost per case to increase.

The duration/intensity trade-off lies at the heart of the problem of using the patient day as the unit of output. As has been shown, a hospital can reduce the duration of treatment and increase its intensity, reflected in an increase in average cost per day, while at the same time reducing average cost per case (again as shown in the move from B to C in Figure 3.2). If the patient day were the unit of output, average cost per unit of output has increased, while the converse is true if the case is the unit of output. This point is clearly critical for interhospital comparisons of productive efficiency. Suppose two hospitals are treating the same volume and composition of cases and providing the same quality of care. If one hospital is at point B in Figure 3.2 and the other is at point D, which one is judged to be more efficient is critically dependent on the unit of output adopted. If comparisons are based on average cost per day, then the hospital at point B would be judged to be more efficient even though its average cost per case is higher.[29]

This problem with the use of the patient day as the unit of output was recognised by Feldstein (1967, p.24): "The possibility of a trade-off between length of stay and cost per week is the most important reason for measuring output in terms of the number of cases treated". It is for this reason also that Fuchs (1974, p.92) makes the following observation: "Another target the press singles out in its coverage of health care problems is high average cost per patient-day ... Such emphasis on cost per day is often misplaced". Beresford (1972, p.165) is also critical of the "almost nineteenth-century concern for costs per in-patient week rather than for costs per case".

The use of the patient day as the unit of output may also explain why some studies have obtained conflicting results on the question of economies of scale in hospitals. Carr and Feldstein (1967) found average cost per day fell as average daily census increased to 190, while Ingbar and Taylor (1968) found that average cost per day increased to a *maximum* at a size of 150 beds and fell thereafter. In neither case need there be any necessary correlation between the behaviour of cost per day and cost per case. In fact, Feldstein (1967, p.24) reported a correlation of only 0.232 between these two magnitudes in his study, while for the Queensland hospitals included in the present study, the correlation coefficient in 1979-80 was only 0.203.

---

[29]   Empirical evidence of this type of situation has been produced by Beresford (1972) in a study of hospitals in England. He finds that "the hospitals with heavy costs per in-patient week are also likely to be the least costly hospitals per case treated" (p.168).

Cullis and West (1979) point out that the reason some studies have used the patient day as the unit of output is that detailed data on the mix of cases have not been available. In this situation, "if the more difficult cases also have a longer stay in hospital (as seems plausible in general) owing to variations in the sophistication of treatment and the time required to recuperate, then the patient day as the unit of output is crudely standardised for case type differences" (Cullis and West 1979, p.149). This argument has also been put by Lave and Lave (1970b). It needs to be emphasised, however, that in such cases the patient day has been employed as a practical expedient rather than a theoretically defensible construct.

In concluding, it should be noted that the treated case has been argued to be a more defensible unit of output than the patient day for treatment provided in *hospitals*. The argument does not necessarily apply to other institutions which may be providing a different type of output. In particular, inpatients in nursing homes do not generally receive treatment for a specific illness or illnesses but are rather being assisted or cared for with regard to matters of everyday living (cooking, bathing, and so on). For such institutions a strong case can be made that a day of care is the unit of output, not a treatment.[30] This can give rise to problems in measuring hospital output, for if nursing home type patients are being cared for in hospitals (along with the usual patients requiring acute care), they should be recognised as receiving a conceptually distinct type of output. This distinction, however, is often more readily drawn in theory than in practice, giving rise to empirical problems as a consequence.

In discussing the concept and measurement of hospital output, this chapter has so far only briefly alluded to the fact that treatments may differ for different illnesses. Under these circumstances, a treated case may not be a homogeneous unit of output even within a hospital. This is another important dimension of the multiproduct nature of the hospital, one which must now be addressed.

---

[30] To quote Beresford (1972, p.165): "Costs per in-patient week and costs per unit are still of some significance as indicators of efficient resource use in long-stay hospitals, where the accent is on maintaining the patient more or less permanently rather than on cure and discharge. In short-stay hospitals, however, it is far more logical and meaningful to consider the patient's stay and the cost of curing and discharging him".

3.4   The Classification of Output

Given the treatment conception of hospital output and its empirically proximate counterpart, the treated case, it must be recognised that not all treatments provided within a hospital are identical. The treatment will vary according to, among other things, the illness of the patient or the patient's diagnosis, so that different treatments will employ different technologies and require different quantities and types of inputs. All treatments cannot then be considered to belong to the same class of output, and allowance must be made for the multiproduct nature of hospital output in this respect.

The term 'case mix' has evolved to describe this phenomenon, but as one author has commented, "no uniform or adequate definition of this term has yet developed" (Hornbrook 1982a, p.1). Generally, it refers to the mix of cases treated by a hospital classified on the basis of those criteria which are significant in explaining the differences in resource usage between the various cases treated. It is the lack of a definitive set of such criteria which has precluded the development of a "uniform or adequate definition" of the term.

Various criteria have been employed by different authors in classifying cases for the purpose of hospital cost analysis. For example, Feldstein (1967) classified cases on the basis of the medical specialty providing the treatment.[31] Lave, Lave and Silverman (1972) classified cases into 17 broad diagnostic classifications and three surgical classifications (no surgery, simple surgery, and complex surgery). They also included four patient characteristics concerned with age and payment status. But however defined, case mix is of fundamental importance and the development of a case mix classification scheme is a central issue.

While this point is widely recognised and agreed upon, there are two divergent approaches to the incorporation of this information into hospital output measurement. One approach is to work with multiple output categories which are constructed on the basis of a case mix classification scheme. The volume of output within each category is then the number of cases treated within that category. The second approach, although taking account of the diagnostic and perhaps other characteristics of patients, seeks to construct a single-valued measure of hospital case mix through the use of a case mix index. In contrast with the first approach, this approach does not result in multiple output categories, instead seeking to capture the influence

---

[31]   The eight medical specialty groups were: general medicine; paediatrics; general surgery; ear, nose and throat; traumatic and orthopaedic surgery; other surgery; gynaecology; and obstetrics.

of case mix in a scalar case mix index. These two approaches will each be discussed in turn.

3.4.1   Case Mix Classification Schemes

Two particularly prominent case mix classification schemes will be discussed—the International Classification of Diseases, and Diagnosis-Related Groups.[32]

(a)   The International Classification of Diseases (ICD)

The ICD codes, as contained in the Manual of the International Statistical Classification of Diseases, Injuries and Causes of Death published by the World Health Organization, provide the most detailed disease classification system currently available. The classification was originally developed as a classification of causes of death by a committee of the International Statistical Institute and was adopted by the Institute in 1893.[33] This first classification was called the Bertillon Classification of Causes of Death after the chairman of the committee responsible for its preparation.

In recommending the adoption of the Bertillon Classification in the United States, Mexico and Canada in 1898, the American Public Health Association also suggested that the classification be revised every 10 years. This suggestion was adopted at a meeting of the International Statistical Institute in 1899, with the first revision being undertaken in 1900. The scope of the classification was broadened to include mortality and morbidity with the sixth revision published in the late 1940s.

The current version of the Manual contains the ninth revision of the codes—ICD-9 (see World Health Organization 1977). This contains approximately 1,000 categories at the three-digit level and a substantially larger number than this at the four-digit level.[34] These categories are

---

[32] Hornbrook (1982b, pp.74-104) also provides a discussion of these and several other case mix classification schemes.

[33] The following historical information has been taken from the Manual containing the eighth revision (see World Health Organization 1967, pp.ix-xiii).

[34] The Commission on Professional and Hospital Activities (CPHA) in the US produces a modified version of ICD-9 for use by US hospitals. A number of the four-digit codes in ICD-9 are further broken down by a fifth digit in this clinically modified version of the codes - ICD-9-CM. This version contains 10,171 categories. A discussion of ICD-9-CM can be found in Hornbrook (1982b, pp.74-6) while some remarks of a comparative nature about ICD-9 and ICD-9-CM can be found in Palmer and Wood (1984, pp.77-9).

contained within 17 major chapter headings representing major classes of diseases and injuries plus a Supplementary Classification of Factors Influencing Health Status and Contact with Health Services (the V codes).

The ICD codes provide a mutually exclusive and exhaustive set of possible output categories for a hospital. These are important characteristics for any output classification scheme for they ensure that all units of output produced are captured and that double counting is avoided. There are, however, some limitations associated with this taxonomy. First, it does not include some dimensions of case mix which may be important sources of heterogeneity between cases. These include age, sex and the presence or type of any surgery performed. Further, "the dimension of severity, i.e. mild, moderate, severe, ... is specified only for a few selected diagnoses" (Hornbrook 1982b, p.75). As a result, cases falling within any particular ICD code may still be heterogeneous with respect to the treatment received on account of these omitted factors.

A second problem arises because of the large number of output categories which arises from this classification. At the four-digit level, zero or small number cells are likely to be common, giving rise to problems of small sample size in statistical analysis. Further, such a large number of output categories would eliminate any possibility of econometrically estimating hospital cost functions in most studies. As pointed out in the previous chapter, the number of independent variables will be equal to the number of output categories even in a restricted specification, and will greatly exceed this in a less constrained specification. Some aggregation of the four-digit or three-digit codes would then be necessary but this could exacerbate the problem of heterogeneity within case types just discussed.

Although from an economist's perspective these are important shortcomings, the ICD codes provide a comprehensive disease classification system and have formed the basis of several other output classification schemes which have been developed. They also form the basis of the output categories employed in the empirical analysis presented in Part B of this book.

(b)   Diagnosis-Related Groups

Of the various case mix classification schemes which have been developed, that based on DRGs has gained particular prominence and is "perhaps the most well known and widely applied case-mix measure" (Hornbrook 1982b, p.83). The scheme has been elucidated by Fetter, Shin, Freeman, Averill and Thompson (1980) who state that "The primary objective in the construction of the DRGs was a definition of case types, each of which could be expected to receive similar outputs or services from a hospital" (p.5).

The original DRGs were constructed using the eighth revision of the ICD, adapted for use in the United States (ICDA-8). However, primary diagnosis was not the only characteristic used in constructing the groups. Other attributes finally employed included some or all of the following: secondary diagnosis; primary surgical procedure; secondary surgical procedure; age; and (for one DRG) clinical service area.[35] Hence the DRGs do not simply represent aggregations of ICD codes.

To begin with, 83 mutually exclusive and exhaustive Major Diagnostic Categories (MDCs) were formed based on primary diagnosis.[36] Each of these MDCs was then subdivided using a statistical algorithm which formed sub-groups so as to maximise the reduction in variance of a particular dependent variable, in this case length of stay.[37] The initial split of an MDC was determined by calculating the percentage reduction in the variance of length of stay which would result by splitting the MDC into two or more sub-groups using each of the attributes mentioned above, together with those that were eventually excluded. An attribute was then selected to form the basis of the first split. "Variables yielding the highest percentage reduction in variance were prime candidates for dividing the data set. However, the number of cells or values for those variables and the number of groups formed were also considered" (Fetter, *et al.* 1980, p.12).

Following the initial split, each sub-group was again divided on the basis of the remaining attributes, the algorithm continuing this iterative process until the final groups were formed. "Subgroups are designated terminal groups when they cannot be partitioned further because the sample sizes are too small or the remaining variation is either too low to be reduced further or unexplainable in terms of the variables in the data base" (Fetter, *et al.* 1980, pp.6-7).[38] The resulting 383 final patient classes were the DRGs.

A tree diagram illustrating the partitioning of MDC 55—Urinary Calculus is contained in Figure 3.4 (taken from Fetter, *et al.* 1980, p.14).

---

[35] Although sex, tertiary diagnosis and tertiary procedure were also included initially as potentially important attributes, empirically they were found not to be important and consequently were not used in defining any of the final groups.

[36] A list of these MDCs can be found in Fetter, *et al.* (1980, pp.9-11).

[37] A discussion of the algorithm, known as the AUTOGRP (autogroup) algorithm, can be found in Mills, Fetter, Riedel and Averill (1976).

[38] The minimum acceptable group size was 100.

The initial split, based on primary surgical procedure and reducing the variance of length of stay by nearly 42 per cent, produced three groups as shown in the diagram. The 'without surgery' group was then split again with four groups being formed on the basis of secondary diagnosis codes. However, two of these had too few observations and so were added in with another group, the three groups then forming one group of patients who shared a common attribute—the presence of a secondary diagnosis. The remaining group had no secondary diagnosis listed. These two groups, along with the two groups which had surgical procedures performed, were terminal groups as further splits were either dubious with respect to medical interpretability or suffered from small cell size. Consequently, from MDC 55 came DRGs 239-242.

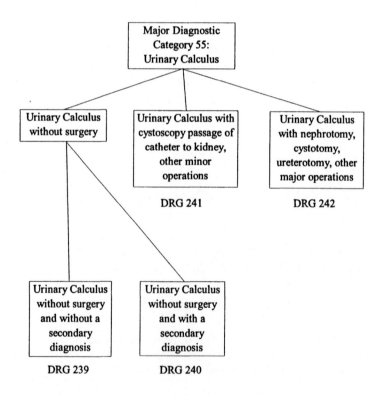

Figure 3.4. The Formation of DRGs From Major Diagnostic Category 55—
Urinary Calculus

The discussion of the foregoing example made reference to medical interpretability, an aspect of the construction of DRGs so far unmentioned. At each step, formation of the groups was subject to the requirement that they be medically meaningful, so that

> when the patient classes are described to physicians, they should be able to relate to these patients and be able to identify a particular patient management process for them ... For example, from the point of view of output utilization, it may be appropriate to form a patient class with hemorrhoids, hypertrophy of tonsils, and normal delivery ... However, the physician who would treat these patients as well as the treatment process of the problems they are presenting are quite different. Therefore, it was felt that including such patients in the same class would not define a medically meaningful category (Fetter, *et al.* 1980, pp.5,8).

This check on medical meaningfulness may also help to ensure economic meaningfulness of the categories. The fact that two items cost the same to produce does not mean they are the same type of output (e.g. a car and an overseas holiday). Medical meaningfulness, by ensuring some degree of medical homogeneity of case types within groups, would also tend to ensure a high degree of homogeneity in the treatment provided, or the output produced, for cases in that group.

In constructing the original set of DRGs, certain cases were excluded. Patients who died were omitted "since their lengths of stay were probably atypical of the disease or problem under consideration" (Fetter, *et al.* 1980, p.8). Records with missing data or coding errors were also deleted, as were cases which had particularly high lengths of stay. The exclusion of deaths can be criticised since it implies "that deaths are counted the same as live discharges or that deaths are not counted as part of the output of the hospital, despite the fact that considerable resources may have been devoted to treating these cases" (Hornbrook 1982b, p.87).

Following the publication of the ninth revision of the ICD (World Health Organization 1977), a revised version of the DRGs was developed. Beginning with a smaller number of 23 MDCs defined mostly in terms of the organ system affected, the revised version contains a total of 467 DRGs plus three additional patient classes for patients who had surgical procedures performed which were unrelated to the their principal diagnosis, and patients with medical record coding errors (see Health Systems International 1984). For most MDCs, the initial split was into two groups based on whether an operating room procedure was or was not performed. In contrast with the derivation of the original DRGs, the revised version embraced discharge status (including death) as a basis for classification, and placed more emphasis on clinical judgement relative to statistical criteria in forming the terminal groups.[39]

Grimaldi and Micheletti (1982) criticised both the original and revised versions of the DRGs because of a lack of economic homogeneity within the groups. "Economic homogeneity pertains to the dollar value of the resources patients consume. A DRG possesses perfect economic homogeneity when patients receive tests, surgical procedures, hours of nursing care, pharmaceuticals etc. with identical dollar values" (Grimaldi and Micheletti 1982, p.59). In other words, it is argued that DRGs do not represent output categories within which each unit of output is homogeneous. Five points are made (p.59).[40]

> The potential for cost differences ... is bolstered by the fact that DRG assignment is not dependent on the number of diagnoses, procedures, complications, and co-morbid conditions that a patient has. A second problem is that the new DRGs do not entirely recognize the severity or stage of a patient's illness. Third, patients with non-operating room procedures will be categorized with medical patients ... Fourth, a principal diagnosis is not necessarily the major diagnosis, or the condition that consumes the most resources. Finally, since the DRGs were not constructed on reabstracted data, the resultant classification scheme probably differs from the "true" scheme, perhaps substantially.

Empirical evidence on the importance of severity of illness as a source of heterogeneity within DRGs has been produced by Horn and Sharkey (1983). A Severity of Illness Index was constructed and used to estimate how much of the variability in charges within selected DRGs (as well as within case mix categories constructed with three other case mix classification schemes) was explained by differences in severity. Data were selected for a sample of 100 admissions for each case type in each of four hospitals. The authors found "that much of the variability (particularly in the university teaching hospital) is accounted for by differences in Severity of Illness ... the 19 DRGs do not account sufficiently for differences in Severity of Illness and hence do not account sufficiently for differences in patient resource

---

[39] Palmer and Wood (1984) provide an overview of the revised version of the DRGs.

[40] Some other criticisms of DRGs are summarised in Hornbrook (1982b, pp.83-91).

utilisation" (Horn and Sharkey 1983, p.320).[41] In a similar vein, a study by Berki, Ashcraft and Newbrander (1984) found that 30-65 per cent of the variation in length of stay within a selected set of DRGs was explicable by indicators of case complexity and severity.

This general problem of within-group heterogeneity of treatments (or cases treated) was noted with respect to the ICD also. The extent to which severity and other factors give rise to heterogeneity is an important matter. The analysis of production and costs for the multiproduct firm presented in Chapter 2 was conducted in terms of output categories within each of which all units of output were homogeneous. Consequently, total output within any category is simply the unweighted sum of these units. In summing output across categories, a more complex aggregator function is required because of heterogeneity between groups. Under certain conditions this function could be linear, or a weighted sum, with the weights being relative average cost per unit of output (see section 2.3).

Strictly speaking, if two units of output are heterogeneous, they belong to different output categories. In the context of hospitals, the problem is that no two patients may receive exactly homogeneous treatments, so that "the hospital may be viewed as a multiproduct firm with a product line that in theory is as extensive as the number of patients it serves" (Fetter, *et al.* 1980, p.1). Given this situation, once cases are aggregated into groups, some within-group heterogeneity is inevitable and will increase with the level of aggregation. It is because of this that the use of a restricted functional form for estimating a hospital cost function is attractive. As was shown in Chapter 2, flexible functional forms are not parsimonious in parameters so that, for any given number of observations, the number of output categories which can be used is restricted. This leads to an increase in within-group heterogeneity. For example, if a case mix classification scheme consisting of four categories defined in terms of sex and the presence or absence of surgery were used, there would be a large amount of heterogeneity between treatments within each group because of wide variations in diagnoses. At the other extreme, of course, a large number of case mix categories, while reducing the problem of within-group heterogeneity, also reduces the number of degrees of freedom and, if sufficiently large, may preclude statistical estimation altogether.

---

[41] The term "I9 DRGs" refers to the DRGs constructed using ICD-9-CM codes. A more detailed discussion of the Severity of Illness Index used in this study is contained in Horn, Sharkey and Bertram (1983). On the concept and measurement of severity of illness, see also Baker, O'Neill, Haddon and Long (1974), Krischer (1976, 1979) and O'Neill, Zador and Baker (1979).

Both the DRGs and the ICD contain too many output categories for the statistical estimations of hospital cost relationships attempted in this study. A more highly aggregated set of output categories is then required. The actual classification schemes used are discussed in Chapter 5, but before proceeding to this it remains to discuss single-valued case mix indexes.

3.4.2   Scalar Case Mix Indexes

A scalar case mix index attempts to provide a single-valued measure of the output composition of a hospital. The multiproduct nature of the hospital is taken into account in constructing the index by the use of weights incorporated into the aggregator function, such weights reflecting the heterogeneity between case mix categories. Hornbrook (1982b, p.104) identifies three components of such an index: a diagnostic classification scheme; a weighting scheme; and an aggregation formula.

Addressing the last of these first, aggregation formulae can generally be either linear or non-linear. "In practice, most authors assume a linear relationship. This assumption reflects the simplicity of a linear index and the lack of *a priori* or empirical support for a more complex formulation." (Klastorin and Watts 1980, p.678). A weighting scheme is necessary to establish relativities between the various case types and so allow meaningful aggregation. An important consideration in establishing these relativities is the objective to be achieved in constructing the index. If it is used in an analysis of hospital costs then the weights would presumably reflect the relative costliness of treating the various case types. If, however, the index is to be used as an indicator of the social benefit resulting from the treatment then the weights would reflect the relative social value placed on the treatment of each case type. The third component of such an index—a diagnostic classification scheme—has been discussed in the first part of this section.

Perhaps the most well known scalar case mix index is the information theory index first developed by Evans and Walker (1972). The information theory approach postulates that the information gain from learning that an event has taken place is inversely related to the prior probability of that event occurring (see Theil 1967; 1971, pp.636-64). If an event is almost certain to take place (i.e. it has a high probability of occurrence) then the information gain from learning that it has in fact taken place is relatively low, and vice versa. This information gain is quantified as

$$\ln\left(\frac{1}{p_i}\right) \qquad\qquad ...(3.5)$$

where p_i is the prior probability of the ith occurrence. The information gain across all events is then given as the probability-weighted sum of these individual gains,

$$\sum_i p_i \ln\left(\frac{1}{p_i}\right) \qquad\qquad ...(3.6)$$

These concepts can also be used as a basis for evaluating the information gain from learning that the probability of occurrence of an event has altered, say to q_i rather than learning whether the event actually took place. If the ith event does take place with probability q_i, the information gain from learning that this has happened will be

$$\ln\left(\frac{1}{q_i}\right) \qquad\qquad ...(3.7)$$

As such, the information gain from learning of the revised probability of occurrence is given by

$$\ln\left(\frac{1}{q_i}\right) - \ln\left(\frac{1}{p_i}\right) = \ln\left(\frac{q_i}{p_i}\right) \qquad\qquad ...(3.8)$$

Again, for the complete series of events, the total information gain from learning of the revised probabilities of occurrence is the probability-weighted sum

$$\sum_i q_i \ln\left(\frac{q_i}{p_i}\right) \qquad\qquad ...(3.9)$$

where the weights are the altered probabilities.

In explaining the construction of the information theory case mix index, consider first the matrix presented in Table 3.1. The columns in this matrix represent diagnostic categories while the rows represent hospitals. Define

$$p_{ij} = \frac{n_{ij}}{N_{i\cdot}}$$

as the proportion of the ith hospital's cases falling in the jth diagnostic category, and

$$q_{ij} = \frac{n_{ij}}{N_{\cdot j}}$$

as the proportion of cases of the jth type being treated in the ith hospital. The following relationships may then be stated:

$$\sum_j p_{ij} = \sum_i q_{ij} = 1$$

$$\sum_i p_{ij} \neq 1 \qquad\qquad\qquad \text{... (3.10)}$$

$$\sum_j q_{ij} \neq 1$$

Also define

$$p_i = \frac{N_{i\cdot}}{N}$$

as the proportion of all cases in the hospital system treated by the ith hospital, and

$$q_j = \frac{N_{\cdot j}}{N}$$

as the proportion of all cases in the hospital system falling in the jth diagnostic category.

Evans and Walker then define two information measures for case type j, of which the first is

$$H_j^1 = \sum_i q_{ij} \ln \left(\frac{q_{ij}}{\frac{1}{I}} \right) \qquad\qquad\qquad \text{... (3.11)}$$

Table 3.1. Hospital Case Mix Data

Diagnostic category

		1	2	·	·	j	·	·	·	J	
	1	n_{11}	n_{12}	·	·	n_{1j}	·	·	·	n_{1J}	$N_{1\cdot}$
	2	n_{21}	n_{22}	·	·	n_{2j}	·	·	·	n_{2J}	$N_{2\cdot}$
	·	·	·			·			·		·
	·	·	·			·			·		·
Hospital	·	·	·			·			·		·
	i	n_{i1}	n_{i2}	·	·	n_{ij}	·	·	·	n_{iJ}	$N_{i\cdot}$
	·	·	·			·			·		·
	·	·	·			·			·		·
	I	n_{I1}	n_{I2}	·	·	n_{Ij}	·	·	·	n_{IJ}	$N_{I\cdot}$
		$N_{\cdot1}$	$N_{\cdot2}$	·	·	$N_{\cdot j}$	·	·	·	$N_{\cdot J}$	N

n^{ij} = number of cases treated in the ith hospital in the jth diagnostic category

$N_i = \sum_{j=1}^{J} n_{ij}$ = total number of cases treated in the ith hospital

$N_{\cdot j} = \sum_{i=1}^{I} n_{ij}$ = total number of cases treated in the jth diagnostic category

$N = \sum_{i=1}^{I} N_i = \sum_{j=1}^{J} N_{\cdot j}$ = total number of cases treated in all hospitals in all diagnostic

categories

This gives "the expected information content of the actual distribution of cases of type j among hospitals, given that our prior knowledge was only that there were I ... active treatment hospitals" (Evans and Walker 1972, p.401).[42] Relating this to equation (3.9), the q_{ij} are the probabilities of occurrence of the event (the event being the treatment of a case of type j in

---

[42]   The authors note that if $q_{ij} = 0$ (i.e. no cases of type j are treated in hospital i), then $Iq_{ij} = 0$ and $\ln(Iq_{ij})$ is undefined. As such, $\ln(Iq_{ij})$ is defined to be zero whenever $q_{ij} = 0$.

hospital i), while $(1/I)$ shows that, in the absence of any information on the actual distribution of cases, the probability of a case going to any hospital is the same for all hospitals and equal to the inverse of the number of hospitals.

If all I hospitals treated the same proportion of cases of type j then $q_{1j} = q_{2j} = ... = 1/I$, that is, each hospital would be treating $(1/I)$ of the total cases of type j. In this situation, the actual distribution of cases is identical to that hypothesised in the absence of any additional information. The information gain would then be expected to be zero, which is the value which results from substituting $q_{ij} = 1/I$ into (3.11). Hence, the more evenly distributed the cases among the hospitals, the lower is the information gain, with a completely equal distribution rendering a zero information gain. Conversely, the more concentrated the cases in a smaller number of hospitals, the larger is the information gain. The following crucial hypothesis then establishes the nexus between concentration, complexity and this measure of information gain: "If concentration is associated with complexity, then the expected information gain of a specific case type is a measure of its complexity" (Evans and Walker 1972, p.401). More complex case types then give rise to a larger information gain.

The second information measure for case type j is as follows:

$$H_j^2 = \sum_i q_{ij} \ln\left(\frac{q_{ij}}{p_i}\right) \qquad\qquad ... (3.12)$$

This differs from the first in that prior knowledge is now of the p_i (the proportion of all cases treated in the ith hospital) and not just I (the number of hospitals). As such, the prior probability is now sensitive to volume rather than assuming that all hospitals would take an equal proportion of all cases (equal to $1/I$). Clearly, the two measures would be equal if $p_1 = p_2 = p_I = 1/I$.

The two information measures are then standardised to have a mean of unity as follows:

$$\overline{H}_j^1 = \frac{H_j^1}{\sum_j H_j^1 q_j}$$

$$\overline{H}_j^2 = \frac{H_j^2}{\sum_j H_j^2 q_j}$$

The standardised measures are then used as weights in a linear aggregation formula to produce two measures of the relative complexity of a hospital's case load:

$$X_i^1 = \sum_j \overline{H}_j^1 p_{ij}$$

$$\qquad \qquad \qquad \qquad \qquad \qquad \qquad ... (3.13)$$

$$X_i^2 = \sum_j \overline{H}_j^2 p_{ij}$$

X_i^1 and X_i^2 are index numbers calculated as a weighted sum of case mix proportions where the weights are the standardised measures of complexity of each case type.[43]

The information theory approach has subsequently been employed in empirical studies by Tatchell (1977), Culyer and Drummond (1978), Horn and Schumacher (1979), Barer (1982), Schapper (1984) and Butler (1988b).[44] It has the general advantage of scalar case mix indexes, namely that it reduces the dimensionality of the data, collapsing a large amount of information into a single index number. Further, it can be applied to any case mix classification scheme. However, as with all single-valued indexes, identical values of the index can be obtained for hospitals with different underlying case mixes (see Klastorin and Watts 1980, p.679 for an example of this).

In addition, the underlying hypothesis that a higher concentration of cases in a smaller number of hospitals implies higher complexity may confuse complexity with rarity. This problem is likely to become more serious the more disaggregated is the underlying case mix classification scheme.[45] Further, the index assumes what Klastorin and Watts (1980) have

---

[43] Derivations of the information theory case mix index can also be found in Horn and Schumacher (1979) and Tatchell (1980).

[44] The study by Schapper also develops an alternative case severity index for a hospital which depends on the case mix of the hospital (using 50 case mix categories), the relative initial dependencies of each case type (estimated on the basis of nurse dependency data), and lengths of stay. The results are compared with those obtained using the Evans-Walker index constructed from the same data. See Schapper (1984, Ch.6).

[45] Tatchell (1977, Ch.9) has produced some empirical evidence on this based on New Zealand hospitals.

termed 'functional homogeneity'—that the relationship embodied in the index is sufficiently similar across institutions to justify using the same aggregation formula and the same weights (see also Hornbrook 1982b, pp.111-16).

In concluding this discussion it should be emphasised that scalar case mix indexes do not vitiate the necessity of classifying output to take account of the multiproduct nature of the hospital. On the contrary, a case mix classification scheme is an essential ingredient in the creation of such an index. It follows, therefore, that scalar case mix indexes will also have built into them any weaknesses or limitations of the underlying output categories used in their construction.

3.5   Summary and Conclusions

This chapter has examined the problems of conceptualising, measuring and classifying hospital output. In common with service industries in general, the outputs of a hospital are intangible, making these problems particularly difficult ones to resolve.

At a conceptual level, two broad schools of thought can be distinguished. One of these argues that hospitals produce health, or more correctly, changes in health status. The other argues that hospitals produce treatment which may or may not change the patient's health status. The health status conception is not operational for two main reasons—first, the empirical measurement of changes in health status is a daunting task, and secondly, even if changes in health status could be measured, it is difficult to separate out the marginal contribution of hospital services from the contributions of other factors which influence the outcome (such as patient compliance, diet, and so on).

In terms of empirical implementation, the treatment conception has a distinct advantage. This does not, however, imply that the health status conception is conceptually superior and that the adoption of the treatment conception in practice is a second-best alternative. In this chapter it has been argued that the treatment conception is defensible on theoretical grounds. This argument is based on the uncertainty which surrounds the impact of treatment on health status and the resulting scope for the provision of insurance cover against the financial loss attendant upon unsuccessful treatment. If patients paid hospitals only for improvements in health status, they would be paying only for successful treatments. Consequently, the hospital would be producing two outputs—treatment, and insurance against the possibility of unsuccessful treatment. Even under these circumstances, then, it can be argued that the output of the hospital is not a change in health status.

Moving on to the problem of measurement, a connection must be established between the abstract concept of a treatment and an empirically workable unit of output measurement. It was argued that an episode of hospitalisation, or a treated case, could be taken as an empirical workable counterpart of the treatment conception. An alternative unit of output—the patient day—was also considered but, in the context of acute inpatient hospital care, was argued to be more of an input-related measure. In particular, it is related to the time dimension over which a unit of output (a treated case) is produced. Interhospital comparisons of average cost per patient day can be quite misleading because of the confounding influence of variations in average length of stay.

The issue of classifying hospital output arises because of the multiproduct nature of inpatient treatment provided by a hospital. Not all treated cases are homogeneous since the treatment produced will depend on, among other things, the patient's diagnosis. The term 'case mix' has evolved to describe the mix of cases treated by a hospital classified according to a set of criteria aimed at achieving homogeneity within case mix categories or output categories. Two broad approaches to the measurement of case mix were then discussed. The first of these adopts a disaggregated approach, aiming to minimise the within-group heterogeneity of treatments provided. The ICD and DRGs were reviewed in this context. The second approach, while employing a case mix classification scheme, attempts to summarise this information in a single-valued measure such as a scalar case mix index. The information theory index developed by Evans and Walker (1972) was discussed to demonstrate this approach.

This and the preceding chapter have attempted to lay the major theoretical foundations for the empirical work presented in Part B of this book. Flexible form multiproduct cost functions which enable jointness and input-output separability to be incorporated as testable hypotheses produce a number of parameters to be estimated which is some multiple of the number of output categories adopted. In the context of hospitals, this is a serious problem, for the number of output categories required to provide within-group homogeneity of treatment may be quite large. Even the DRG classification with its 467 categories has been criticised on the grounds of heterogeneity within categories, and this problem worsens the higher the level of aggregation. But a higher level of aggregation is necessary if the number of output categories is to be reduced. This dilemma will manifest itself in the empirical work presented throughout the remainder of this book.

PART B

EMPIRICAL RESULTS

4

THE QUEENSLAND PUBLIC HOSPITAL

SYSTEM—AN OVERVIEW

4.1   Introduction

This short chapter provides an overview of the development of the public
hospital system in Queensland, Australia, highlighting some distinctive
characteristics of this State's system in comparison with that in other States.
It is descriptive in nature, aiming to provide some institutional background
to the hospital system which is the subject of most of the empirical work
presented in this book. Accordingly, the following two Sections outline the
historical background of the Queensland hospital system and discuss some
interstate differences of relevance to the present study. A summary and
conclusions are presented in Section 4.4.

4.2   Historical Background

The history of Queensland's hospital system is characterised by increasing
government intervention and decreasing reliance on patient charges as a

method of funding. This latter trend culminated in the nationalisation of Queensland's public hospitals in 1944, a feature of the hospital system which has remained to the present day.

Prior to its establishment as a separate colony in 1859, Queensland came under the jurisdiction of the colonial administration of New South Wales. "The first hospital accommodation in Brisbane was made available in 1825, and in 1828 the first hospital for convicts was established" (Hospitals and Health Services Commission 1974, p.156). In these early years, public hospitals were run along the lines of English voluntary hospitals, with funds being provided by subscribers and control resting in the hands of a board elected by the subscribers.

The Government's role in hospital provision became formalised with the passage of the Hospitals Act of 1847. Following its foundation as a separate colony, Queensland established a Select Committee to investigate the hospitals in the colony and subsequently introduced its own Hospitals Act in 1867. This Act has been described by one author as "one of the earliest examples anywhere of legislative intervention in hospital management" (Hielscher 1983, p.77).

The impetus for government involvement in Queensland hospitals was essentially financial. The following quotation from Bell (1968, p.40) summarises the arguments at the time.

> At the hearings of the Select Committee all the hospitals complained of the expense of running a hospital with increasing numbers of patients, more expensive treatments, "cases that would require a great deal of wine and brandy", apathy of subscribers and the need for new buildings.

The upshot was the institutionalisation of Government subsidies to provide financial assistance to hospitals.

By the end of the First World War, hospital finances in Queensland were in a parlous state. The voluntary subscription system had broken down and Government subsidies had increased. The bulk of the proceeds of a lottery established by the Queensland Patriotic Fund during the War (the Golden Casket) was, in 1920, directed to the public hospitals.

The Hospitals Act of 1923 formally ended the necessity for hospitals to rely on subscription revenue.[1] Hospital deficits were to be met by the State

---

[1]   A Hospitals Bill was introduced into Parliament by the Labor Government in the 1916-17 session but was rejected by a hostile upper house. However, the upper house (the Legislative Council) was abolished in 1922, allowing clear passage of the Hospitals Act of 1923.

Government and local authorities contributing 60 per cent and 40 per cent respectively. Except for the Brisbane and South Coast hospitals, this funding mechanism was not forced upon hospitals—they could opt to continue under the voluntary system with Government subsidies. "But gradually hospitals crept in under the sheltering wing of the new system" (Bell 1968, p.44).

The Act also put in place a new system of administration and control of public hospitals in Queensland. The State was divided into hospital districts with a hospital board being set up for each district. A board comprised "three government representatives, three local authority representatives, and three members elected by direct vote ..." (Bell 1968, pp.43-4), giving the Government "dominant power in the operation and administration of public hospitals" (Hielscher 1983, p.78).

Following the defeat of the Labor Government in the 1929 election, the new Government appointed a Royal Commission to examine the public hospital system. The issue of control of the hospital boards proved to be controversial. Two of the three Commissioners recommended that the medical profession be given one of the government positions on certain hospital boards while the third argued against representatives of the medical profession being put on hospital boards. The Commission also recommended that 80 per cent of hospital expenditures be financed by a tax on wage and salary incomes above an exemption level, with the remaining 20 per cent coming from local authorities. But the onset of the depression did not create a favourable economic climate for the adoption of such recommendations, and the Government declined to act on the Commission's findings.

Labor was returned to power in 1932 and in 1936 introduced another Hospitals Act which took further steps toward centralising control of the public hospitals. The Governor-in-Council was given power to appoint the chairman of a hospital board, this person previously being elected by the board itself. In addition, "There were clauses to deal with local authorities who voted against paying hospital precepts and giving the Government power to resume all voluntary hospitals and district them" (Bell 1968, p.47).

While the 1936 Act gave hospital boards the power to change from the honorary system of utilising medical staff to a system of full-time salaried medical staff, the 1944 Act abolished the honorary staff system in most hospitals in the State.[2] Local authorities were relieved of their financial

---

2   The honorary system is a system whereby doctors perform services in public hospitals without remuneration, often in exchange for the right to admit patients to private beds in the same hospital. For a discussion of this system, see Scotton (1974, pp.67-76) and Committee of Inquiry into Rights of Private Practice in Public Hospitals (1984).

responsibilities for hospitals and their representation on hospital boards was cut to one. The Labor policy of a nationalised public hospital system funded fully by the Government and provided free of charge to the whole population had finally been completely implemented.

4.3   Interstate Differences

The hospital system in Queensland developed along markedly different lines to the hospital systems in other States. According to Hielscher, this can be traced to the Hospitals Act of 1923 which "marked the beginning of Queensland's divergence from the Australian norm" (Hielscher 1983, p.77). No other States followed the nationalisation path nor did they adopt such a centralised administrative structure for the control of public hospitals. Queensland was also the only State to discontinue the honorary system of medical staffing, although this system has since been dismantled for the most part in other States also.[3]

This distinctive situation in Queensland has often led to "special provisions" being required in Commonwealth/State negotiations concerning the funding of hospitals. The Commonwealth (Labor) Government first entered the hospital financing arena with the passage of the Hospital Benefits Act of 1946. "This Act required state governments to abolish means tests and to admit patients to public wards free of charge, in return for which the Commonwealth paid a uniform daily benefit on all hospital beds at a rate designed to compensate for fee revenue foregone" (Scotton 1974, p.68).[4] But Queensland had already abolished means tests and was treating public patients free of charge so the conditions had no effect on its hospital system.

This attempt by the Commonwealth was short-lived, however. Following the defeat of the Commonwealth Labor Government at the 1949 elections, the Liberal-Country Party Coalition policy of encouraging individuals to purchase insurance against hospital costs was implemented. "The Hospital Benefits Act of 1951 provided for Commonwealth-State hospital agreements which involved the reimposition both of means tests and fees for

---

[3]   Queensland remains the only State, however, in which rights of private practice are not granted to full-time salaried medical staff (see Committee of Inquiry into Rights of Private Practice in Public Hospitals 1984).

[4]   The rate was initially set at 60 cents per day. It was increased to 80 cents per day in 1948.

public patients" (Scotton 1974, p.68). However Queensland, unlike the other States, did not move to a system of public ward charges, choosing instead to retain its 'free' public hospital system.

This decision saw Queensland disadvantaged under the hospital benefit arrangements which subsequently developed. At the commencement of the scheme in 1952, Queensland health authorities continued to receive 80 cents per day for uninsured public patients, as did hospitals in other States for patients who were not pensioners and did not have hospital insurance. But the Commonwealth benefit for *insured* patients was $1.20 per day, increasing to $2 per day in 1958. The decision by the Queensland Government to provide public ward care free of charge and without means test meant that anyone who was prepared to accept such care had no need for hospital insurance. In the other States, charges for public ward care were reintroduced subject to a means test[5] so that, except for those for whom the means test resulted in no charges, patients had an incentive to purchase hospital insurance. Public patients who were insured then attracted the higher benefit of $2 per day while public patients in Queensland attracted the lower benefit of 80 cents per day.

An indication of Queensland's disadvantaged position under these arrangements is the proportion of bed-days provided to uninsured patients. In 1968, this proportion was 41.1 per cent for Queensland compared with a weighted mean of 15.9 per cent in the remaining States.[6]

This situation continued until 1970. In the previous year, the Commonwealth Government tabled the reports of two separate committees concerned with health insurance. The Labor-controlled upper house established the Senate Select Committee on Medical and Hospital Costs while the Coalition-dominated lower house established a Committee of Inquiry chaired by the Hon. Mr Justice J.A. Nimmo.[7] Both recommended that Queensland be paid the full benefit of $2 per day in respect of all public ward patients.

---

5   A list of hospital charges levied in each State over the period 1952-1970 can be found in Senate Select Committee on Medical and Hospital Costs (1970, Table 27, p.137).

6   These figures are based on data contained in Senate Select Committee on Medical and Hospital Costs (1970, Tables 36 and 37, pp.145-6).

7   See Senate Select Committee on Medical and Hospital Costs (1969) and Commonwealth Committee of Enquiry into Health Insurance (1969). The Senate Select Committee also tabled a more detailed report the following year (see Senate Select Committee on Medical and Hospital Costs 1970).

The last twenty years have witnessed substantial changes in health insurance arrangements in this country.[8] Negotiations between the Queensland and Commonwealth Governments have been strained when hospital funding is involved, the most recent example being Queensland's delay in signing an agreement with the Commonwealth on the matter of Medicare grants. Medicare came into operation in Australia on 1 February 1984, providing universal medical benefits coverage "as well as access without charge to inpatient and outpatient treatment at a public hospital by hospital appointed doctors" (Committee of Inquiry into Rights of Private Practice in Public Hospitals 1984, p.35). The Medicare grants were designed to reimburse the States for both revenue losses and additional medical costs incurred directly as a result of providing public hospital treatment free of charge. But Queensland was already providing this so that its grant was relatively less than the other States since it had no fee revenue to lose. Marshall and Mason (1984, p.36) point out that "This situation lies at the crux of the argument that ensued between the Commonwealth and the Queensland Government before the latter signed the Heads of Agreement".[9]

A particular aspect of the differences between hospital systems in Queensland and the other States which is germane to the present study is the difference in public hospital operating costs. For some decades the average cost per case treated in Queensland has been lower than in any other State, as evidenced by the data in Table 4.1.[10] This Table contains information for each State for the years 1952-53 to 1971-72, the period of time over which the Australian Bureau of Statistics (ABS) maintained an Australia-wide collection of such data. With the exception of 1952-53, Queensland had the lowest average cost per case treated in every year. Furthermore, the margin

---

[8]   These changes are discussed in Marshall and Mason (1984), Committee of Inquiry into Rights of Private Practice in Public Hospitals (1984, pp.32-7) and Palmer and Short (1994, Ch.4).

[9]   The Commonwealth Grants Commission provided an estimate of the extent to which Queensland had been disadvantaged in this case. " ... [T]he Commission concluded that special circumstances existed in the State of Queensland which disturbed the financial relativities between that State and the other States prior to the introduction of Medicare ... [A]fter allowing for the offsetting payments which Queensland had already received, the Commission determined that an additional payment of $10 million would restore Queensland to its previous position" (Commonwealth Grants Commission 1985, Vol.I, p.84). See also Butler (1992).

[10] The following abbreviations have been employed: NSW - New South Wales; Vic - Victoria; Qld - Queensland; SA - South Australia; WA - Western Australia; Tas - Tasmania; ACT - Australian Capital Territory; and NT - Northern Territory.

between Queensland and the other States widened over the period. The data in Table 4.2 compare the average cost per case in Queensland with the average cost per case in all other States. The resulting ratio indicates that, in relative terms, average cost per case in Queensland fell in comparison with the other States.

Comparisons of this kind need to be treated with caution because of the problems associated with the scope and comparability of the statistical collections between States. In fact it was these problems which led to the cessation of the national collection by the ABS in 1974.[11] However, for the financial years 1970-71 to 1976-77, the Hospitals and Allied Services Advisory Council (HASAC) collected data from each State on the net operating expenditures of public hospitals, paying particular attention to problems of consistency between States and between years. From 1977-78, the Commonwealth Grants Commission has produced data for each State on expenditures on General Medical Services (the bulk of which constitutes expenditure on hospitals) or Hospital Services.[12] Because of the absence of data for each State on the number of cases treated, the Grants Commission data have been expressed in per capita terms for comparative purposes (see Table 4.3). For each of the twenty years from 1972-73 to 1991-92 except three (1982-83, 1990-91 and 1991-92), Queensland had the lowest expenditure per capita.

It has been argued that the high degree of centralised control which Queensland excercised over its public hospitals for most of this period, is responsible for this outcome. Queensland itself has put this case to the Commonwealth Grants Commission in the latter's inquiry into State tax sharing and health grants, and the Commission concurred with this view.

> Queensland maintained that the strong degree of departmental control over hospital boards in that State was the major factor contributing to its low per capita expenditure on hospital services. It was pointed out to the Commission that central health authorities in all States were imposing increasing

---

11 The financial year 1971-72 is the last for which data were collected by the ABS. These are contained in the publication *Hospitals and Nursing Homes 1972* published in April 1974.

12 Expenditure on General Medical Services consists of expenditure on the following: country medical services; hospitals; mental health; nursing homes and care of the sick—other; and community health services out of public health—other (see Commonwealth Grants Commission 1981, Vol.I, p.179). The reason for creating this aggregated category was again the interstate differences in the scope and comparability of statistical collections.

Table 4.1. Average Cost per Case[a], Public Hospitals and Nursing Homes, by State, 1952-53 to 1971-72
(A$, current prices)

	1952-53[b]	1953-54[b]	1954-55[b]	1955-56	1956-57	1957-58	1958-59	1959-60	1960-61	1961-62
NSW	n.a.	n.a.	n.a.	134.00	139.34	139.73	140.08	148.28	160.64	170.87
Vic	142.74	151.06	161.98	177.80	189.76	182.26	179.12	192.36	205.70	216.78
Qld	98.20	101.75	110.88	122.07	130.47	125.34	126.65	134.17	147.21	152.17
SA	119.29	118.86	137.58	170.81	220.54	204.80	198.07	202.05	200.10	203.83
WA	117.20	118.04	118.87	133.41	167.09	173.84	167.71	192.48	213.71	225.26
Tas	92.78	103.52	141.52	146.37	166.48	165.22	166.27	173.68	197.01	217.15
ACT & NT	138.07	137.83	131.37	127.22	181.05	174.43	192.87	192.96	229.66	238.49
Australia	n.a.	n.a.	n.a.	143.88	157.71	154.51	153.74	163.84	177.23	178.87

	1962-63[c]	1963-64	1964-65	1965-66	1966-67	1967-68	1968-69	1969-70	1970-71	1971-72
NSW	182.63	193.57	204.46	220.28	236.69	256.82	280.92	306.07	343.76	386.26
Vic	224.07	222.41	235.57	264.52	295.16	308.51	315.87	347.17	412.76	461.27
Qld	155.67	161.89	163.91	174.08	185.96	194.62	204.77	227.00	252.57	296.23
SA	203.99	222.45	235.75	285.82	290.05	253.36	276.57	297.30	381.25	455.06
WA	223.21	225.58	243.90	256.25	282.73	311.73	333.11	373.12	428.60	455.59
Tas	233.20	236.84	288.78	332.33	312.07	346.02	388.24	418.63	458.28	485.10
ACT & NT	276.71	303.12	330.84	364.66	298.54	263.01	260.89	307.16	361.65	571.71
Australia	194.88	202.28	214.38	235.61	252.22	264.98	282.97	310.97	359.32	408.45

Notes: (a) Costs include maintenance expenditure and capital expenditure (purchases of land, costs of new buildings and extensions to buildings).

(b) For 1952-53 and 1953-54, statistics are for the year ended 31 March. For 1954-55, statistics encompass the fifteen months ended 30 June 1955.

(c) During 1962-63, many public and private hospitals were re-classified as nursing homes. Such institutions include those wholly supported by the State, partially subsidised by the State or by State endowments but receiving private aid also, and hospitals established and endowed by individuals for the treatment of the sick generally. Public hospitals are premises of this kind in which patients are received and lodged exclusively for 'hospital' treatment, i.e. nursing care for the purpose of professional attention. Public nursing homes are premises in which patients are received and lodged exclusively for the purpose of nursing home care, i.e. of a kind ordinarily provided in a benevolent home, convalescent home, home for aged care persons or rest home for patients requiring professional attention. The statistics listed after 1962-63 agree in scope with those for earlier years.

Source: Hospitals and Health Services Commission (1974, Table F.7, pp.188-9).

Table 4.2. Average Cost per Case, Public Hospitals and Nursing Homes, Queensland and All Other States, 1955-56 to 1971-72

Year	Qld ($)	All Other States[a] ($)	Ratio of Qld to All Other States
1955-56	122.07	149.13	0.82
1956-57	130.47	164.29	0.79
1957-58	125.34	161.47	0.78
1958-59	126.65	160.09	0.79
1959-60	134.17	170.70	0.79
1960-61	147.21	183.86	0.80
1961-62	152.17	184.83	0.82
1962-63	155.67	203.45	0.77
1963-64	161.89	211.10	0.77
1964-65	163.91	225.35	0.73
1965-66	174.08	248.76	0.70
1966-67	185.96	266.53	0.70
1967-68	194.62	279.62	0.70
1968-69	204.77	298.73	0.69
1969-70	227.00	327.59	0.69
1970-71	252.57	379.44	0.67
1971-72	296.23	429.04	0.69

Notes: (a) This is the weighted average cost per case treated in all other States (including ACT and NT).
Source: As for Table 4.1.

financial constraints on hospital managements in order to contain costs. The Commission concluded that Queensland's management policy, which had been implemented over a long period in the context of the State's free public hospital system, was a major cause of Queensland's relatively low hospital costs (Commonwealth Grants Commission 1982, Vol.I, p.134).

This conclusion was also reached by the Jamison Commission of Inquiry into the Efficiency and Administration of Hospitals. "There is little doubt that centralised administration is advantageous for control and accountability. Queensland provides ample proof of the effectiveness of this approach as a means of constraining costs" (Commission of Inquiry into the Efficiency and Administration of Hospitals 1981, Vol.1, p.65).[13]

---

13 In the late 1980s, Queensland embarked on a policy of decentralising the administration of its public hospitals. It is interesting to note that, of the three years in Table 4.3 in which Queensland did not have the lowest per capita expenditure on hospitals, two of these (1990-91 and 1991-92) were in the post-decentralisation period.

It is possible, however, that the interstate differences in hospital costs may be due to differences in the case mix, or output composition, of hospitals between States. Queensland's relatively low hospital costs may have resulted from its hospitals treating a less costly mix of cases than that treated in other States. This possibility is explored in this study in a comparison of public hospital costs in Queensland and New South Wales. The results of this comparison are presented in Chapter 10.

4.4   Summary and Conclusions

Queensland's public hospital system has, for some decades, provided inpatient treatment to the State's residents free of charge. This, combined with the use of salaried medical practitioners and, and until the late 1980s, a high degree of centralised control, has distinguished this State's hospital system from that of the other States.

These differences have often led to Queensland requiring special consideration in Commonwealth/State negotiations on hospital funding. A particular aspect of these interstate differences which is of interest in this study is the relatively low cost of hospital treatment in Queensland. It seems that this State has had the lowest hospital costs of all the States, and that this situation has persisted for nearly three decades. This particular aspect will be the subject of empirical investigation in a later chapter in this study where the effects of interstate differences in case mix, or output composition, on interstate differences in hospital costs are examined.

Table 4.3. Per Capita Expenditure on Hospitals(a) and General Medical Services(b), by State, 1972-73 to 1991-92 (A$, current prices)

	1972-73	1973-74	1974-75	1975-76	1976-77	1977-78	1978-79	1979-80	1980-81	1981-82
NSW	59.61	74.42	106.91	125.68	158.63	167.91	184.93	202.18	230.27	256.45
Vic	51.83	64.33	82.62	113.07	133.87	158.51	173.62	187.95	215.66	244.42
Qld	43.70	52.90	69.83	89.33	110.48	140.59	156.65	173.29	204.99	228.01
SA	52.53	68.98	99.12	125.97	158.19	199.41	206.31	213.58	243.97	264.31
WA	69.38	87.39	120.12	154.67	175.00	232.11	245.94	272.25	311.32	308.60
Tas	53.56	66.43	104.47	127.53	147.10	196.34	210.20	237.35	260.12	281.60
NT(c)										582.01
ACT(c)										

	1982-83	1983-84	1984-85	1985-86	1986-87	1987-88	1988-89	1989-90	1990-91	1991-92
NSW	244.98	286.06	390.45	434.59	487.25	369.29	408.27	413.90	407.06	412.20
Vic	265.68	300.50	408.63	440.45	507.36	381.85	405.99	438.98	466.13	479.70
Qld	250.94	276.00	319.97	348.45	373.22	348.32	352.38	391.71	430.56	481.77
SA	300.13	338.04	471.87	510.74	560.40	396.41	442.81	477.95	498.33	476.20
WA	330.53	372.39	429.14	465.66	513.79	424.00	454.10	493.84	535.60	557.11
Tas	283.77	319.26	411.21	448.96	498.58	402.52	435.08	497.71	522.62	543.26
NT(c)	558.40	648.59	755.65	800.73	831.28	663.14	678.33	762.68	795.79	826.13
ACT(c)						443.04	479.08	523.59	602.01	554.71

Notes: (a) For the period 1972-73 to 1976-77, the expenditure data pertain to public hospitals, and are net of recoveries from hospital employees for provision by the hospital of meals and accommodation.

(b) For the period 1977-78 to 1986-87, the expenditure data pertain to General Medical Services as defined by the Commonwealth Grants Commission (see text). From 1987-88 onwards, the General Medical Services category was discontinued and Hospital Services, which were previously included in General Medical Services, became a separate category. Up to and including 1983-84, expenditures were net of "all related items of revenue, including those received by way of fees, cost recoupment or charges for services" (Commonwealth Grants Commission 1982, Vol.II, p.1). From 1984-85 onwards, gross expenditures are reported, as hospital revenue was treated as a separate revenue item.

(c) Data for the Northern Territory are included only from 1981-82, and for the Australian Capital Territory from 1987-88.

Source: 1972-73 to 1976-77: Expenditure data obtained from Hospital and Allied Services Advisory Council, Uniform Costing Committee, *Uniform Statements of Cost, Sources of Funds of Hospitals and Nursing Homes, and Government Assistance to Allied Services in Australia,* 1971 to 1977; Population estimates obtained from Commonwealth Grants Commission annual reports on special assistance for States.

1977-78 to 1980-81: Commonwealth Grants Commission (1982, Vol.II, Tables A-17 to A-20).
1981-82 to 1983-84: Commonwealth Grants Commission (1985, Vol.II, Tables B-26, B-28 and B-30).
1984-85 to 1986-87: Commonwealth Grants Commission (1988, Vol.II, Table B-53).
1987-88 to 1991-92: Commonwealth Grants Commission (1993, Vol.II, Table III-30).

5

THE EFFECT OF CASE MIX ON HOSPITAL

COSTS—EVIDENCE FROM QUEENSLAND

5.1   Introduction

This chapter reports the empirical results from an analysis of the effects of case mix on hospital costs using data on Queensland public hospitals. Section 5.2 explains the specification of the multiproduct cost function adopted for this analysis—a non-joint, input-output separable average cost function with overall constant returns to scale. A description of the data sources is provided in Section 5.3 with some descriptive statistics being presented in Section 5.4. The results are presented in Section 5.5. The closing section of the chapter provides a summary and conclusions.

The effects of scale and utilisation, and other factors such as input price variations and teaching status, are not treated in the present chapter. These matters are deferred to Chapters 6 and 7. The current chapter is concerned with measuring, and determining the effect of, case mix composition on hospital costs.

5.2   Specification

In attempting to estimate the influence of output composition on hospital
costs, a specific functional form for the cost-output relationship must be
adopted. In formulating such a cost function for hospitals, it must be borne
in mind that such institutions may not fulfil one of the conditions necessary
for the cost function to represent the dual of the underlying production
technology, *viz.* cost minimisation. The non-profit nature of most hospitals
implies that they have little incentive to minimise costs, so that any
estimated relationship between costs and output may not represent the
minimum attainable cost of producing any particular output level. It is for
this reason that Evans (1971) refers to "behavioural" cost functions for
hospitals, this term being used because of "the possibility of systematic
differences between observed and "minimal" costs due to the behaviour
patterns of the hospital" (Evans 1971, p.200).

From Chapter 2, the general functional form of the multiproduct cost
function is

$$C = C(y_1,...,y_n; w_1,...,w_m)$$
... (5.1)

where C = total costs, y_i = the output level of product i ($i = 1, ..., n$) and
w_j = the per unit price of factor input j ($j = 1, ..., m$). The specific functional
form of the total cost function adopted here takes input prices as given and
assumes non-jointness and overall constant returns to scale. The cost
function can then be written as

$$C = \sum_i a_i y_i$$
... (5.2)

where a_i = the average and marginal cost of product i.

On the basis of the argument presented in Chapter 3, the y_i will be
measured as the number of episodes of hospitalisation, or separations, in
each of a set of mutually exclusive and exhaustive diagnostic categories.
Taking the unweighted sum of all separations as a measure of total output
and dividing equation (5.2) through by this sum gives

$$\frac{C}{y} = ACC = \sum_i a_i p_i$$
... (5.3)

where $y = \sum_i y_i$

$$p_i = \frac{y_i}{\sum_i y_i}$$

ACC = average cost per case.

This corresponds to what Baumol, Panzar and Willig (1982, pp.48-52) call ray average cost, a term used to describe the behaviour of average cost as the overall level of output changes but output proportions remain unchanged (see Chapter 2). In equation (5.3) the output proportions are given by the case mix proportions p_i ($i = 1, ..., n$) which measure the proportion of a hospital's separations in each diagnostic category. If these remain constant as the total volume of cases treated changes, ACC remains constant indicating constant overall returns to scale.

Given data on total costs and the number of cases treated in each diagnostic category, the total cost equation given by (5.2) can be estimated using multiple regression analysis. The parameters so estimated are the average and marginal costs of treating a case for each diagnostic category. The same parameters can also be estimated using the average cost formulation given in equation (5.3), this specification usually being preferred on the grounds that it is more likely to fulfil the ordinary least squares regression assumption of homoscedasticity or constant variance of the error term.[1] Also, Feldstein (1967) found that multicollinearity amongst the case mix proportions was much less severe than amongst the case mix numbers used in the total cost formulation, but other studies such as those by Lave, Lave and Silverman (1972) and Jenkins (1977) have found severe multicollinearity amongst case mix proportions.

With regard to the output classification scheme to be adopted, two diagnostic classification schemes are employed. One of these is an 18 diagnostic category specification using the 17 major chapter headings plus the supplementary classifications of the Eighth and Ninth Revisions of the

---

[1] See Intriligator (1978, p.281). The variance of *total* cost for hospitals treating a relatively small number of cases is likely to be smaller than for hospitals treating large numbers of cases. Estimation using the average cost formulation effectively weights the error term in the total cost function by the inverse of the number of cases. In a study of hospital costs in Ontario, Jenkins found such a procedure to be "an appropriate response to heteroscedasticity" (Jenkins 1977, p.103). On the weighted least squares method see Koutsoyiannis (1977, Ch.9).

International Classification of Diseases (ICD-8 and ICD-9). The other is a
more disaggregated 47 diagnostic category classification used in
constructing a relative stay index for Queensland hospitals, also based on
ICD categories.[2] Both of these sets of categories are mutually exclusive and
exhaustive. Descriptions of the diagnostic categories contained in each of
these classification schemes together with their ICD-8 and ICD-9 codes are
provided in Tables 5.1 and 5.2.

Table 5.1. The 18 Diagnostic Category Classification Scheme

No.	Diagnostic Category	ICD-8 Codes	ICD-9 Codes
1	Infectious & Parasitic Diseases	000 - 136	000 - 139
2	Neoplasms	140 - 239	140 - 239
3	Endocrine, Nutritional & Metabolic	240 - 279	240 - 279
4	Blood	280 - 289	280 - 289
5	Mental Disorders	290 - 315	290 - 319
6	Nervous System	320 - 389	320 - 389
7	Circulatory System	390 - 458	390 - 459
8	Respiratory System	460 - 519	460 - 519
9	Digestive System	520 - 577	520 - 579
10	Genito-Urinary System	580 - 629	580 - 629
11	Complications of Pregnancy, Childbirth & Puerperium	630 - 678	630 - 676
12	Skin & Subcutaneous Tissue	680 - 709	680 - 709
13	Musculoskeletal System	710 - 738	710 - 739
14	Congenital Anomalies	740 - 759	740 - 759
15	Causes of Perinatal Morbidity & Mortality	760 - 779	760 - 779
16	Symptoms & ill-defined	780 - 796	780 - 799
17	Accidents, Poisonings & Violence*	N800 - N999	800 - 999
18	Supplementary Classifications	Y00 - Y89	V01 - V82

Notes: *   This chapter entitled "Injury and Poisoning" in ICD-9.
Source: World Health Organisation (1967, 1977).

The specification of the cost function adopted, i.e. equation (5.3), then
gives rise to a corresponding number of parameters to be estimated (18 and
47 respectively for the two diagnostic classification schemes) since non-

---

[2]   The relative stay index is an index which compares a hospital's actual average length of
stay with its expected average length of stay. The latter is calculated using the hospital's
actual case mix and the state mean length of stay in each case mix category. For an
explanation of this index, see Leigh and McBride (1974).

jointness is incorporated as a maintained hypothesis. However, as argued earlier, this restriction enables a more disaggregated set of output categories to be adopted than would be possible with a less restrictive specification.

It was also pointed out in Chapter 3 that diagnosis may not be the only relevant axis of classification of a hospital's case load. Other factors such as age, sex, separation status and the presence of surgery may affect the type of care provided in addition to the diagnosed illness. It would be possible to subdivide each of the diagnostic categories according to each of these additional criteria but this rapidly multiplies the number of case mix categories and hence the number of explanatory variables. For example, categorisation by sex in addition to diagnosis would approximately double the number of case mix categories.

An alternative method of exploring the effects of these additional dimensions of case mix is to subdivide all cases by each dimension regardless of diagnosis. This enables sex, for example, to be entered with only two additional explanatory variables—the proportions of cases which are male and female. More generally, equation (5.3) becomes

$$ACC = \sum_i a_i p_i + \sum_k b_k v_k + \sum_t c_t s_t + ... \qquad ... (5.4)$$

where v_k represents the proportion of cases in sex category k ($k = 1,2$), s_t represents the proportion of cases in age category t and so on, with an additional set of proportions being added for each additional axis of classification. In this study, hospitals' case loads have also been classified according to the following factors: sex; the presence or absence of surgery; patient payment status (public, intermediate, private);[3] separation status (discharged, transferred, died); and age (0-4, 5-14, 15-40, 41-64, 65+). This gives rise to an additional 15 case mix categories.

While this approach to incorporating additional case mix dimensions is parsimonious in parameters, it incorporates yet another restriction. In effect, what this approach does is "to purge the effects of these other factors in a way that assumes no interaction" (Feldstein and Schuttinga 1977, pp.23-4). That is, it assumes that the effect of sex, for example, is independent of any other factors. If male patients are more expensive to treat, this will be so

---

3   A public patient is treated by a salaried hospital doctor, or a visiting doctor paid by the hospital, free of charge in Queensland (see Chapter 4). Intermediate and private patients both receive treatment by a private doctor of their choice who is then paid by the patient on a fee-for-service basis. Private patients also have a private room whereas intermediate patients are accommodated in a shared ward.

Table 5.2. The 47 Diagnostic Category Classification Scheme

No.	Diagnostic Category	ICD-8 Codes	ICD-9 Codes
1	Investigations, Procedures, Healthy*	Y00 - Y89	V01 - V55
2	Infectious & Parasitic	000 - 007	000 - 007
		010 - 136	010 - 139
3	Enteritis, Diarrhoeal Disease	008 - 00	9008 - 009
4	Malignant Neoplasms	140 - 209	140 - 208
5	Benign Neoplasms	210 - 239	210 - 239
6	Endocrine & Metabolic	240 - 279	240 - 279
7	Blood	280 - 289	280 - 289
8	Psychiatric	290 - 315	290 - 319
9	Other CNS & Nerves	320 - 358	320 - 359
10	Eye & Ear	360 - 389	360 - 389
11	Other Heart, Hypertension	390 - 404	390 - 405
		411 - 426	411 - 425
		428 - 429	429
12	Acute Myocardial Infarction	410	410
13	Symptomatic Heart Disease	427	426 - 428
14	Cerebrovascular Disease	430 - 438	430 - 438
15	Circulation	440 - 458	440 - 459
16	Upper Respiratory	460 - 474	460 - 466
			487
17	Pneumonia	480 - 486	480 - 486
18	Bronchitis, Emphysema, Asthma	490 - 493	490 - 493
			495 - 496
19	Tonsils & Adenoids	500	474
20	Other Respiratory	501 - 519	470 - 473
			475 - 478
			494
			500 - 519
21	Dental	520 - 529	520 - 529
22	Upper Gastrointestinal	530 - 537	530 - 537
23	Appendicitis	540 - 543	540 - 543
24	Hernia	550 - 553	550 - 553
25	Other Gastrointestinal	560 - 577	555 - 579
26	Nephritis & Nephrosis	580 - 584	580 - 589
			V56
27	Other Urinary	590 - 599	590 - 599
28	Male Genital	600 - 607	600 - 608
29	Other Female Genital	610 - 625	610 - 625
		627 - 629	627 - 629
30	Disorders of Menstruation	626	626
31	Complications of Pregnancy		
	& Puerperium	630 - 639	640 - 648
		670 - 678	670 - 676
32	Abortion	640 - 645	630 - 639
33	Normal Delivery	650	650
34	Delivery Complications	651 - 662	651 - 669
35	Skin Disease	680 - 709	680 - 709

Table 5.2 (cont.)

No.	Diagnostic Category	ICD-8 Codes	ICD-9 Codes
36	Orthopaedic	710 - 738	710 - 739
37	Congenital Malformation	740 - 759	740 - 759
38	Perinatal	760 - 776	760 - 764
		778 - 779	766 - 770.3
			770.5 - 779
39	Immaturity	777	765
			770.4
40	Symptoms, ill-defined	780 - 793	780 - 796
		795	798
41	Long Stay, ill-defined	794	797
		796	799
42	Other Fractures (excl. Femur)	N800 - N819	800 - 819
		N821 - N829	821 - 829
			905.0 - 905.2
			905.4 - 905.5
43	Fracture of Neck of Femur	N820	820
			905.3
44	Dislocations	N830 - N848	830 - 848
			905.6 - 905.7
45	Internal Injury	N850 - N869	850 - 869
			907.0
			908.0 - 908.2
46	External Injury	N870 - N959	870 - 904
			910 - 959
			905.8 - 905.9
			906
			907.1 - 907.9
			908.3 - 908.9
47	Poisoning	N960 - N999	960 - 999
			909

Notes: * This category entitled "Factors influencing Health States" in ICD-9.
Sources: Queensland Department of Health (1980); World Health Organisation (1967, 1977).

regardless of diagnosis, age and so on. Alternatively, the additional expense of treating a male patient will be the same no matter what his diagnosis, age, separation status or whatever.

The expansion of the average cost equation (5.3) to include additional sets of mutually exclusive and exhaustive output categories changes the interpretation of the coefficients. Since any one case is now classified along a number of different axes, the average and marginal cost of a particular case type (e.g. eye & ear, male, age 38, discharged, private patient) is now the sum of the coefficients of each relevant dimension, i.e. $a_i + b_k + c_t + ...$ for the ikt^{th} case type. The simple summation of coefficients in this way reflects the absence of any interaction between the various axes of classification, with the effects of each additional dimension on average and marginal cost being independent and additive.

The average cost equation (5.4) contains no constant term and hence passes through the origin. Indeed, equation (5.4) cannot be estimated with a constant term included, for the inclusion of such a term would result in linear dependence between the columns in the data matrix, or perfect multicollinearity. A constant term can be entered, however, if one category from each case mix classification is suppressed. The effect of this can be demonstrated simply with the following example based on two sets of case mix proportions each of which contains two categories. The average cost equation can be written as

$$ACC = a_1 p_1 + a_2 p_2 + b_1 v_1 + b_2 v_2 \qquad\qquad ... (5.5)$$

where $p_1 + p_2 = 1, \quad 0 < p_1, p_2 < 1;$

and $v_1 + v_2 = 1, \quad 0 < v_1, v_2 < 1.$

Now (5.5) can be rewritten as

$$ACC = a_1 p_1 + a_2(1 - p_1) + b_1 v_1 + b_2(1 - v_1)$$

which, when rearranged, gives

$$ACC = (a_2 + b_2) + (a_1 - a_2) p_1 + (b_1 - b_2) v_1 \qquad\qquad ... (5.6)$$

The constant term $(a_2 + b_2)$ is now the average cost of a case in the excluded category. Notice also that the coefficients on the remaining parameters represent the differential impact on average cost of changing one of the characteristics of the excluded case type.

An advantage of allowing the constant term to enter in this way is that, where there are two or more axes of classification, it economises on the number of parameters to be estimated. The reduction in the number of parameters to be estimated is $(x - 1)$ where x is the number of different classification schemes employed. For example, equation (5.5) is based on two axes of classification (age and sex) so that $x = 2$. Suppressing one category from each classification and allowing a constant term to enter then reduces by one the number of parameters to be estimated, as is evident in equation (5.6).

5.3   The Data

The data used for this study are drawn from two separate statistical collections—a Hospital Morbidity Data collection and a Hospital Finance Data collection. The Hospital Morbidity Data comprise a unit record for each separation from every acute hospital in Queensland. The unit record on each episode of hospitalisation contains information on, among other things, date of admission and separation, demographic information on the patient (notably age, sex, and Local Authority Area of usual residence), the identity of the hospital, and summary information on the principal diagnosis and principal medical procedure (if any) pertaining to the episode of hospitalisation. The Hospital Finance Data, on the other hand, comprise aggregated budgetary information about each public hospital.

5.3.1   Hospital Morbidity Data

The Hospital Morbidity Data are collected on a calendar year basis while the Hospital Finance Data are compiled on a financial year basis. However, it was possible to split the former into half years and combine these so as to construct a financial year Hospital Morbidity Data file. This procedure then synchronised the two data sets.

For this study, the following details for each separation from each hospital were extracted from the Hospital Morbidity Data: principal diagnosis; length of stay; age; sex; presence or absence of surgery; separation status (discharged, transferred, died); and payment status (public, intermediate, private). For each hospital, separations were then aggregated into the 47 diagnostic categories listed in Table 5.2, then aggregated again into the 18 diagnostic categories listed in Table 5.1. Separations for each hospital were also aggregated into the three payment status categories, the three separation status categories and the five age groups (0-4, 5-14, 15-40, 41-64, 65+). The same information was extracted and the same aggregations performed for occupied bed days.

This information was initially extracted for the year 1977-78, and subsequently for the three years 1978-79 to 1980-81. The adoption of the ICD-9 codes in 1979 presented a problem for this study in the construction of the Hospital Morbidity Data file for the financial year 1978-79, since the second half of 1978 was coded under ICD-8 while the first half of 1979 was coded under ICD-9. To achieve the melding of these two half years, the 18 and 47 diagnostic category classifications were maintained and defined in terms of ICD-9 codes also. The corresponding ICD-9 codes adopted in this study are shown in Tables 5.1 and 5.2.

5.3.2   Hospital Finance Data

The Hospital Finance Data collection contains information on every public hospital in the State. While there is an expenditure category entitled "Interest and Redemption", this bears no necessary relationship to the opportunity cost of capital. This item pertains merely to the interest on and repayment of debt and so cannot be used as a measure of the annual cost of capital. In the absence of any economically meaningful estimates of interest and depreciation charges, the cost data employed in this study include maintenance costs only, i.e. they include all costs except capital charges.

The total maintenance expenditure for each hospital is dissected into costs of services to other hospitals, inpatient, outpatient, dental clinic, and ambulance expenditure. This dissection is undertaken by each hospital individually and is not subject to a uniform basis of apportionment across hospitals. Since this study is concerned primarily with the costs of inpatient treatment, and in the absence of any more reliable estimates of expenditure on these various services, the estimates of costs constructed by the hospitals have been employed.[4]

A 'treated case' in this data is defined as an inpatient rather than a separation, and this difference gives rise to different numbers of total cases treated in the Hospital Morbidity and Hospital Finance Data collections. The difference between the two relates to patients who are in hospital at the end of the year and consequently have not been discharged. Since the Hospital Finance Data pertain to all patients treated in a hospital in a given financial year, the figure for total inpatients from this data set was taken as the measure of the total volume of cases treated, rather than total separations from the Hospital Morbidity Data collection. It should be noted, however, that in using case mix proportions obtained from the Hospital Morbidity Data set, it is then assumed that the case mix of patients in hospital at the end of the year is the same as those discharged during the year.

---

[4]   Note that, in accepting each hospital's apportionment of its costs between services to other hospitals, inpatients, outpatients, dental clinic and ambulance services, it is being assumed that the cost function is non-joint and input-output separable as between each of these output categories.

5.4 Descriptive Statistics

The sample of hospitals used in this study consists of 121 Queensland public hospitals with data for each of the four financial years 1977-78 to 1980-81. This sample was selected on the basis of the 1977-78 data, and includes all public hospitals which treated inpatients in that year and for which reliable data were available.[5] The composition of this sample was then maintained for the remaining three years also. Some descriptive statistics relating to these hospitals for the year 1977-78 are presented in Tables 5.3 to 5.6.[6]

The mean, standard deviation, coefficient of variation (standard deviation/mean) and maximum value of the case mix proportions based on the 18 diagnostic category classification for 1977-78 are presented in Table 5.3.[7] These data have the following salient features:

- The following three categories had a mean proportion of cases treated of less than one per cent: 4 Blood; 14 Congenital Anomalies; and 15 Causes of Perinatal Morbidity and Mortality. This was also the case in the other three financial years. Further, these were the only categories in any of the four years which had a mean proportion of less than one per cent.

- Two of these categories—14 Congenital Anomalies and 15 Causes of Perinatal Morbidity and Mortality—also had the highest coefficients of variation in each of the four years, i.e. had the highest degree of dispersion around their respective means in relative terms.

- The category with the highest mean proportion of cases treated in every financial year was 17 Injury and Poisoning with a mean of between 15 and 16 per cent of cases treated in each year.

---

5   Only one hospital was excluded because of data problems.

6   The descriptive statistics for the remaining three years are available from the author on request.

7   Unless otherwise indicated, the mean of the case mix proportions is the unweighted mean, i.e. it is calculated as the sum of the case mix proportions divided by the number of hospitals. The maximum value only of the case mix proportions in each category is reported in this and the following Table as, with only a few exceptions, the minimum value is always zero, i.e. in virtually every category there is at least one hospital which has not treated any cases in that category in each financial year.

Table 5.3. Mean, Standard Deviation, Coefficient of Variation and Maximum Value of Case Mix Proportions, 18 Diagnostic Categories, Queensland Public Hospitals, 1977-78

No.	Diagnostic Category	Mean	SD	CV	Max.
1	Infectious & Parasitic Diseases	.0496	.0312	.6289	.182
2	Neoplasms	.0204	.0224	1.1022	.139
3	Endocrine, Nutritional, Metabolic	.0159	.0095	.5958	.060
4	Blood	.0043	.0040	.9286	.026
5	Mental Disorders	.0361	.0247	.6830	.137
6	Nervous System	.0388	.0206	.5303	.145
7	Circulatory System	.0782	.0409	.5232	.256
8	Respiratory System	.1445	.0657	.4546	.442
9	Digestive System	.0632	.0329	.5210	.148
10	Genito-Urinary System	.0532	.0350	.6576	.211
11	Complications of Pregnancy, Childbirth & Puerperium	.1218	.1398	1.1484	.961
12	Skin & Subcutaneous Tissue	.0272	.0176	.6459	.095
13	Musculoskeletal System	.0255	.0153	.5987	.083
14	Congenital Anomalies	.0042	.0105	2.4833	.084
15	Causes of Perinatal Morbidity & Mortality	.0036	.0077	2.1406	.055
16	Symptoms & ill-defined	.1294	.0690	.5334	.429
17	Accidents, Poisonings & Violence	.1547	.0547	.3538	.321
18	Supplementary Classifications	.0295	.0215	.7284	.111

Notes: SD = standard deviation.
              CV = coefficient of variation.
Source: Hospital Morbidity Data, Queensland Department of Health.

• The degree of dispersion within each diagnostic category, as measured by the coefficient of variation, varies between categories, ranging from a low of 0.35 to a high of 2.48 in 1977-78.

The descriptive statistics for the case mix proportions based on the 47 diagnostic category classification for 1977-78 are presented in Table 5.4. As can be expected, this lower level of aggregation generally reduces the mean proportion of cases treated in each diagnostic category. The following points emerged from these data:

• Category 39 Immaturity had the lowest mean proportion of cases treated in each of the four financial years. It also had a relatively high coefficient of variation.

- Category 40 Symptoms, ill-defined had the highest mean proportion of cases treated in every year, ranging from just under 10 per cent up to 11.7 per cent.

- There is again substantial variation in the degree of dispersion within each diagnostic category.

A possible source of concern here might be the fact that, on average, around 10 per cent of cases are assigned to one category out of the 47, and that this category is an amorphous one labelled 'Symptoms, ill-defined'. The reasons for this are not known. It may be a reflection of the uncertainty surrounding the formation of a diagnosis in medicine, although it is interesting to note in this context that hospitals which have medical school affiliation have a substantially lower proportion of cases in this category compared with other hospitals (see Chapter 7). Alternatively, this category may contain a high proportion of elderly patients suffering from general ailments connected with ageing. Whatever the reason, it seems that the composition of this category may well be quite heterogeneous.

Table 5.5 presents the descriptive statistics for 1977-78 for the additional dimensions of case mix employed in this study, *viz.* sex, the presence or absence of surgery, payment status,[8] separation status and age. The following points can be made about each of these:

- The mean proportion of male patients in each year was in the range 48 to 49 per cent.

- The mean proportion of cases for which surgery was performed was consistently in the region 16 to 17 per cent over the four years.

- The average proportion of public patients, i.e. patients who pay no charges and are treated by a doctor employed by the hospital, is 75 to 76 per cent over the four years.

- The mean proportion of patients discharged ranges from 89 to 92 per cent with a low degree of dispersion (CV = 0.076 - 0.125). There is considerably more dispersion, in relative terms, in the proportion of cases transferred although the average proportion of such cases is only in the range four to eight per cent over the four years.

---

8   For 1979-80 and subsequent years, it was not possible to separate intermediate and private patients.

Table 5.4. Mean, Standard Deviation, Coefficient of Variation and Maximum Value of Case Mix Proportions, 47 Diagnostic Categories, Queensland Public Hospitals, 1977-78

No.	Diagnostic Category	Mean	SD	CV	Max.
1	Investigative Procedures, Healthy	.0295	.0215	.7284	.111
2	Infectious & Parasitic	.0214	.0158	.7412	.106
3	Enteritis, Diarrhoeal Disease	.0282	.0229	.8101	.123
4	Malignant Neoplasms	.0158	.0189	1.1966	.126
5	Benign Neoplasms	.0046	.0050	1.0880	.029
6	Endocrine & Metabolic	.0159	.0095	.5958	.060
7	Blood	.0043	.0040	.9286	.026
8	Psychiatric	.0361	.0247	.6830	.137
9	Other CNS & Nerves	.0219	.0128	.5871	.091
10	Eye & Ear	.0169	.0165	.9735	.096
11	Other Heart, Hypertension	.0284	.0230	.8108	.150
12	Acute Myocardial Infarction	.0087	.0072	.8286	.029
13	Symptomatic Heart Disease	.0170	.0151	.8883	.125
14	Cerebrovascular Disease	.0106	.0080	.7524	.036
15	Circulation	.0136	.0096	.7098	.049
16	Upper Respiratory	.0449	.0338	.7524	.165
17	Pneumonia	.0237	.0293	1.2382	.226
18	Bronchitis, Emphysema, Asthma	.0449	.0297	.6625	.170
19	Tonsils & Adenoids	.0088	.0142	1.6182	.083
20	Other Respiratory	.0224	.0229	1.0263	.122
21	Dental	.0055	.0072	1.3040	.036
22	Upper Gastrointestinal	.0139	.0113	.8117	.064
23	Appendicitis	.0116	.0111	.9544	.066
24	Hernia	.0089	.0088	.9962	.053
25	Other Gastrointestinal	.0233	.0137	.5902	.055
26	Nephritis & Nephrosis	.0055	.0200	3.6483	.154
27	Other Urinary	.0162	.0091	.5627	.042
28	Male Genital	.0061	.0048	.7998	.028
29	Other Female Genital	.0197	.0180	.9163	.106
30	Disorders of Menstruation	.0058	.0057	.9911	.023
31	Complications of Pregnancy & Puerperium	.0348	.0306	.8781	.259
32	Abortion	.0080	.0062	.7714	.042
33	Normal Delivery	.0724	.1000	1.3815	.792
34	Delivery Complications	.0065	.0235	3.6028	.255
35	Skin Disease	.0272	.0176	.6459	.095
36	Orthopaedic	.0255	.0153	.5987	.083
37	Congenital Malformation	.0042	.0105	2.4833	.084
38	Perinatal	.0022	.0049	2.2550	.038
39	Immaturity	.0014	.0039	2.8303	.037
40	Symptoms, ill-defined	.1172	.0661	.5636	.429
41	Long Stay, ill-defined	.0121	.0141	1.1639	.115

Table 5.4 (cont.)

No.	Diagnostic Category	Mean	SD	CV	Max.
42	Other Fractures (excl. Femur)	.0378	.0260	.6863	.214
43	Fracture of Neck of Femur	.0020	.0030	1.5147	.021
44	Dislocations	.0083	.0066	.7967	.034
45	Internal Injury	.0304	.0182	.5985	.088
46	External Injury	.0454	.0266	.5849	.182
47	Poisoning	.0307	.0170	.5528	.105

Source: Hospital Morbidity Data, Queensland Department of Health.

Table 5.5. Mean, Standard Deviation, Coefficient of Variation and Range of Case Mix Proportions, Additional Case Mix Dimensions, Queensland Public Hospitals, 1977-78

Case Mix Category	Mean	SD	CV	Range Min.	Max.
Male separations	.4789	.099	.207	.001	.786
Surgery performed	.1615	.135	.836	0	.544
Payment status					
- public	.7504	.195	.260	0	1.000
- intermediate	.2120	.181	.854	0	.997
- private	.0376	.035	.931	0	.173
Separation status					
- discharged	.9190	.070	.076	.556	1.000
- transferred	.0652	.071	1.089	0	.444
- died	.0158	.011	.696	0	.050
Age bracket					
- 0-4	.1228	.082	3.596	0	.537
- 5-14	.1117	.066	.591	0	.492
- 15-40	.3982	.125	.314	.001	.984
- 41-64	.2072	.075	.362	0	.420
- 65+	.1601	.073	.456	0	.373

Source: Hospital Morbidity Data, Queensland Department of Health.

- The age bracket with the highest average proportion of cases in each of the four years is 15-40, with a mean ranging from 38 to 40 per cent.

As indicated earlier in this chapter, the Hospital Morbidity Data were used to obtain the case mix *proportions* for each hospital and are hence the source of Tables 5.3 to 5.5. Information on costs and the *number* of cases treated and days of care provided was obtained from the Hospital Finance

Data. Some descriptive statistics for a selection of variables from this data set for the year 1977-78 are provided in Table 5.6.[9]

Table 5.6. Mean, Standard Deviation, Coefficient of Variation and Range of Cost/Volume Variables, Queensland Public Hospitals, 1977-78

				Range	
	Mean	SD	CV	Min.	Max.
Average Cost per Case($)	546.83	238.90	.44	34.71	1361.16
Average Cost per Day($)	79.93	35.64	.45	16.71	220.09
Average Length of Stay	7.44	3.54	.48	1.00	19.48
Occupancy	.43	.20	.47	.006	1.075*
Case Flow Rate	23.33	14.34	.61	1.50	77.70
Inpatients	2725	5677	2.08	14	39907
Beds	98	175	1.79	2	1234

Notes: *   This figure relates to a maternity hospital where days of care to "qualified babies" are added to the occupied bed days provided to the mother.
Source: Hospital Finance Data, Queensland Department of Health.

While the coefficients of variation do not indicate a high degree of dispersion, the range of values for each of these variables indicates the diversity of some hospitals with respect to these measures. There are hospitals in the sample which have an average cost per case as low as $33, an average cost per day of just over $16 and an average length of stay of one day. At the other extreme, there are hospitals with an average cost per case of nearly $4,900, an average cost per day of nearly $1,900 and an average length of stay of 127 days.

The diverse situations of some hospitals are also borne out in the remaining data in Table 5.6. While the mean occupancy rate was 43 per cent, there was one hospital which had 0.6 per cent occupancy. The mean case flow rate (case flow rate = inpatients/beds) was 23.33 but one hospital treated as few as 1.50 cases per bed. Large ranges of values are also evident in the number of inpatients treated and the number of beds.

---

[9]   The mean average cost per case is not equal to the product of the mean average cost per day and mean average length of stay because these are unweighted means.

5.5   Empirical Results

5.5.1   18 and 47 Diagnostic Categories and Additional Case Mix Dimensions

Linear average cost equations were initially estimated using the 18 and 47 diagnostic category classification schemes. In estimating such equations, one case mix proportion was suppressed and a constant term allowed to enter.[10] Summary statistics for each of the estimated equations for each of the four financial years are presented in Table 5.7.

Overall for every equation there was a statistically significant relationship between average cost per case and case mix. Using the 18 diagnostic category classification of output, the amount of variation in average cost per case explained by variation in the case mix proportions ranged from 22 to 30 per cent, after adjusting for degrees of freedom. Using the more disaggregated 47 diagnostic category classification, the amount of variation so explained increased for every year, ranging from 33 to 60 per cent. This increase in explanatory power was statistically significant for three of the four years, as indicated by the F-statistic in the last column of Table 5.7.[11] The improvement is also evident in the lower standard errors of estimate for the 47 diagnostic category specification.

---

10   When only one axis of case mix classification is employed, there is no gain in degrees of freedom by suppressing one category and allowing a constant to enter. There is still a statistical advantage, however, because most computer packages do not compute the correct coefficient of determination (R^2) when the constant term is suppressed. The reason for this can be found in Maddala (1977, p.108).

11   It might be objected that the F-statistic is inappropriate for testing the significance of the increase in explanatory power because the two equations contain two different sets of variables, i.e. the 47 diagnostic category specification is not obtained by adding additional variables to the 18 diagnostic specification. The F-test is designed to test the improvement of fit from adding additional explanatory variables (see Koutsoyiannis, 1977, pp.158-64). In other words, the two models are non-nested, and the "variants of the various F norm test statistics ... cannot in general be used for hypotheses of the *non-nested* type" (Judge, Griffiths, Hill and Lee 1980, p.436, emphasis in original). However, to quote Feldstein (1967, p.39, n.26), substituting where appropriate, "since the [18] variables are linear combinations of the [47], the [47] could be specified in terms of the [18] variables and [29] others. This equivalence assures us that the two chi-square distributions are independent". For a discussion of the R^2 and other criteria for selecting regressors, see Judge, *et al.* (1980, Ch.11).

Table 5.7. Summary Statistics for Estimated Cost Functions using 18 and 47 Diagnostic Categories, Queensland Public Hospitals, 1977-78 to 1980-81

Year	18DCs (d.f. = 103)			47DCs (d.f. = 74)			$F^{(a)}$ (47/18)
	$\overline{R}^2$	F	SEE	$\overline{R}^2$	F	SEE	
1977-78	.22	3.01*	210.77	.33	2.29*	195.51	1.58
1978-79	.30	4.08*	241.89	.60	4.86*	184.15	3.58*
1979-80	.30	4.09*	413.31	.58	4.62*	320.83	3.34*
1980-81	.23	3.16*	407.83	.43	2.97*	351.87	2.22*

Notes: *   Significant at 1% level.
        (a)   The F-statistic calculated to test the statistical significance of the increase in explanatory power of the 47DC specification over the 18DC specification.
        d.f. = degrees of freedom.
        SEE = standard error of the estimate.
Source: Regression results.

The greater explanatory power of a specification with a more detailed output classification is theoretically plausible and accords with the results obtained in other studies. The higher the level of aggregation of output, the more heterogeneous the output categories are likely to be. In a comparative study of the ability of 10 different case mix variables to explain interhospital variation in average cost per case, Watts and Klastorin (1980) found that, in general, "the detailed variables were able to explain more interhospital cost variation than the single-valued indices ... " (p.366). In a similar vein, Feldstein (1967) found that, in comparison with a nine category output specification, "the explanatory power of the 28 variable equation is somewhat greater (adjusted R^2 = .320); an F-test shows that this difference is "significant" at the 10 per cent level" (p.39).[12]

Turning now to the individual parameter estimates, Tables 5.8 and 5.9 contain the estimated coefficients from the 18 and 47 diagnostic category specifications respectively for 1977-78. These Tables also present the t-statistics and the implied average and marginal cost per case. These latter values are obtained by adding each estimated coefficient to the constant term since the constant term represents the estimated average and marginal cost per case of the suppressed category and the estimated coefficients

---

[12]   Feldstein also tried several more highly aggregated specifications obtained by various groupings of the nine categories and found a significant reduction in explanatory power. See Feldstein (1967, p.41).

represent the difference between the cost per case of each category and that of the excluded category. Under these circumstances, the t-values are in effect testing whether the *difference* between the cost per case of each category and the excluded category is significantly different from zero.[13]

Considering first the 18 diagnostic category parameter estimates (see Table 5.8), only one estimated coefficient is significantly different from zero, i.e. only for category 5 Mental Disorders is there a significant difference between average and marginal cost per case and the average and marginal cost per case of category 1 Infectious and Parasitic Diseases (the excluded category). While it seems unlikely that the average and marginal costs of all cases in 17 of the 18 categories are the same, it is even more implausible when one considers that the estimated average and marginal cost of the excluded category is negative (−$296.28). Even ignoring the significance of the individual parameter estimates, the implied figures for average and marginal cost per case are implausible. Five of the 18 values are negative and a number of the positive values are very large in relation to the mean average cost per case for 1977-78 of $546.83 (see Table 5.6).

A similar pattern emerges for the parameter estimates from the 47 diagnostic category specification (see Table 5.9). Only two estimated coefficients are significantly different from zero (categories 12 Acute Myocardial Infarction, and 27 Other Urinary), and 19 of the 47 values of implied average and marginal cost per case are negative. Further, the estimated coefficients from this specification are generally inconsistent with those obtained from the 18 diagnostic category specification. For example, the category Endocrine and Metabolic has exactly the same ICD codes in the two specifications (see Tables 5.1 and 5.2) but has an implied average and marginal cost per case of $4,075 in the 18 category specification and $2,737 in the 47 category specification.

---

[13] The t-statistic for each parameter estimate can be converted to a t-statistic for the corresponding estimate of average and marginal cost by computing the estimated variance for the sum of two coefficients as follows:

$$\text{estimated variance } (a_k + a_i) = \text{variance } (a_k) + \text{variance } (a_i) \\ + 2 \text{ covariance } (a_k a_i)$$

where a_k and a_i are the constant term and the estimated coefficient respectively ($i = 1,...,17$ for the 18 diagnostic category specification). The information required for this calculation can be obtained from the variance-covariance matrix of the parameter estimates. A statistical discussion of this can be found in Johnston (1972, pp.176-86). On the interpretation of the t-statistic in equations of the type estimated here, with particular reference to hospital costs, see Lee and Wallace (1973).

Table 5.8. Parameter Estimates, 18 Diagnostic Category Specification, Queensland Public Hospitals, 1977-78

No.	Diagnostic Category	Estimated Coefficient	t-value	Implied Average & Marginal Cost per Case ($)
	Constant[a]	-296.28		-296.28
2	Neoplasms	266.82	0.19	-29.46
3	Endocrine, Nutritional, Metabolic	4371.31	1.79	4075.03
4	Blood	1463.92	0.24	1167.64
5	Mental Disorders	3707.51	3.00*	3411.23
6	Nervous System	1390.17	0.93	1093.89
7	Circulatory System	1314.03	1.39	1017.75
8	Respiratory System	-71.09	-0.08	-367.37
9	Digestive System	867.86	0.77	571.58
10	Genito-Urinary System	263.23	0.26	-33.05
11	Complications of Pregnancy, Childbirth & Puerperium	952.29	1.20	656.01
12	Skin & Subcutaneous Tissue	1282.19	0.71	985.91
13	Musculoskeletal System	3190.94	1.75	2894.66
14	Congenital Anomalies	2544.06	1.03	2247.78
15	Causes of Perinatal Morbidity & Mortality	-1864.54	-0.45	-2160.82
16	Symptoms & ill-defined	262.31	0.31	-33.97
17	Accidents, Poisonings & Violence	720.40	0.84	424.12
18	Supplementary Classifications	1050.90	0.77	754.62

Notes: *   Significant at 5% level.
            (a)   Suppressed category is Infectious and Parasitic Diseases.
Source: Regression results.

The parameter estimates for each of the specifications for each of the other three years 1979-80 to 1980-81 were found to exhibit similar behaviour. These estimates will not be presented here.

These two specifications are based on only one axis of classification of hospital output, *viz.* diagnosis. Each can be expanded by including the additional dimensions of case mix which were used to classify cases in this study—sex, surgical status, payment status, separation status and age. Summary statistics for each of the estimated equations for each of the four years are presented in Table 5.10.

Taking the 18 diagnostic category specification first, the addition of the extra case mix dimensions resulted in a statistically significant improvement in the explanatory power of each equation, as indicated by the F(18+/18)-statistic.[14] Including the additional case mix dimensions increased the amount of explained variation in average cost per case to a range of 43 to 62 per cent. A similar result emerged when the additional case mix dimensions were added to the 47 diagnostic category specification. The improvement in explanatory power was significant in three of the four years as indicated by the F(47+/47)-statistic.[15] After including the additional case mix dimensions, the amount of variation in average cost per case explained by case mix ranged from 46 to 75 per cent. Overall, each of the expanded specifications showed a statistically significant relationship between average cost per case and case mix in each year, as indicated by the F-statistics. In general it seems that a classification of hospital output based solely on diagnosis does not capture all of the dimensions of case mix which are relevant in explaining interhospital variation in average cost per case.

Another comparison of interest in Table 5.10 is that between each of the expanded specifications. Does the more finely disaggregated output classification based on diagnosis, i.e. the 47 diagnostic category classification, add significant explanatory power *after* the additional case mix dimensions have been added to the 18 diagnostic category specification? Put another way, does it make any difference if cases are more finely classified on the basis of diagnosis after the effect of the other case mix dimensions has been taken into account? The F(47+/18+)-statistic provides evidence on this, comparing the explanatory power of the expanded 47 diagnostic category specification with the expanded 18 diagnostic category specification. For all years other than 1977-78, the increase in explanatory power is statistically significant. Hence the more detailed diagnosis classification scheme continues to significantly enhance our ability to explain the interhospital variation in average cost per case even after the effects of the other dimensions of case mix (age, sex, etc.) have been incorporated.

Turning to the individual parameter estimates in the expanded specifications, again the problems of insignificance and incorrect signs are manifest. Table 5.11 presents such estimates for the expanded 18 diagnostic category specification for 1977-78. Only five of the 28 categories have

---

14 The 18DC+ specification included a constant term, allowing one category from each of the extra five case mix classifications to be suppressed. The expanded specifications contained 10 extra variables (93 degrees of freedom) for 1977-78 and 1978-79, and nine extra variables (94 degrees of freedom) for the remaining two years (the intermediate/private payment category was conflated in 1979-80 and 1980-81).

15 There were 64 degrees of freedom in estimating the equations for the first two years and 65 degrees of freedom for the last two years.

Table 5.9. Parameter Estimates, 47 Diagnostic Category Specification, Queensland Public Hospitals, 1977-78

No.	Diagnostic Category	Estimated Coefficient	t-value	Implied Average & Marginal Cost per Case ($)
	Constant[a]	995.30		995.30
2	Infectious & Parasitic	1024.52	0.47	2019.82
3	Enteritis, Diarrhoeal Disease	-2057.21	-1.25	-1061.91
4	Malignant Neoplasms	-468.72	-0.22	526.58
5	Benign Neoplasms	1098.11	0.15	2093.41
6	Endocrine & Metabolic	1741.90	0.48	2737.20
7	Blood	-8638.75	-1.32	-7643.45
8	Psychiatric	2030.61	1.26	3025.91
9	Other CNS & Nerves	-1134.31	-0.45	-139.01
10	Eye & Ear	1372.61	0.68	2367.91
11	Other Heart, Hypertension	803.51	0.54	1798.81
12	Acute Myocardial Infarction	8593.93	2.02*	9589.23
13	Symptomatic Heart Disease	1139.02	0.50	2134.32
14	Cerebrovascular Disease	-2763.03	-0.62	-1767.73
15	Circulation	-4415.16	-1.13	-3419.86
16	Upper Respiratory	-1116.30	-0.83	-121.00
17	Pneumonia	-845.91	-0.62	149.39
18	Bronchitis, Emphysema, Asthma	-2427.75	-1.54	-1432.45
19	Tonsils & Adenoids	-4262.40	-1.84	-3267.10
20	Other Respiratory	-1095.88	-0.74	-100.58
21	Dental	-259.93	-0.07	735.37
22	Upper Gastrointestinal	-678.03	-0.29	317.27
23	Appendicitis	380.54	0.14	1375.84
24	Hernia	-8.49	-0.002	986.81
25	Other Gastrointestinal	2500.66	0.93	3495.96
26	Nephritis & Nephrosis	-451.07	-0.25	544.23
27	Other Urinary	7242.38	2.40*	8237.68
28	Male Genital	344.29	0.05	1339.59
29	Other Female Genital	-2035.49	-0.77	-1040.19
30	Disorders of Menstruation	-8362.86	-1.61	-7367.56
31	Complications of Pregnancy & Puerperium	-472.30	-0.24	523.00
32	Abortion	-2455.86	-0.46	-1460.56
33	Normal Delivery	-294.14	-0.25	701.16
34	Delivery Complications	578.52	0.25	1573.82
35	Skin Disease	-1170.66	-0.56	-175.36
36	Orthopaedic	1178.85	0.53	2174.15
37	Congenital Malformation	4919.51	1.19	5914.81
38	Perinatal	-5584.18	-0.80	-4588.88
39	Immaturity	-163.64	-0.02	831.66

Table 5.9 (cont.)

No.	Diagnostic Category	Estimated Coefficient	t-value	Implied Average & Marginal Cost per Case ($)
40	Symptoms, ill-defined	-774.21	-0.61	221.09
41	Long Stay, ill-defined	-1121.43	-0.52	-126.13
42	Other Fractures (excl. Femur)	-1485.42	-0.95	-490.12
43	Fracture of Neck of Femur	-11821.93	-1.18	-10826.63
44	Dislocations	5284.24	1.19	6279.54
45	Internal Injury	-1073.44	-0.66	-78.14
46	External Injury	-90.34	-0.05	904.96
47	Poisoning	-3790.48	-1.59	-2795.18

Notes: * Significant at 5% level.
(a) Suppressed category is Investigations, Procedures, Healthy.
Source: Regression results.

estimated coefficients which are significantly different from zero, implying that for most case types the average cost per case is the same as that of the excluded category.

This set of parameter estimates implies a particular average and marginal cost per case for each possible combination of diagnosis, sex, surgical status, and so on.[16] An illustrative set of such figures is tabulated in Table 5.11 for cases with age 5-14.[17] While most of these estimates are positive, again they seem large relative to the mean average cost per case for 1977-78 of $546.83. Further, some of the estimates implied for the other possible combinations of case mix categories (not given here) are quite unreasonable.

The parameter estimates obtained from the expanded 47 diagnostic category specification are presented in Table 5.12. Only three of the 57 categories have estimated coefficients which are significantly different from zero, implying again that for most case types the average cost per case is equal to that of the excluded category. For the diagnostic categories, only one coefficient is significantly different from zero—that for category 27

---

16 Some of these combinations are, of course, likely to be empty cells. For example, it is difficult to imagine a male with diagnosis 11 Complications of Pregnancy, Childbirth & Puerperium, at least under the existing state of technology!

17 These figures are obtained by adding the constant term and the parameter estimate for the age 5-14 category to the parameter estimate for each category.

Table 5.10. Summary Statistics for Estimated Cost Functions using 18 and 47 Diagnostic Categories plus Additional Case Mix Dimensions, Queensland Public Hospitals, 1977–78 to 1980-81

Year	18DCs	18DCs+(a)			F(b) 18+/18	47DCs	47DCs+			F 47+/47	F 47+/18+
	$\bar{R}^2$ (1)	$\bar{R}^2$ (2)	F (3)	SEE (4)	(5)	$\bar{R}^2$ (6)	$\bar{R}^2$ (7)	F (8)	SEE (9)	(10)	(11)
1977-78	0.33	0.44	4.48*	178.89	5.00*	0.33	0.46	2.85*	175.06	2.83*	1.14
1978-79	0.30	0.62	8.21*	179.06	9.50*	0.60	0.75	7.48*	144.55	5.61*	2.71*
1979-80	0.30	0.43	4.46*	374.70	3.48*	0.58	0.59	4.10*	318.36	1.13	2.25*
1980-81	0.23	0.45	4.75*	346.16	5.44*	0.43	0.58	4.00*	302.39	3.91*	2.01**

Notes: *   Significant at 1% level.
         **   Significant at 5% level.
         (a)   The "+" sign means that the additional case mix dimensions have been added to the specification.
         (b)   "F 18+/18" refers to the F-statistic calculated to test the statistical significance of the increase in explanatory power of the 18DC+ specification over the 18DC specification. The other F-statistics have an analogous interpretation.
               SEE = standard error of the estimate.

Source: Regression results.

Table 5.11. Parameter Estimates, 18 Diagnostic Category plus Additional Case
Mix Dimensions Specification, Queensland Public Hospitals, 1977-78

No.	Case Mix Category	Estimated Coefficient	t-value	Implied Average & Marginal Cost per Case with Age 5-14 ($)
	Constant[a]	924.80		2326.07
2	Neoplasms	-3245.64	-2.11*	-919.57
3	Endocrine, Nutritional & Metabolic	1260.77	0.56	3586.84
4	Blood	-3151.22	-0.57	-825.15
5	Mental Disorders	110.27	0.09	2436.34
6	Nervous System	-305.57	-0.21	2020.50
7	Circulatory System	-1714.52	-1.52	611.55
8	Respiratory System	-1939.81	-2.13*	386.26
9	Digestive System	-1700.47	-1.44	625.60
10	Genito-Urinary System	-1275.72	-1.20	1050.35
11	Complications of Pregnancy, Childbirth & Puerperium	-369.89	-0.40	1956.21
12	Skin & Subcutaneous Tissue	-1067.72	-0.60	1258.35
13	Musculoskeletal System	-1691.57	-0.89	634.50
14	Congenital Anomalies	7111.41	2.24*	9437.48
15	Causes of Perinatal Morbidity & Mortality	-5193.20	-1.30	-2867.13
16	Symptoms & ill-defined	-1245.67	-1.52	1080.40
17	Accidents, Poisonings & Violence	-294.72	-0.32	2031.35
18	Supplementary Classifications	-1552.34	-1.04	773.73
	Sex - male	-698.25	-1.32	1627.82
	Surgery present	-134.84	-0.41	2191.23
	Intermediate patient	-142.80	-1.07	2183.27
	Private patient	28.70	0.04	2354.77
	Patient transferred	-798.06	-1.61	1528.01
	Patient died	6365.44	2.55*	8691.51
	Age 5-14	1401.27	1.66	-
	Age 15-40	368.06	0.73	-
	Age 41-64	2775.74	4.56*	-
	Age 65+	600.10	1.12	-

Notes: *   Significant at 5% level.
   (a)   Suppressed categories are: Infectious and Parasitic Diseases; Sex - female;
       Surgery absent; Public patient; Patient discharged; and Age 0-4.
Source: Regression results.

Table 5.12. Parameter Estimates, 47 Diagnostic Category plus Additional Case Mix Dimensions Specification, Queensland Public Hospitals, 1977-78

No.	Case Mix Category	Estimated Coefficient	t-value	Implied Average & Marginal Cost per Case with Age 5-14 ($)
	Constant[a]	-474.39		1043.58
2	Infectious & Parasitic	2544.55	1.18	3588.39
3	Enteritis, Diarrhoeal Disease	124.19	0.06	1168.03
4	Malignant Neoplasms	-979.18	-0.45	64.66
5	Benign Neoplasms	862.33	0.11	1906.17
6	Endocrine & Metabolic	2364.64	0.67	3408.48
7	Blood	-7928.57	-1.26	-6884.73
8	Psychiatric	1853.40	1.10	2897.24
9	Other CNS & Nerves	585.03	0.19	1628.87
10	Eye & Ear	2064.32	0.90	3108.16
11	Other Heart, Hypertension	48.78	0.03	1092.62
12	Acute Myocardial Infarction	5634.65	1.38	6678.49
13	Symptomatic Heart Disease	1594.50	0.69	2638.34
14	Cerebrovascular Disease	-5672.86	-1.18	-4629.02
15	Circulation	-1532.32	-0.40	-488.48
16	Upper Respiratory	-1034.02	-0.76	9.82
17	Pneumonia	44.06	0.03	1087.90
18	Bronchitis, Emphysema, Asthma	-695.07	-0.41	348.77
19	Tonsils & Adenoids	-3519.29	-1.49	-2475.45
20	Other Respiratory	-656.74	-0.43	387.10
21	Dental	-240.24	-0.07	803.60
22	Upper Gastrointestinal	369.68	0.16	1413.52
23	Appendicitis	1827.98	0.69	2871.82
24	Hernia	862.44	0.20	1906.28
25	Other Gastrointestinal	777.76	0.30	1821.60
26	Nephritis & Nephrosis	-626.78	-0.35	417.06
27	Other Urinary	6298.99	2.11*	7342.83
28	Male Genital	-2917.02	-0.43	-1873.18
29	Other Female Genital	-592.65	-0.23	451.19
30	Disorders of Menstruation	-6192.87	-1.30	-5149.03
31	Complications of Pregnancy & Puerperium	1778.80	0.89	2822.64
32	Abortion	-22.10	-0.004	1021.74
33	Normal Delivery	549.59	0.46	1593.43
34	Delivery Complications	463.42	0.22	1507.26
35	Skin Disease	234.59	0.11	1278.43
36	Orthopaedic	-930.72	-0.44	113.12
37	Congenital Malformation	7747.07	1.66	8790.91

Table 5.12 (cont.)

No.	Case Mix Category	Estimated Coefficient	t-value	Implied Average & Marginal Cost per Case with Age 5-14 ($)
38	Perinatal	-8726.59	-1.26	-7682.75
39	Immaturity	3918.55	0.49	4962.39
40	Symptoms, ill-defined	447.41	0.31	1491.25
41	Long Stay, ill-defined	-1323.23	-0.56	-279.39
42	Other Fractures (excl. Femur)	840.82	0.44	1884.66
43	Fracture of Neck of Femur	-11144.13	-1.07	-10100.29
44	Dislocations	4864.04	1.06	5907.88
45	Internal Injury	194.03	0.10	1237.87
46	External Injury	1753.00	0.96	2796.84
47	Poisoning	-2367.58	-0.99	-1323.74
	Sex - male	-603.89	-0.79	439.95
	Surgery present	229.19	0.40	1273.03
	Intermediate patient	-192.94	-1.13	850.90
	Private patient	177.91	0.28	1221.75
	Patient transferred	-753.40	-1.31	290.44
	Patient died	9624.61	2.90*	10668.45
	Age 5-14	1517.97	1.37	-
	Age 15-40	505.44	0.67	-
	Age 41-64	2294.72	2.65*	-
	Age 65+	179.41	0.22	-

Notes: * Significant at 5% level.
(a) Suppressed categories are: Investigations, Procedures, Healthy; Sex - female; Surgery absent; Public patient; Patient discharged; and Age 0-4.
Source: Regression results.

Other Urinary—and this category is not a subset of any of the diagnostic categories which had significant coefficients in the expanded 18 diagnostic category specification. However, the two additional case mix dimensions which do have statistically significant coefficients in this specification— Patient died, and Age 41-64—were also significant in the expanded 18 diagnostic category specification. The significant positive coefficients here indicate that patients in these categories have a significantly higher average cost per case than the excluded category.

The parameter estimates for the remaining three years will not be presented in detail here. In general, the number and composition of diagnostic categories which are significant vary from one year to the next, as do the number and composition of significant additional case mix dimensions. For example, in the expanded 47 diagnostic category classification in 1978-79, 11 diagnostic categories were significant and four additional case mix dimensions were significant.

Overall it appears that, for each specification for each year, there is a statistically significant relationship between average cost per case and case mix, whether the latter is restricted to a diagnosis classification scheme or expanded to include additional case mix dimensions. But also, in each specification, there is a large number of output categories which have insignificant coefficients. This suggests a possible underlying problem in the data—multicollinearity.

This possibility is further enhanced when the estimated relationship between average cost per case and the number of cases *without* case mix adjustment is considered. Recall that the cost relationships estimated so far allow for no influence of the number of cases treated on average cost per case, only the mix of cases. The following are some estimated relationships between average cost per case (ACC) and the number of cases treated (y) using the 1977-78 data (t-values in parentheses; *, ** = significant at one and five per cent levels respectively).

$$ACC = 526.08 + 0.007613\, y$$
$$(2.01**)$$

$$\overline{R}^2 = .02; \ \text{d.f.} = 119.$$

$$ACC = 523.28 + 0.009522\, y - (0.6114 \times 10^{-7})y^2$$
$$\qquad\qquad (1.00) \qquad\qquad (-0.22)$$

$$\overline{R}^2 = .02; \ \text{d.f.} = 118.$$

$$ACC = 578.38 - 7433.63\,(1/y)$$
$$(-4.01*)$$

$$\overline{R}^2 = .11; \ \text{d.f.} = 119.$$

Generally these results compare poorly with those arising from the equations containing case mix variables, lending further credence to the overall significance of the relationship between average cost per case and case mix discussed above. The problem of multicollinearity therefore warrants further discussion.

5.5.2 The Multicollinearity Problem

In multiple regression analysis, the F-statistic provides a *joint* test of significance of all the variables in the equation, i.e. it involves testing the null hypothesis

$$H_0: a_1 = a_2 = a_3 = ... = a_n = 0$$

against the alternative hypothesis

$$H_i: \text{ not all } a_i \text{ are zero.}$$

Since the relevant F-statistics for the equations estimated here all exceed their critical value (see Tables 5.7 and 5.10), the null hypothesis is rejected. At the same time, however, the individual tests of significance of individual parameter estimates suggest that a large number are not significantly different from zero.[18] Hence while the overall relationship is significant, the source of variation in average cost per case cannot be assigned to individual case mix categories. This situation often arises in the presence of multicollinearity, a term used to describe the problem where, "because of strong interrelationships among the independent variables, it becomes difficult to disentangle their separate effects on the dependent variable" (Maddala 1977, p.183).

The behaviour of the confidence region for joint tests of significance in the presence of multicollinearity has been well documented (see Kennedy 1992, pp.55-61; Judge, Hill, Griffiths, Lütkepohl and Lee 1982, pp.177-86). The joint confidence region can indicate rejection of the null hypothesis H_0 above even though individual hypothesis tests would accept the null hypothesis $H_0: a_i = 0$ $(i = 1, ..., k)$. A diagrammatic exposition of this possibility for two parameter estimates B_1 and B_2 is depicted in Figure 5.1. The rectangle *abcd* is formed by the confidence intervals for each estimate based on individual tests of significance. As drawn, the null hypotheses

---

[18] Recall that, in the specifications employed here which include a constant term, a coefficient being equal to zero does not imply the average and marginal cost of that case type is zero, but rather that it does not differ significantly from the average and marginal cost of the excluded category. If all the coefficients were zero, this would imply all case types have the same average and marginal cost, thus precluding any effect of case mix on average cost per case.

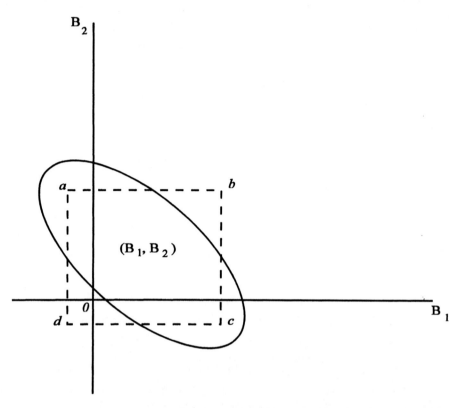

Figure 5.1. Individual and Joint Confidence Regions for Two Parameter Estimates

H_0: $B_1 = 0$ and H_0: $B_2 = 0$ would be accepted. This area, however, does not define the correct confidence region for a *joint* test of significance, i.e. a test of the null hypothesis H_0: $B_1 = B_2 = 0$. If B_1 and B_2 had equal variances and zero covariance, the joint confidence region would be given by a circle centred on (B_1, B_2) and the rectangular region *abcd* would approximate this correct region. But as the variances of B_1 and B_2 differ and covariance between them is admitted, the joint confidence region becomes an ellipse. With negative covariance, the ellipse tilts as shown in Figure 5.1, increasing the likelihood that the joint test of significance will reject the null hypothesis H_0: $B_1 = B_2 = 0$ even though the individual confidence regions both encompass the origin (see Judge, *et al.* 1982, p.179).[19]

---

[19]   It is, of course, possible that the multicollinearity may give rise to positive covariance
between the parameter estimates, resulting in an ellipse tilting in the opposite direction
to that shown in Figure 5.1. In this case it is possible that the joint confidence region
will encompass the origin while each of the individual confidence regions do not. Hence

The presence of multicollinearity in the case mix data is suggested by a number of other factors also. *First,* the parameter estimates and associated t-values were highly unstable when the relationship was estimated using forward stepwise regression. As additional case mix categories were added into the equation, the parameter estimates and t-values of categories already in the equation fluctuated considerably. If there were zero collinearity between the case mix categories, then parameter estimates and t-values of categories already in the equation would be unaffected by the addition of further case mix categories.

Second, when the equation was estimated stepwise with a critical t-value of 1.2, the final equation contained different case mix categories depending upon which category was entered first, i.e. selectivity bias was present (see Jenkins 1977, pp.62-3). If the independent variables were orthogonal, the parameter estimates would be independent of the order of entry.

Third, the determinant of the correlation matrix of the 47 diagnostic categories in 1977-78 was $(0.19571408 \times 10^{-16})$. A value of zero for this determinant indicates perfect multicollinearity. Using Bartlett's formula to transform this determinant into a chi-square statistic, statistically significant dependence between the explanatory variables was indicated.[20]

Fourth, an examination of the correlation matrices revealed a high degree of correlation between some variables and a number of statistically

---

the null hypothesis H_0: $B_1 = B_2 = 0$ would be accepted while H_0: $B_2 = 0$ would be rejected. This situation is not encountered very often and is clearly not the case which has arisen in this study. For a discussion, see Geary and Leser (1968).

[20] The determinant of a correlation matrix lies in the interval [0,1], being zero if perfect multicollinearity is present and unity if there is no multicollinearity. Bartlett's transformation converts this determinant into a chi-square statistic using the following formula:

$$\chi^2 = -[(T-1) - ((2K+5)/6)]\ln|\mathbf{X'X}|$$

with $K(K-1)/2$ degrees of freedom, where $T =$ the number of observations, $K =$ the number of independent variables, and $|\mathbf{X'X}|$ is the determinant of the correlation matrix $\mathbf{X'X}$ with $\mathbf{X}$ being the standardised data matrix (see Farrar and Glauber 1967, pp.99-101). This statistic can then be used to test the null hypothesis that $|\mathbf{X'X}| = 1$, a rejection of the null hypothesis implying that the explanatory variables are not independent. Haitovsky (1969) suggested that the null hypothesis should be $|\mathbf{X'X}| = 0$ since this is more likely to indicate whether multicollinearity is a problem, while Willan and Watts (1978) have provided an interpretation of $\sqrt{|\mathbf{X'X}|}$ in terms of the joint confidence region. For further discussion see also Judge, *et al.* (1980, pp.460-1).

significant correlation coefficients. For example, of the 153 correlation coefficients in the 18 diagnostic category correlation matrix for 1977-78, 82 or nearly 54 per cent were statistically significant at the 5 per cent level.

A *fifth* indication of the extent of linear dependencies amongst the data is the behaviour of the characteristic roots of the **X'X** matrix (**X** is the data matrix). For 47 independent variables there are 47 characteristic roots which have the property that, if the data are standardised, their sum will be equal to the number of independent variables (i.e. 47). Further, if the case mix categories are orthogonal, i.e. there is no multicollinearity, these characteristic roots will all equal unity, while the existence of one or more exact linear dependencies will result in one or more characteristic roots being zero.[21]

Using the 47 diagnostic category output classification for 1979-80, the characteristic roots were calculated. Since there is an exact linear dependence among the 47 categories (they all sum to unity), the first category was suppressed and 46 characteristic roots were obtained.[22] These roots are presented in descending order in Table 5.13. The value of the largest characteristic root relative to the value of each of the others is also presented in this Table.

The characteristic roots range in value from 6.26 down to 0.02 indicating some degree of linear dependence in the data. The ratio of the largest to the smallest characteristic root is 381.68. This ratio, termed the "condition number" of the **X'X** matrix by Belsley, Kuh and Welsh (1980, Ch.3), is of a magnitude which suggests serious collinearity. It should be noted, however, that our data have been standardised, i.e. scaled and centred. Belsley, *et al.* (1980, pp.98-9) argue that uncentred data should be used "since centering can mask the role of the constant in any underlying near dependencies and produce misleading diagnostic results". This was not pursued though, because as Judge, *et al.* (1982, p.621) point out, any rule for determining the presence of serious multicollinearity based on a particular value of the condition number "is still just a rule of thumb".

As pointed out in Appendix 5.I, a large degree of inequality in the characteristic roots does not *per se* indicate that large standard errors will attach to the parameter estimates—multicollinearity does not necessarily imply imprecise estimation. There is, however, sufficient evidence to

---

[21]   The concepts of characteristic roots and characteristic vectors, and their relationship to the multicollinearity problem, are discussed more thoroughly in Appendix 5.I.

[22]   Including the 47th category would simply have resulted in a 47th characteristic root equal to zero.

warrant the conclusion that the parameter estimates presented so far in this chapter have large variances arising from multicollinearity in the underlying data.

Table 5.13. Characteristic Roots of $\mathbf{X'X}$ Matrix Using 46 Diagnostic Categories, 1979-80[a]

	Value	λ_1/λ_i		Value	λ_1/λ_i
λ_1	6.25581		λ_{24}	0.52890	11.83
λ_2	5.43634	1.15	λ_{25}	0.47102	13.28
λ_3	3.06902	2.04	λ_{26}	0.45979	13.61
λ_4	2.64327	2.37	λ_{27}	0.42251	14.81
λ_5	2.48113	2.52	λ_{28}	0.40057	15.62
λ_6	2.40210	2.60	λ_{29}	0.39265	15.93
λ_7	1.86460	3.36	λ_{30}	0.35778	17.49
λ_8	1.72320	3.63	λ_{31}	0.32307	19.36
λ_9	1.47517	4.24	λ_{32}	0.31076	20.13
λ_{10}	1.40467	4.45	λ_{33}	0.28931	21.62
λ_{11}	1.36968	4.57	λ_{34}	0.25797	24.25
λ_{12}	1.14472	5.46	λ_{35}	0.22583	27.70
λ_{13}	1.04189	6.00	λ_{36}	0.21369	29.28
λ_{14}	1.01427	6.17	λ_{37}	0.20119	31.09
λ_{15}	0.99493	6.29	λ_{38}	0.19634	31.86
λ_{16}	0.97114	6.44	λ_{39}	0.15358	40.73
λ_{17}	0.87697	7.13	λ_{40}	0.14624	42.78
λ_{18}	0.76826	8.14	λ_{41}	0.13119	47.69
λ_{19}	0.71048	8.81	λ_{42}	0.11939	52.40
λ_{20}	0.69240	9.03	λ_{43}	0.08407	74.41
λ_{21}	0.65623	9.53	λ_{44}	0.07442	84.06
λ_{22}	0.59411	10.53	λ_{45}	0.05441	114.98
λ_{23}	0.57849	10.81	λ_{46}	0.01639	381.68

Notes: (a) Data have been standardised.
Source: Statistical Results obtained using BMDP4R.

While multicollinearity can, and often does, result in large standard errors for the parameter estimates, it will not affect the precision of the predicted values of the dependent variable obtained from the equation "as long as the values of the independent variables from which a prediction is desired obey the same near exact restrictions as the original [data] matrix" (Judge, *et al.* 1980, p.458). That is, as long as the underlying pattern of multicollinearity in the data from which a prediction is being obtained is the same as in the data from which the relationship was estimated, the precision of the prediction will not be impaired. As will be seen in Chapter 10, this explains why the predicted values of average cost per case obtained from the estimated case-mix-based equations presented in this chapter are relatively precise if they are obtained using the data from which the equation was estimated.

Returning to the problem of imprecise parameter estimates, what can be done to improve this precision? Broadly, there are two approaches. *First*, since multicollinearity is a problem in the data, the traditional approach is to supplement the original data with more information. Such extra information may take the form of either additional observations, or *a priori* restrictions on the values of the parameters, e.g. an inequality constraint or a linear restriction. *Second*, the dimensionality of the data can be reduced, generally either by deleting variables from the specified equation on the basis of economic theory or by the use of an *ad hoc* statistical procedure designed to collapse the original set of independent variables into a smaller set of variables.

With regard to the first approach, it is possible to expand the number of observations by pooling two or more years of data, or by expanding the sample of hospitals in any year by incorporating hospitals from other States. This latter possibility is investigated in Chapter 9 where data from Queensland and New South Wales for 1979-80 are pooled, but as will be seen, this does not alleviate the problem. On the possibility of incorporating restrictions, Chant (1986), using the same data sets employed in the present study, utilised a multiplicative model of average cost per *day* which guarantees positive parameter estimates. However the resulting estimates, although positive, are unrealistic or unstable from year to year.[23]

With regard to the second approach—reducing the dimensionality of the data—it must be emphasised that deletion of variables from an equation

---

[23] In the field of agricultural economics, Dixon, Batte and Sonka (1984) have suggested that estimates of average costs by product type be obtained by treating the multiproduct total cost function as a random coefficients model. They obtained positive, plausible estimates of average costs using this approach but only for firms producing two outputs (corn and soybeans). In dealing with firms producing many outputs (such as hospitals) the computational requirements may become excessive. Nevertheless, this approach could provide a promising avenue for future research on hospital costs.

whose parameter estimates are affected by multicollinearity can be a dangerous procedure. This is particularly so if there is a strong case on theoretical grounds for believing that the variables are related to the dependent variable. To quote Fomby, Hill and Johnson (1984, p.297):

> One especially dangerous approach to "curing" multicollinearity is to delete, on the basis of t-values, one or more variables involved in a multicollinear relation from a model, [using] a stepwise regression routine of some sort or simply on an *ad hoc* basis. While the standard errors of the parameter estimates in the reduced model will certainly be lower (but only conditionally correct), the omission of relevant explanatory variables simply because the data will not allow precise estimation of their parameters is unsatisfactory.

Certainly in the context of this study such deletion of variables would be a haphazard procedure because of the selectivity bias noted earlier and because of the strong theoretical supposition that output produced in any of the output categories will affect total cost.

The remainder of this chapter presents results using two other means of reducing the dimensionality of the data. The first of these utilises an *ad hoc* statistical procedure known as principal components analysis. The second uses the information theory approach to case mix measurement as discussed in Chapter 3 to construct a single-valued case mix index. Each of these will be discussed in turn.

5.5.3   Principal Components Analysis

The method of principal components analysis, or the more general method of factor analysis from which it is derived, has been employed in several studies of hospital costs, such as those by Lave, Lave and Silverman (1972), Evans (1971), Feldstein and Schuttinga (1977), Jenkins (1977, 1980) and Nicholson (1983). Its aim is to form a new set of synthetic variables from linear combinations of the original set of independent variables in such a way that the new variables—the principal components—are orthogonal or uncorrelated.

Consider the first principal component P_1. This can be written as a weighted linear sum of the independent variable (the Xs) as follows:

$$P_1 = \ell_{11}X_1 + \ell_{21}X_2 + ... + \ell_{K1}X_K \qquad\qquad ... (5.7)$$

where there are K independent variables. The results presented below pertain to the 47 diagnostic category classification so $K = 47$ in the current context. Suppose there are T observations ($T = 121$ in the data set used here). Then equation (5.7) can be used to produce T observations $(P_{11}, P_{12}, \ldots, P_{1T})$ on the first principal component. In this way the 121 observations on 47 variables can by synthesised into the same number of observations on the first principal component.

The obvious question then is how are the weights in equation (5.7) —the $\ell_{11}, \ell_{21}, \ldots, \ell_{K1}$—determined? The answer is that P_1 is constructed in such a way that it accounts for the largest amount of the total variation in the data. The values are obtained as the solution to the problem of maximising the sum of squares of P_1 subject to the constraint that the sum of the squared values of the weights be unity,[24] i.e. subject to

$$\ell_{11}^2 + \ell_{21}^2 + \ldots + \ell_{K1}^2 = 1.$$

A more detailed account of this process is provided in Appendix 5.II.

Having derived the first principal component P_1, the procedure can be repeated to construct a second principal component P_2 which captures the maximum amount of variation in the data remaining after the construction of P_1. The solution is again that of a constrained maximisation problem, but for the second (and subsequent) principal components, a further constraint is added, *viz.* that the principal components be orthogonal or uncorrelated. In this way a set of synthetic variables which exhibit zero multicollinearity is constructed from the original variables.

If there is substantial multicollinearity in the data, a small number of principal components may account for a large proportion of the variation in the data. It is in such cases that principal components can be used to reduce the dimensionality of the data. The original variables in the relationship to be estimated can be replaced by a smaller number of principal components which also have the property that they are orthogonal. In the context of this study the average cost function to be estimated would become

$$ACC = \alpha_0 + \alpha_1 P_1 + \ldots + \alpha_j P_j \quad (j < K) \qquad \ldots (5.8)$$

---

[24] This constraint is necessary otherwise the problem becomes the trivial one of unconstrained maximisation of the sum of squares of P_1, the solution to which is to make the values of the weights as large as possible.

where P_i is the ith principal component and $j < K$ indicates that the number of principal components retained is smaller than the original number of independent variables.

It is often the case that the principal components, being 'artificial' variables, have no economic meaning. A particular value of a principal component arises as a weighted sum of each value of the independent variables and the resulting number can be difficult to interpret. For instance, Maddala (1977, p.193) asks "what is the meaning of 2(income) + 3(price)?", and Koutsoyiannis (1977, p.436) states categorically that the components "are artificial orthogonal variables not directly identifiable with a particular economic magnitude".

For this reason attention is not usually focussed on the principal component values or the parameter estimates of equation (5.8). Rather, having obtained the principal component parameter estimates, a further transformation of such estimates back to estimates of the original parameters is undertaken, i.e. having estimated equation (5.8) it is possible to retrieve estimates of the original parameters. By substituting equation (5.7) into equation (5.8) and rearranging terms, expressions for each of the original parameters in terms of the ℓs (the weights) and the αs (the principal component parameter estimates) can be found (see Koutsoyiannis 1977, pp.435-6; Chatterjee and Price 1977, Ch.7). The use of this approach in hospital cost analysis has been forcefully advocated by Jenkins (1977).

A possible advantage of this procedure is that it may result in estimates of the original parameters which have smaller mean square errors. The mean square error of an estimator is the sum of its variance and the square of its bias (see Dutta 1975, pp.63-4). Ordinary least squares (OLS) estimators have the property of being best linear *unbiased* estimators so they are also the minimum mean square error estimators in the set of *unbiased* estimators. Now the parameter estimates retrieved from the principal component parameter estimates are likely to be biased, but they may also have smaller variances. Hence by trading off increased bias in favour of lower variance, it might be possible to reduce the mean square error of the original estimates. The conditions under which this will be true have been investigated by McCallum (1970) and Cheng and Iglarsh (1976) and are discussed in Fomby, Hill and Johnson (1984, pp.298-300).

It should be noted that the values obtained for principal components as in equation (5.7) and the principal component parameter estimates as in equation (5.8) are not independent of the scale of measurement of the independent variables. The solutions will differ according to whether the data are expressed in original units, deviation form or standardised form. "In other words, the solution obtained using a correlation matrix as input will differ from the solution obtained from a covariance matrix and—more importantly—there is no simple way of translating one solution to the other" (Dillon and Goldstein 1984, p.27).

The results presented here use the correlation matrix as input. This corresponds to standardising each independent variable by subtracting its mean and dividing by its standard deviation. The variance of any particular principal component is then given by its characteristic root, and since the components are orthogonal, the sum of these characteristic roots for all components gives the total variation in the data which, because of the use of standardised data, is equal to the number of independent variables (see Appendix 5.II).

The results are again derived from the 47 diagnostic category classification for 1979-80 with the first category suppressed. The characteristic roots are then those which have been presented in Table 5.13. The cumulative proportion of the total variance of the independent variables explained by the first j principal components ($j = 1, ..., 46$) is shown in Table 5.14. This cumulative proportion is calculated as the sum of the first j characteristic roots divided by the sum of all the roots (which is 46). The first seven principal components capture over 50 per cent of the total variance of the 46 diagnostic categories, while the first 15 components capture nearly 75 per cent.

Which and how many components should be retained as independent variables? Given that the objective of using principal components regression is to increase the precision of the original parameter estimates by reducing their mean square errors, this would be the logical criterion to use in deciding which components to retain. Unfortunately such a decision rule is not operational because it requires a knowledge of the true values of the original parameters, the very magnitude for which estimates are being sought (McCallum 1970, pp.111-12).

Alternative criteria are based on either the characteristic roots of the principal components or the correlations of the principal components with the dependent variable (average cost per case). The former results in the deletion of those components "that are relatively unimportant as predictors of the *original independent variables*" (Massy 1965, p.241, emphasis in original), i.e. those components which have low characteristic roots and so account for a small proportion of the total variance of the independent variables. The latter results in the deletion of components "that are relatively unimportant as predictors of the *dependent variable*" (Massy 1965, p.241, emphasis in original), i.e. those components which have relatively low correlation coefficients with the dependent variable. As can be seen from Table 5.14, the components which have the largest characteristic roots do not necessarily have the largest correlations with average cost per case. Consequently, these two decision rules will result in a different order of entry of the components into the regression equation.

Table 5.14. Cumulative Percentage of Total Variance of Independent Variables and Correlation with Average Cost Per Case for Principal Components extracted from 46 Diagnostic Categories, 1979-80

	Cumulative Percentage of Total Variance	Correlation with Average Cost per Case		Cumulative Percentage of Total Variance	Correlation with Average Cost per Case
P_1	13.60	-.040	P_{24}	88.47	-.142
P_2	25.42	.004	P_{25}	89.50	-.111
P_3*	32.09	.196	P_{26}	90.50	-.112
P_4	37.84	.092	P_{27}	91.42	.075
P_5*	43.23	-.403	P_{28}	92.29	-.016
P_6*	48.45	.190	P_{29}	93.14	-.018
P_7*	52.50	.187	P_{30}	93.92	.043
P_8*	56.25	.255	P_{31}	94.62	.023
P_9*	59.46	-.163	P_{32}	95.30	-.019
P_{10}	62.51	.140	P_{33}	95.93	-.004
P_{11}*	65.49	-.323	P_{34}	96.49	-.043
P_{12}*	67.98	-.186	P_{35}	96.98	.003
P_{13}*	70.24	.180	P_{36}	97.44	.006
P_{14}*	72.45	-.144	P_{37}	97.88	-.043
P_{15}	74.61	.070	P_{38}	98.31	-.063
P_{16}	76.72	.029	P_{39}	98.64	-.018
P_{17}*	78.63	-.213	P_{40}	98.96	-.006
P_{18}	80.30	.007	P_{41}	99.24	-.075
P_{19}	81.84	-.020	P_{42}	99.50	-.090
P_{20}	83.35	-.011	P_{43}	99.68	-.027
P_{21}	84.78	.004	P_{44}	99.85	-.116
P_{22}	86.07	-.068	P_{45}	99.96	.035
P_{23}	87.32	.092	P_{46}	100.00	.004

Notes: * Entered in principal components regression.
Source: As for Table 5.13.

The criterion employed here is that based on the correlations of the components with average cost per case. Since the predictive value of the average cost equation is important in the context of hospital payment schemes to be discussed later, it was decided that the attempt to obtain positive estimates of average and marginal cost by case type should be undertaken using a decision rule related to the overall goodness-of-fit of the equation. Entering the components in the order of their correlation with average cost per case is equivalent to maximising the value of R^2 at each step, and so seems more in keeping with the purpose of the analysis.

This resolves the problem of determining the order of entry of the components into the equation, but leaves unresolved the problem of how many to enter.[25] At this juncture it is useful to recall that, on *a priori* grounds, average and marginal costs should be non-negative. Consequently, in entering successive components, the resulting original parameter estimates can be observed to see if they give rise to non-negative values of average and marginal cost. The computer package used to produce these results (BMDP4R) facilitated this analysis because, as each successive component was entered, the retrieved estimates of the 47 original parameters were printed.[26] Hence it is possible to observe how these estimates react to the entry of successive components.

Overall the results of the principal components regression are disappointing. While the variances of a number of parameter estimates were reduced and t-values consequently increased, large numbers of negative values for average and marginal cost were still implied. Regression of average cost per case on the first principal component gave rise to 17 negative values for average and marginal cost, and the entry of successive components did not improve this situation. As such, the *a priori* expectation of non-negative values gave little guidance as to the number of components to enter.

The parameter estimates and implied values of average and marginal cost per case retrieved from the entry of eleven principal components are presented in Table 5.15. For comparative purposes, the estimates which resulted from ordinary least squares regression are also included in this

---

25   It might be thought that all components can be entered because, since they are orthogonal, this may result in estimates of the original parameters with lower mean square errors. This is not so, however. While the principal component parameter estimates (the αs in equation (5.8)) will be unaffected by the number of components entered because of the orthogonality of the components, the use of all components will result in exactly the same original parameter estimates as the straightforward application of the classical least squares technique to the original data (see Massy 1965).

26   Principal components with a correlation with average cost per case less than .01 were not entered. This constraint resulted in 38 components eligible for entry.

Table. The 11 components were entered in decreasing order of correlation with average cost per case, and all except one had characteristic roots greater than unity. The components entered are those marked with an asterisk in Table 5.14.

The success of principal components regression in reducing the variance of parameter estimates is evident in Table 5.15—the number of categories with t-values significant at the five per cent level increased from one using ordinary least squares to 21 using principal components regression.[27] However, the problem of negative values for average and marginal cost is also evident in this Table—21 such values arise in the estimates retrieved from principal components regression compared with 22 under ordinary least squares. The technique has thus been unsuccessful in eliminating this problem.

A similar analysis of hospital costs in Ontario undertaken by Jenkins (1977, 1980) also failed to completely eliminate negative average and marginal cost estimates. In addition to 41 diagnostic classification variables, Jenkins also included eight scale-related variables in the derivation of the principal components, and retained 24 of the 48 principal components in the case-type average cost equation. Upon retrieving the original parameter estimates, seven of the 41 implied average and marginal costs were negative.

In a study of Western Australian hospitals using principal components analysis, Nicholson (1983) was more fortunate. Beginning with an 18 diagnostic category classification, results were reported based on the inclusion of one and two principal components. Positive and meaningful

---

27   The variances of the original parameter estimates are retrieved from the principal components regression by the use of the following formula:

$$\text{var}(a_i) = s^2 \sum_{j=1}^{m} (v_{ij}^2 / \lambda_j)$$

where m is the number of components entered in the regression, v_{ij} is the jth element in the ith row of the matrix whose columns are the characteristic vectors of the components entered, j is the jth characteristic root, and s^2 is the error variance from the regression on principal components ($s^2 = .005514679$ for the eleven principal components regression reported here). a_i represents a standardised regression coefficient because the components are constructed from standardised data. Hence the variance calculated is the variance of the standardised original parameter estimate. It can be transformed to the variance of the unstandardised parameter estimate by multiplying by (σ_y^2/σ_i^2) where σ_y^2 is the variance of the dependent variable and σ_i^2 is the variance of the ith independent variable.

Table 5.15. Parameter Estimates for 47 Diagnostic Categories obtained from Ordinary Least Squares Regression and Regression on Eleven Principal Components, Queensland Public Hospitals, 1979-80

No.	Ordinary Least Squares			Principal Components		
	Estimated Coefficient	t-value	Implied Average & Marginal Cost per Case ($)	Estimated Coefficient	t-value	Implied Average & Marginal Cost per Case ($)
C[a]	729.62		729.62	1165.91		1165.91
2	2455.06	0.88	3184.68	-328.55	-0.32	837.36
3	2513.60	-0.88	-1783.98	-2185.84	-2.86*	-1019.93
4	985.76	0.20	1715.38	5229.48	5.70*	6395.39
5	12729.52	0.82	13459.14	6717.55	2.62*	7883.46
6	-5453.02	-1.16	-4723.40	-7404.38	-4.25*	-6238.47
7	-9340.43	-1.18	-8610.81	-9381.71	-3.72*	-8215.80
8	-992.72	-0.45	-263.10	-1177.77	-1.39	-11.86
9	6976.55	1.85	7706.17	1487.29	1.04	2653.20
10	-849.54	-0.23	-119.92	80.16	0.12	1246.07
11	-275.63	-0.10	453.99	-508.77	-0.55	657.14
12	-3784.28	-0.49	-3054.66	-5932.96	-2.33*	-4767.05
13	10521.36	2.55*	11250.98	9739.28	7.63*	10905.19
14	2496.32	0.66	3225.94	3492.38	4.58*	4658.29
15	-2083.91	-0.33	-1354.29	-6854.18	-4.73*	-5688.27
16	-4030.48	-1.25	-3300.86	-2109.56	-4.36*	-943.65
17	-3048.13	-1.00	-2318.51	231.28	0.20	1397.19
18	2312.00	0.98	3041.62	-749.55	-1.34	416.36
19	-3.17	-0.001	726.45	-3372.02	-2.35*	-2206.11
20	-1622.80	-0.41	-893.18	-488.27	-0.43	677.64
21	-1967.80	-0.36	-1238.18	-1698.61	-0.51	-532.70
22	1237.68	0.28	1967.30	584.69	0.47	1750.60
23	-1865.77	-0.35	-1136.15	-1670.43	-1.20	-504.52
24	1755.77	0.21	2485.39	-3524.96	-3.56*	-2359.05
25	5826.05	-1.79	-5096.43	-1221.75	-1.21	-55.84
26	-2321.60	-0.91	-1591.98	1217.04	1.68	2382.95
27	4557.37	0.88	5286.99	-2855.23	-1.77	-1689.32
28	-11748.43	-1.26	-11018.81	-11242.75	-4.75*	-10076.84
29	-4143.35	-0.97	-3413.73	-2363.60	-3.02*	-1197.69
30	1248.92	0.15	1978.54	-3429.94	-1.14	-2264.03
31	-1599.98	-0.41	-870.36	-729.92	-2.17*	435.99
32	151.04	0.02	880.66	-1321.26	-0.92	-155.35
33	-942.48	-0.60	-212.86	-23.48	-0.33	1142.43
34	2955.21	1.21	3684.83	43.16	0.22	1209.07
35	-1908.92	-0.66	1179.30	-714.35	-0.85	451.56
36	2409.76	0.78	3139.38	-747.04	-0.97	418.87
37	-12195.62	-1.50	-11466.00	2505.27	1.18	3671.18
38	3415.01	0.40	4144.63	-3825.29	-1.80	-2659.38
39	20895.37	0.77	21624.99	-29946.77	-2.71*	-28780.86

Table 5.15 (cont.)

No.	Ordinary Least Squares			Principal Components		
	Estimated Coefficient	t-value	Implied Average & Marginal Cost per Case ($)	Estimated Coefficient	t-value	Implied Average & Marginal Cost per Case ($)
40	706.85	0.42	1436.47	481.30	2.18*	1647.21
41	20460.96	4.98	21190.58	8913.19	7.33*	10079.10
42	-349.31	-0.10	380.31	51.64	0.08	1217.55
43	-20258.46	-0.98	-19528.84	8391.88	0.99	9557.79
44	11022.53	1.55	11752.15	15636.62	4.02*	16802.53
45	733.19	0.28	1462.81	-2926.40	-4.62*	-1760.49
46	-1207.30	-0.55	-477.68	-476.18	-1.07	689.73
47	-2883.78	-0.75	-2154.16	-3285.84	-4.21*	-2119.93

Notes: *   Significant at 5% level.
          (a)   Constant term (suppressed category is Investigations, Procedures, Healthy).
Source: Regression results.

average and marginal cost estimates emerged from the use of only one principal component.

Principal components regression is one approach to breaking the multicollinearity deadlock. "... [It] should be stressed that the optimal properties of principal component regression are concerned with the variance component of the mean squared error" (Greenberg and Webster 1983, p.175). Countering this, the retrieved parameter estimates may be severely biased, the principal components are not invariant to the units of measurement, and the use of this technique actually involves working with a reduced amount of information since the retained principal components capture less than 100 per cent of the variation in the original independent variables. Clearly the technique cannot be regarded as a panacea for the multicollinearity problem.

The principal component technique is an *ad hoc* data reduction technique which constructs synthetic variables on purely statistical criteria. Before concluding this chapter, some results based on the theoretical constructs of information theory will be presented.

5.5.4   Information Theory Indexes

An explanation of the information theory approach to constructing a scalar case mix index was provided in Chapter 3. Recall that the unstandardised weights originally proposed by Evans and Walker (1972) were

$$H_j^1 = \sum_i q_{ij} \ln\left(\frac{q_{ij}}{\frac{1}{I}}\right)$$

$$= \sum_i q_{ij} \ln(Iq_{ij}) \qquad\qquad\qquad ...(5.9)$$

$$H_j^2 = \sum_i q_{ij} \ln\left(\frac{q_{ij}}{p_i}\right)$$

where q_{ij} is the proportion of all cases of the jth type being treated in the ith hospital, I is the number of hospitals in the state and p_i is the proportion of all cases in the state being treated in the ith hospital.

The weights are designed to give a measure of the complexity of each particular case type on the hypothesis that the treatment of more complex cases tends to be concentrated in a smaller number of hospitals than the treatment of less complex cases. Consider *first* the weight H_j^1. Suppose first that all cases of a particular type are evenly distributed over all hospitals. Then $q_{1j} = q_{2j} = ... = 1/I$ and H_j^1 has a value of zero (since ln 1 = 0). This would be classified as a non-complex case type. Now suppose that all cases of a particular type are treated in one hospital, i.e. the cases are highly concentrated. Then $q_{ij} = 0$ for all but one hospital and in that hospital $q_{ij} = 1$. The weight H_j^1 then takes on a maximal value of ln I. As such, H_j^1 will have a minimum value of zero for the least complex (least concentrated) case types and ln I for the most complex (most concentrated) case types. Given that in this study there are 121 hospitals, H_j^1 then has a lower bound of zero and an upper bound of 4.8 (= ln 121). The actual values of H_j^1 for the 18 and 47 diagnostic category classifications for 1977-78 are contained in Tables 5.16 and 5.17 respectively.

Table 5.16. Unstandardised and Standardised Complexity Measures for 18
Diagnostic Categories, Queensland Public Hospitals, 1977-78

No.	Diagnostic Category	H_j^1	$\overline{H}_j^1$	H_j^2	$\overline{H}_j^2$
1	Infectious & Parasitic Diseases	0.67	0.52*	0.24	0.92
2	Neoplasms	2.09	1.62**	0.31	1.22
3	Endocrine, Nutritional & Metabolic	1.10	0.86	0.09	0.33*
4	Blood	1.23	0.96	0.16	0.62
5	Mental Disorders	1.79	1.39	0.41	1.61**
6	Nervous System	1.43	1.11	0.17	0.66
7	Circulatory System	1.33	1.03	0.18	0.71
8	Respiratory System	0.75	0.58*	0.22	0.85
9	Digestive System	1.22	0.95	0.09	0.35*
10	Genito-Urinary System	1.82	1.41**	0.22	0.87
11	Complications of Pregnancy, Childbirth & Puerperium	1.42	1.11	0.69	2.72**
12	Skin & Subcutaneous Tissue	0.88	0.68*	0.14	0.54
13	Musculoskeletal System	1.43	1.11	0.14	0.54
14	Congenital Anomalies	2.19	1.70**	0.89	3.47**
15	Causes of Perinatal Morbidity & Mortality	2.22	1.73**	1.06	4.15**
16	Symptoms & ill-defined	0.72	0.56*	0.12	0.47*
17	Accidents, Poisonings & Violence	1.01	0.78	0.07	0.29*
18	Supplementary Classifications	1.39	1.08	0.13	0.51

Notes: *   one of the four lowest standardised complexity values.
         **   one of the four highest standardised complexity values.
Sources: Hospital Morbidity Data and information theory index calculations.

For the 18 diagnostic categories, the complexity values range from a low
of 0.67 for category 1 Infectious and Parasitic Diseases, to a high of 2.22 for
category 15 Causes of Perinatal Morbidity and Mortality. For the 47
diagnostic categories (Table 5.17), the category with the lowest complexity
rating (0.55) is 16 Upper Respiratory, while category 26 Nephritis and
Nephrosis has the highest complexity value (3.24).

A problem with the unstandardised weights is that, "if hospitals are of
very different sizes (and the q_{ij} vary greatly for a given j), then H_j^1 will be
large even if cases of type j are distributed across hospitals in exactly the
same way as total cases" (Horn and Schumacher 1979, p.386). In other
words, a hospital may have high values of q_{ij} because it treats a high
proportion of the total cases in the state. However, the H_j^1 measure reads
this as high concentration even though it might be attributable solely to the

Table 5.17. Unstandardised and Standardised Complexity Measures for 47 Diagnostic Categories, Queensland Public Hospitals, 1977-78

No.	Diagnostic Category	H_j^1	$\overline{H}_j^1$	H_j^2	$\overline{H}_j^2$
1	Investigations, Procedures, Healthy	1.39	1.01	0.13	0.39
2	Infectious & Parasitic	0.88	0.64	0.18	0.55
3	Enteritis, Diarrhoeal Disease	0.56	0.41*	0.44	1.31
4	Malignant Neoplasms	2.22	1.62	0.37	1.01
5	Benign Neoplasms	1.67	1.22	0.20	0.59
6	Endocrine & Metabolic	1.10	0.81	0.09	0.25*
7	Blood	1.23	0.90	0.16	0.47
8	Psychiatric	1.79	1.31	0.41	1.22
9	Other CNS & Nerves	1.27	0.93	0.11	0.33*
10	Eye & Ear	1.71	1.24	0.36	1.06
11	Other Heart, Hypertension	1.25	0.91	0.34	0.99
12	Acute Myocardial Infarction	1.49	1.08	0.23	0.68
13	Symptomatic Heart Disease	1.13	0.82	0.23	0.67
14	Cerebrovascular Disease	1.54	1.12	0.23	0.67
15	Circulation	1.67	1.22	0.22	0.65
16	Upper Respiratory	0.55	0.40*	0.50	1.48
17	Pneumonia	0.68	0.49*	0.25	0.73
18	Bronchitis, Emphysema, Asthma	0.89	0.65	0.32	0.95
19	Tonsils & Adenoids	1.50	1.09	0.58	1.71
20	Other Respiratory	1.03	0.75	0.20	0.58
21	Dental	1.23	0.90	0.41	1.20
22	Upper Gastrointestinal	1.30	0.95	0.16	0.47
23	Appendicitis	1.15	0.84	0.19	0.57
24	Hernia	1.37	1.00	0.16	0.47
25	Other Gastrointestinal	1.37	1.00	0.15	0.43
26	Nephritis & Nephrosis	3.24	2.37**	0.95	2.82**
27	Other Urinary	1.28	0.93	0.13	0.38
28	Male Genital	1.51	1.10	0.15	0.45
29	Other Female Genital	1.39	1.01	0.23	0.67
30	Disorders of Menstruation	1.63	1.19	0.29	0.85
31	Complications, Pregnancy & Puerperium	1.22	0.89	0.60	1.77
32	Abortion	1.19	0.87	0.24	0.71
33	Normal Delivery	1.60	1.17	0.85	2.52
34	Delivery Complications	2.33	1.70**	1.61	4.75**
35	Skin Disease	0.88	0.64	0.14	0.41
36	Orthopaedic	1.43	1.04	0.14	0.41
37	Congenital Malformation	2.19	1.60	0.88	2.61
38	Perinatal	2.23	1.63**	1.04	3.08**
39	Immaturity	2.63	1.92**	1.51	4.47**
40	Symptoms, ill-defined	0.72	0.53*	0.12	0.37
41	Long Stay, ill-defined	0.85	0.62	0.29	0.85
42	Other Fractures (excl. Femur)	1.25	0.91	0.10	0.30*
43	Fracture of Neck of Femur	2.00	1.46	0.41	1.21
44	Dislocations	0.92	0.67	0.20	0.58
45	Internal Injury	1.01	0.74	0.14	0.42

Table 5.17 (cont.)

No.	Diagnostic Category	H_j^1	$\overline{H}_j^1$	H_j^2	$\overline{H}_j^2$
46	External Injury	0.83	0.61	0.14	0.41
47	Poisoning	0.97	0.71	0.09	0.27*

Notes: *   one of the four lowest standardised complexity values.
          **   one of the four highest standardised complexity values.
Source: As for Table 5.16.

size distribution of hospitals. "But this systematic upward bias is general across all *j*, and is removed in going from H_j^1 to $\overline{H}_j^1$" (Evans and Walker 1972, p.402), $\overline{H}_j^1$ being the standardised measure. The standardised values for the 18 and 47 diagnostic category classifications, which have a weighted mean of unity, are also presented in Tables 5.16 and 5.17 respectively.[28]

For the 18 diagnostic category classification the categories with the *lowest* standardised complexity values are:

1   Infectious and Parasitic Diseases (0.52);
16 Symptoms and ill-defined (0.56);
8   Respiratory System (0.58); and
12 Skin and Subcutaneous Tissue (0.68).

The categories with the *highest* standardised complexity values are:

15 Causes of Perinatal Morbidity and Mortality (1.73);
14 Congenital Anomalies (1.70);
2   Neoplasms (1.62); and
10 Genito-Urinary System (1.41).

These generally accord with what would be expected, e.g. neoplasms and diseases of the urinary system (which includes renal dialysis) come up as complex case types.

For the 47 diagnostic category classification the categories with the *lowest* standardised complexity values are (see Table 5.17):

---

[28]   The formulae for calculating the standardised values of H_j^1 and H_j^2 are given in Chapter 3, p.80.

16   Upper Respiratory (0.40);
3   Enteritis, Diarrhoeal Disease (0.41);
17   Pneumonia (0.49); and
40   Symptoms, ill-defined (0.53).

The categories with the *highest* standardised complexity values are:

26   Nephritis and Nephrosis (2.37);
39   Immaturity (1.92);
34   Delivery Complications (1.70); and
38   Perinatal (1.63).

   The results from the two diagnostic classifications are highly consistent
—the categories with the lowest complexity values in the 47 diagnostic
category classification are all subsets of the lowest complexity value
categories in the 18 diagnostic category classification, and similarly for the
high complexity value categories.[29] This result, together with the intuitive
plausibility of the rankings, is pleasing for it indicates that the 47 diagnostic
category classification is not sufficiently disaggregated to be confusing
'rarity' with 'complexity'. The chances of this problem arising increase with
the level of disaggregation of the classification scheme, as detected by
Tatchell (1977, Ch.9) who compared a 50 with a 150 diagnostic category
classification scheme and found the latter to suffer from the 'rarity' effect.[30]
   Consider now the *second* weight H_j^2 (see equation (5.9)). In contrast
with H_j^1, this measure is sensitive to the volume of cases treated, since the
prior knowledge incorporated is now of the p_i (the proportions of all cases
in the state treated in the ith hospital) and not simply the number of hospitals
I. The value of H_j^2 depends upon the value of q_{ij} *relative to* p_i, i.e. it

---

[29]   The results are also generally in accord with those produced by Evans and Walker
(1972) who found that "the highest complexities are recorded by list numbers (63)
nephritis and nephrosis, (35) diseases of the eye, (2) poliomyelitis and encephalitis, and
(6)-(18) malignant neoplasms. At the bottom end are the variants of upper respiratory
disease, skin infections, and stomach troubles" (p.402). These authors were working
with a 98 diagnostic category classification. Horn and Schumacher (1979) also found
that the information theory complexity measure correlated very highly with an
independently constructed clinical measure of complexity.

[30]   Tatchell also produced results for two years and found the index numbers to be
intertemporally stable.

depends upon the proportion of cases of the jth type treated by the ith hospital *relative to* the proportion of all cases in the state treated by the ith hospital. If these two values are equal for all hospitals—if the proportionate distribution of a particular case type is the same as the proportionate distribution of all cases—then H_j^2 will equal zero, since $q_{ij} = p_i$ for all i. The complexity measure H_j^2 is thus sensitive to deviations of the q_{ij} away from the p_i and increases as the dispersion of the q_{ij} around the p_i increases.

The values of H_j^2, together with the standardised values of this index $\overline{H_j^2}$, for the 18 and 47 diagnostic category classifications are presented in Tables 5.16 and 5.17 respectively. Comparing these standardised values with those of the first complexity index $\overline{H_j^1}$, there are a number of similarities but there are also a few differences. Under the 18 diagnostic category classification, for instance, category 10 Genito-Urinary System receives a significantly lower complexity value with the second index as does category 9 Digestive System. Similar differences between the indexes can also be found in the 47 diagnostic category classification.

The standardised complexity values presented in Tables 5.16 and 5.17 provide the weights used in the construction of the information theory case mix index. The following aggregation formulae are used:

$$X_i^1 = \sum_j \overline{H_j^1}\, \pi_{ij} \quad (i = 1, ..., 121)$$

$$\quad ... (5.10)$$

$$X_i^2 = \sum_j \overline{H_j^2}\, \pi_{ij} \quad (i = 1, ..., 121)$$

where π_{ij} is the proportion of the ith hospital's case load in the jth diagnostic category. Since two different diagnostic classification schemes are employed, use of the formulae in equation (5.10) gives rise to four case complexity index numbers for each hospital. While the complete set of resulting index numbers is not reproduced here, Table 5.18 tabulates the minimum and maximum values which arose for each index and the size of the hospital (measured in beds) which recorded the particular result. The same hospital scored the highest complexity value in three of the four indexes, while two hospitals each recorded the lowest complexity values on two of the indexes.

Table 5.18. Minimum and Maximum Values for Information Theory Case Mix
Indexes, Queensland Public Hospitals, 1977-78[a]

Index[b]	Minimum	Maximum
X181	0.67 (12)	1.14 (1234)
X182	0.58 (4)	2.72 (80)
X471	0.63 (12)	1.24 (80)
X472	0.59 (4)	2.80 (80)

Notes: (a)   Figures in brackets are sizes of hospitals (measured by number of beds) with
the particular result.
(b)   X181 = information theory index based on 18 diagnostic categories and first
information theory index formula. The other symbols in this column have an
analogous interpretation.
Source: Hospital Morbidity Data and information theory index calculations.

It remains to be seen how well these case mix indexes perform in
explaining the interhospital variation in average cost per case. Clearly the
use of a scalar case mix index is extremely parsimonious in parameters
compared with the use of more disaggregated case mix classification
schemes and also by-passes the multicollinearity problem. Estimation of the
cost function is reduced to a bivariate regression of average cost per case on
the particular case mix index.

The correlation matrix for the four information theory indexes and
average cost per case is presented in Table 5.19. Considering first the
correlations between the indexes, it can be seen that the type of index
employed—X^1 or X^2—has a much more important influence on the value of
a hospital's complexity index number than the diagnostic classification
scheme. Indexes constructed using the same type of weights correlate much
more closely than indexes constructed using different types of weights. The
X181 and X471 indexes have a correlation coefficient of 0.97, and the
X182 and X472 indexes have a correlation coefficient of 0.98. The X^1 and
X^2 indexes are much less closely correlated—X471 and X472 have a
correlation coefficient of 0.67 while X181 and X182 have a coefficient of
0.61.

Turning to the correlations between each of the indexes and average cost
per case, the type of index again has a more important influence than the
diagnostic classification scheme. The X181 and X471 indexes have
correlations with average cost per case of 0.38 and 0.34 respectively,
compared with 0.09 for each of the X^2 indexes.

In the estimated cost functions, the X^1 indexes then outperform the X^2
indexes in explaining interhospital variation in average cost per case. The

Table 5.19. Correlation Matrix, Information Theory Indexes and Average Cost Per Case

	X181	X182	X471	X472	ACC
X181	1.00	0.61	0.97	0.62	0.38
X182		1.00	0.64	0.98	0.09
X471			1.00	.67	0.34
X472				1.00	0.09
ACC					1.00

Source: Regression Results.

results are as follows (t-values in parentheses, * = significant at one per cent level; 119 degrees of freedom for each equation):

$$ACC = -377.44 + 1039.24 \ X181$$
$$(4.48*)$$

$$\bar{R}^2 = .14; \ SEE = 221.93.$$

$$ACC = 484.85 + 67.41 \ X182$$
$$(0.96)$$

$$\bar{R}^2 = -.001; \ SEE = 238.99.$$

$$ACC = -99.60 + 759.86 \ X471$$
$$(3.97*)$$

$$\bar{R}^2 = .11; \ SEE = 225.43.$$

$$ACC = 484.34 + 70.55 \ X472$$
$$(0.94)$$

$$\bar{R}^2 = -.001; \ SEE = 239.02.$$

The X181 and X471 indexes explain 14 and 11 per cent of the variation in average cost per case respectively (after adjustment for degrees of freedom) and this is statistically significant in each case. The X^2 indexes, however, actually have negative adjusted R^2 values and are statistically insignificant. All coefficients have the expected positive sign, indicating that hospitals with a higher complexity index have a higher predicted average cost per case.

This superior performance of the X^1 index was also found by Evans and Walker (1972, p.408): "By far the strongest variable ... is the first definition of complexity ... ".[31] Tatchell (1977), who also constructed four indexes based on two different diagnostic classifications, found that "the two measures based on the assumption of no prior knowledge of the hospital system ... appear to perform the better of the four measures ... " (pp.295-6). The X^1 index is that which assumes "no prior knowledge". Horn and Schumacher (1979, p.386) reported that the X^2 index "did not perform as well in the original regression equations" and consequently excluded it from the remainder of their study. Watts and Klastorin (1980) found their information theory index to be a poor explanator of average cost per case but it is not clear from their paper which index (X^1 or X^2) was constructed. Hardwick (1986) included only the X^1 index in her study, finding that this index on its own explained 24 per cent of the variation in average cost per case (adjusted $R^2 = .24$) for 111 acute care hospitals in Alberta, Canada, for the year 1978-79.

The X^1 index, however, does not explain as much of the interhospital variation in average cost per case as the more disaggregated diagnostic classification schemes. The R^2 values of .14 and .11 reported above can be compared with those reported earlier in this chapter based upon the 18 and 47 diagnostic category classification schemes (see Table 5.7). As such, the use of this scalar case mix index does result in a loss of explanatory power and hence predictive accuracy although the standard errors of estimate are not greatly in excess of those obtained with the more disaggregated classifications (see Table 5.7).

While the use of a scalar case mix index in the cost functions estimated in this chapter collapses the regression problem from one of multivariate analysis to bivariate analysis, it is still possible to retrieve estimates of the average and marginal cost by case type. Consider the following specification of average cost per case as a linear function of the information theory case mix index:

---

[31] Evans and Walker do not actually present results equivalent to those presented here, reporting only equations which include various scale and activity variables along with the information theory index. This quotation then pertains to a set of equations all of which include the effects of other factors. The effects of scale and other factors will be considered in Chapter 6.

$$ACC = \phi X_i^1 \qquad \qquad \text{... (5.11)}$$

Now recall from equation (5.10) that

$$X_i^1 = \sum_j \overline{H}_j^1 \pi_{ij} \qquad \qquad \text{... (5.12)}$$

Substituting equation (5.12) into equation (5.11) gives

$$ACC_i = \phi \sum_j \overline{H}_j^1 \pi_{ij}$$

$$= \phi \overline{H}_1^1 \pi_{i1} + \phi \overline{H}_2^1 \pi_{i2} + ... + \phi \overline{H}_n^1 \pi_{in} \qquad \qquad \text{... (5.13)}$$

where n is the number of diagnostic categories. But equation (5.13) is equivalent to equation (5.3) with the terms $\phi \overline{H}_j^1$ providing an estimate of the a_j, i.e. $a_j = \phi \overline{H}_j^1$. Given that the original specification incorporated non-jointness as a result of which the a_j are the average and marginal costs in each diagnostic category, $\phi \overline{H}_j^1$ provides an estimate of average and marginal cost for the jth case type.

To obtain such estimates, two cost functions of the form given by equation (5.11) were estimated using the X^1 information theory indexes X181 and X471. This provided the following parameter estimates $\phi(18) = 618.87$; $\phi(47) = 644.61$.[32] These were then multiplied by the standardised weights $\overline{H}_j^1(18)$ and $\overline{H}_j^1(47)$ from Tables 5.16 and 5.17 respectively. The resulting estimates are presented in Tables 5.20 and 5.21. The relative values of these estimates are, of course, exactly the same as the relative values of the weights which underlie their construction.

A refreshing characteristic of these estimates is that they are positive and have plausible values. The 18 diagnostic category estimates range from $323.98 (category 1) up to $1,067.62 (category 18) while the 47 diagnostic category estimates range from $257.53 (category 16) up to $1,524.57

---

[32] Since these estimates are obtained from regression through the origin, the R^2 values are not reported as they are not comparable to those obtained when an intercept term is included. On this point see Aigner (1971, pp.85-90), Stewart (1976, pp.73-4) and Maddala (1977, p.108).

(category 26). Given the state mean cost per case of $546.83 for 1977-78, these figures are generally quite reasonable. Because of the dependence on the relative values of the underlying weights, the credibility of any particular estimate depends directly on the credibility of the underlying case complexity weight (the $\overline{H_j^1}$). Such weights have already been found to be generally plausible.

Table 5.20. Values of Average and Marginal Cost implied by Information Theory Index Regression Results, 18 Diagnostic Categories, Queensland Public Hospitals, 1977-78

No.	Description	Implied Average and Marginal Cost per Case ($)
1	Infectious & Parasitic Diseases	323.98
2	Neoplasms	1004.05
3	Endocrine, Nutritional & Metabolic	531.26
4	Blood	592.44
5	Mental Disorders	861.11
6	Nervous System	687.16
7	Circulatory System	638.28
8	Respiratory System	358.79
9	Digestive System	586.39
10	Genito-Urinary System	874.74
11	Complications of Pregnancy, Childbirth & Puerperium	684.19
12	Skin & Subcutaneous Tissue	423.31
13	Musculoskeletal System	687.96
14	Congenital Anomalies	1053.58
15	Causes of Perinatal Morbidity & Mortality	1067.62
16	Symptoms & ill-defined	344.47
17	Accidents, Poisonings & Violence	484.07
18	Supplementary Classifications	667.83

Sources: Table 5.16 and regression results.

The scalar case mix indexes constructed on the assumption of no prior knowledge of the distribution of cases between hospitals have been found to explain a small (11 to 14 per cent) but statistically significant amount of interhospital variation in average cost per case. They also give rise to a credible set of estimates of average and marginal cost by case type in contrast to the estimates produced by the other techniques employed in this chapter. The estimates are credible in terms of both their range and the values attaching to particular case types. The problem of multicollinearity is side-stepped by the construction of a set of complexity weights from *a priori* reasoning based on information theory.

5.6   Summary and Conclusions

Case mix has been found to exert a statistically significant influence on interhospital variation in average cost per case. Further, this influence generally increases significantly when a more disaggregated diagnostic classification scheme is employed and additional dimensions of case mix are added.

The ordinary least squares parameter estimates, however, are plagued by insignificance and incorrect signs implying negative values for average and marginal cost by case type. The overall significance of the relationships considered, coupled with insignificant coefficient estimates, is suggestive of multicollinearity. This is supported by other evidence including selectivity bias, a correlation matrix determinant approaching zero, and inequality in the characteristic roots derived from the correlation matrix. Deletion of particular output categories under these circumstances is likely to be a dangerous and haphazard procedure.

Use of the *ad hoc* data reduction technique of principal components analysis failed to improve the credibility of the parameter estimates although the variances of many were reduced. It is suggested that the attainment of positive, plausible, significant estimates via this procedure would be fortuitous. A critical weakness of the technique is its sensitivity to scale, i.e. the results vary according to the units of measurement of the original variables.

An output index based upon information theory was found to explain less of the variation in average cost per case than the disaggregated output classifications but resulted in positive, credible estimates of average and marginal cost by case type. This approach reduces considerably the number of parameters to be estimated by the construction of an index based upon *a priori* reasoning as opposed to the *ad hoc* parameter reduction arising from principal components regression.

It may be the case, and this possibility cannot be ignored, that the problem of misbehaved parameter estimates arises because of misspecification of the underlying cost function. The warning given by Maddala (1977, p.186) must be heeded: "Sometimes it is easy to lay the blame for wrong signs for coefficients and implausible values of

Table 5.21. Values of Average and Marginal Cost implied by Information Theory Index Regression Results, 47 Diagnostic Categories, Queensland Public Hospitals, 1977-78

No.	Description	Implied Average and Marginal Cost per Case ($)
1	Investigations, Procedures, Healthy	652.68
2	Infectious & Parasitic	412.69
3	Enteritis, Diarrhoeal Disease	262.36
4	Malignant Neoplasms	1043.02
5	Benign Neoplasms	785.45
6	Endocrine & Metabolic	519.21
7	Blood	579.01
8	Psychiatric	841.58
9	Other CNS & Nerves	598.85
10	Eye & Ear	802.11
11	Other Heart, Hypertension	587.48
12	Acute Myocardial Infarction	698.42
13	Symptomatic Heart Disease	531.71
14	Cerebrovascular Disease	725.16
15	Circulation	786.54
16	Upper Respiratory	257.53
17	Pneumonia	318.70
18	Bronchitis, Emphysema, Asthma	419.34
19	Tonsils & Adenoids	703.91
20	Other Respiratory	481.99
21	Dental	579.70
22	Upper Gastrointestinal	613.25
23	Appendicitis	542.93
24	Hernia	644.86
25	Other Gastrointestinal	643.01
26	Nephritis & Nephrosis	1524.57
27	Other Urinary	602.55
28	Male Genital	712.03
29	Other Female Genital	653.34
30	Disorders of Menstruation	766.84
31	Complications, Pregnancy & Puerperium	574.06
32	Abortion	558.99
33	Normal Delivery	752.21
34	Delivery Complications	1093.17
35	Skin Disease	413.71
36	Orthopaedic	672.36
37	Congenital Malformation	1029.69
38	Perinatal	1049.85
39	Immaturity	1236.29
40	Symptoms, ill-defined	340.49
41	Long Stay, ill-defined	399.48
42	Other Fractures (excl. Femur)	589.67
43	Fracture of Neck of Femur	939.29

Table 5.21 (cont.)

No.	Description	Implied Average and Marginal Cost per Case ($)
44	Dislocations	433.17
45	Internal Injury	475.32
46	External Injury	390.69
47	Poisoning	457.67

Source: Table 5.17 and regression results.

coefficients on multicollinearity when in fact the problem may have been a poor specification of the model." The results presented in this chapter pertain to a non-joint, input-output separable cost function incorporating overall constant returns to scale. While the former restrictions will be maintained, the following chapter expands the analysis undertaken in this chapter by attempting to incorporate scale effects and the effects of other factors which may be relevant to the cost function.

Appendix 5.I

Characteristic Roots, Characteristic Vectors and Multicollinearity[1]

Begin with the classical linear regression model

$$y = XB + e \qquad\qquad ...(1)$$

where y is a $(T \times 1)$ vector of observations of the dependent variable, X is a $(T \times K)$ matrix of T observations on each of K independent variables, and B is a $(K \times 1)$ vector of unknown regression coefficients. The OLS estimates of B are given by

$$\hat{B} = (X'X)^{-1}X'y \qquad\qquad ...(2)$$

The $(X'X)$ matrix is a square $(K \times K)$ symmetric matrix with a trace (the sum of the elements in the principal diagonal) equal to the sum of the squares of all the observations on the K independent variables.

The characteristic roots (or eigenvalues or latent roots) of any square matrix A and the associated characteristic vectors (or eigenvectors or latent vectors) are found as the solution to the following problem: is it possible to find a column vector v (a characteristic vector) and a scalar λ (a characteristic root) such that

$$Av = \lambda v \qquad\qquad ...(3)$$

---

[1] The material contained in this Appendix is based on Johnston (1972, pp.102-5), Glaister (1978, Ch.9), Dowling (1980, pp.244-6), Judge, *et al.* (1982, pp.614-19) and Fomby, Hill and Johnson (1984, pp.283-7).

That is, can a value for the scalar λ and the vector $\mathbf{v}$ be found so that post-multiplication of $\mathbf{A}$ by $\mathbf{v}$ is equal to the scalar times the vector $\mathbf{v}$? The answer is 'yes', and there are in fact as many characteristic roots and vectors as there are columns or rows in $\mathbf{A}$, i.e. if $\mathbf{A}$ is $(n \times n)$ there will be n characteristic roots and vectors. The reason for this can be seen by considering the solution of equation (3). Rearranging this equation gives

$$\mathbf{A}\mathbf{v} - \lambda\mathbf{v} = \mathbf{0}$$

or $\qquad (\mathbf{A} - \lambda\mathbf{I})\mathbf{v} = \mathbf{0}$ $\qquad\qquad\qquad\qquad$ ... (4)

where $\mathbf{I}$ is the identity matrix. If $(\mathbf{A} - \lambda\mathbf{I})$ is non-singular, equation (4) has the trivial solution that $\mathbf{v} = \mathbf{0}$. Hence if $\mathbf{v} \neq \mathbf{0}$ then $(\mathbf{A} - \lambda\mathbf{I})$ must be singular, i.e. its determinant must be zero. In this case the solution to equation (4) is obtained by solving

$$|\mathbf{A} - \lambda\mathbf{I}| = \mathbf{0} \qquad\qquad\qquad\qquad \text{... (5)}$$

The expansion of this determinant yields an nth degree polynomial in λ. The n roots of this polynomial are then the characteristic roots (or eigenvalues or latent roots) of $\mathbf{A}$, denoted $\lambda_1, \lambda_2, \cdots, \lambda_n$.

Associated with each characteristic root λ_i there will be a characteristic vector $\mathbf{v}$ such that equation (3) is satisfied, i.e.

$$\mathbf{A}\mathbf{v}_i = \lambda_i\mathbf{v}_i \qquad\qquad\qquad\qquad \text{... (6)}$$

In solving for $\mathbf{v}$ recall that $(\mathbf{A} - \lambda\mathbf{I})$ is singular, implying that its columns are linearly dependent. Consequently there is no unique solution for $\mathbf{v}$ but an infinite number of solutions each differing by a scalar multiple. Alternatively, the solution for $\mathbf{v}$ is unique only up to a scalar multiple. To force a unique solution, the normalisation condition is often imposed on the elements of $\mathbf{v}_i$ so that $\sum v_i^2 = 1$, i.e. the sum of squares of the elements of

$\mathbf{v}_i$ is set at unity. The column vector $\mathbf{v}_i$ is the characteristic vector associated with the characteristic root λ_i.

An important property of the characteristic vectors is that they are orthogonal so that $\mathbf{v}_i'\mathbf{v}_j = 0$ ($i \neq j$) and $\mathbf{v}_i'\mathbf{v}_i \neq 0$. This says that the sum of the cross-products of the corresponding elements of any two characteristic vectors is zero, while the sum of the squares of the elements of any characteristic vector is non-zero. If the characteristic vectors have been normalised so that $\sum v_i^2 = 1$ then $\mathbf{v}_i'\mathbf{v}_i = 1$.

Now consider the $(K \times K)$ matrix $\mathbf{V}$ which has as its columns the characteristic vectors $\mathbf{v}_1, \mathbf{v}_2, \cdots, \mathbf{v}_K$ each of which has been normalised, i.e. $\mathbf{V} = (\mathbf{v}_1, \mathbf{v}_2, \cdots, \mathbf{v}_K)$. Then $\mathbf{V'V} = \mathbf{VV'} = \mathbf{I}$. The matrix $\mathbf{V}$ is then said to be an orthogonal matrix.

Consider next the product $\mathbf{v}_i'\mathbf{Av}_j$. From equation (6) this is equal to $\mathbf{v}_i'\lambda_j\mathbf{v}_j$ or $\lambda_j\mathbf{v}_i'\mathbf{v}_j$ since λ_j is a scalar. Therefore, $\mathbf{v}_i'\mathbf{Av}_j = 0$ if $i \neq j$ and $\mathbf{v}_i'\mathbf{Av}_j = \lambda_j$ if $i = j$. Extending this result to the product $\mathbf{V'AV}$, we have the following:

$$\mathbf{V'AV} = \begin{bmatrix} \lambda_1 & 0 & 0 & . & . & 0 \\ 0 & \lambda_2 & 0 & . & . & 0 \\ 0 & 0 & \lambda_3 & . & . & 0 \\ . & . & . & . & . & . \\ . & . & . & . & . & . \\ 0 & 0 & 0 & . & . & \lambda_K \end{bmatrix} \qquad \ldots (7)$$

That is, the product $\mathbf{V'AV}$ results in a diagonal matrix with the characteristic roots of $\mathbf{A}$ on the principal diagonal.

Relating this to the classical linear regression model, recall that $\mathbf{X'X}$ is a square $(K \times K)$ matrix. This matrix then has K characteristic roots $\lambda_1, \cdots, \lambda_K$ and K characteristic vectors $\mathbf{v}_1, \cdots, \mathbf{v}_K$ with

$$\mathbf{X'Xv}_i = \lambda_i\mathbf{v}_i \quad (i = 1, \cdots, K) \qquad \ldots (8)$$

Pre-multiplying both sides by $\mathbf{v}_i'$ gives

$$\mathbf{v}_i'\mathbf{X}'\mathbf{X}\mathbf{v}_i = \mathbf{v}_i'\lambda_i\mathbf{v}_i = \lambda_i \qquad \ldots (9)$$

since $\mathbf{v}_i'\mathbf{v}_i = 1$ and λ_i is a scalar.

Again letting $\mathbf{V}$ be the orthogonal (K x K) matrix whose columns are the characteristic vectors of $\mathbf{X}'\mathbf{X}$, we know that

$$\mathbf{V}'\mathbf{X}'\mathbf{X}\mathbf{V} = \mathbf{Z} \qquad \ldots (10)$$

where $\mathbf{Z}$ is a diagonal matrix with elements $\lambda_i (i = 1,\cdots,K)$. Let $\mathbf{V}$ be constructed so that in the matrix $\mathbf{Z}$, $\lambda_1 \ge \lambda_2 \ge \cdots \ge \lambda_K$. Rearranging equation (10) gives

$$\mathbf{X}'\mathbf{X} = \mathbf{V}\mathbf{Z}\mathbf{V}' \qquad \ldots (11)$$

so that

$$(\mathbf{X}'\mathbf{X})^{-1} = (\mathbf{V}\mathbf{Z}\mathbf{V}')^{-1} = \mathbf{V}'^{-1}\mathbf{Z}^{-1}\mathbf{V}^{-1} \qquad \ldots (12)$$

Recall that, because $\mathbf{V}$ is orthogonal, $\mathbf{V}'\mathbf{V} = \mathbf{I}$ and so $\mathbf{V}' = \mathbf{V}^{-1}$. Applying this to equation (12) gives

$$(\mathbf{X}'\mathbf{X})^{-1} = \mathbf{V}\mathbf{Z}^{-1}\mathbf{V}' \qquad \ldots (13)$$

Since $\mathbf{Z}$ is a diagonal matrix with elements $\lambda_1,\lambda_2,\cdots,\lambda_K$, its inverse will be a diagonal matrix with elements $1/\lambda_1,1/\lambda_2,\cdots,1/\lambda_K$. $\mathbf{V}'$ can be written as

$$\mathbf{V}' = \begin{bmatrix} \mathbf{v}_1' \\ \mathbf{v}_2' \\ . \\ . \\ \mathbf{v}_K' \end{bmatrix}$$

so that

$$\mathbf{ZV'} = \begin{bmatrix} \dfrac{\mathbf{v_1'}}{\lambda_1} \\ \dfrac{\mathbf{v_2'}}{\lambda_2} \\ \cdot \\ \cdot \\ \dfrac{\mathbf{v_K'}}{\lambda_K} \end{bmatrix}$$

Finally,

$$\mathbf{VZ^{-1}V'} = \frac{\mathbf{v_1v_1'}}{\lambda_1} + \frac{\mathbf{v_2v_2'}}{\lambda_2} + \cdots + \frac{\mathbf{v_Kv_K'}}{\lambda_K}$$

$$= \sum_{i=1}^{K} \lambda_i \mathbf{v_i v_i'}$$

$$= (\mathbf{X'X})^{-1}$$

In the classical linear regression model, the variance-covariance matrix of parameter estimates is given by

$$\text{cov}(\hat{\mathbf{B}}) = \sigma^2 (\mathbf{X'X})^{-1}$$

which can now be written as

$$\text{cov}(\hat{\mathbf{B}}) = \sigma^2 \sum_{i=1}^{K} \lambda_i^{-1} \mathbf{v_i v_i'}$$

The variance of any particular parameter estimate $\hat{B}_j$ is given by the jth diagonal element in this covariance matrix and may be written as follows:

$$\text{var}(\hat{B}_j) = \sigma^2 \left[\frac{v_{j1}^2}{\lambda_1} + \frac{v_{j2}^2}{\lambda_2} + \cdots + \frac{v_{jK}^2}{\lambda_K} \right] \qquad \ldots (14)$$

Equation (14) shows that the variance of the jth parameter estimate depends upon three factors: first, the error variance σ^2; second, the magnitude of the jth element in each of the K characteristic vectors; and third, the magnitudes of the characteristic roots (the λs).

The effect of the error variance is straightforward. As the error variance increases, the explained variation in the dependent variable decreases, *ceteris paribus*, and so does the precision with which any particular parameter can be estimated. It remains to explain the effects of the last two factors and their connection with the multicollinearity problem.

The effect of the last two factors depends on the size of the characteristic roots *relative to* the size of the jth element in each of the corresponding characteristic vectors. While it is the case that, *ceteris paribus*, smaller characteristic roots tend to increase the variance of the parameter estimates, a small value for any particular characteristic root may be offset by a small value of v_{ji}^2.

That multicollinearity gives rise to small values of the characteristic roots will now be established. Referring back to equation (8), consider the extreme case where $\lambda_i = 0$, i.e. a characteristic root has a value of zero. Equation (8) then becomes

$$\mathbf{X'Xv}_i = \mathbf{0}$$

which can be written as

$$v_{i1}\mathbf{x}_1 + v_{i2}\mathbf{x}_2 + \cdots + v_{iK}\mathbf{x}_K = \mathbf{0} \qquad \ldots (15)$$

where v_{ij} is the jth element in the ith root and $\mathbf{x}_j$ is the jth column in the $\mathbf{X'X}$ matrix $(j = 1, \cdots, K)$. But this specifies precisely perfect multicollinearity— there is a perfect linear dependence among the columns of the $\mathbf{X'X}$ matrix. Hence if any characteristic root is zero, perfect multicollinearity is present while small values of such roots indicate a near exact linear relationship of the kind indicated by equation (15).

Again, however, it must be noted that small characteristic roots do not *necessarily* lead to parameter estimates with high variances. As equation (14) shows, the small characteristic roots may be offset by small values of the relevant elements in the corresponding characteristic vector, so that precise estimates may be obtained even in the presence of extreme multicollinearity. This would explain why, for example, some studies of production functions have obtained highly significant parameter estimates even though the correlation coefficients between labour and capital have been in the range 0.8 to 0.9 (see Klein 1962, p.101).

Appendix 5.II

The Derivation of Principal Components[1]

Begin with a data matrix $\mathbf{X}$ containing standardised values of T observations on each of K independent variables. The problem is to construct a set of new variables which are a weighted linear sum of the original variables. Denote the first new such variable by P_1. Then in matrix form what is required is

$$\mathbf{P}_1 = \mathbf{X}\ell_1 \qquad \qquad \dots (1)$$

where $\mathbf{P}_1$ is a T-element column vector of observations on P_1 and ℓ_1 is a K-element vector of weights. Equation (1) could alternatively be written as

$$P_{1t} = \ell_{11}X_{1t} + \ell_{21}X_{2t} + \cdots + \ell_{K1}X_{Kt} \quad (t = 1, \cdots, T)$$

The weights are to be constructed in such a way that P_1 accounts for the maximum possible variation in the data (the Xs). The weights are then found as the solution to a constrained maximisation problem—maximise the sum of squares of the elements of $\mathbf{P}_1$ (given by $\mathbf{P}_1'\mathbf{P}_1$) subject to the constraint that the sum of the squared values of the weights be equal to unity, i.e. $\ell_1'\ell_1 = 1$. This constraint is necessary otherwise the variance of P_1 can be made infinitely large simply by increasing the values of the weights.

The sum of squares of $\mathbf{P}_1$ can then be expressed as

$$\mathbf{P}_1'\mathbf{P}_1 = \ell_1'\mathbf{X}'\mathbf{X}\ell_1 \qquad \qquad \dots (2)$$

The problem then is to maximise equation (2) subject to $\ell_1'\ell_1 = 1$. The solution, obtained by forming the relevant Lagrange expression and differentiating, gives

$$\mathbf{X}'\mathbf{X}\ell_1 = \lambda_1\ell_1 \qquad \qquad \dots (3)$$

---

[1] The material contained in this Appendix is based on Johnston (1972, pp.322-31), Morrison (1976, Ch.8), Stopher and Meyburg (1979, Ch.11) and Schuerman (1983, Ch.6).

Now it can be seen that λ_1 is a characteristic root and ℓ_1 a characteristic vector of $\mathbf{X'X}$ (see Appendix 5.I). Further, substituting equation (3) into equation (2) gives

$$\mathbf{P_1'P_1} = \ell_1'\lambda_1\ell_1 = \lambda_1\ell_1'\ell_1 \qquad\qquad \text{... (4)}$$

Therefore, the weights which maximise the variance of $\mathbf{P_1}$ are the elements of the characteristic vector of $\mathbf{X'X}$ associated with the largest characteristic root of $\mathbf{X'X}$, i.e. maximising $\mathbf{P_1'P_1}$ requires selecting the largest λ_1 and its associated characteristic vector ℓ_1. Substituting ℓ_1 into equation (1) then produces the first principal component $\mathbf{P_1}$.

The second principal component can then be derived by a similar procedure but the maximisation of $\mathbf{P_2'P_2}$ is now subject to two constraints— the normalisation condition $\ell_2'\ell_2 = 1$, and the additional constraint that $\ell_1'\ell_2 = 0$. This latter condition ensures that the two principal components $\mathbf{P_1}$ and $\mathbf{P_2}$ are uncorrelated. To see this, recall that $\mathbf{P_2} = \mathbf{X}\ell_2$ so that the covariance between $\mathbf{P_1}$ and $\mathbf{P_2}$ and is given by

$$\mathbf{P_1'P_2} = \ell_1'\mathbf{X'X}\ell_2 \qquad\qquad \text{... (5)}$$

Setting equation (5) equal to zero ensures orthogonality between $\mathbf{P_1}$ and $\mathbf{P_2}$. Therefore, orthogonality requires

$$\ell_1'\mathbf{X'X}\ell_2 = 0$$

but from equaton (3)

$$\ell_1'\mathbf{X'X} = \lambda_1\ell_1'$$

so orthogonality requires

$$\lambda_1\ell_1'\ell_2 = 0$$

which will be satisfied if and only if $\ell_1'\ell_2 = 0$.

Again the solution is found by forming the appropriate Lagrangean expression and differentiating which gives

$$\mathbf{X'X}\ell_2 = \lambda_2\ell_2 \qquad\qquad \text{... (6)}$$

Substituting this into $\mathbf{P_2'P_2}$ (the expression for the variance of P_2) gives

$$\mathbf{P_2'P_2} = \ell_2'\lambda_2\ell_2 = \lambda_2 \qquad \qquad \text{... (7)}$$

From equation (7), maximising the variance of P_2 then requires that the second largest characteristic root λ_2 and its associated characteristic vector ℓ_2 be selected to calculate the second principal component.

This procedure can be continued, with the maximum number of principal components extracted being equal to the rank (R) of the data matrix $\mathbf{X}$. In the absence of perfect multicollinearity, $\mathbf{X}$ will be of full rank ($R = K$) and hence K principal components could be extracted. Letting $\mathbf{P}$ represent the matrix of principal components, it could then be written as

$$\mathbf{P} = (\mathbf{P_1}, \mathbf{P_2}, \dots, \mathbf{P_K})$$

The $\mathbf{P}$ matrix would thus have as its columns the principal component values obtained as the weighted sum of each set of observations on the independent variables. With the data matrix $\mathbf{X}$ of full rank, K principal components are needed to capture all of the variation in the original K variables.

If the data matrix $\mathbf{X}$ has less than full rank ($R < K$), one or more exact linear dependencies exist among the variables and the variation in the independent variables can be captured with only R principal components.

This does not imply that principal components may not be useful if the data matrix is of full rank. Often the existence of near-exact linear dependencies will mean that a small number of principal components can capture *most* of the variation in the data. As was seen in Appendix 5.I, one or more characteristic roots with values close to zero imply the existence of near-exact linear dependencies and it is in those situations that a small number of principal components may be usefully substituted for a large number of the independent variables.

In fact, the amount of variation in the original data which can be captured by any given number of principal components is related to the values of the characteristic roots. To establish this, recall first that the trace of the $\mathbf{X'X}$ matrix is the sum of the elements in the main diagonal in that matrix. What this sum specifically represents will depend upon the form of the data in the $\mathbf{X}$ matrix. The relationship can be summarised as follows:

If the data matrix **X** contains data in	The trace of the **X'X** matrix equals
Raw Form	The sum of squares of the original observations
Deviation Form	The sum of squared deviations
Standardised Form (deviation divided by square root of sum of squares)	The number of independent variables (since **X'X** is the correlation matrix)

Hence the trace of **X'X** provides a measure of the total variation in the data. If the data are in raw form, the trace is equal to the total sum of squares. Now if the data have been standardised, the total variation in the data is equal to the number of independent variables K since the **X'X** matrix in this case is the correlation matrix.

From equations (2) to (4), the variation captured by the first principal component P_1 is given by $P_1'P_1$ which is equal to λ_1, the largest characteristic root. Also recall that $P_i'P_j = 0$ for $i \neq j$—the principal components are orthogonal. It follows from this that

$$\mathbf{P'P} = \begin{bmatrix} \lambda_1 & 0 & . & . & 0 \\ 0 & \lambda_2 & . & . & 0 \\ . & . & & & . \\ . & . & & & . \\ 0 & 0 & . & . & \lambda_K \end{bmatrix}$$

and trace $(\mathbf{P'P}) = \sum_{i=1}^{K} \lambda_i$.

Further, this trace must be equal to K because K is the total variation in the standardised data and λ_1 represents the amount of that variation captured by the ith principal component. Therefore, the *proportion* of the total variation in the data captured by any particular principal component is λ_1/K, and the cumulative proportion attributable to the first j principal components is given by $\left(\lambda_1 + \lambda_2 + \cdots + \lambda_j\right) / K$.

It can now be seen that the extent to which a small number of principal components can capture a large proportion of the variation in the data depends on the degree of inequality in the characteristic roots (the λs) which in turn reflect the extent to which there are near-exact linear dependencies in the data. If the degree of multicollinearity is high, a large proportion of the variation may be captured by a small number of principal components.

6

THE EFFECTS OF SCALE, UTILISATION AND

INPUT PRICES ON HOSPITAL COSTS—

EVIDENCE FROM QUEENSLAND

6.1   Introduction

Is the production of inpatient treatment subject to economies or diseconomies of scale? The following oft quoted response by Berki (1972) to this question foreshadows the difficult task ahead: " ... depending on the methodologies and definitions used, economies of scale exist, may exist, may not exist, or do not exist, but in any case, according to theory, they ought to exist" (p.115). This should not come as a surprise. Surveys of empirical studies seeking to answer this question for other industries have found the conclusions "indefinite and disappointing" (Smith 1955, p.213), the field "still fairly blank" (Weiss 1971, p.297), the findings "few and debatable" (Shepherd 1979, p.259) and the empirical research characterised by "pervasive inadequacies" (Gold 1981, p.21). One can be forgiven for being pessimistic at the outset!

In using the term 'scale', the concepts of economies and diseconomies of scale should not be confused with the concept of returns to scale. The former relate to the behaviour of cost as a function of output, with economies of scale being present when long run average cost declines as output increases and conversely for diseconomies of scale. Returns to scale are defined in terms of the effects of an equal proportionate change in all inputs on the level of output produced, i.e. input proportions are fixed. If the proportionate change in output exceeds the equi-proportionate change in all inputs, increasing returns to scale are present, and similarly for constant and decreasing returns to scale.

The concept of returns to scale, then, involves a movement along a ray through the origin in input space whereas economies or diseconomies of scale concern a movement along the long run cost curves in cost/output space or the expansion path in input space. Since the expansion path need not be a ray, the two concepts generally differ. There is, however, a special case for which the two coincide. "Homothetic production functions have isoquants which remain parallel along rays, so the rate of technical substitution between inputs remains constant along any activity ray. Thus, any expansion path derived for the homothetic case will coincide with a ray through the origin" (Solberg 1982, p.270).[1]

Determining the degree of scale economies requires that the *ceteris paribus* assumption be fulfilled. In particular, input prices and the state of technology should be held constant and, for a multiproduct firm, the product mix also. If input prices vary, the behaviour of costs will reflect pecuniary as well as technical economies and diseconomies. In the words of Shepherd (1979, p.243), "removing the pecuniary economies is the whole point of the exercise. If optimal scale were defined to include pecuniary economies, then the measures of "efficient" scale may just reflect the firm's ability to exploit the market rather than its ability to produce efficiently."

Attempting to standardise for technology across firms is a difficult matter (see Gold 1981), particularly so for hospitals. At what point do different plant sizes incorporate 'different' technology? How can such differences be measured? In hospitals, it is reasonable to expect that production

---

[1]   For a discussion of homogeneous and homothetic production functions, see Baumol (1977, pp.280-6). The difference between economies of scale and returns to scale has been analysed rigorously by Hanoch (1975), who argues that economies of scale "is the more relevant concept for micro-economic analysis" (p.492). In a survey concerning the concept of scale, Gold (1981, p.14) reports that fixed factor proportions are "seldom encountered in actual cases involving substantial increases in scale, precisely because such restrictions tend to minimize or prevent the benefits whose expected realization is a primary motive for considering increases in scale".

technologies will differ—the treatment provided for a particular case type, e.g. a malignant neoplasm, may be based on quite different technologies in a small country hospital and a large metropolitan hospital. Such differences may have a substantial impact on hospital costs (see Russell and Burke 1975; Russell 1979).

The importance of allowing for product mix in estimated cost functions has already been discussed and will not be dwelt on in this chapter.[2] Section 6.2 addresses some issues of definition and measurement with respect to scale, utilisation and input price differences in hospital cost analysis. Section 6.3 provides a specification of the hospital cost function which includes scale and utilisation and discusses some issues concerning the specification of scale and utilisation in hospital cost functions. Sections 6.4 and 6.5 present the empirical results for the Queensland hospitals included in the study. The chapter finishes with a summary and conclusions.

6.2 Definition and Measurement Issues

6.2.1 Defining Scale and Utilisation

The difficulty associated with the concept of returns to scale for a multiproduct production function has been discussed in Chapter 2. It was pointed out there that, in general, an equal proportionate change in all inputs need not give rise to a uniform proportionate change in all outputs unless the production function is homogeneous. This difficulty does not, however, arise with the multiproduct cost function where economies or diseconomies of scale are defined with reference to the proportionate change in total costs associated with a uniform proportionate change in all outputs. Further, since output mix is held constant, the concepts of economies and diseconomies of scale can be illustrated using the cost curves analogous to those for a single output production process.

In Figure 6.1, the horizontal axis shows the output vector y with some particular level and mix of the outputs being designated arbitrarily as the unit bundle of outputs y^0. Variations in y then occur through a proportionate change in all outputs in the vector represented by t ($t \geq 0$). From Chapter 2, and assuming input prices and the state of technology are constant,

---

2   Gold (1981, p.17) indentifies the failure to allow for product mix as a serious shortcoming of "most recent empirical research".

$$RAC = \frac{C(y)}{t}$$

where RAC is ray average cost and $C(y)$ is the total cost of the output vector y. The behaviour of the RAC curve drawn in Figure 6.1 shows the familiar U-shape of the long run average cost curve of the single output production process, manifesting economies of scale over some initial range of values of the output vector and diseconomies of scale thereafter.

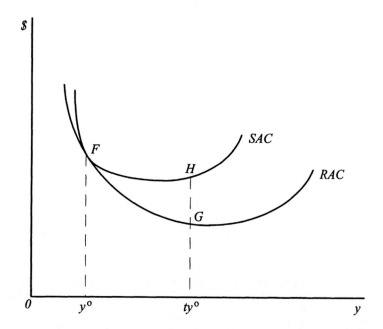

Figure 6.1. Economies of Scale, Short Run Average Cost and Ray Average Cost

   The RAC curve is a long run construct, showing the minimum attainable ray average cost of producing any output vector when all inputs are variable. In the short-term, when one or more inputs are fixed, movement along the RAC curve may not be possible. Changes in the value of the output vector can be obtained only by varying the quantities of the variable inputs used in conjunction with the fixed inputs. Since the resulting input combination will in general, be non-optimal, average cost in the short run will then usually be higher than ray average cost , as shown by the SAC curve in Figure 6.1. The level of the fixed inputs associated with the SAC curve is optimal for the production of the unit bundle of outputs y^0 and hence RAC is obtained. However, it is non-optimal for the production of ty^0 so that $SAC > RAC$ if ty^0 is produced with that level of the fixed inputs.

The foregoing analysis provides the basis for the distinction between scale effects and the effects of utilisation for a multiproduct cost function. Scale effects arise when all outputs change by the same proportion and all inputs are variable. Utilisation effects arise when all outputs change by the same proportion and at least one input is fixed, so that variation is possible only in the extent to which that fixed input is utilised rather than in the quantity of that input.

6.2.2   Measuring Scale and Utilisation

In some circumstances, it is necessary to incorporate measures of scale and utilisation in hospital cost analysis in addition to measures of hospital output. Recall from Chapter 2 that the general functional form of a multiproduct cost function includes only outputs and input prices. However, this specification of the cost function assumes all inputs are variable and is therefore a long run cost function. If this assumption is fulfilled then scale effects can be assessed by estimating the behaviour of ray average cost, and no measures of scale and utilisation in addition to the output measures are required.

In practice, all firms in an industry may not be on the long run cost curve. The quantities of the fixed inputs which they have in the short run may not be the long run optimal levels of such inputs for the output levels they are producing. Under these circumstances it is necessary to incorporate measures of the quantities and utilisation of the fixed inputs in the cost function. This is so even if the data comprise a cross-section of firms in the industry. While cross-section data may provide observations of firms of widely differing sizes, it will still not necessarily be the case that all such firms will be on the long run cost curve.

This argument can be illustrated easily in terms of Figure 6.1. A firm producing the unit bundle of outputs y^0 with the level of fixed inputs underlying the short run cost curve SAC will be at point F which is also a point on the RAC curve. But now suppose another firm with the same level of fixed inputs is observed producing ty^0 at point H. If long run cost minimisation is assumed, point H will incorrectly be interpreted as being on the RAC curve and diseconomies of scale will appear to be present. In fact, the long run cost minimising point for output level ty^0 is G and the firm is operating in a region of economies of scale. Measures of scale and utilisation in addition to output will be necessary to detect this difference.

The most common measure of size of a hospital is the number of beds. This proxy is, of course, an imperfect measure of the scale of a hospital's operations because hospitals with the same number of beds can differ widely in the other capital equipment and fixed factors which they employ. Deeble (1983, p.321) expresses this well.

> But we have all been using an increasingly unsatisfactory unit of capacity—the bed available. For low-intensity, nursing-home type institutions bed availability may well be the main constraint on output; this was undoubtedly true of hospitals generally in the past. But admission to hospital no longer signifies the presence of serious, disabling illness for which bed care is the principal treatment. Increasingly it is for the support of medical procedures —diagnostic and surgical—for which admission is sought, and the functions related to these activities play an increasing role in hospital structure. Capacity can thus be thought of in two ways: capacity to accommodate and capacity to treat. The former is measured by beds available, the second by the capacity of operating theatres, radiology and pathology facilities and so on.

Even as a measure of capacity to accommodate, however, the number of beds may be deficient—"there are surgical beds and medical beds, and they are not always interchangeable: and there are obstetrical beds, maternity beds, pediatric beds, intensive care beds, and none of these beds are usually substitutable for either medical or surgical beds" (Berki 1972, p.104).[3]

An advantage of the use of the number of beds as a measure of size is that it bears no necessary relationship to output and so avoids the "regression fallacy" identified by Friedman (1955). "Insofar as size itself is measured by actual output, or an index related to it, a much more serious bias is introduced tending toward an apparent decline of costs as size increases" (Friedman 1955, p.236). The reason for this is that, as output increases, per unit capital costs will decline if capital is fixed. But if the output level itself is taken as the measure of size then, by definition, size has increased. As such, this could give a misleading indication of the existence of economies of scale.[4]

---

[3]   Berki (1972, pp.100-15) provides a penetrating discussion of capacity, size and economies of scale in hospitals, including a comprehensive overview of previous studies.

[4]   For a more detailed, and critical, discussion of the regression fallacy, see Johnston (1958, pp.348-50). See also Walters (1960), Borts (1960) and Meyer and Kraft (1961). In the context of hospitals see Feldstein (1967, Ch.3) and Hornbrook and Monheit (1985).

The number of beds also has the advantage that it gives rise to some readily measurable concepts of utilisation. For this purpose, it is convenient to transform the number of beds into the number of rated bed days (*RBD*) as follows:

$$RBD = 365\,B$$

This defines the technical capacity of the hospital to accommodate patients. The case flow rate (*CFR*) can be defined as the number of cases treated in a hospital per bed per year:

$$CFR = \frac{y}{B}$$

where *y* is the total number of cases treated. *CFR* is related to average length of stay (*ALS*) and the occupancy rate (*OCC*) in the following manner:

$$CFR = \frac{OCC}{ALS} \times 365 \qquad\qquad \text{... (6.1)}$$

where $\quad OCC = \dfrac{OBD}{RBD}$

$$ALS = \frac{OBD}{y}$$

(*OBD* = total number of occupied bed days in the hospital per year). *CFR* has a maximum value of 365, achieved when the occupancy rate reaches 100 per cent (*OCC* = 1.0) and average length of stay is at its minimum of one day.

For any given number of beds, an increase in the number of cases treated will cause an increase in *CFR*. From equation (6.1), this increase in *CFR* can be accommodated either by an increase in the occupancy rate or a reduction in average length of stay or some combination of the two. It is possible that the marginal cost of treating an additional patient will differ according to the changes in *OCC* and/or *ALS* which occur in accommodating that patient. It is important to bear this in mind when deciding how to incorporate these measures of utilisation in the cost function, a matter discussed in Section 6.3 below.

6.2.3   Measuring Input Price Differences

The problem of allowing for input price differences arises only if firms do actually pay different prices for the same factors of production. If input prices are the same for all firms then they cannot possibly be a source of cost variation between firms and so can be ignored. This was the case, for example, in the study by Feldstein (1967, p.12).

If factor prices do vary, there are generally three methods of adjusting for the differences (Lave and Lave 1979, p.966). *First*, the sample can be subdivided on a regional basis if input prices vary geographically, and dummy variables can be used to test for significant differences between regions. *Second*, factor price indexes can be constructed as was done, for example, for the price of fuel in the study of US electric power generation by Christensen and Greene (1976). The *third* approach involves adjusting the cost data for each firm by applying a standard set of input prices to the quantities of inputs purchased.

Of these three approaches, the last might seem to be the most desirable for it apparently accurately standardises each firm's costs for input price differences. It suffers from a limitation, however, arising out of the possibility that input substitution may have taken place in response to the different input prices. Consider Figure 6.2 which depicts an isoquant for an output level Q_1 produced using two inputs L and K. Suppose two firms each producing this output level are identical in all respects except for the factor prices which they face. Firm 1 pays relative input prices given by the slope of AA' (an isocost constraint) while Firm 2 pays relative input prices given by the slope of BB'. The firms are then producing at points V and W respectively. Now suppose that the input combination used by Firm 2 (point W) is valued at the input prices paid by Firm 1. This places Firm 2 on the constraint ZZ' passing through W and would give Firm 2 a higher level of total cost than Firm 1, indicating it to be less efficient. But this is an erroneous result. Point W represents an inefficient input combination at *the factor prices paid by Firm 1* but is an efficient combination for Firm 2 *given the input prices actually paid by Firm 2*. In fact, Firm 2 has efficiently substituted its inputs in response to the different input prices which it faces.

The conclusion of this argument is clear. Adjusting each firm's costs based on a common set of input prices does not completely eliminate the effects of different input prices and can actually produce inflated estimates of the costs of some firms.

The actual extent of the inaccuracy arising out of this kind of calculation is directly related to the elasticity of substitution. If there is no input substitution in response to the different factor prices, i.e. if the elasticity of

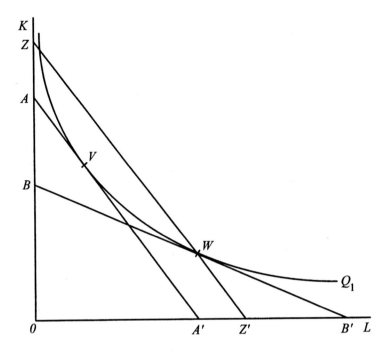

Figure 6.2. Input Price Differences and Input Substitution

substitution is zero, the inaccuracy will disappear. In terms of Figure 6.2, the isoquants become L-shaped in this case and points V and W converge. Conversely, the inaccuracy will be larger the larger is the elasticity of substitution.

Keeping this limitation in mind, this approach to the incorporation of factor price differences was attempted in this study. The results are discussed later in this chapter.

6.3 Specification

The total cost formulation of the cost function as specified in Chapter 5, equation (5.2), incorporated overall constant returns to scale as a maintained hypothesis since an equal proportionate change in all outputs results in an equal proportionate change in total cost. To allow for scale effects, scale terms measured in terms of 'rated bed days' (*RBD*) can be added to allow for the impact of size in addition to the number of cases in each diagnostic category. The cost function can then be expressed as

$$C = \sum_{i=1}^{n} a_i y_i + r_1 RBD + r_2 RBD^2 \qquad \qquad \text{... (6.2)}$$

where y_i is the number of cases treated in the ith diagnostic category. Dividing equation (6.2) through by the total number of cases y gives the average cost formulation as

$$ACC = \sum_{i=1}^{n} a_i p_i + r_1 \left(\frac{RBD}{y} \right) + r_2 \left(\frac{RBD^2}{y} \right)$$

$$= \sum_{i=1}^{n} a_i p_i + r_1 \left(\frac{365}{CFR} \right) + r_2 \left(\frac{365 RBD}{CFR} \right) \qquad \text{... (6.3)}$$

where *CFR* is the case flow rate.

This specification of the average cost function embodies an assumption that any given change in the case flow rate, whether brought about by a change in occupancy or average length of stay, has the same effect on average cost. For any given size (number of beds), an increase in the number of cases treated increases the case flow rate. "We are interested in the cost of treating an additional patient. But this can be done in two ways, either by shortening the length of stay of patients or by increasing the occupancy of the hospital's capacity" (Cullis and West 1979, p.155). It is possible that the marginal cost of each of these options is different.

This problem can be resolved by including an additional average length of stay term in equation (6.3) which then becomes

$$ACC = \sum_{i=1}^{n} a_i p_i + r_1 \left(\frac{365}{CFR} \right) + r_2 \left(\frac{365 RBD}{CFR} \right) + r_3 ALS \qquad \text{... (6.4)}$$

Differentiating (6.4) gives

$$\frac{\partial ACC}{\partial ALS} = r_3 \qquad \qquad \text{... (6.5)}$$

$$\frac{\partial ACC}{\partial CFR} = -\frac{(365 r_1 + +365 RBD r_2)}{CFR^2} \qquad \qquad \text{... (6.6)}$$

Equation (6.5) indicates the effect of a change in length of stay on average cost per case holding the case flow rate, size (beds) and case mix (the p_i) constant. Given that the case flow rate (the number of cases per bed per year) is held constant, this implies that the change in *ALS* is accompanied by an equal proportionate change in occupancy in the same direction (see equation (6.1)). As such, the coefficient r_3 measures the effect of a change in *ALS* on *ACC* when the size of the hospital, the number of patients treated and the case mix of those patients remain constant. In other words it relates to a change in the average length of stay of the existing number and composition of patients.

The sign of r_3 may be positive or negative. Recall from Chapter 3 that a change in average length of stay may increase or reduce average cost per case depending upon the duration/intensity elasticity. If an increase in the duration of treatment (*ALS*) is more than offset by a reduction in intensity of treatment (*ACD*), then average cost per case will fall. Conversely, if such an increase is less than offset by a reduction in intensity, average cost per case will rise.

Equation (6.6) gives the rate of change of average cost per case with respect to a change in the case flow rate with average length of stay, size and case mix constant. With average length of stay constant, the case flow rate can change only if there is a change in occupancy (see equation (6.1)) so this expression shows how average cost per case varies with changes in occupancy. It tells us how average cost per case reacts to a change in the number of cases treated when average length of stay, size and case mix are constant, since a change in the case flow rate with given average length of stay and size can only come about through a change in the number of cases treated.[5]

The sign of this expression will depend on the values of the coefficients r_1 and r_2 and beds (*B*). It is tempting to speculate that the derivative will be negative because increased utilisation of existing capacity spreads the fixed

---

5   If desired, equation (6.6) can be expressed as the rate of change of average cost per case with respect to the number of cases treated. This is done by substituting (y/B) for *CFR* in equation (6.4) and differentiating with respect to y. This gives

$$\frac{\partial ACC}{\partial y} = -\frac{(365r_1 + 365RBDr_2)}{CFRy}$$

This differs from equation (6.6) by a factor of *B*, i.e.

$$B(\partial ACC / \partial y) = (\partial ACC / \partial CFR)$$

because it shows the effects on average cost per case of a one unit change in the number of cases treated rather than a one unit change in the case flow rate.

costs of capital over a larger output. The cost data employed in this study, however, do not include any capital charges. It is likely, nevertheless, that certain maintenance costs do not vary greatly with changes in the number of cases, in which case increases in the case flow rate will tend to reduce average cost per case.

If the expression in equation (6.6) does turn out to be negative, then its value will be less the larger is the size of the hospital. That is, any given increase in the case flow rate will reduce average cost per case more in larger hospitals than smaller ones. Again this lends itself to an interpretation in terms of 'fixed' costs, suggesting that such costs represent a larger proportion of total costs in large institutions. This may well be the case. Staffing levels, for example, may be less sensitive to changes in the number of cases treated in large institutions because of tenure conditions, whereas smaller hospitals may be more flexible in this regard.

A weakness of this specification is that it does not allow a turning point in the relationship between average cost per case and the case flow rate. Given that RBD and CFR must be positive in equation (6.6), the sign then depends on the sign of the numerator which is fixed once the values of r_1 and r_2 are ascertained.[6] As such, average cost per case either continuously declines or continuously increases as the case flow rate increases. This will be discussed further in Section 6.4 where some evidence is presented on a specification incorporating linear and quadratic terms in the case flow rate as was done by Feldstein (1967).

A further effect on average cost per case not covered in equations (6.5) and (6.6) is the effect of a change in average length of stay holding occupancy constant, or alternatively a change in the case flow rate accommodated by a change in average length of stay holding occupancy constant. It is possible for a hospital to increase the number of cases treated per bed per year without increasing occupancy by reducing the average length of stay of all cases. The effect of such a change on average cost per case can be obtained by substituting equation (6.3) into equation (6.4) which gives[7]

---

[6]   The numerator will be positive if $r_1 > RBDr_2$.

[7]   Note that this substitution does not result in *CFR*, *OCC* and *ALS* all appearing in the one equation. It actually results in *ALS* and *OCC* appearing with *CFR* suppressed. Given that these terms are related as in equation (6.1) it is necessary that no more than two of them appear in any particular formulation of the cost function.

$$ACC = \sum_{i=1}^{n} a_i p_i + r_1\left(\frac{ALS}{OCC}\right) + r_2 RBD\left(\frac{ALS}{OCC}\right) + r_3 ALS \qquad \dots (6.7)$$

Differentiating equation (6.7) with respect to average length of stay then gives

$$\frac{\partial ACC}{\partial ALS} = r_1\left(\frac{1}{OCC}\right) + r_2\left(\frac{RBD}{OCC}\right) + r_3 \qquad \dots (6.8)$$

It can be expected that the sign of equation (6.8) will be the opposite of equation (6.6). Both relate to the effects of a change in the case flow rate, one by changing occupancy and the other by changing average length of stay. While the magnitudes of these two effects may well differ, it seems unlikely that their directions would differ also. The same signs would indicate that, say, an increase in the case flow rate may increase or reduce average cost per case depending on whether it is accommodated by an increase in occupancy or a reduction in average length of stay.

If the sign of equation (6.8) is positive, then increasing average length of stay (and hence reducing the case flow rate) increases average cost per case, and this increase in *ACC* will be larger the bigger the hospital. This is in accord with the effects of a change in the case flow rate on average cost per case accommodated by a change in occupancy as given by equation (6.6). The gradient of the cost function is steeper for hospitals with more beds.

The effects discussed above describe short run cost behaviour in the sense that they relate to changes in cost per case arising from changes in the utilisation of given capacity. That is, they are concerned with the effects of changing average length of stay, occupancy and the case flow rate with size (beds) held constant. Long run cost behaviour is concerned with the effects of a change in size or capacity on average cost per case, i.e. size becomes variable. Before developing this, however, the *a priori* legitimacy of the average cost equations (6.4) and (6.7) will be discussed further.

The specification developed so far incorporates reciprocal terms in the case flow rate and occupancy. This implies that, if the coefficient is positive, increases in the case flow rate and occupancy reduce average cost per case but such reductions are smaller the larger are the case flow and occupancy rates. This formulation is similar to that adopted by Jenkins (1977, 1980) and Hardwick (1986) and, without the case mix terms, by Deeble (1965, 1980). It has been argued cogently by Jenkins (1977, pp.31-6) that this kind of specification is superior to one which enters these terms in linear form as has been done, for example, by Ingbar and Taylor (1968), Ro (1969), Evans

(1971), Lave, Lave and Silverman (1972) and Nicholson (1983). The reasons given for this are threefold. *First,* linear terms in occupancy or the case flow rate are inconsistent with linear terms in rated bed days in the total cost function. *Second,* a linear term in occupancy fails to reflect "the likelihood that the reduction in average costs associated with a given increase (5 per cent) in occupancy rates will be larger when occupancy rates are low (50 per cent) rather than high (90 per cent)" (Jenkins 1977, p.35). *Third,* the terms are often entered in the same manner in both an average cost per case equation and an average cost per day equation. This implies that "two *different* total cost equations apply to the same sample of hospitals" (Jenkins 1977, p.35, emphasis in original).

The addition of a linear average length of stay term in the average cost function corresponds to adding a linear term in occupied bed days to the total cost function. Given the argument in Chapter 3 that patient days of care are essentially an input into the provision of treatment, does this amount to including an input in the total and average cost function? While the arguments advanced in this book suggest an affirmative answer to this question, average length of stay enters the cost function as a dimension of the *utilisation of capacity* and, as has been shown, is necessary if the various ways of altering the case flow rate are to be distinguished. Whether average length of stay should enter the cost function if this function is to be used for reimbursement purposes is another matter, however, which will be taken up in Part C of this book.

Schuttinga (1976) rejects the use of average length of stay in the average cost function, stating categorically that "the average length of stay is not an acceptable regressor if the method of ordinary least squares is used to estimate the parameters of [an] average cost equation" (p.26). His reasoning is as follows.

> If there is a non-zero elasticity of demand for hospital care with respect to price, the decision to spend an extra day in the hospital depends upon the price charged. Because the price charged is presumably related to average costs per day, a hospital's average length of stay is jointly determined with average costs and cannot be presumed exogenous. (p.27)

Schuttinga then opts to use a measure of *expected* average length of stay "which can be taken as exogenous with respect to the hospital's average cost ... " (p.27). Friedman and Pauly (1983) worked with two models of hospital costs, one being a single-equation model treating average length of stay as exogenous and the other being a two-equation model with average length of stay endogenous. Robinson and Luft (1985), in analysing the effect of market structure on patient volume, average length of stay, average cost per case and average cost per day, also use a multi-equation model in which average length of stay is endogenous. Palmer (1986) also suggests that average length of stay may be endogenous to the hospital.

Generally, for hospital cost functions, "there is a problem in determining whether some of the variables are endogenous or exogenous" (Pauly 1978, p.80), and average length of stay is one of these variables. In contrast to Schuttinga's position, it is possible to interpret average length of stay as a surrogate for complexity, or as an indicator of the health of the patient at the time of discharge (Lave and Lave 1970b, p.298). Average length of stay may also reflect the availability of post-discharge care or the degree of vertical integration, as suggested by Evans (1981).[8] One can conclude from this that the inclusion of average length of stay in hospital cost functions is problematic and needs to be handled with care.

Turning to long run cost behaviour, differentiating equation (6.4) with respect to beds (holding the case flow rate constant) gives

$$\frac{\partial ACC}{\partial B} = \frac{133225\, r_2}{CFR}$$

For a given case flow rate, this expression will be positive or negative depending on the sign of r_2. As such, it implies that average cost per case will either increase or decrease continuously as size increases. Since no turning point can occur, this specification precludes the possibility of a conventional U-shaped cost curve. To allow for this possibility, equation (6.4) can be expanded to include linear and quadratic terms in beds, giving

$$ACC = \sum_{i-1}^{n} a_i p_i + r_1\left(\frac{365}{CFR}\right) + r_2\left(\frac{365 RBD}{CFR}\right) + r_3 ALS$$

$$+ r_4 B + r_5 B^2 \qquad\qquad \text{... (6.9)}$$

Differentiating equation (6.9) with respect to beds then gives

$$\frac{\partial ACC}{\partial B} = 133225\, r_2 CFR + r_4 + 2 r_5 B \qquad\qquad \text{... (6.10)}$$

---

8   See also McGuire (1985b, pp.37-8) for a discussion of these points.

Two points can be made about the behaviour of average cost per case as size varies in equation (6.10). *First*, the rate of change of average cost per case with respect to size depends upon the case flow rate. If r_2 is positive, then the larger the case flow rate the smaller will be the responsiveness of average cost per case to a change in size. In other words, the higher is the level of utilisation of capacity, the 'shallower' will be the average cost curve. The inclusion of linear and quadratic size terms in equation (6.9) is equivalent to including interactive terms in size and the number of cases treated in the total cost function, i.e. the total cost function will now contain terms in yB and yB^2.

Second, since the case flow rate and hence utilisation of capacity are held constant, changes in size are accompanied by an equal proportionate change in the number of cases treated. It is also possible to ascertain the effects of a change in size with a fixed number of cases treated. Substituting (y/B) for *CFR* in equation (6.9) and differentiating with respect to beds (B) gives

$$\frac{\partial ACC}{\partial B} = r_1 \left(\frac{365}{y} \right) + 2B \left[\left(\frac{133225 r_2}{y} \right) + r_5 \right] + r_4 \qquad \ldots (6.11)$$

Given that y and B are positive the sign of this expression depends on the signs of the coefficients r_1, r_2, r_4 and r_5. If negative, this indicates that, for any given number of patients treated, increases in size or capacity reduce average cost per case, and conversely if the sign is positive. In this way, some insight is gained into whether capacity has been overexpanded or underexpanded. A negative coefficient indicates that, for the given number of cases treated, existing capacity is too small and average cost per case can be reduced by increasing the size of the hospital. That is, hospitals on average are producing at a point on their short run average cost curves to the left of the tangency with the long run average cost curve.[9]

Equation (6.9), then, provides the specification upon which most attention will be focused in the empirical work in Section 6.5. In addition, as already mentioned, an equation which includes linear and quadratic terms in the case flow rate in addition to case mix will be considered. Also, an equation which includes linear terms in occupancy and average length of stay, as done by Evans (1971) and others, will be estimated for comparative purposes.

---

[9]   See Borts (1960, pp.108-12) for a discussion of the interpretation of size terms in cost functions. In the context of hospitals, see Cowing, Holtmann and Powers (1983, pp.264-9).

6.4 Descriptive Statistics

The empirical analysis is again based on the 121 Queensland public hospitals as described in Chapter 5. The mean, standard deviation, coefficient of variation and range of the relevant scale variables for these hospitals for 1977-78 are presented in Table 6.1 (reproduced from Table 5.7).

Table 6.1. Mean, Standard Deviation, Coefficient of Variation and Range of Cost/Volume Variables, Queensland Public Hospitals, 1977-78

	Mean	SD	CV	Range Min.	Max.
Average Cost per Case($)	546.83	238.90	.44	34.71	1361.16
Average Cost per Day($)	79.93	35.64	.45	16.71	220.09
Average Length of Stay	7.44	3.54	.48	1.00	19.48
Occupancy	.43	.20	.47	.006	1.075*
Case Flow Rate	23.33	14.34	.61	1.50	77.70
Inpatients	2725	5677	2.08	14	39907
Beds	98	175	1.79	2	1234

Notes: * This figure relates to a maternity hospital where days of care to "qualified babies" are added to the occupied bed days provided to the mother.
Source: See Table 5.6.

Note first of all that occupancy is relatively low (mean = 0.43), in contrast to occupancy rates of 0.81 in the 65 Western Pennsylvanian hospitals studied by Lave, Lave and Silverman (1972, p.168), 0.72 to 0.80 over the period 1963-64 to 1973-74 in the ten Victorian Country Base Hospitals studied by Deeble (1980, p.42) and 0.68 and 0.76 for all California hospitals and all US hospitals respectively for a three-month period in 1975 (Pauly 1978, p.83).

This relatively low mean occupancy, however, needs to be interpreted in the context of the average size of the hospitals included in the study, *viz.* 98 beds. This compares with 246 beds in the Lave, Lave and Silverman study, 235 to 260 beds in Deeble's study, and 149 and 158 beds for all California hospitals and all US hospitals respectively as reported in Pauly's study.

The reason why size needs to be taken into consideration in interpreting occupancy rates relates to the probability of overcrowding, i.e. the probability that, on any particular day, all beds will be full. This problem arises because occupancy is not stable through time. The demand for admission exhibits peaks and troughs, fluctuating according to the day of the week and the month of the year.[10] To the extent that daily case loads are Poisson-distributed, the number of beds required to achieve any particular probability of overcrowding can be calculated. It can be shown that, to attain any given probability of overcrowding, average occupancy needs to be maintained at a *lower* level the *smaller* is the number of beds in the hospital (Blumberg 1961; Joskow 1980).[11]

The correlation between size and occupancy in the hospitals included in this study in 1977-78 was 0.42 (see Table 6.2), indicating that larger hospitals within the sample do tend to have higher occupancy rates. The mean levels of occupancy and size in the system may well then be a reflection of an underlying objective to prevent the probability of overcrowding from rising above some particular level. The Queensland situation, for instance, is more akin to that in Newfoundland cottage hospitals where a mean size of 28 beds was associated with a mean occupancy of 0.49 (Brown 1980, p.270).[12]

The frequency distributions of hospitals by occupancy, case flow rate and size are generally skewed to the left. Nearly 64 per cent of hospitals have an occupancy rate less than 50 per cent, while 93 per cent of hospitals have occupancy rates less than 70 per cent. The relatively low occupancy rates are reflected in the case flow rates also. For a hospital with an average length of stay equal to the mean of 7.44 days, 100 per cent occupancy would give a case flow rate of 49.1, and 50 per cent occupancy a case flow rate of

---

[10] Some evidence on this, together with a discussion of the economic consequences, can be found in Weisbrod (1965, pp.23-8). Friedman and Pauly (1981, 1983) have addressed the problem of estimating hospital cost functions when demand is stochastic, allowing also for the possibility that in periods of unusually high demand the hospital may permit some aspects of quality of care to deteriorate. See also Cowing, Holtmann and Powers (1983, pp.273-5).

[11] The applicability of the Poisson distribution depends on the randomness of the variable, in this case admissions. To the extent that admissions can be scheduled, e.g. those requiring non-urgent surgery, variations in occupancy through time can be smoothed out. But emergency cases are a different matter—admission cannot be postponed. For further discussion of this problem see Bailey (1956), Thompson, Fetter, McIntosh and Pelletier (1963) and Feldstein (1983, pp.248-60). See also Long (1964) and Long and Feldstein (1967).

[12] Brown uses the term 'excess bed capacity' to describe what is termed 'occupancy' in this study. A note to his Table 2 makes it clear that the concepts are identical.

Table 6.2. Correlation Matrix for Cost/Volume Variables, Queensland Public Hospitals, 1977-78

	ACC	ALS	OCC	CFR	Inpatients	Beds
ACC	1.00	0.61	0.08	-0.32	0.18	0.26
ALS		1.00	0.34	-0.34	0.02	0.12
OCC			1.00	0.67	0.46	0.42
CFR				1.00	0.29	0.17
Inpatients					1.00	0.97
Beds						1.00

Source: Hospital Finance Data and statistical results.

24.5.[13] Nearly 65 per cent of hospitals treated less than 25 cases per bed per year and nearly 30 per cent treated less than 15 cases per bed per year. With regard to size, although the mean is 98 beds, nearly half the hospitals have less than 40 beds and about 75 per cent of hospitals are below average size.

The correlation matrix for the cost/volume variables is presented in Table 6.2. Considering first the case flow rate/occupancy/average length of stay relationship (see equation (6.1)), the point made above about low case flow rates reflecting low occupancy rates is confirmed by the correlation coefficient between them of 0.67. Variation in average length of stay is negatively associated with the case flow rate, as expected, but its association is much weaker (−0.34).

Turning to average cost per case, this is most closely associated with average length of stay with which it is positively correlated, and the case flow rate with which it is negatively correlated. Size and the number of cases treated are highly correlated, but neither is particularly strongly associated with average cost per case. Occupancy and average cost per case are almost unassociated.

These are, of course, simple correlation coefficients. The examination of any chains of causation involved here requires the theoretical apparatus discussed earlier and the inclusion of these factors in an appropriately specified cost function. The results of such an analysis are now considered.

---

[13] Note that, because the means in Table 6.1 are unweighted means, the values for the case flow rate, average length of stay and occupancy do not satisfy the relationship given in equation (6.1).

6.5   Empirical Results

6.5.1   Scale and Utilisation with Disaggregated Case Mix Classifications—1977-78

Before presenting the results with the preferred functional form, it is interesting to note that size alone is a very poor explanator of variation in average cost per case between hospitals. This is confirmed by the following estimated equations (t-values in parentheses, *, ** = significant at one and five per cent levels respectively):

$$ACC = 511.33 + 0.3611\,B$$
$$(3.00^*)$$

$$\overline{R}^2 = .06; \quad SEE = 231.34; \quad \text{d.f.} = 119.$$

$$ACC = 492.55 + 0.6982\,B - 0.0003582\,B^2$$
$$(2.25^{**}) \quad (-1.18)$$

$$\overline{R}^2 = .07; \quad SEE = 230.97; \quad \text{d.f.} = 118.$$

The linear function gives a small but statistically significant proportion of the variation in average cost per case being explained by size, while the addition of a quadratic term does not improve the result. The quadratic formulation implies average cost per case rises to a maximum then falls as size increases. Similarly poor results were found by Feldstein (1967) who emphasised that such equations "make no allowance for the association between hospital size and case mix composition" (p. 64).

   Moving on to the preferred specification given by equation (6.9), the scale and utilisation terms given in that specification were included with the 18 and 47 diagnostic categories and the additional case mix dimensions also. The parameter estimates for the scale terms for each of these equations are presented in Table 6.3.[14]

   Overall the addition of the five scale and utilisation terms to both the specifications results in a statistically significant increase in the proportion of the variation in average cost per case explained by each equation.

---

[14]   The parameter estimates for the case mix terms continued to be plagued by incorrect signs and statistical insignificance. As such, they are of little interest and are not included here.

Table 6.3. Scale and Utilisation Parameter Estimates obtained using 18 and 47 Diagnostic Categories and Additional Case Mix Dimensions, Queensland Public Hospitals, 1977-78[a]

	$\dfrac{365}{CFR}$	$\dfrac{365RBD}{CFR}$	ALS	B	B^2	$\bar{R}^2$	SEE	F
18DCs+[b] (d.f.=88)	3.115 (3.67*)	0.00027 (3.18*)	14.459 (2.53**)	-2.035 (-3.43*)	0.00065 (2.41**)	.69	133.72	9.22*
47DCs+[b] (d.f.=59)	4.136 (3.85*)	0.00031 (3.28*)	17.368 (2.42**)	-2.634 (-3.56*)	0.00092 (2.58**)	.77	115.23	7.49*

Notes: * Significant at 1% level.
        ** Significant at 5% level.
        (a) t-values in parentheses.
        (b) The "+" sign indicates that the additional case mix dimensions have been added to the specification.
        d.f. = degrees of freedom.
Source: Regression results.

Without these terms, the 18 diagnostic categories together with the additional case mix dimensions explained 44 per cent of the variation in average cost after adjusting for degrees of freedom (see Table 5.10). The addition of the scale and utilisation terms increases this to 69 per cent, and this increase is statistically significant at the one per cent level (incremental $F = 15.69$). A noticeable improvement in explanatory power also occurs when the scale and utilisation terms are added to the 47 diagnostic categories and additional case mix dimensions, with adjusted R^2 increasing from 0.46 (see Table 5.10) to 0.77. This increase is again statistically significant at the one per cent level (incremental $F = 17.74$).

Comparing the results of the two specifications presented in Table 6.3, the more disaggregated case mix classification scheme again outperforms the more highly aggregated categories. The specification containing 47 as opposed to 18 diagnostic categories explains more variation in average cost per case (adjusted $R^2 = 0.77$ compared to adjusted $R^2 = 0.69$) and an incremental F test of the additional 29 variables shows the improvement to be statistically significant at the five per cent level (incremental $F = 2.05$). Henceforth scale and utilisation parameter estimates from this equation will be used in discussing short run and long run cost behaviour. It is evident from Table 6.3, though, that the values of the coefficients do not differ markedly between the two equations so the cost behaviour implied by the two specifications is similar.

Turning now to the individual parameter estimates for the scale and utilisation variables, all of these estimates are statistically significantly different from zero at the five per cent level (see Table 6.3). These coefficients will be interpreted in terms of their implications for short run and long run cost behaviour respectively.

(a)   Short run cost behaviour

Short run cost behaviour refers to changes in the utilisation of existing capacity and is thus concerned with the behaviour of average cost per case for any given size hospital. From equation (6.5), the effect of a change in average length of stay on average cost, holding the case flow rate, size and case mix constant, is given by the coefficient attaching to the *ALS* term in the equation. From Table 6.3, the effect of an increase in average length of stay of one day under these conditions would be to increase average cost per case by \$17.37. Note that, since the case flow rate is constant, such an increase in average length of stay would be accompanied by an equal proportionate increase in occupancy. This result indicates that the duration/intensity elasticity (as defined in Chapter 3) is greater than unity in absolute value, i.e. an increase in average length of stay will be accompanied by a less than proportionate reduction in average cost per day.

Considering now the effects of a change in the case flow rate, recall that case flow can be increased either by increasing occupancy with average length of stay constant, or reducing average length of stay with occupancy constant. The effect of the former change is captured by equation (6.6). Inserting the relevant parameter estimates from Table 6.3 into this equation gives

$$\frac{\partial ACC}{\partial CFR} = -\frac{(1509.64 + 41.3B)}{CFR^2} < 0 \qquad\qquad ... (6.12)$$

Since this is negative, increasing the case flow rate by increasing occupancy with average length of stay constant reduces average cost per case. In other words, hospitals can reduce average cost per case by treating more cases per bed and allowing occupancy rates to increase even with a constant average length of stay.

Inserting the mean size (98 beds) and case flow rate (23.33) from Table 6.1 into equation (6.12) gives a value of \$10.21. Hence in a hospital of average size and case flow, treating one more case per bed per year, with average length of stay given, would reduce average cost per case by just over \$10. A hospital with these characteristics and the State mean length of stay of 7.44 days would have an occupancy rate of 0.48. Increasing the case flow rate by one under these conditions implies increasing the occupancy rate to 0.50 or fifty per cent.

The reduction in average cost per case is larger the bigger the hospital and the smaller the initial case flow rate. For example, a 200 bed hospital with the State mean case flow rate of 23.33 could expect a decline of $17.95 per case by increasing case flow to 24.33. If such a hospital's case flow rate was initially 15.00, the decline in average cost per case arising from a one unit increment in the case flow rate would be $43.42.

These relationships can be depicted graphically if case mix is specified. For illustrative purposes, the mean case mix proportions (see Tables 5.4 and 5.5) and mean length of stay were substituted into the estimated average cost function as specified by equation (6.9) giving

$$ACC = 481.19 + 4.136\left(\frac{365}{CFR}\right) + 0.00031\left(\frac{365RBD}{CFR}\right)$$

$$- 2.634\,B + 0.00092\,B^2 \qquad\qquad ...\,(6.13)$$

This relationship was then plotted for three different size hospitals—50, 98 and 200 beds. The resulting cost curves are shown in Figure 6.3.[15] Note that, for a movement along any of these curves, the volume of cases treated is changing but case mix is constant.

It is evident from Figure 6.3 that these short run cost curves are L-shaped —increasing the case flow rate will always produce some reduction in average cost per case. Such a result is not uncommon in studies of other industries (see Walters 1963), and "There are many reasons to expect an L-shaped curve for hospitals, the prime one being that hospitals tend to staff for a higher than average level of utilisation so they can be ready on a stand-by basis" (Lave and Lave 1970a, p.381). Nevertheless, as pointed out in Section 6.3, the specification of the average cost function adopted here does not allow a turning point in the average cost/case flow relationship.

To gain some insight into the problem, a specification similar to that employed by Feldstein (1967, Ch.5) in his study of capacity utilisation was

---

[15] In this diagram average cost per case could have been shown as a function of the number of cases treated rather than the case flow rate, giving a conventional short run cost curve. This would simply result in a change in the units of measurement on the horizontal axis since, for any given size, the case flow rate can be translated directly into a number of cases treated (see footnote 5). The present format was chosen because it facilitates a comparison of the effects of size on the average cost/case flow relationship.

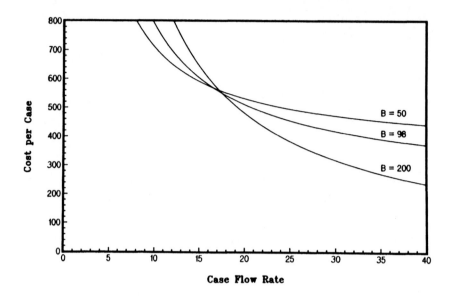

Figure 6.3. Relationship between Cost per Case and Case Flow Rate for Hospitals
of different Size, Length of Stay constant

estimated. This involved including linear and quadratic terms in the case
flow rate with the case mix proportions.[16] The results are presented as
equation I in Table 6.4. Both case flow rate terms are highly significant as is
the overall relationship. The equation indicates a U-shaped relationship
between average cost and case flow. Performing the relevant differentiation
shows the turning point occurs at a case flow rate of 53.14.

While this evidence supports a U-shaped curve, minimum average cost
per case occurs at a case flow rate far beyond that of most hospitals in the
study—only five hospitals out of the 121 have a case flow rate exceeding
53.14. Feldstein (1967) found a similar result and suggested that the
continuously declining curve might be appropriate. "Because only seven
hospitals have [CFR] values exceeding the implied turning point of the
short-run average-cost-per-case curve, it is difficult to infer from their
residuals ... whether the U-shaped curve is a better hypothesis than a curve
that is monotonically decreasing with a positive second derivative"
(Feldstein 1967, p.133). Hence it seems that the cost behaviour depicted in

---

[16] Feldstein also included linear and quadratic terms in size but these were found to be
insignificant. This was tested in the present study also and the same result emerged (see
equation (6.22) and discussion later in this chapter).

Figure 6.3 is reasonable, at least for the great majority of hospitals in this sample.

Table 6.4. Scale and Utilisation Parameter Estimates using Alternative Specifications with 47 Diagnostic Categories and Additional Case Mix Dimensions, Queensland Public Hospitals, 1977-78[a]

Equation	CFR	CFR^2	B	B^2	$\bar{R}^2$	SEE	F
I (d.f.=62)	-31.66 (-7.68*)	0.29791 (5.74*)			.76	117.87	7.43*
II (d.f.=60)	-30.43 (-7.07*)	0.28527 (5.17*)	-0.04437 (-0.10)	-0.00010 (0.31)	.73	124.08	6.41*

Equation	OCC	ALS	B	B^2	$\bar{R}^2$	SEE	F
III (d.f.=62)	-738.002 (-6.17*)	47.15 (7.36*)			.75	119.64	7.18*
IV (d.f.=60)	-749.43 (-5.71*)	48.46 (7.11*)	-0.3903 (-0.94)	0.00034 (1.06)	.74	120.54	6.60*

Notes: *   Significant at 1% level.
           **   Significant at 5% level.
          (a)   t-values in parentheses.
Source: Regression results.

The marginal cost of treating additional cases can also be estimated from the results in Table 6.3. Substituting the mean size, case flow rate, average length of stay and 47+ case mix proportions into equation (6.13) gives a predicted average cost per case of $470.09 increasing the case flow rate by one reduces this to $460.30 or by $9.79 per case. Given that this involves increasing the number of patients treated from 2,286 to 2,384, the implied marginal cost is $231.90, about 50 per cent of average cost.

Before turning to the effects of accommodating a change in the case flow rate by a change in average length of stay, the foregoing results can be used to further illuminate the first aspect of short run cost behaviour considered— the effects of an equal proportionate change in average length of stay and occupancy with the case flow rate held constant. Recall that this change was estimated to increase average cost per case by $17.37. The analysis of changes in occupancy with constant average length of stay just undertaken now clarifies this result. An increase in occupancy with constant length of stay will reduce average cost per case, but if average length of stay and occupancy are increased in the same proportion, the cost-reducing effect of higher occupancy is more than offset by the cost-increasing effect of a higher average length of stay.

The effect of a change in average length of stay with occupancy constant is ascertained by considering the third aspect of short run cost behaviour—the effect of a change in the case flow rate accommodated by a change in average length of stay with constant occupancy. Equation (6.8) describes the effect of this kind of change in terms of the coefficients to be estimated. Substituting in the relevant values of the coefficients from Table 6.3 gives

$$\frac{\partial ACC}{\partial ALS} = \frac{4.136}{OCC} + 0.00031\left(\frac{RBD}{OCC}\right) + 17.368 > 0 \qquad \text{... (6.14)}$$

The positive sign of this expression indicates that increasing average length of stay with constant occupancy (and hence a reduced case flow rate) will increase average cost per case. For a hospital of mean size (98 beds) and mean occupancy (0.43), equation (6.14) predicts that increasing average length of stay by one day would increase average cost per case by \$52.77. Conversely, a one day reduction in average length of stay would reduce average cost per case by \$52.77.

It is useful for comparative purposes to relate the change in average cost per case to the change in the case flow rate rather than directly to the change in average length of stay as in equation (6.14). This can be achieved by substituting the term $365(OCC/CFR)$ in equation (6.4) and differentiating with respect to CFR. This gives

$$\frac{\partial ACC}{\partial CFR} = -\frac{\left(365r_1 + 365RBDr_2 + 365OCCr_3\right)}{CFR^2} \qquad \text{... (6.15)}$$

Substituting the estimated values of r_1, r_2 and r_3 from Table 6.3 gives

$$\frac{\partial ACC}{\partial CFR} = -\frac{\left(1509.64 + 41.3\,B + 6339.32\,OCC\right)}{CFR^2} < 0 \qquad \text{... (6.16)}$$

For a hospital with the mean occupancy rate of 0.43, equation (6.16) becomes

$$\frac{\partial ACC}{\partial CFR} = -\frac{(4235.5476 + 41.3\,B)}{CFR^2} < 0 \qquad\qquad \dots (6.17)$$

This gives the effect of a change in the case flow rate when occupancy is held constant and average length of stay is varied. It shows that an increase in case flow, which requires a reduction in the average length of stay, will reduce average cost per case.

Again the relationship between average cost per case and the case flow rate can be plotted if the case mix is specified. For this purpose the mean case mix proportions and mean occupancy were used and the resulting average cost function plotted for three different hospital sizes—50, 98 and 200 beds. The resulting curves are shown in Figure 6.4.

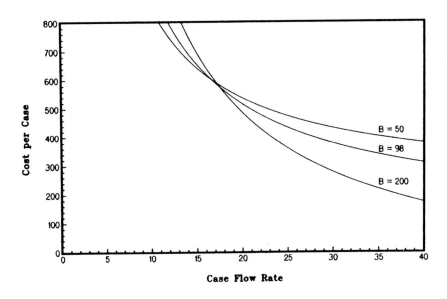

Figure 6.4. Relationship between Cost per Case and Case Flow Rate for Hospitals of different Size, Occupancy constant

It is tempting to interpret the cost curves in Figures 6.3 and 6.4 as supporting Alchian's rate/volume theory of costs (Alchian 1959). In the short run, the increase in the case flow rate is brought about by an increase in the volume of cases treated. The continuously declining average cost per case may appear to support Alchian's contention that marginal cost is a decreasing function of the volume of output when the rate of output is held constant. However, 'volume' in Alchian's theory is a *stock* concept referring to the total stock of output to be produced by a firm, while the rate of output is a *flow* concept measuring output per time period. The term 'volume' in our analysis is a flow concept measuring cases treated per year while the case flow *rate* is the rate at which cases are treated per unit of capacity (beds) per year. Although it has been suggested that Alchian's theory may be applicable to hospitals (see Mann and Yett 1968; Finkler 1979), it is debatable whether the production characteristics of hospitals actually fit the process analysed by Alchian. In particular, Hirshleifer (1962, p.236) has argued that the theory is most applicable to "establishments producing to unique customer order" where the (stock) concept of volume is unambiguous. Mann and Yett's suggestion that the number of beds be used as a proxy for volume (in Alchian's sense) can be debated on conceptual grounds and Finkler seems to confuse the stock and flow concepts of volume.

Comparing Figures 6.3 and 6.4, it seems that increasing the case flow rate will reduce average cost per case, whether this is accommodated by allowing occupancy to increase or average length of stay to decrease. But the cost consequences of these two actions are not the same. It has already been shown that equal proportionate changes in average length of stay and occupancy do not offset each other in their effect on average cost per case, and the result indicated that the change in average length of stay was more expensive. That this is the case can now be demonstrated more specifically.

Figure 6.5 compares the *ACC-CFR* relationship for a hospital of mean size (98 beds) when the case flow change is accommodated alternatively by a change in occupancy and a change in average length of stay.[17] It is immediately evident that any given increase in case flow will reduce average cost per case by a greater amount if it is accommodated by a reduction in average length of stay rather than an increase in occupancy.[18]

The comparative magnitudes of the two effects can be illustrated by considering a hospital with the State mean values of all variables and a predicted average cost per case of $470.09. It was shown earlier that if the case flow rate was increased by one to 24.33 by allowing occupancy to increase, the predicted cost per case would fall to $460.30, or by $9.79 per case. This implied a marginal cost of $231.90 which is about 50 per cent of

---

[17]   In other words this Figure contains, on the one diagram, the 98 bed curves from Figures 6.3 and 6.4.

[18]   This result is also evident from a comparison of the partial differentials in equations (6.12) and (6.17). The latter, which shows the effects of a case flow change via a change in *ALS*, will always be larger in absolute value for any given *CFR* change.

average cost. Now if the same increase in case flow is achieved by allowing average length of stay to fall, average cost per case would fall to $454.83 or by $15.26 per case. The marginal cost of treating extra patients is therefore lower if these patients are accommodated by reducing the average length of stay of all patients rather than increasing occupancy and is estimated to be $98.81 or about 22 per cent of average cost. These estimated marginal/average cost ratios are generally in accord with those found in other studies (see Lipscomb, Raskin and Eichenholz 1978; Lave and Lave 1979, p.967).[19]

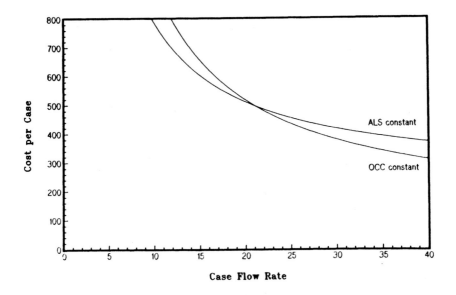

Figure 6.5. Comparative effects of increasing Case Flow Rate by increasing Occupancy and reducing Length of Stay, Size constant (*B*=98)

For purposes of comparison with the sign and magnitude of the above results, an average cost function including case mix (47 diagnostic categories and other dimensions) and linear terms in occupancy and average length of stay, as done for example by Evans (1971), was also estimated. The results are presented as equation III in Table 6.4. The directions of the

---

[19] Feldstein (1967, pp.138-9) estimated the two marginal costs directly from a total cost equation which included only size and volume terms, i.e. no adjustment was made for case mix. The difference in magnitude of the two estimates and their relationship to average cost were similar to that found here.

effects of a change in occupancy or average length of stay are the same as in the specification adopted above—increasing occupancy reduces average cost while increasing length of stay increases it.

To compare the magnitudes of the effects in the two specifications, the implied changes in occupancy and average length of stay for a one unit change in case flow in an average hospital will be used. A hospital with a case flow rate of 23.33 and average length of stay of 7.44 days will have an occupancy rate of 0.476. An increase in the case flow rate to 24.33 can be achieved by increasing occupancy to 0.496 (*ALS* constant) or by reducing average length of stay to 7.13 days. From equation III in Table 6.4, the first of these changes would reduce average cost by $15.66, the second by $14.62. In contrast to the results presented above, the second option— increasing case flow by reducing length of stay—now reduces average cost by a slightly smaller amount and will consequently have a higher marginal cost. It was argued earlier, however, that this specification was theoretically inferior because of the nature of the relationship it postulates between average cost and utilisation.

The foregoing results imply that substantial cost savings can be had by increasing the case flow rate in hospitals with relatively low case flow rates. If the total volume of cases treated in the State remains the same, then this implies reducing the number of beds. But while this is certainly a relevant consideration in deciding upon the configuration of the hospital system, it is not the only consideration. As discussed earlier, the probability of overcrowding must be considered. Further, a smaller number of hospitals will increase travel costs incurred by patients. These points will be raised again after long run cost behaviour has been considered.

(b)   Long run cost behaviour

Cost behaviour in the long run pertains to the relationship between average cost per case and size. The general effects of a change in size in the specification adopted here are given by equations (6.10) and (6.11). Substituting into these equations the relevant parameter estimates from Table 6.3 gives

$$\frac{\partial ACC}{\partial B} = \frac{41.30}{CFR} - 2.634 + 0.00184B \qquad \text{... (6.18)}$$

$$\frac{\partial ACC}{\partial B} = \frac{1509.64}{y} + 2B\left[\left(\frac{41.30}{y}\right) + 0.00092\right] - 2.634 \qquad \text{... (6.19)}$$

Considering first equation (6.18), recall that this indicates the effect of a change in size with case flow held constant, i.e. size and the volume of cases treated change proportionately. Under these conditions, equation (6.18) indicates that, for a hospital with the mean case flow rate of 23.33, average cost per case falls up to a size of 469 beds and increases thereafter.

It must be noted, however, that in the specification adopted here, the rate of change of average cost per case with respect to size is dependent on the case flow rate. As such, the size at which average cost is minimised will depend upon the case flow rate. In particular, the higher the case flow rate, the larger will be the size required to exhaust the economies of scale. For example, with a case flow rate of 30, average cost is minimised at a size of 683 beds. Further, if the case flow rate does not exceed 15.67 cases per bed per year, there are no economies of scale to be reaped. Such hospitals need to either increase the number of patients treated or be reduced in size if average cost per case is to be reduced.

To illustrate these effects diagrammatically, the mean case mix proportions and average length of stay were again substituted into the estimated average cost equation and the resulting relationship between average cost per case and size plotted for various case flow rates. Figure 6.6 depicts the curves so plotted.[20] Given the mean size of hospitals in the sample of 98 beds and mean case flow of 23.33, these curves indicate that many Queensland public hospitals could reap economies of scale from an expansion of capacity (or an increase in the number of beds). The predicted average cost per case at 98 beds is $465.50 which is 36 per cent higher than the predicted average cost per case of $343.16 at the cost-minimising size of 469 beds.

Considering now equation (6.19), recall that, in contrast to the adjustments just considered, this relates to a change in the size of the hospital with the number of cases treated and their case mix being held constant. Evaluating this at the mean size (98 beds) and volume of cases treated (2,725) gives a figure of $1.07, i.e. one extra bed added to this hospital with volume constant would increase average cost by $1.07 per case. This result is consistent with the results already presented in this section. It indicates that, for the given average volume of cases, a 98 bed hospital is too large and that average cost could be reduced by reducing size. Of course, reducing size with a given volume of cases increases the case flow rate and so the predicted cost reducing effects of this have the same

---

20   This is, in fact, another plot of equation (6.13) but this time depicting the average cost/size relationship. Since average length of stay is fixed, the different case flow rates reflect a change in occupancy.

direction as increasing the case flow rate by increasing volume with a given size.

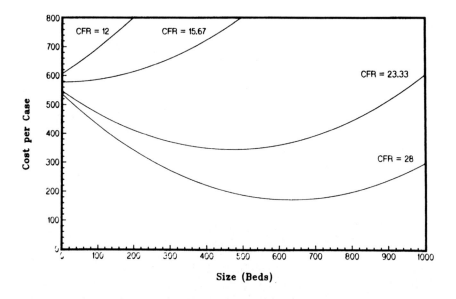

Figure 6.6. Relationship between Cost per Case and Size for varying Case Flow Rates, Length of Stay constant

Generally, the findings on economies of scale presented here indicate that minimum average costs are achieved at higher sizes than in most other studies, although it must be borne in mind that 'optimal' size in the current study does depend on the case flow rate. In reviewing the evidence on economies of scale, Lave and Lave (1979, p.966) report: "Economies of scale in the production of hospital services have not been found to be important. A number of studies have suggested that there may be economies of scale up to about 150-200 beds; but not beyond." Feldstein (1993, p.212) reports "there are some slight economies of scale; hospitals with approximately 200 to 300 beds appear to have the lowest average costs".

Some studies, however, have found evidence that economies of scale may be attained in hospitals of a larger size than suggested by these reviews. A study of optimal hospital size employing the 'survivor technique' has suggested that scale economies may be attainable in hospitals up to 450 beds. The survivor technique to estimating minimum efficient scale was pioneered by Stigler (1958). "Its fundamental postulate is that the competition of different sizes of firms sifts out the more efficient enterprises" (Stigler 1958, p.55). Hence, by observing the sizes of surviving firms through time, it may be possible to infer the size range of firms over which economies of scale are attainable.

> The survivor technique proceeds to solve the problem of determining the optimum firm size as follows: Classify the firms in an industry by size, and calculate the share of industry output coming from each class over time. If the share of a given class falls, it is relatively inefficient, and in general is more inefficient the more rapidly the share falls. (Stigler 1958, p.56).

An advantage of the technique is that it does not require data on firm costs as such—only data on the size distribution of firms through time are required. However, as has been pointed out by Shepherd (1967), the existence of economies of scale is but one reason why firms survive. The pursuit of entry-deterring strategies and government regulations, for example, may also be important determinants of survival.

Bays (1986) employed the survivor technique in a study of the changing size distribution of over 3,000 short-term, private (voluntary non-profit or profit), non-teaching hospitals in the US over the period 1971 to 1977. "For the combined sample, hospitals of less than 100 beds and more than 500 beds declined in frequency and the range of surviving sizes is from 100 to 449 beds" (Bays 1986, p.362). However, for the non-profit hospitals (which comprised nearly 80 per cent of the sample), only the size range 200 to 299 beds had a statistically significant increase in relative frequency.[21]

Another approach which has been applied to the analysis of hospital costs is based on frontier models. These models are concerned with estimating production or cost functions which show the maximum output attainable from a given set of inputs, or the minimum costs which must be incurred to produce any given output level, i.e. frontier production or cost functions. Conventional regression analyses provide estimates of the *mean* output attainable, or cost incurred, rather than estimates of the *maximal* output attainable or *minimal* cost incurred as provided by frontier models. Schmidt (1986) provides a useful overview of frontier production functions.

---

21   Bays also found significant regional differences in survival patterns. In an analysis of the determinants of surviving hospital size, he found that interstate variations in competition (specifically from HMOs), regulation and demographic factors were all related to the size distribution of hospitals. The survivor technique has also been used to analysis other parts of the health care industry, e.g. commercial health insurers (Blair and Vogel 1978) and medical practices (Frech and Ginsburg 1974; Marder and Zuckerman 1985).

There have been relatively few empirical applications of frontier models in the health sector, and those studies which have been done have generally been concerned with estimating production rather than cost frontiers (e.g. Grosskopf and Valdmanis 1987; Johnson and Lahiri 1992). However, Wagstaff (1989) has employed three different statistical cost frontier models, in addition to a non-frontier model of the kind used in the present study, in an analysis of 49 Spanish public hospitals. Only six case mix categories were included in the study—a high level of aggregation of hospital outputs—and the size terms were statistically significant in only the panel data model. In that model, scale economies were evident in the "within" (fixed effects) model up to 589 beds, and in the generalised least squares (random effects) model up to 540 beds (Wagstaff 1989, p.669). These results must be treated with caution, as time series data on case mix for the panel data model were unavailable, necessitating an assumption that case mix remained unchanged over the five-year period for the panel data model.

There is, therefore, some evidence to suggest that economies of scale may exist in hospitals with sizes up to 500+ beds. But even if one accepted the lower size limits on economies of scale of 150-200 beds, Queensland public hospitals still appear to be too small on average to exhaust the potential scale economies.

The relatively few Australian studies undertaken to date generally do not provide results comparable to those produced in the present study. The studies by Deeble (1965, 1980) use average cost per *day* as the dependent variable and do not adjust for case mix. Higham and Robb (1977) found evidence of scale economies in Queensland country hospitals but this study, along with a study by the Health Commission of New South Wales (1978), employs a questionable specification of the cost function (see Richardson and Wallace 1983, pp.141-2). The latter did produce some evidence of scale economies for hospitals up to 140-190 beds. Nicholson (1983), in a study of Western Australian hospitals, does adjust for case mix but uses only a linear term in size. As such, no turning point in the average cost/size relationship is allowed for. The size coefficient, which was statistically significant, indicated diseconomies of scale.

Finally, for comparative purposes, linear and quadratic terms in beds were added to the Feldstein- and Evans-type specifications estimated earlier (see equations I and III in Table 6.4). The results are presented as equations II and IV in Table 6.4. The size terms in each of these equations have the expected signs, implying that minimum average cost is attained at 223 beds in equation II and at 574 beds in equation IV. None of the size terms are, however, statistically significantly different from zero. These results agree with those of Feldstein (1967, p.75) and Evans and Walker (1972) who conclude that there is "little evidence of impact on costs from scale of plant once diagnostic and age-sex mix and other sorts of activities are adjusted for" (p.417).

Given these conclusions and the relatively weak evidence which other studies seem to have found on the existence of economies of scale, one may well query whether the results reported here are robust. To check on this, the cost functions were re-estimated for each of another three years using data for the years 1978-79 to 1980-81. These results will be presented in the following sub-section.

In concluding this discussion of our results on economies of scale for 1977-78, two important limitations must be stressed. First, the findings provide no guidance as to the appropriate *composition* of a hospital of any given size, i.e. they provide no evidence on the cost-minimising *mix* of facilities and services. As mentioned earlier in this chapter, using beds as a measure of capacity ignores the different *kinds* of beds a hospital may have, and also ignores the other types of capital which can be employed. In this sense the results are quite aggregative.

The second limitation relates to the problems of travel costs, the probability of overcrowding and the overall configuration of the hospital system. To illustrate this, consider that the findings of this study imply that, if all the 329,725 patients treated in the hospitals in this study in 1977-78 were treated in hospitals with an average case flow rate of 23.33 cases per bed per year, the system would require 14,133 beds. If all of these were to be configured in hospitals of optimal size for this case flow rate (469 beds), about 30 hospitals would be required compared to 121 in the sample. Could this seriously be put forward as a policy recommendation?

The answer must be 'no', because the overall design of the system also requires information on travel costs and the costs associated with various probabilities of overcrowding, in addition to information on facility costs. Average travel cost per case rises as the size of hospitals increases and the number of hospitals decreases because patients must travel greater distances for services. Average penalty cost, which is the cost "incurred by those inconvenienced when the absence of facilities necessitates a departure from regular procedures" (Long and Feldstein 1967, p.121), falls as the size of the facility increases because, for any given occupancy rate, the probability of overcrowding diminishes. The optimal size of a facility depends upon the behaviour of each of the three components of cost.[22]

---

22   For a diagrammatic exposition of this argument and further discussion of facility planning, see Long and Feldstein (1967) and Feldstein (1983, Ch.11).

6.5.2   Scale and Utilisation with Disaggregated Case Mix Classifications—1978-79 to 1980-81

Interesting though the foregoing results might be, the preferred specification has been estimated for one financial year only. If these results are an accurate reflection of the underlying cost behaviour of the hospitals in this sample, one can reasonably expect that they will hold for other years also. Given the recent concern about applied econometrics in general (Leamer 1983; McAleer, Pagan and Volker 1985; Leamer 1985) and the possibility of replicating particular studies to ascertain the veracity of the results (Kane 1984; Mittelstaedt and Zorn 1984; Dewald, Thursby and Anderson 1986), an examination of whether the results obtained here are reproducible for other years is important.

Consequently, the specification given in equation (6.9) was re-estimated using data from each of the financial years 1978-79 to 1980-81.[23] The coefficient estimates for the scale and utilisation variables for each of these years, together with those already obtained for 1977-78, are presented in Table 6.5. While the explanatory power of the equation is high and significant in every year, only two of the five scale and utilisation terms retained their statistical significance over the whole period—the inverse of the case flow rate, and average length of stay.[24] The remaining terms lacked significance in every additional year. The signs of the coefficients remained the same each year with some variation in magnitude.

Of the results presented in the previous sub-section, these estimates considerably weaken the evidence of any scale effects and the presence of any interaction between the case flow rate and size. They do, however, strongly support the estimated utilisation effects. Increasing the case flow rate with length of stay constant reduces the predicted average cost per case in every year, with this reduction being greater in 1979-80 and 1980-81 compared with the two previous years. Increasing average length of stay with a constant case flow rate increases the predicted average cost, again by a larger amount in the last two years.

For comparative purposes the scale and utilisation terms as incorporated into the alternative specifications in equations II and IV in Table 6.4 were also re-estimated for each of the years 1978-79 to 1980-81. The parameter

---

[23]   The 47 diagnostic categories and the additional case mix dimensions were again used to measure output mix, but the individual parameter estimates have not been included here.

[24]   The coefficient on the inverse of the case flow rate in 1978-79 is significant at the 10 per cent level.

Table 6.5. Scale and Utilisation Parameter Estimates obtained using 47 Diagnostic Categories and Additional Case Mix Dimensions, Queensland Public Hospitals, 1977-78 to 1980-81[a]

Year	$\dfrac{365}{CFR}$	$\dfrac{365RBD}{CFR}$	ALS	B	B^2	$\bar{R}^2$	SEE	F
1977-78	4.136 (3.85*)	0.00031 (3.28*)	17.368 (2.42**)	-2.634 (-3.56*)	0.00092 (2.58**)	.77	115.23	7.49*
1978-79	2.883 (1.76)	0.00012 (1.26)	17.970 (3.14*)	-1.0279 (-1.49)	0.00051 (1.49)	.82	121.86	10.17*
1979-80	9.323 (6.32*)	0.00005 (0.35)	35.711 (8.37*)	-0.1465 (-0.16)	0.00042 (0.99)	.92	139.83	24.12*
1980-81	7.371 (4.74*)	0.00010 (0.62)	35.109 (5.21*)	-0.4221 (-0.43)	0.00027 (0.67)	.89	152.21	17.74*

Notes: *   Significant at 1% level.
          **   Significant at 5% level.
         (a)   t-values in parentheses.
Source: Regression results.

estimates for these terms for these years together with the estimates for 1977-78 are presented in Table 6.6. The scale terms, although often having the correct signs indicating a U-shaped long run average cost curve, were always statistically insignificant. In contrast, the utilisation terms had the expected signs every year and were always highly significant.

In the specification incorporating the case flow rate terms, average cost per case is predicted to decline with increasing case flow up to 53.34 cases per bed per year in 1977-78, 51.43 in 1978-79, 52.62 in 1979-80 and 52.74 in 1980-81. As discussed earlier, these figures are well in excess of the case flow rates currently experienced by most hospitals in Queensland.

In the specification including linear terms in occupancy and average length of stay, increases in occupancy with constant average length of stay are predicted to reduce average cost per case in every year, although the magnitude of the coefficient varies from year to year. Increases in average length of stay with constant occupancy (which means reducing the case flow rate) increase predicted average cost per case in every year.

The significant and consistent influence of the utilisation terms in all specifications lends credence to the result that increased case flow, whether accommodated by increased occupancy or reduced length of stay, can be expected to reduce average cost per case. The effects of changing scale with a given case flow rate are, however, less clear.

Table 6.6. Scale and Utilisation Parameter Estimates from Alternative
Specifications using 47 Diagnostic Categories and Additional Case Mix
Dimensions, Queensland Public Hospitals, 1977-78 to 1980-81[a]

Year	CFR	CFR^2	B	B^2	$\bar{R}^2$	SEE	F
1977-78	-30.43 (-7.07*)	0.28527 (5.17*)	-0.04437 (-0.10)	0.00010 (0.31)	.73	124.08	6.41*
1978-79	-22.57 (-5.96*)	0.21943 (5.45*)	-0.13946 (-0.30)	-0.00018 (0.52)	.84	116.98	10.80*
1979-80	-47.38 (-4.86*)	0.45024 (3.96*)	-0.50165 (-0.46)	-0.00133 (1.41)	.72	264.46	5.86*
1980-81	-33.77 (-3.16*)	0.32018 (2.63**)	0.00886 (0.001)	0.00049 (0.64)	.66	272.44	4.73*

Year	OCC	ALS	B	B^2	$\bar{R}^2$	SEE	F
1977-78	-749.43 (-5.71*)	48.46 (7.11*)	-0.3903 (-0.94)	0.00034 (1.06)	.74	122.54	6.60*
1978-79	-408.44 (-2.97*)	30.17 (5.32*)	-0.41548 (-0.84)	0.00051 (1.39)	.83	121.18	10.00*
1979-80	-811.72 (-4.53*)	47.17 (12.22*)	0.48408 (0.71)	0.00025 (0.41)	.89	166.93	16.12*
1980-81	-390.39 (-2.07**)	57.58 (9.86*)	0.68313 (0.99)	-0.00032 (-0.61)	.85	182.53	11.68*

Notes: *   Significant at 1% level.
            **   Significant at 5% level.
            (a) t-values in parentheses.
Source: Regression results.

To gain further insight into the sensitivity of the scale and utilisation
effects to changes in the case mix specification employed, terms in scale and
utilisation were employed in conjunction with the information theory scalar
case mix indexes for the year 1977-78. These results will now be discussed.

6.5.3   Scale and Utilisation with Information Theory Case Mix Indexes—1977-78

Recall from Chapter 5 that two scalar case mix indexes were constructed
using the information theory approach adopted by Evans and Walker (1972),
and that each of these two indexes was constructed using the 18 and 47

diagnostic category classifications. These indexes were then used to replace the 18 and 47 diagnostic categories in the estimated cost functions with the scale and utilisation terms included. This gave the following general formulation:

$$ACC = a_0 + a_1 X + \sum_{i=2}^{11} a_i p_i + r_1 \left(\frac{365}{CFR}\right) + r_2 \left(\frac{365\, RBD}{CFR}\right) \quad \dots (6.20)$$

$$+ r_3 ALS + r_4 B + r_5 B^2$$

where X is the scalar case mix index and p_i is the proportion of the hospital's case load in the ith additional case mix category (see Table 5.5 for the descriptions of these additional categories).

Given that there are two indexes and two diagnostic classifications are used to construct each, there are four separate index numbers for each hospital, labelled X181, X182, X471 and X472. The parameter estimates for each of the scale and utilisation terms in equation (6.20) obtained from the use of each of these four indexes are presented in Table 6.7.[25]

Note first of all that the overall explanatory power of these equations is less than the equivalent equations which employ the disaggregated diagnostic classifications (see Table 6.3). This reinforces the conclusion in Chapter 5 that the more aggregated the case mix classification scheme, the less is its ability to explain interhospital variation in average cost per case. Note also that the poorer performance of the second type of case mix index (X182 and X472) is again evident in the results in Table 6.7 as it was in the results presented in the previous chapter. Taken together, these two outcomes indicate that the additional case mix dimensions along with scale and utilisation do not compensate for the loss of detail in the more aggregated diagnostic classification scheme, and do not compensate for the poor performance of the second type of information theory index.

Turning to the individual parameter estimates in Table 6.7, the signs, magnitude and significance of all the estimates *except* that for the quadratic term in size accord with those found using the more disaggregated diagnostic classification schemes in 1977-78 (see Table 6.3). While the quadratic size term has the same sign and similar magnitude to those found using the 18 and 47 diagnostic categories, it is now insignificantly different

---

[25] The estimates of the constant terms, the case mix index and additional case mix dimension coefficients are not included here.

Table 6.7. Scale and Utilisation Parameter Estimates obtained using Information Theory Case Mix Index and Additional Case Mix Dimensions, Queensland Public Hospitals, 1977-78[a]

Index[b]	$\dfrac{365}{CFR}$	$\dfrac{365RBD}{CFR}$	ALS	B	B^2	$\bar{R}^2$	SEE	F
X181	2.749 (3.71*)	0.00022 (3.18*)	18.416 (3.46*)	-1.411 (-2.56**)	0.00022 (0.78)	.65	141.33	14.93*
X182	2.180 (2.75*)	0.00020 (2.74*)	18.578 (3.27*)	-1.318 (-2.24**)	0.00037 (1.19)	.60	150.76	12.33*
X471	2.352 (3.08*)	0.00023 (3.18*)	19.785 (3.59*)	-1.537 (-2.66*)	0.00026 (0.87)	.63	146.28	13.51*
X472	2.278 (2.81*)	0.00020 (2.68*)	18.383 (3.16*)	-1.214 (-2.01**)	0.00027 (0.86)	.58	154.54	11.42*

Notes: *   Significant at 1% level.
           **   Significant at 5% level.
           (a)   t-values in parentheses. Each equation is estimated with 104 degrees of freedom.
           (b)   Case mix index (see Chapter 5 for explanation).
Source: Regression results.

from zero. Two conclusions emerge. *First*, the important influence of utilisation is again evident. Increasing case flow can again be expected to reduce average cost per case whether this is accommodated by increasing occupancy or reducing length of stay. *Second*, the evidence supporting a U-shaped long run average cost curve in 1977-78 presented earlier in this chapter is weakened. The size terms suggest only economies of scale as the quadratic size term is insignificant. Taking this in conjunction with the results presented in Section 6.5.2 for other years (see Table 6.5), the results originally obtained pertaining to long run cost behaviour do not appear to be robust.

For comparative purposes again, the two alternative specifications given by equations II and IV in Table 6.4 were re-estimated using the information theory indexes in place of the 47 diagnostic category classification scheme. The parameter estimates for the scale and utilisation terms arising from these specifications are presented in Table 6.8.[26] These estimates can be compared with those obtained when the 47 diagnostic categories were adopted as given in Table 6.6.

---

[26] The remaining parameter estimates from these specifications are not presented here.

Table 6.8. Scale and Utilisation Parameter Estimates from Alternative Specifications using Information Theory Case Mix Indexes and Additional Case Mix Dimensions, Queensland Public Hospitals, 1977-78[a]

Index[b]	CFR	CFR^2	B	B^2	$\bar{R}^2$	SEE	F
X181	-27.903 (-7.75*)	0.26847 (5.67*)	0.10701 (0.33)	-0.00018 (-0.71)	.65	141.86	15.69*
X182	-25.888 (-6.87*)	0.24518 (4.94*)	0.02993 (0.09)	-0.00001 (0.04)	.62	147.61	13.69*
X471	-26.868 (-7.21*)	0.25233 (5.13*)	0.04358 (0.13)	-0.00016 (-0.59)	.68	146.88	14.16*
X472	-26.267 (-6.77*)	0.25084 (4.90*)	0.15387 (0.44)	-0.00010 (-0.35)	.60	151.86	12.80*

Index[b]	OCC	ALS	B	B^2	$\bar{R}^2$	SEE	F
X181	-707.36 (-6.93*)	42.531 (8.78*)	-0.12354 (-0.40)	0.00001 (0.04)	.67	137.92	17.00*
X182	-734.95 (-7.19*)	41.479 (8.59*)	-0.27916 (-0.89)	0.00026 (1.01)	.67	137.72	17.07*
X471	-722.02 (-7.02*)	43.898 (8.96*)	-0.23158 (-0.74)	0.00003 (0.14)	.66	138.73	16.72*
X472	-734.11 (-6.91*)	41.408 (8.25*)	-0.15938 (-0.49)	0.00014 (0.53)	.64	143.03	15.32*

Notes: *   Significant at 1% level.
(a) t-values in parentheses. Each equation is estimated with 104 degrees of freedom.
(b) Case mix index (see Chapter 5 for explanation).
Source: Regression results.

Before discussing the individual parameter estimates, it is interesting to note again that the overall explanatory power of these equations is smaller compared with those using a more disaggregated diagnostic classification scheme. Further, the second type of information theory index (X182 and X472) generally records poorer performance again.

Considering first the case flow rate specification, the individual parameter estimates paint a very similar picture of hospital cost behaviour. This is true as between the four sets of estimates in Table 6.8 and in comparison with the estimates in Table 6.6. The case flow rate terms invariably have the expected sign and are always highly significant. Regardless of which case mix index is used, average cost per case is predicted to decline with increases in case flow up to a case flow rate of about 52 to 53 cases per bed per year. This result is virtually identical to that obtained earlier. Also, the size terms are both insignificant and have implausible signs in every equation, again casting doubt on the presence of any scale effects.

Considering the occupancy/average length of stay specification, the utilisation terms are again highly significant and have the expected sign, and compare well with the estimates in Table 6.6. For a given length of stay, higher occupancy is predicted to reduce average cost per case while increases in average length of stay with given occupancy will increase average cost per case. The size terms lack significance in every equation, and while their signs are plausible, the implied cost minimising size varies greatly between equations because of the variability in the magnitudes of the coefficients.[27]

This concludes our discussion of the evidence produced in this study on the effects of scale and utilisation on average cost per case.[28] Before drawing the main findings together to conclude this chapter, it remains to discuss briefly one outstanding matter—the effect of input price differences between hospitals.

---

[27] The results of this section accord with those obtained by others using the information theory indexes, e.g. Evans and Walker (1972) and Hardwick (1976). In comparing results care must be exercised in interpreting the coefficients. For example, Hardwick includes occupancy and the case flow rate as measures of utilisation, suppressing average length of stay. The resulting *positive* coefficient is consistent with the *negative* coefficient obtained here, however, because in her study the coefficient relates to a change in occupancy with constant case flow and hence involves an equal proportionate change in average length of stay. The positive coefficient then indicates that increasing occupancy and average length of stay in the same proportion will increase average cost per case, the same result as obtained here. See Hardwick (1976, p.53) for a discussion of the effects of such changes in her specification.

[28] It should be noted that the results presented in this chapter should not suffer greatly from the potential bias suggested by Bays (1980) arising from the exclusion of the cost of physician input from the cost data. As pointed out in Chapter 4, Queensland public hospitals employ salaried medical staff to treat patients in public wards and such salaries are included in the cost data at least as far as public patients are concerned. The only physician costs which are not included are those incurred by intermediate and private patients who pay their doctors on a fee-for-service basis. Given that about 75 per cent of patients in public hospitals are public patients (see Table 5.5) most physician costs have been included.

6.5.4   Input Price Differences

As discussed in Chapter 2, the cost function, which can be derived as the dual of the underlying production function, expresses total cost as a function of output levels and input prices. If all firms pay the same input prices, this can be ignored since input prices cannot be a source of variation in costs between firms in this case. If, however, input prices vary between firms, allowance should be made for this.

In Queensland, hospitals outside the south-east corner of the State pay higher per unit prices for labour for one or more of the following reasons:

- locality allowances—payable to hospital managers and full-time medical staff located in towns deemed to be disadvantaged by a higher cost of living;

- district allowances—payable to most other staff outside the Southern Division of the Eastern District; and

- an additional week's leave—allowable to managerial, medical and clerical staff in certain parts of the State.

Per unit input prices of other inputs may also vary between regions in the State, although differences in wage rates are likely to be the most important since wages and salaries account for over 70 per cent of total hospital maintenance costs in the State.

Subject to the problem of input substitution which may have occurred in response to factor price differences (see Section 6.2.3), it was decided to estimate the extra costs incurred by hospitals which had to pay locality and district allowances and grant an extra week's leave. This was done by ascertaining the number of staff in each category eligible for these extra emoluments in 1977-78 and using these in conjunction with the allowances to estimate the total extra payments incurred. In 1977-78, locality allowances ranged up to $47.50 per fortnight and district allowances up to $6.50 per fortnight. The estimate of the total extra payments so calculated was $446,309—about 0.17 per cent of total maintenance costs for the year, or about $1.35 per case treated. The unweighted State mean cost per case in 1977-78 was $546.83 (see Table 6.1).

Another estimate of this total was produced by the Queensland Department of Health for 1978-79 in its submission to the Commonwealth Grants Commission. This estimate amounted to $693,855. Even without allowing for inflation, this amounts to only 0.27 per cent of total maintenance costs in 1977-78, or about $2.10 per case treated.

Given these results it was decided that input price differences were unlikely to be an important source of interhospital cost variation in Queensland. While input prices are not strictly constant across the State, the variation does seem quite small. As such, the inaccuracy introduced into the results by ignoring input price differences can be expected to be minimal.

6.6   Summary and Conclusions

This chapter has been concerned primarily with estimating the effects of scale and utilisation on average cost per case. Ascertaining the presence or otherwise of economies of scale is a difficult matter not least because of the problems associated with measuring capital input. The use of a one-dimensional measure of hospital capacity such as beds represents a substantial over-simplification of the problem, effectively assuming that all beds are homogeneous and hence are perfectly substitutable. Further, it may fail to represent adequately differences in the other kinds of capital employed by a hospital.

In addition to this, scale economies are not the only consideration in determining the optimal size and configuration of a hospital system. Penalty costs associated with increasing the probability of overcrowding also need to be considered, as do the travel costs associated with different locations of hospitals. Be that as it may, and bearing in mind the limitations mentioned above, findings on economies of scale can be a useful input into policy-making concerning hospitals.

In examining the effects of scale on costs, it is necessary to distinguish between the effects of changes in the utilisation of any given level of capacity (short run cost behaviour) and changes in the level of capacity or scale of plant (long run cost behaviour). A measure of capacity utilisation is the case flow rate—the number of cases treated per bed per year—which in turn is related to occupancy and average length of stay. It was argued that a specification of the cost function which allowed for non-linearity between average cost per case and case flow was theoretically more defensible and a 'preferred' specification was developed along these lines. For comparative purposes, two other specifications were also examined, one incorporating linear and quadratic terms in the case flow rate and the other incorporating linear terms in occupancy and average length of stay. Non-linearity in the average cost/size relationship was allowed for in all specifications by using linear and quadratic terms in beds.

Three major sets of results have been presented. *First*, using the 18 and 47 diagnostic category classifications along with additional case mix dimensions as the case mix measure, the specifications were estimated using data for the year 1977-78. *Second*, to see if the results so generated could be replicated, the three specifications using only the 47 diagnostic categories and other case mix dimensions were re-estimated using data for each of the years 1978-79 to 1980-81. *Third*, the three specifications were re-estimated for 1977-78 using the information theory indexes in place of the 18 and 47 diagnostic categories.

The first major set of results with the 'preferred' specification gave significant results for both short run and long run cost behaviour. In the short run, increased case flow was predicted to reduce average cost per case whether this was accommodated by increased occupancy or reduced length of stay, although the latter could be expected to reduce average cost by more than the former. The marginal cost of accommodating an extra patient by reducing average length of stay was estimated to be 22 per cent of average cost compared with a marginal cost equal to 50 per cent of average cost if, instead, occupancy was increased. An interaction between case flow and scale was also detected, indicating that increases in the case flow rate could be expected to reduce average costs by more in larger hospitals. In the long run, a U-shaped average cost curve was detected with the cost-minimising size being positively related to the case flow rate. A hospital with the mean case mix proportions, average length of stay and case flow was predicted to minimise average cost per case at a size of 469 beds. The two alternative specifications confirmed the pattern of short run cost behaviour detected here but did not indicate economies or diseconomies of scale in the long run.

The second major set of results, relating to cost behaviour in three subsequent years, confirmed the pattern of short run cost behaviour found in 1977-78 with the exception of the interaction between case flow and size. This was true in all three specifications. No evidence of significant economies or diseconomies of scale was found in any specification.

The third major set of results again confirmed the pattern of short run cost behaviour between average cost and case flow in 1977-78 for all specifications, but only in the 'preferred' specification was any evidence of economies of scale produced, and here the previously found U-shape of the long run average cost curve was not confirmed. The alternative specifications produced no evidence of economies or diseconomies of scale.

To summarise, the evidence that increasing capacity utilisation will reduce average cost per case is overwhelming, arising in every specification in every year. This confirms what Richardson and Wallace (1983, p.142) have suggested is "the chief expected source of improved hospital efficiency

—increased occupancy rate ... ". The evidence of any economies or diseconomies of scale is much weaker, with the patterns of long run cost behaviour being neither consistent nor significant across different specifications or years.

Finally, some evidence on input price differences between hospitals was presented. While input prices are not constant across the sample, they are nearly so as evidenced by the quite small reduction in overall average cost per case if the cost data are purged of input price variations (specifically variation in the price of labour). Consequently it was argued that the inaccuracies arising from an assumption that input prices are constant would be minimal and could be ignored.

7

A COMPARISON OF THE COSTS OF TEACHING

AND NON-TEACHING PUBLIC HOSPITALS

IN QUEENSLAND

7.1   Introduction

So far the empirical work in this study has failed to take into account
another output commonly produced by hospitals—teaching. As will be seen
in Section 7.2, this activity has certainly not been ignored in other studies of
hospital costs. Indeed, an attempt has even been made to construct a specific
theoretical model of the teaching hospital (see Dusansky and Kalman 1974).
The purpose of this chapter is to fill this gap in the empirical analysis
undertaken up to this point.

This and the remaining two chapters in Part B of this book share the
common characteristic of analysing the impact of differences between two
groups of hospitals on hospital costs. In this chapter, the sample of 121
Queensland public hospitals is effectively split into two groups on the basis
of the presence or absence of a teaching program. In Chapter 8, some private
hospitals are included in the sample and the differences between the two

groups—public and private—are analysed. In Chapter 9, the initial sample is expanded to include New South Wales public hospitals, the objective being to analyse the differences between public hospitals in the two States.

The chapter comprises a discussion of the relationship between teaching and hospital costs and of the evidence to date (Section 7.2), a documentation of the differences in case mix, scale and utilisation between teaching and non-teaching hospitals in the sample (Section 7.3) and an analysis of the independent influence of teaching status on hospital costs (Section 7.4). A summary and conclusions are provided in Section 7.5.

7.2   Theory and Specification

7.2.1   The Nexus between Teaching and Hospital Costs

The effect of a hospital's teaching activities on its costs of production depends upon whether teaching is jointly produced with the other hospital outputs in fixed proportions. In this extreme case, and with no separable costs, teaching could have no impact on a hospital's costs—eliminating teaching would not change the costs incurred. This is, however, an unlikely occurrence because it would imply that all hospitals could mount teaching programs at no extra cost.

A more realistic possibility is where teaching and the other hospital outputs are produced jointly in variable proportions and some portion of the hospital's costs incurred in providing teaching is incurred in common with the production of other outputs. The problem then becomes one of ascertaining the separable costs of teaching—the costs which could be avoided if teaching were not undertaken.

It is of course possible, although again unlikely, that the production of teaching and the other hospital outputs could be characterised by non-jointness. This implies that the costs of producing the teaching output and the other hospital outputs are independent of whether these outputs are produced by one combined process or two separate processes. All teaching costs would be separable and, if estimated, could be deducted from the costs of producing the other outputs in the same way that outpatient cost estimates have been deducted to give a hospital's inpatient costs.

If teaching is jointly produced then the common costs cannot be allocated between the outputs in any economically meaningful way. In commenting on 'time and motion' studies which have attempted to separate out the time devoted to teaching in hospitals, Sloan, Feldman and Steinwald

(1983, pp.1-2) argue that "Patient care, teaching, and research are jointly produced in teaching hospitals, and there is no unambiguous way to identify the amount of time devoted to each". In the words of Hadley (1983, p.77), "the jointness-in-production of education and patient care make any accounting approach to allocating costs between education and patient care essentially arbitrary".

In comparing costs in teaching and non-teaching hospitals, Sloan, *et al.* (1983, p.9) identify three important criteria which they argue should be fulfilled. *First*, the hospital cost data should include costs of medical staff. *Second*, the sample should include a number of hospitals and the analysis should identify where *within* a hospital, i.e. in which departments or wards, teaching has its major impact on costs. *Third*, case mix and other factors affecting costs must be taken into account. This third point is particularly important. Teaching hospitals may treat a more expensive mix of cases, and if this case mix difference is not adjusted for, these higher costs may be incorrectly ascribed as being the separable costs of teaching.

The evidence on the magnitude of the impact of teaching on hospital costs is mixed, even from studies which control for case mix variations. Frick, Martin and Shwartz (1985) reported the results of a comparison of 11 teaching hospitals and 20 non-teaching hospitals in New York state. Case mix differences were examined in both the 19 Major Diagnostic Groups from which the Diagnosis Related Groups (DRGs) were first derived, and the 30 highest volume DRGs. Estimates of the direct costs of teaching programs, e.g. salaries of residents and interns, were also available. The average cost per case in the teaching hospitals was $2,734, 68 per cent higher than the average cost per case of $1,625 in non-teaching hospitals (maternity, newborn and mental disorder DRGs excluded). This difference was then sourced to either differences in case mix composition or differences in the average cost of treating particular case types. The result: "Most of the overall difference in resource use between teaching and nonteaching hospitals is attributable to differences in average cost per case within DRGs, rather than case mix differences" (Frick, *et al.* 1985, p.290). Only 23 per cent of the $1,109 difference was explained by case mix differences. A similar result was found when the estimates of direct teaching costs were excluded from the cost data.

What, then, accounts for the cost differences within DRGs between teaching and non-teaching hospitals? Frick, *et al.* (1985, p.292) suggest four possibilities. *First*, there may be indirect teaching costs associated with the learning process.[1] *Second*, teaching hospitals may be treating more complex

---

[1]   Patients in teaching hospitals may receive more ancillary services, such as laboratory tests and X-rays, because of the teaching function. See Busby, Leming and Olson

or severe cases within any given DRG.[2] *Third*, teaching hospitals may be providing a higher quality of care in terms of patient outcomes. *Finally*, teaching hospitals may simply be less efficient.

A significant residual effect of teaching status even after adjustment for differences in case mix and other factors has also been found in other studies such as those by Pauly (1978), Culyer, Wiseman, Drummond and West (1978), Watts and Klastorin (1980), Sloan and Steinwald (1980), Jones (1985) and Cameron (1985). Distinguishing between teaching and research, Sloan and Becker (1981) found that the effect of teaching was reduced and the dummy variable identifying the presence of funded medical reserach was significant.

Where the results of these studies differ, however, is with respect to the *magnitude* of the effect of teaching. Frick, *et al.* (1985), for instance, suggest that case mix accounts for only about one-quarter of a 68 per cent difference in average cost per case between teaching and non-teaching hospitals, an estimate in line with that produced by Culyer, *et al.* (1978, p.78). Yet a study by Sloan, *et al.* (1983) finds the following:

> Holding casemix and other factors constant greatly reduces the difference attributable to teaching. Non-physician expense in medical school-affiliated, non-COTH [Council of Teaching Hospitals] hospitals is less than 10 per cent higher on average, ceteris paribus, than in non-teaching hospitals; the difference is *at most* 20 per cent for COTH hospitals. The magnitude of these teaching effects on hospital costliness is in line with some previous estimates from multivariate cost analysis [e.g. Sloan and Steinwald (1980)], but is far lower than many discussions of this subject have implied (p.24, emphasis in original).

Horn (1983) also found that, after adjustment for severity of illness, the cost differences between major teaching hospitals and other community hospitals either disappear or become much smaller. Robinson and Luft (1985, p.153) conclude that "Bed size, medical school affiliation, and the ratio of housestaff to hospital beds all play smaller roles in explaining differences in hospital costs once case mix is directly controlled for". Cameron (1985), after adjusting for case mix and including full physician

---

(1972), Schroeder and O'Leary (1977), Martz and Ptakowski (1978) and Cameron (1985) for evidence of this.

[2]   Becker and Steinwald (1981) have produced evidence that case mix complexity is positively associated with the level of teaching commitment.

costs in hospital costs, found that "university hospitals were 26 per cent more costly than nonteaching hospitals for the same mix of patients, whereas major teaching hospitals were 10 per cent more costly, and minor teaching hospitals 8 per cent more costly" (p.1236). Garber, Fuchs and Silverman (1984) found that, within one hospital, patients admitted by university faculty physicians were 10.8 per cent more costly than those admitted by community service physicians, but a more recent study in the same hospital by Jones (1985) found a larger difference. Using more severity of illness control variables, Jones found the cost of treating faculty service patients exceeded that of treating community service patients by 26 and 18 per cent before and after omitting death and transfer cases.

The effect of teaching has also been found to vary considerably between departments in a hospital. Sloan, *et al.* (1983, p.25) found that "Part of the cost differential is attributable to higher ancillary costs, but also teaching institutions have higher costs on the non-clinical side in dietary, plant operations, and housekeeping departments". In a detailed study of the effects of teaching on the costs of a radiology department, Hosek and Palmer (1983) found that the costs of some outputs were actually lower in teaching hospitals—" ... a major result is that for several outputs there appear to be cost savings associated with teaching in VA [Veterans Administration] radiology departments" (p.45). Their model suggests that the cost savings arose because of substitution of students for physicians. Culyer, *et al.* (1978) have also produced evidence of the differential effects of teaching on departmental costs.

In summary, the overseas evidence generally supports the hypothesis that teaching does affect hospital costs, or that there are positive separable costs associated with teaching in hospitals. Different studies have produced different estimates of the magnitude of this effect, although it does seem that the effect is greater in hospitals which have a larger teaching commitment. The effect of teaching also varies by department.

The only attempt in Australia to estimate the impact of teaching on hospital costs using multivariate techniques was that by the Health Commission of New South Wales (1978). Two variables—the number of staff designated as nurse educators, and a teaching/non-teaching dummy variable—were included in an average cost per case equation along with measures of case mix, size and utilisation. Both variables had significant coefficients indicating higher average costs per case in teaching hospitals.

In a paper on hospital staffing and hospital costs, Andrew (1976) compared average costs per day in teaching hospitals associated with Monash University and large non-teaching metropolitan hospitals over the period 1964-74. While bed day costs were much higher in the teaching hospitals (about 45 per cent greater in 1974-75), Andrew could find no evidence from this study or from a more detailed study of indirect teaching costs at one of the teaching hospitals (see Andrew and Nehrmann 1977) that the higher costs could be attributed to undergraduate teaching.[3] In concluding the latter study, the authors suggest five possible sources of the teaching/non-teaching hospital cost differential (Andrew and Nehrmann 1977, pp.825-6). *First*, teaching hospitals attract well qualified doctors who in turn can exert pressure for expenditure on the latest developments in medicine. *Second*, teaching hospitals have more doctors per bed. *Third*, teaching hospitals have research with its associated indirect costs. *Fourth*, teaching hospitals have a large and growing component of postgraduate education. *Finally*, there could be a differential in administrative, nursing and paramedical costs not captured by their study.

This analysis, however, can only be taken as suggestive because it makes no adjustment for differences in case mix between the hospitals, and because of its reliance on average cost per day rather than per case as a basis for making cost comparisons.

In its report on expansion of medical education, the Committee on Medical Schools (1973) considered briefly the causes of the higher average costs per day in teaching hospitals. The Committee suggested two kinds of costs incurred by a teaching hospital as a result of training medical students (Committee on Medical Schools, 1973, p.23). *First*, there are costs (such as cleaning, power and administration) of operating areas of the hospital occupied solely by university staff and students. *Second*, there are additional costs incurred in areas such as pathology, anaesthetics, radiology and so on which arise as a result of medical teaching. These latter costs, the indirect costs of teaching, were considered difficult to isolate. However, quoting the estimate provided in the Second Report of the Committee on Teaching Costs of Medical Hospitals in 1965 that undergraduate teaching costs amount to about four per cent of a hospital's expenditure, the Committee decided that

> the evidence available suggests that the teaching of medical students itself does not constitute a major part of the additional costs of running a teaching hospital, these additional costs being principally associated with the provision of specialist services by highly qualified staff who engage in research and postgraduate training in addition to their responsibilities for patient care, and

---

3   It should be borne in mind that, as argued in detail in Chapter 3, cost comparisons based on average cost per *day* are not really considering average cost per unit of output since the case is a more appropriate unit of output than the day.

with the level of other services provided by those activities. (Committee on Medical Schools, 1973, p.23).

Again, however, it must be noted that the Committee did not explicitly address the question of case mix differences between teaching and non-teaching hospitals, and was again concerned with average cost per day comparisons.

In examining teaching and hospital costs in Australia, it must be borne in mind that the institutional arrangements in this country for the funding of medical education are such that the additional staffing costs associated with teaching hospitals are borne primarily by the university medical schools. As such, the salaries of the academics are funded by the universities and not by the hospital. Under these circumstances, teaching may well result in only a small increase in hospital costs. This does not, of course, mean that teaching *per se* is a low cost activity but that the costs of teaching are borne to some degree by an institution other than the hospital and hence will not show up in the hospital's accounts.[4]

7.2.2 Teaching Output and the Specification of the Cost Function

In attempting to assess the impact of teaching on hospital costs, one immediately comes up against the problem of defining and measuring teaching output. But as Kershaw (1969, p.309) says, "Educational output ... is a slippery notion indeed". A full treatment of this issue lies outside the scope of this study,[5] but one critical issue must be mentioned. Whatever definition and measure of output is adopted, it should not be input-related. This is for the obvious reason that, if output is defined in terms of inputs, no meaningful measures of productivity can be developed

---

[4] Andrew and Nehrmann (1977, p.823) offer the following comment on this situation compared with that in the United States. "The somewhat meagre literature from the United States is largely irrelevant to our scene because, in Australia, the medical schools are formed separately, and the funds expended on teaching and research, in the teaching hospitals identifiable, are known. These are direct costs which in America are usually inextricably mixed in total hospital budgets, frequently university owned and operated." The authors provide some data on the costs of university medical schools in Table 1 of their paper.

[5] For a discussion of production and cost functions in education, see Cohn (1979, Ch.8) and Culyer (1980, Ch.9). Further references can be found in Blaug (1978).

and the cost function becomes nothing other than a relationship between costs and inputs.

In the context of the teaching hospital, it is important to avoid input-related measures of teaching output such as the number of doctors (or equivalent full-time doctors) involved in teaching activities. One particular measure of teaching output which has been subject to criticism is the number of students. Hosek and Palmer (1983) argue convincingly that students, along with doctors, are inputs into the production function. If the number of students is entered into a cost function as a measure of output and the coefficient is found to be positive, the conclusion is that teaching increases hospital costs. But this makes no allowance for the fact that students may actually be substituted for doctors in the performance of various tasks so that more students result in lower costs.

Perhaps the most common approach to assessing the impact of teaching using multivariate analysis is to incorporate a dummy variable to indicate the presence or absence of teaching activity. A shortcoming of this approach is that it makes no allowance for variations in the *level* of any particular kind of teaching activity which is taking place. The presence of a particular type of teaching program is assumed to result in a uniform change in average and total costs for all hospitals pursuing the program. It is, of course, possible to allow for the presence of more than one type of program, or for different types of teaching hospital, by the use of additional dummy variables (see, for example, Sloan and Steinwald 1980). However, this still does not allow for variations of activity *within* any particular teaching classification.

In the absence of any better measure of teaching output, the dummy variable approach has been adopted in this study. Dummy variables reflecting the presence or absence of a number of different types of teaching program in Queensland public hospitals (to be discussed in the next section) have been used in the specifications of the average cost function discussed in Chapters 5 and 6. This then produces some insight into whether teaching has any effect on costs after allowing for differences in case mix, scale and utilisation.

7.3   Differences Between Teaching and Non-Teaching Hospitals

7.3.1   The Teaching/Non-Teaching Dichotomy

Traditionally the term 'teaching hospital' refers to a hospital which is used for training students to become doctors and, in order to carry out this task, has an affiliation with a university medical school. "The teaching hospitals associated with a university medical school are often situated at considerable distances from the university campus ... The association between a university and a teaching hospital may be the subject of a formal agreement between the two bodies although this is not always the case" (Committee on Medical Schools 1973, pp.16-17). In 1977-78, eight hospitals in Queensland were teaching hospitals in this sense.

But the training of medical students is not the only teaching carried out by hospitals. Until the late 1980s in Australia, nurse education was also carried out in a number of hospitals.[6] To carry out nurse education in 1977-78, a hospital must have been recognised as a Training School by The Nurses Registration Board of Queensland for the purposes of the *Nursing Act* 1976. Training Schools could be for General Nurses (3 year course), Midwifery Nurses, Child Health Nurses, Psychiatric Nurses, and Enrolled Nurses—General (1 year course). Of these, General Nurse and Enrolled Nurse—General courses accounted for the largest number of training schools and so were adopted as two further bases of classification of teaching hospitals in this study. Of the 121 hospitals in the sample, 27 were recognised Training Schools for General Nurses and 53 were recognised Training Schools for Enrolled Nurses—General.[7]

The remainder of this section is concerned with presenting some data on the differences between teaching and non-teaching hospitals classified on each of the three bases just discussed.

7.3.2   Cost/Volume Differences

Using data for 1977-78, the unweighted means of a number of cost and volume variables were computed for the hospitals in the teaching/non-teaching sub-samples. The results are presented in Table 7.1. Considering first the dichotomy based on medical school affiliation, it can be seen that, on average, teaching hospitals have a cost per case which is over $210 or just over 40 per cent greater than that in non-teaching hospitals. With only a slight difference in average length of stay, most of this difference in cost per

---

6   Since then, nurse education has been transferred to colleges of advanced education and universities. Palmer and Short (1994, pp.136-8) provide a discussion of this transfer.

7   The two types of courses are not mutually exclusive. Some hospitals are recognised Training Schools for both courses and also have medical school affiliation.

Table 7.1. Cost/Volume Differences between Teaching and Non-Teaching Hospitals, Queensland Public Hospitals, 1977-78[a]

| | Medical School Affiliation | | | | | |
| | Teaching (n=8) | | | Non-Teaching (n=113) | | |
	Mean	Min.	Max.	Mean	Min.	Max.
Av. Cost per Case ($)	745.97	450.14	1361.17	532.73	34.71	1284.74
Av. Cost per Day ($)	107.02	86.90	136.03	78.02	16.71	220.09
Average Length of Stay	7.23	3.31	13.52	7.46	1.00	19.48
Occupancy	.72	.51	1.075	.41	.006	.84
Case Flow Rate	41.44	17.24	66.25	22.04	1.50	77.70
Inpatients	16780	4854	39907	1730	14	17243
Beds	496	80	1234	70	2	613

| | General Nurse (3 year) Course | | | | | |
| | Teaching (n=27) | | | Non-Teaching (n=94) | | |
	Mean	Min.	Max.	Mean	Min.	Max.
Av. Cost per Case ($)	570.15	355.90	809.19	540.13	34.71	1361.17
Av. Cost per Day ($)	74.04	48.35	105.44	81.63	16.71	220.09
Average Length of Stay	7.89	5.22	11.75	7.32	1.00	19.48
Occupancy	.58	.35	.83	.39	.006	1.075
Case Flow Rate	28.17	16.55	46.36	21.93	1.50	77.70
Inpatients	8299	1274	39907	1124	14	11434
Beds	275	76	1234	48	2	609

| | Enrolled Nurse—General (1 year) Course | | | | | |
| | Teaching (n=53) | | | Non-Teaching (n=68) | | |
	Mean	Min.	Max.	Mean	Min.	Max.
Av. Cost per Case ($)	592.89	336.09	1361.17	510.93	34.71	1233.64
Av. Cost per Day ($)	71.47	34.80	128.45	86.54	16.71	220.09
Average Length of Stay	8.74	4.27	19.48	6.44	1.00	18.37
Occupancy	.51	.19	.83	.37	.006	1.075
Case Flow Rate	23.55	6.08	46.36	23.15	1.50	77.70
Inpatients	4922	225	39907	1013	14	11434
Beds	177	22	1234	37	2	356

Note: (a) Means are unweighted means.
Source: Queensland Hospital Finance Data.

case is reflected in the difference in average cost per day.[8] The non-teaching hospitals encompass a much wider range of values of these variables,

---

[8] Note that, because these are unweighted means, average cost per case is not equal to the product of average cost per day and average length of stay.

however, with the maximum average cost per case in the non-teaching sub-sample ($1,284.74) being almost as high as that in the teaching sub-sample ($1,361.17).

Occupancy rates in the teaching hospitals are, on average, also substantially greater than in the non-teaching hospitals (0.72 compared to 0.41) with minimum occupancy in the teaching sub-sample being 0.51. The case flow rate is, on average, nearly 90 per cent greater in teaching hospitals, such hospitals also treating a substantially greater number of inpatients and being much larger in size. The general picture which emerges here is not surprising. The hospitals with medical school affiliation are the major metropolitan hospitals which are, on average, larger in size and have higher utilisation rates and costs.

These differences are much less in the other two classifications of teaching/non-teaching hospitals. Those hospitals which are recognised Training Schools for General Nurses have a mean cost per case only $30 or 5.5 per cent in excess of that in the non-teaching hospitals. Again, the non-teaching sub-sample encompasses institutions with a much wider range of values for the teaching sub-sample. Occupancy and case flow rates and the number of inpatients and beds are all greater on average in the teaching group although the differences are not as stark as in the medical school affiliation categorisation.

Turning to the Enrolled Nurse—General classification, average cost per case here is about $82 or 16 per cent greater in the teaching hospitals. While average cost per day is lower, average length of stay is about 36 per cent greater in the teaching group. Occupancy rates are again greater in the teaching sub-sample but the differential is narrower than in the previous two classifications. Case flow rates are similar in the two groups so the higher occupancy and average length of stay almost 'cancel out' in their effect on case flow. There is again a difference in the number of inpatients treated and size (both larger in the teaching group) but the difference is again less than in the other two classifications.

Clearly there are differences in the cost/volume characteristics of teaching and non-teaching hospitals, with the most marked differences being between hospitals with and without medical school affiliation, followed by differences between hospitals with and without Training Schools for General Nurses. But to what extent are these differences due to teaching status? The differences may in part be explained by the differences in size and utilisation, although the results of the previous chapter would suggest that hospitals with higher occupancy and case flow rates and more beds would have a *lower* average cost per case for any *given* case mix. This brings us to the next aspect of differences in the two types of hospital—differences in case mix or output composition.

7.3.3   Case Mix Differences—18 and 47 Diagnostic Categories

The unweighted mean case mix proportions in each of the 18 and 47 diagnostic categories for the teaching and non-teaching sub-samples are presented in Tables 7.2 and 7.3 respectively. Considering first the teaching/non-teaching classification based upon *medical school affiliation* in each of these two Tables, the following points emerge.

- In the 18 diagnostic category classification, teaching hospitals have over twice the proportion of cases compared to non-teaching hospitals in the following categories:

Diagnostic Category	*Complexity Ranking based on type 1 information theory index (see Table 5.16)*
2 Neoplasms	3
11 Complications of Pregnancy, Childbirth & Puerperium	6
14 Congenital Anomalies	2
15 Causes of Perinatal Morbidity & Mortality	1

  When viewed in conjunction with the complexity measures based on the information theory index developed in Chapter 5, this suggests that teaching hospitals tend to specialise in the treatment of the more complex case types.

- These differences are also evident in the more disaggregated 47 diagnostic category classification, where teaching hospitals have over twice the proportion of cases in the following categories:

Table 7.2. Differences in Case Mix Proportions Between Teaching and Non-Teaching Hospitals, 18 Diagnostic Categories, Queensland Public Hospitals, 1977-78(a)

No.	Diagnostic Category	Medical School Affiliation			General Nurse (3yr)			Enrolled Nurse—Gen.		
		T (n=8)	NT (n=113)	Diff. (%)	T (n=27)	NT (n=94)	Diff. (%)	T (n=53)	NT (n=68)	Diff. (%)
1	Infectious & Parasitic Diseases	.0234	.0514	-54.5	.0325	.0545	-40.4	.0417	.0557	-25.1
2	Neoplasms	.0624	.0174	258.6	.0438	.0136	222.1	.0314	.0117	168.4
3	Endocrine, Nutritional, Metabolic	.0145	.0160	-9.4	.0159	.0159	0.0	.0165	.0154	7.1
4	Blood	.0051	.0042	21.4	.0060	.0038	57.9	.0048	.0038	26.3
5	Mental Disorders	.0389	.0359	8.4	.0337	.0368	-8.4	.0382	.0345	10.7
6	Nervous System	.0533	.0378	41.0	.0387	.0389	-0.5	.0383	.0392	-2.3
7	Circulatory System	.0710	.0788	-9.9	.0848	.0764	11.0	.0920	.0676	36.1
8	Respiratory System	.0991	.1477	-32.9	.0980	.1579	-37.9	.1240	.1605	-22.7
9	Digestive System	.0525	.0640	-18.0	.0900	.0555	62.2	.0785	.0513	53.0
10	Genito-Urinary System	.0696	.0520	33.8	.0926	.0418	121.5	.0662	.0429	54.3
11	Complications of Pregnancy, Childbirth & Puerperium	.2324	.1139	104.0	.1323	.1187	11.5	.1105	.1305	-15.3
12	Skin & Subcutaneous Tissue	.0139	.0282	-50.7	.0209	.0290	-27.9	.0231	.0305	-24.3
13	Musculoskeletal System	.0354	.0248	42.7	.0339	.0231	46.8	.0315	.0208	51.4
14	Congenital Anomalies	.0267	.0027	888.9	.0049	.0041	19.5	.0060	.0029	106.9
15	Causes of Perinatal Morbidity & Mortality	.0147	.0028	425.0	.0045	.0033	36.4	.0032	.0039	-17.9
16	Symptoms & ill-defined	.0511	.1349	-62.1	.0916	.1402	-34.7	.1134	.1418	-20.0
17	Accidents, Poisonings, Violence	.1018	.1584	-35.7	.1351	.1603	-15.7	.1471	.1605	-8.3
18	Supplementary Classifications	.0339	.0291	16.5	.0409	.0262	56.1	.0336	.0262	28.2

Note: (a) Proportions are unweighted means. T = teaching; NT = non-teaching; Diff. = difference = (T-NT)/NT.
Source: Queensland Hospital Morbidity Data.

Table 7.3. Differences in Case Mix Proportions Between Teaching and Non-Teaching Hospitals, 47 Diagnostic Categories, Queensland Public Hospitals, 1977-78(a)

No	Diagnostic Category	Medical School Affiliation			General Nurse (3yr)			Enrolled Nurse—Gen.		
		T (n=8)	NT (n=113)	Diff. (%)	T (n=27)	NT (n=94)	Diff. (%)	T (n=53)	NT (n=68)	Diff. (%)
1	Investigations, Procedures, Healthy	.0339	.0291	16.5	.0409	.0262	56.1	.0336	.0262	-20.6
2	Infectious & Parasitic	.0155	.0218	-28.9	.0174	.0225	-22.7	.0208	.0218	-4.6
3	Enteritis, Diarrhoeal Disease	.0079	.0297	-73.4	.0150	.0320	-53.1	.0209	.0339	-38.3
4	Malignant Neoplasms	.0518	.0132	292.4	.0338	.0106	218.9	.0243	.0092	164.1
5	Benign Neoplasms	.0106	.0041	158.5	.0100	.0030	233.3	.0071	.0026	173.1
6	Endocrine & Metabolic	.0145	.0160	-9.4	.0159	.0159	0.0	.0165	.0154	7.1
7	Blood	.0051	.0042	21.4	.0060	.0038	57.9	.0048	.0038	26.3
8	Psychiatric	.0389	.0359	8.4	.0337	.0368	-8.4	.0382	.0345	10.7
9	Other CNS & Nerves	.0219	.0219	0.0	.0196	.0225	-12.9	.0211	.0225	-6.2
10	Eye & Ear	.0315	.0159	98.1	.0190	.0163	16.6	.0172	.0167	3.0
11	Other Heart, Hypertension	.0273	.0285	-4.2	.0241	.0296	-18.9	.0324	.0253	28.1
12	Acute Myocardial Infarction	.0088	.0087	1.1	.0124	.0076	63.2	.0115	.0065	76.9
13	Symptomatic Heart Disease	.0117	.0174	-32.8	.0156	.0174	-10.3	.0181	.0161	12.4
14	Cerebrovascular Disease	.0076	.0108	-29.6	.0136	.0097	40.2	.0138	.0082	68.3
15	Circulation	.0157	.0134	17.2	.0190	.0120	58.3	.0162	.0115	40.9
16	Upper Respiratory	.0162	.0469	-65.5	.0220	.0515	-57.3	.0356	.0521	-31.7
17	Pneumonia	.0076	.0248	-69.4	.0156	.0260	-40.0	.0164	.0293	-44.0
18	Bronchitis, Emphysema, Asthma	.0428	.0450	-4.9	.0293	.0493	-40.6	.0414	.0476	-13.0
19	Tonsils & Adenoids	.0180	.0081	122.2	.0164	.0066	148.5	.0122	.0060	103.3
20	Other Respiratory	.0144	.0229	-37.1	.0146	.0246	-40.7	.0183	.0255	-28.2
21	Dental	.0030	.0057	-47.4	.0083	.0047	76.6	.0080	.0035	128.6
22	Upper Gastrointestinal	.0100	.0142	-29.6	.0144	.0138	4.3	.0155	.0127	22.0
23	Appendicitis	.0068	.0120	-43.3	.0165	.0103	60.2	.0146	.0094	55.3
24	Hernia	.0144	.0085	69.4	.0163	.0067	143.3	.0121	.0063	92.1
25	Other Gastrointestinal	.0183	.0236	-22.5	.0346	.0200	73.0	.0283	.0194	45.9

Table 7.3 (cont.)

No	Diagnostic Category	Medical School Affiliation			General Nurse (3yr)			Enrolled Nurse—Gen.		
		T (n=8)	NT (n=113)	Diff. (%)	T (n=27)	NT (n=94)	Diff. (%)	T (n=53)	NT (n=68)	Diff. (%)
26	Nephritis & Nephrosis	.0290	.0038	663.2	.0180	.0019	847.4	.0104	.0016	550.0
27	Other Urinary	.0117	.0165	-29.1	.0171	.0160	6.9	.0163	.0161	1.2
28	Male Genital	.0074	.0060	23.3	.0101	.0049	106.1	.0073	.0051	43.1
29	Other Female Genital	.0153	.0200	-23.5	.0356	.0151	135.8	.0241	.0162	48.8
30	Disorders of Menstruation	.0063	.0057	10.5	.0118	.0040	195.0	.0081	.0039	107.7
31	Comp. Pregnancy/Puerperium	.0542	.0334	62.3	.0298	.0363	-17.9	.0284	.0398	-28.6
32	Abortion	.0090	.0079	13.9	.0105	.0073	43.8	.0090	.0073	23.3
33	Normal Delivery	.1322	.0682	93.8	.0854	.0687	24.3	.0682	.0756	-9.8
34	Delivery Complications	.0370	.0044	740.9	.0066	.0065	1.5	.0049	.0078	-37.2
35	Skin Disease	.0139	.0282	-50.7	.0209	.0290	-27.9	.0231	.0305	-24.3
36	Orthopaedic	.0354	.0248	42.7	.0339	.0231	46.8	.0315	.0208	51.4
37	Congenital Malformation	.0267	.0027	888.9	.0049	.0041	19.5	.0060	.0029	106.9
38	Perinatal	.0078	.0018	333.3	.0031	.0019	63.2	.0022	.0022	0.0
39	Immaturity	.0068	.0010	580.0	.0014	.0014	0.0	.0010	.0017	-41.2
40	Symptoms, ill-defined	.0476	.1222	-61.0	.0829	.1271	-34.8	.1020	.1291	-21.0
41	Long Stay, ill-defined	.0036	.0128	-71.9	.0086	.0132	-34.8	.0114	.0127	-10.2
42	Other Fractures (excl. Femur)	.0338	.0381	-11.3	.0415	.0368	12.8	.0380	.0377	0.8
43	Fracture of Neck of Femur	.0046	.0018	155.6	.0033	.0016	106.3	.0027	.0014	92.9
44	Dislocations	.0037	.0086	-57.0	.0062	.0089	-30.3	.0079	.0086	-8.1
45	Internal Injury	.0196	.0312	-37.2	.0291	.0308	-5.5	.0303	.0306	-1.0
46	External Injury	.0202	.0472	-57.2	.0307	.0497	-38.2	.0400	.0497	-19.5
47	Poisoning	.0199	.0315	-36.8	.0244	.0325	-24.9	.0282	.0326	-13.5

Note: (a) Proportions are unweighted means. T = teaching; NT = non-teaching; Diff. = difference = (T-NT)/NT.
Source: Queensland Hospital Morbidity Data.

Diagnostic Category	*Complexity Ranking based on type 1 information theory index (see Table 5.17)*
4 Malignant Neoplasms	5
5 Benign Neoplasms	10
19 Tonsils and Adenoids	15
26 Nephritis and Nephrosis	1
34 Delivery Complications	3
37 Congenital Malformation	6
38 Perinatal	4
39 Immaturity	2
43 Fracture of Neck of Femur	7

Again there is an association between medical school affiliation and complexity.[9]

Turning next to the teaching classification based on hospital's which offer the *General Nurse (3 year) course*, the following points can be gleaned from Tables 7.2 and 7.3.

- In the 18 diagnostic category classification, teaching hospitals have over twice the proportion of cases in the following categories (complexity rankings based on Table 5.16 in brackets): 2 Neoplasms (3); and 10 Genito-Urinary System (4). Again there is an association between teaching status and complexity.

- In the 47 diagnostic category classification, teaching hospitals have over twice the proportion of cases in the following categories (complexity rankings based on Table 5.17 in brackets): 4 Malignant Neoplasms (5); 5 Benign Neoplasms (10); 19 Tonsils and Adenoids (15); 24 Hernia (19); 26 Nephritis and Nephrosis (1); 28 Male Genital (14); 29 Other Female Genital (18); 30 Disorders of Menstruation (11); and 43 Fracture of Neck of Femur (7).

---

[9]   It might be argued that these conclusions are self-fulfilling since the information theory index accords a high complexity weight to cases whose treatment is concentrated in a small number of hospitals. While this is a characteristic of these weights, it does not necessarily follow that the small number of hospitals which account for the majority of treatments of these case types are teaching hospitals. Hence the association noted here is not tautological.

Generally there is some overlap here with the results for hospitals affiliated with medical schools, but the association between teaching status and complexity is not as marked in the 47 diagnostic category classification.

Finally, consider the teaching classification based on hospitals which offered the *Enrolled Nurse—General (1 year) course*. Tables 7.2 and 7.3 indicate the following patterns.

- In the 18 diagnostic category classification, teaching hospitals have over twice the proportion of cases in the following categories (complexity rankings again in brackets): 2 Neoplasms (3); and 14 Congenital Anomalies (2). Teaching status and complexity again appear to be related.

- In the 47 diagnostic category classification, teaching hospitals have over twice the proportion of cases in the following categories (complexity rankings in brackets): 4 Malignant Neoplasms (4); 5 Benign Neoplasms (10); 19 Tonsils and Adenoids (15); 21 Dental (26); 26 Nephritis and Nephrosis (1); 30 Disorders of Menstruation (11); and 37 Congenital Malformation (6). Again an association between teaching status and complexity is evident.

The general picture which emerges is one of substantial differences in the diagnostic mix of patients between teaching and non-teaching hospitals, whichever basis of classifying teaching and non-teaching hospitals is used.[10] Further, there is overall a strong association between the case types which teaching hospitals tend to treat and case complexity as indicated by the type 1 information theory case mix complexity measures.

---

[10] The importance of case mix differences between the two types of hospital was also investigated in this study by estimating a two group linear discriminant function. (For an explanation of this technique see Morrison 1969; Morrison 1976, Ch.6; Kleinbaum and Kupper 1978, Ch.22; Stopher and Meyburg 1979, Ch.12; Srivastava and Carter 1983, Ch.8; Schuerman 1983, Ch.9; and Dillon and Goldstein 1984, Ch.10). These results also support the conclusion that differences in the 18 and 47 diagnostic category proportions between the two types of hospital in each teaching/non-teaching classification can be used to discriminate between the two types of hospital.

7.3.4   Case Mix Differences—Other Case Mix Dimensions

Teaching and non-teaching hospitals also differ with respect to some of the other case mix dimensions examined in this study. Such differences are evidenced by the data in Table 7.4 which have the following features.

- Teaching hospitals, on average, treat a smaller proportion of male patients with the greatest difference being between hospitals with and without medical school affiliation. This would be a reflection of the concentration of the complex childbirth and associated cases in the teaching hospitals noted in the foregoing sub-section.

- More surgery is performed on patients in teaching hospitals. The difference is again greatest in hospitals with a medical school affiliation.

- Hospitals with medical school affiliation have a much higher proportion of public patients than their non-teaching counterparts, and a very low proportion of private patients. This pattern, however, is not replicated in the other two classifications where the teaching hospitals have lower proportions of public patients and higher proportions of intermediate and private patients than their non-teaching counterparts.

- The most substantial differences in separation status arise in the proportions of patients discharged and transferred. In all three teaching classifications, teaching hospitals discharge a higher proportion of their cases and transfer a lower proportion than the non-teaching hospitals. This is to be expected. The higher concentration of more complex cases in teaching hospitals would arise in part because of the referral of such cases from the non-teaching hospitals.

- With regard to the age of patients, hospitals with medical school affiliation, on average, have higher proportions of their patients in the 0-40 age brackets and less in the 41-64 and 65+ age brackets. The pattern is almost exactly the opposite of this in the other two types of teaching hospital. In the General Nurse and Enrolled Nurse training classifications, teaching hospitals have *lower* proportions of cases in the 0-14 age brackets and *higher* proportions in the 41-64 and 65+ age brackets.

Table 7.4. Differences in Other Case Mix Dimensions between Teaching and Non-Teaching Hospitals, Queensland Public Hospitals, 1977-78[a]

Case Mix Category	Medical School		General Nurse		Enrolled Nurse	
	T (n=8)	NT (n=113)	T (n=27)	NT (n=94)	T (n=53)	NT (n=68)
Male discharges	.412	.484	.453	.486	.472	.484
Surgery performed	.391	.145	.333	.112	.237	.103
Payment status						
- public	.834	.745	.655	.778	.692	.796
- intermediate	.165	.215	.296	.188	.257	.177
- private	.001	.040	.049	.034	.052	.027
Separation status						
- discharged	.975	.915	.957	.908	.940	.903
- transferred	.010	.069	.023	.077	.040	.085
- died	.014	.016	.021	.014	.020	.012
Age bracket						
- 0-4	.152	.121	.082	.135	.107	.135
- 5-14	.134	.110	.083	.120	.105	.117
- 15-40	.410	.397	.416	.393	.382	.411
- 41-64	.194	.208	.245	.196	.228	.191
- 65+	.110	.164	.175	.156	.178	.146

Note: (a) T = Teaching; NT = Non-Teaching.
Source: Hospital Morbidity Data.

Clearly there are differences in the diagnostic and other case mix characteristics of patients between teaching and non-teaching hospitals. These differences are evident in all three teaching classifications but are generally more pronounced in hospitals with medical school affiliation. It remains to examine the extent to which teaching status, as opposed to case mix, scale and utilisation, accounts for the difference in average cost per case between the two types of institution.

7.4 Empirical Results on the Effects of Teaching on Hospital Costs

It is useful to begin by considering more formally the patterns of association between teaching status, cost, scale and utilisation, and case mix. Table 7.5 presents the correlation matrix for average cost per case, scale and utilisation, teaching status and the two type 1 information theory case mix indexes. In all the results presented in this section, the presence or absence of a teaching program is taken into account by the use of a dummy variable which takes a value of zero if the hospital is non-teaching and unity if it is teaching.

Table 7.5. Correlation Matrix, Three Teaching Categories, Average Cost Per Case, Information Theory Case Mix Indexes, Size and Utilisation, Queensland Public Hospitals, 1977-78[a]

	ACC	X181	X471	ALS	OCC	CFR	Beds	T1	T2	T3
ACC	1.00	0.38*	0.34*	0.61*	0.08	-0.32*	0.26*	0.22*	0.05	0.17
X181		1.00	0.97*	0.17	0.60*	0.35*	0.62*	0.47*	0.50*	0.36*
X471			1.00	0.13	0.60*	0.37*	0.67*	0.54*	0.50*	0.35*
ALS				1.00	0.34*	-0.34*	0.12	-0.02	0.07	0.32*
OCC					1.00	0.67*	0.42*	0.39*	0.41*	0.36*
CFR						1.00	0.17	0.34*	0.18	0.01
Beds							1.00	0.61*	0.54*	0.40*
T1								1.00	0.10	0.10
T2									1.00	0.53*
T3										1.00

Note: *   Significant at 1% level.
  (a) *ACC* = average cost per case; *X181, X471* = type 1 information theory case mix indexes based on 18 and 47 diagnostic categories respectively; *ALS* = average length of stay; *OCC* = occupancy; *CFR* = case flow rate; *T1* = medical school affiliation; *T2* = General Nurse training; *T3* = Enrolled Nurse—General training (0= non-teaching status for all teaching dummies).
Source: Queensland Hospital Finance Data and statistical results.

It is interesting to note first of all that average cost per case is positively correlated with teaching status but the association is not particularly strong. As expected from the discussion in the previous section, medical school affiliation has the highest correlation with average cost out of the three teaching types. Teaching status—particularly medical school affiliation and General Nurse training—is much more highly positively correlated with the case mix indexes and size, and less so with occupancy and case flow.

The correlation coefficients between each of the three teaching types and the 18 and 47 diagnostic categories were also investigated. Considering first the 18 diagnostic categories, the following statistically significant associations emerged (see Table 7.2 for descriptions for the diagnostic category numbers and note (a) to Table 7.5 for teaching status codes).[11]

---

11   In the following discussion of correlation coefficients, it should be borne in mind that 'significantly positive' and 'significantly negative' do not mean 'large'. The sample of 121 hospitals results in correlations of about 0.2 and higher (in absolute terms) being

Diagnostic Categories from 18DCs with Significant Positive Correlations with Teaching Status			Diagnostic Categories from 18DCs with Significant Negative Correlations with Teaching Status		
T1	T2	T3	T1	T2	T3
2	2	2	1	1	1
11	4	7	16	8	8
14	9	9	17	16	
15	10	10			
	13	13			
	18				

These results highlight the significant overall association of teaching status and case mix, but also show that the different types of teaching hospital are generally associated with different case mix categories. Only one category in each of the positive and negative groups is common across all three teaching categories.

Considering now the 47 diagnostic categories, the statistically significant associations which emerged are listed overleaf (see Table 7.3 for the descriptors for the diagnostic category numbers; + = common across all three teaching types). Again the results are in accord with those from Table 7.3. Teaching status and case mix are clearly associated although, as with the 18 diagnostic category results, the case mix categories associated with teaching status tend to differ somewhat between the different teaching classifications.

The last correlation coefficients to consider are those between the type of teaching hospital and the additional case mix dimensions. The most significant correlations are those with 'surgery performed', indicating that teaching status however defined is positively correlated with the proportion of cases on whom surgery is carried out (Butler 1988a). This is consistent with the difference in mean proportions noted in Table 7.4 and the hypothesis that teaching hospitals tend to treat more complex cases. The other correlations also support the earlier discussion—hospitals with medical school affiliation tend to have a higher proportion of public patients and a lower proportion of private patients while the converse is true of the other two teaching types, and teaching hospitals in general tend to transfer a smaller proportion of their patients. There is only a small amount of

statistically significant at the one per cent level. The correlation coefficients discussed here can be found in Butler (1988a).

Diagnostic Categories from 47DCs with Significant Positive Correlations with Teaching Status			Diagnostic Categories from 47DCs with Significant Negative Correlations with Teaching Status		
T1	T2	T3	T1	T2	T3
4+	1	4	3+	3	3
5+	4	5	16+	16	16
10	5	12	40	18	17
26+	7	14	46	40	
34	12	15		46	
37	15	19			
38	19	21			
39	23	23			
43+	24	24			
	25	25			
	26	26			
	28	28			
	29	29			
	30	30			
	32	36			
	36	43			
	43				

significant systematic variation between teaching status and the age of patients.

The foregoing results indicate that there is a substantial amount of correlation between teaching status, case mix and size. The remainder of this section is concerned with attempting to estimate the influence of teaching status, *ceteris paribus*, on average cost.

Teaching status alone explains very little of the interhospital variation in average cost per case as can be seen by examining the first four estimated average cost equations in Table 7.6. Medical school affiliation alone explains only a small (four per cent) but significant (at the five per cent level) amount of variation in average cost per case (see equation I). The other two teaching dummies explain only a very small and insignificant amount of such variation (see equations II and III). The three teaching dummies together account for only five per cent of average cost variation (see equation IV).

This cannot, of course, be taken as strong evidence that teaching has no influence on hospital costs because differences in other factors have not been taken into account. For example, recall that teaching hospitals tend to have higher occupancy rates (see Tables 7.1 and 7.5). From the analysis of the previous chapter it seems that higher occupancy will reduce average cost per case so this effect could be mitigating any cost-increasing effect of teaching status. Hence it is necessary to allow for differences in other relevant factors.

Equations V - IX include the teaching dummy variables with various measures of case mix. In equations V and VI the type 1 information theory indexes are used based on the 18 and 47 diagnostic categories respectively.[12] These equations explain 16 and 12 per cent respectively of the variation in average cost per case and the coefficient on the second teaching variable (TEACH2), which reflects the presence of General Nurse training, is negative and significant in both. This suggests that, holding case mix constant, the implementation of a General Nurse training program will *reduce* average cost per case. The estimated magnitude of this reduction is in the range of $130 to $150 per case. It suggests that input substitution may be at work in these hospitals—lower paid trainee nurses may be substituted for fully trained nurses in such a way as to reduce average cost per case. This would be consistent with the findings of Hosek and Palmer (1983) discussed earlier in this chapter.[13]

An alternative explanation of the negative effect of General Nurse training on average cost per case is that it is actually picking up the effect of the higher proportions of intermediate and private patients in these hospitals. The presence of General Nurse training is significantly positively correlated with intermediate and private payment status, and such patients pay private doctors on a fee-for-service basis. Hence for these patients the physician cost is not included in hospital costs. This possibility will be discussed again later in this section.

The TEACH2 (General Nurse training) coefficient, however, loses significance and decreases considerably in magnitude (in absolute terms) when the more disaggregated case mix classifications are employed. Equation VII incorporates the 18 diagnostic category classification and the additional case mix dimensions. None of the teaching dummies now has a significant coefficient. Nor do they have significant coefficients in equations VIII and IX which use the 47 diagnostic categories, and the 47 diagnostic

---

[12] The type 1 information theory index was selected because of its better explanatory power as detailed in Chapter 5.

[13] If robust, this finding would imply that the transfer of nurse education from hospitals to colleges of advanced education and universities in Australia will *increase* costs in those hospitals which are losing General Nurse training programs.

Table 7.6. Parameter Estimates from Various Specifications of Average Cost
Functions including Teaching Dummies, Queensland Public Hospitals, 1977-78[a]

	I	II	III	IV	V	VI
Constant	523.73	540.13	510.93	503.13	-548.82	-201.67
TEACH1	213.23 (2.49**)			201.60 (2.35**)	18.54 (0.20)	15.97 (0.16)
TEACH2		30.02 (0.57)		-37.06 (-0.62)	-145.67 (-2.33**)	-129.59 (-2.02**)
TEACH3			81.96 (1.89)	88.23 (1.76)	67.04 (1.41)	73.23 (1.51)
X181					1234.09 (3.98*)	
X471						874.89 (3.26*)
18DCs						
47DCs						
Add. CM						
ALS						
OCC						
CFR						
CFR^2						
$\frac{365}{CFR}$						
$\frac{365RBD}{CFR}$						
Beds						
Beds^2						
$\bar{R}^2$	.04	-.006	.02	.05	.16	.12
F	6.2**	0.33	3.58	3.16**	6.63*	5.22*

Table 7.6 (cont.)

	VII	VIII	IX	X	XI	XII
Constant	871.73	1407.52	-515.03	406.85	85.16	-422.79
TEACH1	188.73 (1.42)	151.57 (1.10)	121.75 (0.89)	190.58 (1.70)	36.54 (0.35)	90.67 (0.85)
TEACH2	-66.87 (-1.00)	-28.44 (-0.41)	-47.35 (-0.71)	-88.60 (-1.62)	-86.13 (-1.63)	-43.83 (-0.79)
TEACH3	-21.88 (-0.46)	56.71 (0.95)	-21.88 (-0.35)	-60.21 (-1.69)	-71.22 (-1.95**)	-42.50 (-0.89)
X181						
X471						
18DCs	in			in	in	
47DCs		in	in			in
Add. CM	in		in	in	in	in
ALS				11.82 (2.05**)	20.59 (3.84*)	18.01 (2.33**)
OCC						
CFR						
CFR^2						
$\frac{365}{CFR}$				3.671 (4.43*)	4.464 (5.62*)	4.328 (3.83*)
$\frac{365RBD}{CFR}$				0.00023 (2.84*)	0.00003 (0.97)	0.00024 (2.32**)
Beds				-0.86 (-1.30)		-1.348 (-1.58)
Beds^2				-0.00022 (-0.64)		0.00022 (0.51)
$\overline{R}^2$	.45	.32	.46	.72	.69	.75
F	4.26*	2.16*	2.74*	9.85*	9.17*	6.73*

Table 7.6 (cont.)

	XIII	XIV	XV	XVI	XVII	XVIII
Constant	-898.55	643.63	-420.99	-1322.02	-80.82	-517.39
TEACH1	22.23 (0.23)	159.22 (1.15)	65.91 (0.45)	155.98 (1.83)	184.16 (2.15**)	259.54 (3.24*)
TEACH2	-58.29 (-1.20)	-105.47 (-1.83)	-49.78 (-0.82)	-59.45 (-1.11)	-98.00 (-1.96**)	-51.31 (-1.06)
TEACH3	-82.30 (-1.87)	-29.94 (-0.81)	-42.46 (-1.13)	-51.57 (-1.44)	-16.23 (-0.46)	-39.23 (-1.16)
X181				1486.66 (3.83*)	1237.12 (3.28*)	1084.10 (3.03*)

(X471 case mix index and 18DCs not entered in equations XIII-XVIII)

	XIII	XIV	XV	XVI	XVII	XVIII
47DCs	in	in	in			
Add. CM	in	in	in	in	in	in
ALS	24.11 (3.31*)		48.46 (6.81*)	19.43 (3.73*)		41.33 (8.97*)
OCC			-803.11 (-6.16*)			-705.93 (-7.34*)
CFR		-30.64 (-7.39*)			-25.09 (-7.09*)	
CFR^2		0.28016 (5.31*)			0.22813 (4.86*)	
$\frac{365}{CFR}$	5.327 (5.05*)			2.803 (3.84*)		
$\frac{365RBD}{CFR}$	0.00004 (0.90)			0.00017 (2.44**)		
Beds		0.266 (0.48)	-0.359 (-0.61)	-0.863 (-1.45)	0.285 (0.86)	0.050 (0.16)
Beds^2		-0.00023 (-0.54)	0.00028 (0.62)	-0.00010 (-0.32)	-0.00039 (-1.52)	-0.00024 (-0.97)
$\bar{R}^2$	.74	.77	.75	.67	.68	.71
F	6.57*	7.27*	6.86*	13.91*	15.17*	17.37*

Table 7.6 (cont.)

	XIX	XX	XXI	XXII	XXIII	XXIV
Constant	-668.06	-648.19	-784.27	268.91	686.06	317.24
TEACH1	94.01 (1.03)	86.74 (0.86)	188.31 (2.30**)	171.12 (1.81)	193.06 (1.71)	248.80 (2.70*)
TEACH2	-45.52 (-0.74)	-123.05 (-1.96**)	-32.13 (-0.61)	-6.74 (-0.10)	-78.19 (-1.10)	4.02 (0.07)
TEACH3	-49.32 (-1.23)	31.40 (0.75)	-37.65 (-1.06)	-56.98 (-1.34)	33.10 (0.69)	-45.61 (-1.13)
X181	1098.29 (3.94*)	1702.67 (5.92*)	1385.99 (5.74*)			

(No case mix measures other than X181 entered equations XIX-XXIV)

	XIX	XX	XXI	XXII	XXIII	XXIV
ALS	33.16 (6.12*)		48.91 (11.00*)	35.69 (6.24*)		48.77 (9.68*)
OCC			-618.58 (-6.47*)			-424.34 (-4.19*)
CFR		-19.14 (-4.43*)			-11.82 (-2.50**)	
CFR^2		0.14785 (2.47**)			0.06727 (1.01)	
$\dfrac{365}{CFR}$	0.031 (0.04)			-0.787 (-1.10)		
$\dfrac{365RBD}{CFR}$	0.00021 (2.65*)			0.00019 (2.25**)		
Beds	-1.156 (-1.84)	0.37 (0.93)	0.173 (0.53)	-0.60 (-0.92)	1.076 (2.45**)	0.706 (1.98**)
$Beds^2$	0.00027 (0.85)	-0.0003 (-0.97)	-0.00015 (-0.60)	-0.00002 (-0.07)	-0.00071 (-2.11**)	-0.00046 (-1.65)
$\bar{R}^2$	.50	.42	.60	.44	.24	.49
F	14.35*	11.76*	23.96*	12.57*	6.48*	17.67*

Notes: *   Significant at 1% level.   **   Significant at 5% level.
     (a)   t-values in parentheses. Add. CM = additional case mix dimensions.
         in = included
Source: Regression results.

categories and additional case mix dimensions respectively.[14] Interestingly, the magnitude of the second teaching dummy decreases further in these latter two equations and its standard error increases.

It seems that the negative influence of the General Nurse training program on average cost per case may have been reflecting part of the influence of case mix not captured by the scalar case mix indexes. Certainly the disaggregated case mix classifications possess more explanatory power, explaining from 32 to 46 per cent of the variation in average cost per case (after adjusting for degrees of freedom—see Table 7.6). Further, an incremental F test on the set of three teaching dummies revealed no significant increase in explanatory power in equations VII - IX so it is unlikely that their parameter estimates have high standard errors because of collinearity between them.[15]

The next step in the analysis involved the inclusion of scale and utilisation terms in the average cost equation. Equation X incorporates the 18 diagnostic categories, the additional case mix dimensions, the 'preferred' scale and utilisation terms and the teaching dummies. While none of the teaching dummies is significant at the five per cent level, their t-values have increased considerably and the scale terms have lost the significance which they had before teaching status was included (see Table 6.3). Also the squared size term now has the wrong sign.

Perhaps the scale effects found in 1977-78 were capturing some influence of teaching status? To allow for this, equation X was re-estimated deleting the 'pure' size terms (see equation XI). This resulted in the coefficient on the third teaching dummy (TEACH3), reflecting the presence of the Enrolled Nurse—General training program, attaining significance at the five per cent level. The negative coefficient again indicates that the presence of such a program *reduces* average cost, holding case mix and utilisation constant.

An unexpected result here is that medical school affiliation (TEACH1) did not prove to be significant. This was the teaching category most highly correlated with size (see Table 7.5), but after eliminating the pure scale terms the value of its coefficient and its associated t-value dropped substantially.

---

[14] None of the diagnostic category parameter estimates are included here or in the remainder of this chapter.

[15] The lack of increase in explanatory power arising from the inclusion of teaching dummies can be seen by comparing the results of equations VII - IX with the results presented in Table 5.10.

The 'preferred' scale and utilisation terms were then included with the 47 diagnostic categories, additional case mix dimensions and teaching dummies giving the parameter estimates of equation XII. The teaching dummies are again insignificant and the size terms again lose significance. Eliminating the two 'pure' size terms again increases the significance of Enrolled Nurse —General training (TEACH3) which is now significant at the ten per cent level (see equation XIII). The effect of such training programs on average cost per case is again negative.

Equations XIV and XV again include the 47 diagnostic categories, other case mix dimensions and size terms but this time incorporate alternative specifications of the utilisation terms along with the teaching dummies. Equation XIV includes linear and squared terms in the case flow rate and size, with the size terms being insignificant and the teaching dummies also, although the General Nurse training coefficient (TEACH2) is significant at the ten per cent level and is again negative in sign. Equation XV uses linear terms in average length of stay and occupancy in place of the case flow terms in equation XIV. Neither the teaching dummies nor the scale terms even approach a satisfactory level of statistical significance. Both of these equations were re-estimated excluding the scale terms but again the results (not included here) showed no significant effect of teaching status.

The final aspect of this investigation considers the effects of teaching using the scale and utilisation terms together with the scalar case mix indexes in place of the diagnostic categories and other case mix dimensions. The results so far have included scale and utilisation only with the disaggregated case mix classifications. What are the effects of teaching status if scale and utilisation are held constant and case mix is measured by an aggregated case mix index? Could teaching status be used as a complete substitute for case mix once scale and utilisation effects are taken into account?

Evidence on the first of these questions is provided by equations XVI - XVIII. Equation XVI replaces the disaggregated diagnostic classification with a scalar case mix index (X181), retaining the other case mix dimensions and the 'preferred' scale terms. The linear and squared terms in size are insignificant at the five per cent level as are the three teaching dummies, but medical school affiliation (TEACH1) is significant and positive at the ten per cent level. Equation XVII uses linear and quadratic terms in case flow in place of the three utilisation terms in equation XVI. Both medical school affiliation (TEACH1) and General Nurse training (TEACH2) are now significant at the five per cent level, the former being positive and the latter being negative. Medical school affiliation is also highly significant in equation XVIII which incorporates linear terms in average length of stay and occupancy in place of the case flow terms in equation XVII. General Nurse training, though, is insignificant.

Two points can be made about these results. *First*, the large magnitudes of the TEACH1 coefficients in equations XVII and XVIII suggest that medical school affiliation increases average cost by \$185 to \$260 per case. However, it must be remembered that this variable has become significant only after using a scalar case mix index, suggesting that it is more a proxy for case mix complexity than a measure of the effect of medical school affiliation, *ceteris paribus*. *Second*, the significant negative sign for General Nurse training in equation XVII, an equation which also contains the other case mix dimensions *including payment status*, suggests that the alternative explanation of this negative sign advanced previously is not supported. This estimate indicates that General Nurse training is predicted to reduce average cost per case even when the payment status of patients (public, intermediate, private) remains constant.

The last six equations (XIX - XXIV) continue to explore the extent to which teaching status can be substituted for more direct case mix measures when scale and utilisation are taken into account. In equations XIX - XXI, the other case mix dimensions are dropped leaving the information theory index based on 18 diagnostic categories as the only case mix variable in the equation. The explanatory power of each of these equations is significantly lower than its counterpart which included the other case mix dimensions. General Nurse training (TEACH2) remained significant at the five per cent level and negative in equation XX as it was in equation XVII, although its magnitude has increased suggesting it might be capturing some influence of patient payment status lost by the exclusion of the other case mix dimensions. Medical school affiliation (TEACH1) is positive and significant in equation XXI but this is the only one of these three equations where it is significant and, as already mentioned, it does not compensate for the loss of explanatory power occasioned by the exclusion of the other case mix dimensions. In none of the three equations is there any evidence of significant 'pure' scale effects.

Equations XXII - XXIV then drop the information theory case mix index (X181) also, leaving only the teaching dummies as possible proxies for case mix. The explanatory power of each equation is further reduced compared with the corresponding equation which included the case mix index. Medical school affiliation (TEACH1) is the only teaching dummy which is significant at the five per cent level, and this only once in equation XXIV. It is, however, significant at the ten per cent level in equations XXII and XXIII also, suggesting that it is partially capturing the effect of case mix. Generally, however, the results are poor and counter-intuitive. The non-linear term in case flow loses significance for the first time in equation XXIII, and while the two size terms are significant they have the wrong sign, implying an inverted U-shaped long run average cost curve. Similar results on scale are found in equation XXIV although the non-linear size term here is insignificant.

In concluding this section, it is reassuring to note that the strong evidence of the effects of utilisation on average cost per case found in the previous chapter is again evident in virtually all of the results presented here. Increased average length of stay is always associated with increased average cost per case, and increased occupancy and case flow rates with reduced average cost per case (at least up to the turning point in the average cost/case flow relationship).

7.5 Summary and Conclusions

The evidence to date has generally found teaching status to have a significant effect on hospital costs, although the magnitude of this effect has varied considerably between studies. More recent studies, particularly those which have adjusted for case mix and other relevant differences between hospitals, have tended to suggest that the impact of teaching is somewhat less than was found in earlier studies. One study (Hosek and Palmer 1983) has even found that teaching status tended to reduce hospital costs in radiology departments primarily, it seems, because of input substitution in favour of the lower priced student inputs.

Little evidence on this matter has been produced for Australian hospitals, but the bulk of that which has suggests that the influence of teaching on hospital costs is quite small. This may be explained by the differences in the funding arrangements for medical education in this country. The medical schools are actually funded as part of the university budget, so there may not be any reason to expect that teaching status will dramatically increase hospital costs. Even the indirect costs of teaching arising from factors such as increased use of pathology and other ancillary services have been found to be quite small.

This chapter has classified Queensland public hospitals on the basis of the presence or absence of three separate teaching programs: doctor education (medical school affiliation); a General Nurse (3 year) program; and an Enrolled Nurse—General (1 year) program. The presence of each of these was found to be positively correlated with the proportion of cases treated in various diagnostic categories, and these categories tended to rank high in a complexity ordering based on the information theory complexity measure. This is in accord with the statement by Lave and Lave (1979, p.968) that "Teaching hospitals treat *more difficult* cases" (emphasis in original). Teaching status was also found to be associated with other case mix dimensions, and with scale and utilisation.

The approach adopted in this chapter to assessing the independent influence of teaching status on hospital costs was to estimate various specifications of an average cost function for hospitals. These functions generally included case mix, scale and utilisation terms along with dummy variables to indicate the presence of one or more of the three teaching programs in a hospital.

Overall, the conclusion is· that there is only limited evidence of any independent influence of any kind of teaching on hospital costs once case mix, scale and utilisation are taken into account. What evidence there is suggests that medical school affiliation has a positive effect on average cost per case, and General Nurse training a negative effect. This evidence, however, arises for the most part in equations where an aggregated scalar case mix index is used in place of a disaggregated set of diagnostic or other case mix categories.

This suggests that teaching may serve as a proxy for case mix. However, it was found not to be a particularly good proxy since the equations in which teaching status appeared as the only case mix indicator, along with scale and utilisation, had substantially inferior explanatory power compared with those which incorporated more detailed case mix measures. It seems, then, that if detailed adjustments are made for the influence of case mix, scale and utilisation, teaching status has virtually no impact on hospital costs. This would indicate that most of the costs involved in this production process are common costs and that the separable costs of teaching are quite small.

8

A COMPARISON OF PUBLIC AND PRIVATE

HOSPITAL COSTS IN QUEENSLAND

8.1   Introduction

Suppose there are two firms identical in all respects except that one is a public enterprise while the other is a private enterprise. Will this difference in ownership cause one firm to achieve a higher level of productive efficiency than the other and, if so, which form of ownership is more conducive to the attainment of productive efficiency? This chapter attempts to bring some empirical evidence to bear on this question by comparing the relative costliness of public and private hospitals in Queensland.

Our concern in this chapter is exclusively with the question of relative productive efficiency and not allocative efficiency. The latter concept relates to the attainment of the welfare maximising composition of commodities produced by an economy. As is well known, some commodities will not be supplied by the private sector because they are 'public' in nature or will be supplied in non-optimal quantities because of the existence of externalities (Winch 1971, Ch.7). In such cases, private provision may be allocatively inefficient, even though the firms may be productively efficient, i.e. producing their particular output levels at minimum attainable per unit cost.[1]

The subject matter of this chapter can perhaps be characterised as subject to an excess supply of ideology and an excess demand for empirical evidence, particularly with regard to some of the arguments which have been put forward for privatisation (see Kay and Thompson 1986; Kolsen 1986). In the words of one author,

> [T]he subject matter of public versus private production of services abounds with ideological overtones, and despite the considerable heat generated about this topic, there has been relatively little light shed on it. In particular, there have been few studies that have attempted to compare the performances of the public and private sectors in supplying the same specific service. (Savas 1980, p.254).

8.2 Theoretical Background

A theoretical argument that private enterprises can be expected to be more efficient than public enterprises producing similar commodities has been put by Davies (1971). This argument is based upon the ability of the private owner to sell ownership rights to private property, an ability not possessed by the public owner. Because of this, poor performance in the private sector will be reflected in reduced prices of ownership rights (reduced share prices). In the case of public ownership,

> ... inability to exchange ownership claims along with lack of specialization inhibits inexpensive detection and rectification of poor management ... Therefore, as a result of transferability and changing values of private shares, it is not as costly either to perceive or eradicate poor management in the private sector as it is in the public sphere. (Davies 1971, pp.150-1).

---

[1] The terminology used here differs from that adopted by Farrell (1957) in his discussion of productive efficiency. Farrell defines allocative inefficiency as one of two components of productive inefficiency, the other component being technical inefficiency. Allocative inefficiency arises if the firm is producing on an isoquant but has an input combination which differs from that which is optimal. Technical inefficiency arises if the firm is producing at a point off the isoquant.

Davies argues that this conclusion applies even if the private firm is regulated, provided that shares in the firm are transferable and have a fluctuating monetary value.[2]

Although Davies does not explicitly consider private non-profit firms, his argument implies that, to the extent that they are not characterised by transferable share ownership and flexible share prices, they too could be expected to be less efficient than their for-profit counterparts. This theme has been taken up by Frech (1976) who argued that the attenuation of property rights in a non-profit firm reduces the price of non-pecuniary amenities (pleasant offices, shorter working hours) relative to firm wealth, and reduces the gains from the takeover of poorly managed firms. His position is aligned with that of Alchian and Demsetz (1972) who conclude that 'shirking' can be expected to be greater in non-profit firms.

An implication of the above argument is that non-profit firms can be expected to be driven out of an industry when faced with competition from the more efficient profit-seeking firms. Frech offers two explanations as to why this may not happen. *First*, "government regulation may cause cost disadvantages for profit-seeking firms" (Frech 1976, p.145). *Second*, the behaviour of a non-profit firm is constrained by the desires of its donors who may wish to see their contributions employed to increase output rather than increasing the firm's owners' wealth.

In addition to the property rights argument, the public choice literature also leads to the expectation that private firms will be relatively more efficient. In particular, the budget-maximising model of bureaucracy as developed by Niskanen (1971) suggests that government bureaus have little incentive to be efficient and "the monopoly nature of most bureaus also frees them from competitive pressure to be efficient" (Mueller 1989, p.251).

A counter to the property rights and public choice arguments arises from the theory of regulation. While this theory supports the general contention that regulation can lead to inefficiency, this contention applies to *both* public and private firms. If one is then dealing with private firms which are subject to regulation, "the case for relatively higher efficiency levels in private firms is no longer so clear-cut" (Byrnes, Grosskopf and Hayes 1986, p.337). For example, the regulation might be such as to erect substantial barriers to entry so that private ownership *per se* may not lead to productive efficiency.

Empirical evidence has been produced which supports the arguments outlined above concerning the superior productive efficiency of private firms. Frech (1976) found that private non-profit health insurance firms

---

2   For an elaboration of the property rights argument in the context of hospitals, see
     Clarkson (1972).

processing claims for the Social Security Administration in the US had significantly higher average processing time and made significantly more errors per 1,000 claims processed. Spann (1977) assesses the empirical evidence on the relative efficiency of public and private production in five areas—airline services, fire protection, health care and hospitals, electric utilities, and garbage collection. He concludes that "For the majority of activities, private producers can provide the same services at the same or lower costs than can public producers" (Spann 1977, p.88). Savas (1980), in surveying eight studies which have compared the cost of household refuse collection by municipal authorities with systems where the municipality contracts with private firms for such services or where private collection is used, found that "only one study ... is inconsistent with the conclusion that the price of contract collection is less than the cost of municipal collection of residential refuse" (Savas 1980, p.263).

In comparing the costs of for-profit and non-profit hospitals, Bays (1979) found that chain for-profit hospitals, i.e. those owned by large corporate chains, were significantly less costly than either non-chain for-profit or non-profit hospitals. This study is important because it took into account differences in case mix, or the composition of output, of the various firms. Failure to hold case mix constant was argued by Bays to be a serious weakness of earlier studies in this area.[3] Also with respect to hospitals, Clarkson (1972) found significant differences in "the variance of input combinations used to produce similar products" (p.379) in non-proprietary hospitals.

Knapp (1986) undertook a study of the relative costs of residential child care services in three sectors—local authority, voluntary and private—in England and Wales. The study was based upon data collected in a survey of 789 children's homes, and included information on the characteristics of children, such as age, sex, and the presence or otherwise of mental and physical handicap. "The *tentative* conclusion to be drawn ... is that in the privatization of *production* the private and voluntary sectors are more cost-effective than the public sector in the sense that they employ more efficient 'technologies' of care" (Knapp 1986, p.195, emphasis in original). A similar study by Judge (1986) of residential accommodation for the elderly in the public and private sectors in England and Wales concluded that "the apparent cost advantage in the private sector is striking" (p.215).

In Australia, evidence that the interstate private enterprise airline Ansett is more efficient than the public enterprise Trans Australian Airlines (now

---

3   Among the earlier studies are those by Cohen (1963), Berry (1967), Carr and Feldstein (1967), Ingbar and Taylor (1968), Francisco (1970) and Cohen (1970).

QANTAS) has been produced by Davies (1971, 1977).[4] A later study of this industry by Mackay (1979) also demonstrated that while both airlines were relatively inefficient in comparison with overseas airlines, Ansett was slightly more efficient than TAA.

Empirical evidence has also been produced, however, which has found no significant difference in efficiency between public and private firms. Some interesting studies in this regard relate to the water utility industry in the US. These studies have produced conflicting results on the effect of ownership even though their samples were drawn from the same data. Crain and Zardkoohi (1978), using a dummy variable in a cost function to distinguish between public and private ownership, found public water utilities to have statistically significantly higher costs than private firms while Bruggink (1982) found ownership had no effect. In a later study, Feigenbaum and Teeples (1983) re-examined this data using a translog cost function and also attempted to capture the effect of quality differences. They too found no significant effect of ownership on costs.

Byrnes, *et al.* (1986) have undertaken a further analysis of this industry using more recent data. Their study differs from the other three in that it estimates a production function rather than a cost function. Further, a frontier production function is estimated using linear programming techniques, thus avoiding the imposition of any particular functional form.[5] "By focusing directly on the production relationship we compare the total factor productivity of water utilities, which is clearly related to costs. More productive firms have lower costs, ceteris paribus" (Byrnes, *et al.* 1986, p.338).[6] In other words, the study concentrated on identifying differences in

---

4   His evidence has been critically appraised by Forsyth and Hocking (1980). See also the reply by Davies (1980).

5   The mathematical programming approach to frontier estimation is known as Data Envelopment Analysis (DEA). In contrast to the econometric approach, "DEA is a methodology directed to frontiers rather than central tendencies. Instead of trying to fit a regression plane through the *center* of the data, one 'floats' a piecewise linear surface to rest *on top* of the observations" (Seiford and Thrall 1990, p.8, emphasis in original). For further discussion and applications, see Färe, Grosskopf and Lovell (1985) and Dogramaci and Färe (1988). An application of DEA to hospital production is provided by Banker, Conrad and Strauss (1986).

6   The authors argue that one of the main advantages of estimating a production function is that it avoids the use of data which "do not correspond to the economist's notion of costs. For example, these data do not include economic or opportunity costs of capital and land" (Byrnes, *et al.* 1986, p.338). As has already been noted, the same could be said about the cost data used in the present study.

technical efficiency between the two types of firm. But none were found—
"we find no evidence that publicly owned utilities are more wasteful or
operated with more slack than privately owned utilities" (Byrnes, *et al.*
1986, p.341).

Evidence that ownership type does not affect costs has also been
produced for hospitals. Renn, Schramm, Watt and Derzon (1985) undertook
a detailed study of the effects of ownership and chain-affiliation on 24
different hospital performance measures in the following five categories:
revenues and expenses; markups and profitability; productivity and activity;
capital structure; and patient and payer mix. Five hospital types were
distinguished—chain-affiliated and freestanding investor owned (for profit),
chain-affiliated and freestanding not-for-profit, and government hospitals—
with dummy variables being used to indicate hospital type. Differences in
case mix, scale, utilisation, teaching commitments, the extent of competition
and the use of contract management were all taken into account. The initial
sample consisted of about 800 hospitals from a national population of nearly
4,500 hospitals in the US in 1980, with about 500 hospitals having useable
data for each estimated relationship.

The results of this study showed that "In the case of 20 of the 24
dependent performance measures examined, the combination of ownership
and system affiliation, as defined by our five hospital types, was a
statistically significant factor in explaining differences among hospitals"
(Renn, *et al.* 1985, p.230). But the four performance measures on which
ownership and affiliation had no effect included the most comprehensive
average cost measure (total patient care expenses per adjusted admission).
To quote the authors,

> ... no type of hospital incurred significantly different costs for
> delivering comparable patient care services. More importantly,
> the differences that did exist in length of stay or cost per case
> were not explained by ownership type or system affiliation, but
> rather by other factors. Specifically, in the equations predicting
> length of stay and patient care costs per admission, the construct
> of hospital type, as defined by ownership and system affiliation,
> had no significant explanatory power. (Renn, *et al.* 1985, p.231).

These results contrast with those obtained in the study by Bays (1979)
discussed earlier in this chapter. In a discussion of the literature in this area,
Culyer (1990, p.36) states that "Detailed microeconomic evidence casts
serious doubts on the empirical validity of the claim that public provision is
relatively X-inefficient".

Bearing these conflicting results in mind, attention is now turned to public and private hospitals in Queensland.

8.3   Differences between Public and Private Hospitals in Queensland

8.3.1   The Public/Private Dichotomy

All public hospitals in Queensland with the exception of the Mater hospitals at South Brisbane are owned by the State Government. Private hospitals are regulated under the *Health Act* 1937-81 which gives the Director-General of Health power to issue or refuse a licence to operate a private hospital (s.64).[7] The sale or transfer of ownership of a private hospital licence is subject to approval by the Director-General of Health (s.71) and no such hospitals in Queensland are public limited liability corporations. Any additions or alterations "to, in or about the premises of a licenced private hospital" must receive the prior written approval of the Director-General of Health (s.70).

This immediately suggests that the incentives to efficiency in private firms arising from the ability to sell ownership rights are absent. Private hospital activities are highly regulated in a number of dimensions and barriers to entry are substantial.

The Australian Bureau of Statistics (ABS) distinguishes between acute hospitals on the basis of their being recognised (i.e. public), non-profit or private enterprise. The last two categories constitute the private hospital sector, with non-profit hospitals being those owned by registered religious or charitable organisations. The number and size of each of these hospital types in Queensland in 1977-78 are given in Table 8.1. Private enterprise hospitals account for less than six per cent of the number of institutions and less than three per cent of total acute hospital beds. The private sector in total accounts for 28 per cent of institutions and 21 per cent of total beds.[8]

---

7   For more detail see Queensland Department of Health (1982).

8   In 1991-92, there were 46 private acute hospitals in Queensland compared with 50 in 1977-78. However, the number of private enterprise (or for-profit) hospitals increased from 10 to 17, while the number of beds increased from 3,066 to 3,868 (Australian Bureau of Statistics 1993, Table 2).

Table 8.1. Number and Size of Acute Hospitals in Public and Private Sectors, Queensland, 1977-78

	Hospitals		Total Beds		Average size (beds)
	No.	%	No.	%	
Recognised (public)	131	72.4	11,847	79.4	90
Non-Profit[a]	40	22.1	2,652	17.8	66
Private enterprise	10	5.5	414	2.8	41
All hospitals	181	100.0	14,913	100.0	82

Note: (a) Includes, in addition to those regarded as private hospitals under the Medibank agreement, three Commonwealth Government repatriation hospitals, four hospitals operated by the State Government, and four hospitals operated by religious authorities.

Source: Australian Bureau of Statistics (1981, Table 2).

8.3.2   Private Hospital Data

Disaggregated data on the hospitals described in Table 8.1 are unavailable from the ABS. However, the Queensland Department of Health made available data on the case mix of discharges from each hospital—public and private—from the Hospital Morbidity Data collection. For the year 1977-78, this data set contained information on 42 private hospitals. Of these, one was not in operation for the full financial year, two were catering for long-stay nursing home type patients, and the Queensland Department of Health could provide no financial data on another (a State prison hospital).

Unfortunately the Queensland Department of Health could not provide financial data on any of the other private hospitals either, so this information was solicited from the remaining 38 private hospitals by mail. Only three responses were received. The ABS then agreed to provide financial information in aggregate form for the remaining 35 hospitals, effectively giving one observation on financial data for the remainder of the private sector. As such, there were only four observations to include for the private sector—three pertaining to individual private hospitals and one aggregated observation for the remainder of the private sector.

This dearth of private hospital cost data severely hampers any empirical analysis of the cost differences between public and private hospitals. As well as curtailing the number of observations, the aggregated observation clouds the ownership issue because it includes two Commonwealth Government repatriation hospitals which are classified as private because they cater for a restricted clientele. These limitations need to be borne in mind.

8.3.3   Cost/Volume Differences

Some descriptive statistics on the cost/volume characteristics of the public and private hospitals included in this study are presented in Table 8.2. It can be seen that the 35 private hospitals included in the aggregate observation, on average, discharged about the same number of patients as public hospitals but were somewhat smaller in size. In combination with a lower average length of stay, this has given the private hospitals substantially higher occupancy and case flow rates. The individual private hospital observations are seen to exhibit considerable variation around the means of the aggregate group.

Table 8.2. Cost/Volume Characteristics of Public and Private Hospitals, Queensland, 1977-78

	Public Hospitals[a] (n=121)	Aggregate Private Hospitals[a] (n=35)	Individual Private Hospitals A	B	C
Av. Cost per Case ($)	636.11	423.36	498.22	334.35	1607.47
Av. Cost per Day ($)	83.68	65.99	65.95	47.43	130.63
Av. Length of Stay	7.6	6.4	7.6	7.1	12.3
Occupancy	.58	.72	.67	.66	.71
Case Flow Rate	27.7	41.0	32.2	34.4	21.0
Separations	2635.3	2592.8	2424	963	10259
Beds	98.3	63.2	74	28	488

Note: (a)   These figures are the weighted means of the hospitals in each group.
Source: Queensland Hospital Finance and Hospital Morbidity Data and data supplied by the Australian Bureau of Statistics.

A crude comparison of average cost per case in the two hospital types indicates private hospitals are relatively less expensive, but such a comparison is subject to three serious shortcomings. *First*, the cost data are not strictly comparable because the public hospital figures include medical salaries whereas the private hospital figures do not. Patients in private hospitals choose their own doctor who is then paid by the patient on a fee-for-service basis. For the public hospitals in the sample, medical salaries cost per case (including payments to visiting medical staff) amounted to $52.41 per case, giving a weighted mean public hospital cost per case of $583.70 excluding medical salary costs.

Second, the private hospital cost data include outpatient costs, but such costs have been deducted from the public hospital cost data. Any adjustment for outpatient costs would, of course, reduce private hospital cost per case. This point will be taken up again below.

A *third* and more serious shortcoming of this crude cost comparison, mentioned earlier with respect to other studies, is that it does not take into account differences in the composition of output between the public and private sectors. It is now well established that the composition of a hospital's case load is an important determinant of its costs. The lower cost per case in private hospitals may well be a reflection of their treating a relatively less costly mix of cases. Some authors have argued that for-profit hospitals selectively admit case types with relatively high price-cost margins leaving the less profitable cases to be treated by non-profit or public hospitals—so-called 'cream skimming' behaviour (see Steinwald and Neuhauser 1970; Bays 1977, and references cited therein). Any meaningful cost comparison must take such variations in the composition of output into consideration.

Differences in scale and utilisation could also partially account for the lower average cost per case in private hospitals. Strong evidence that higher case flow and occupancy rates reduce average cost per case was presented in Chapter 6, and private hospitals do have higher such rates (see Table 8.2). Consequently it is important that these factors also be taken into consideration.

The next sub-section presents evidence on differences in the composition of output between the 121 public and 38 private hospitals in this study. A series of cost equations are then estimated to take account of output and other differences between the public and private sectors. This enables some insight to be gained into the relative costliness of public and private hospitals.

8.3.4   Case Mix Differences

Data on the proportion of each hospital's case load falling in each of the 47 mutually exclusive and exhaustive diagnostic categories are presented in Table 8.3. A chi-square test of homogeneity indicates a highly significant difference between the overall composition of cases in the two hospital types. However, it is also of interest to know within which diagnostic categories significant differences occur. To ascertain this, a statistical test on the difference between the proportions in each diagnostic category was carried out. The resulting t-values are also presented in Table 8.3.[9] The

---

9   The test statistic is that used to test the difference between two population proportions (see, for example, Pfaffenberger and Patterson 1977, pp.348-51). In this context it

differences in proportions are significant at the 0.5 per cent level in all but four categories, and is significant at the one per cent level in one of these. Public hospitals treat a significantly lower proportion of cases in 18 diagnostic categories (indicated by a negative t-value) and a significantly higher proportion in 26 diagnostic categories compared with the private hospitals.

The five diagnostic categories in which the public hospitals' proportion of cases is most significantly less than, and the five categories in which the public hospitals' proportion is most significantly greater than, that of the private hospitals are as follows (t-values in parentheses):

Public Hospital Proportion less than Private Hospital Proportion	*Public Hospital Proportion greater than Private Hospital Proportion*
Diagnostic Category	*Diagnostic Category*
29 Other Female Genital (−88.2)	26 Nephritis and Nephrosis (58.98)
1 Investigations, Procedures, Healthy (−79.87)	45 Internal Injury (45.11)
19 Tonsils and Adenoids (−55.54)	33 Normal Delivery (42.13)
21 Dental (−31.16)	42 Other Fractures (excl. Femur Neck) (33.34)
10 Eye and Ear (−27.94)	46 External Injury (30.19)

Of those categories where private hospitals treat a significantly greater proportion of cases than public hospitals, categories 29 Other Female Genital and 1 Investigations, Procedures, Healthy Persons, together account for nearly 20 per cent of the private hospitals' case load, compared with seven per cent in public hospitals. The five categories together account for nearly 30 per cent of the private hospitals' case load. Turning to categories where the public hospitals treat a significantly greater proportion of their cases than private hospitals, 26 Nephritis and Nephrosis and 33 Normal

should be noted that the proportions given in Table 8.3 are weighted means, i.e. they give the proportion of total public (or private) hospital cases contained in each diagnostic category and are not simply the sum of each hospital's proportion in a category divided by the number of hospitals. This latter mean is the one used if a one way analysis-of-variance is used to test for significant differences between diagnostic categories (as in Bays 1977, 1979).

Table 8.3. Proportionate Case Mix Composition in Public and Private Hospitals, 47 Diagnostic Categories, Queensland, 1977-78

No.	Diagnostic Category	Public Hospitals (%)	Private Hospitals (%)	t-value
1	Investigations, Procedures, Healthy	4.04	10.62	-79.87*
2	Infectious & Parasitic	1.71	1.01	15.76*
3	Enteritis, Diarrhoeal Disease	1.32	0.56	20.09*
4	Malignant Neoplasms	4.36	3.71	8.98*
5	Benign Neoplasms	0.98	1.92	-23.87*
6	Endocrine & Metabolic	1.56	1.31	5.66*
7	Blood	0.55	0.57	-0.62
8	Psychiatric	4.14	4.17	-0.55
9	Other CNS & Nerves	2.17	1.68	9.66*
10	Eye & Ear	2.57	4.27	-27.94*
11	Other Heart, Hypertension	2.51	1.59	17.28*
12	Acute Myocardial Infarction	1.18	0.67	14.07*
13	Symptomatic Heart Disease	1.45	0.99	11.24*
14	Cerebrovascular Disease	1.30	1.04	6.60*
15	Circulation	1.96	2.86	-17.32*
16	Upper Respiratory	2.14	0.91	25.72*
17	Pneumonia	1.32	0.81	13.07*
18	Bronchitis, Emphysema, Asthma	3.22	1.76	24.59*
19	Tonsils & Adenoids	1.37	4.18	-55.54*
20	Other Respiratory	1.67	2.32	-13.50*
21	Dental	0.57	1.57	-31.16*
22	Upper Gastrointestinal	1.40	0.89	12.94*
23	Appendicitis	1.25	1.91	-15.59*
24	Hernia	1.43	2.29	-19.19*
25	Other Gastrointestinal	2.96	4.23	-20.03*
26	Nephritis & Nephrosis	3.45	0.09	58.98*
27	Other Urinary	1.65	1.76	-2.53**
28	Male Genital	0.96	1.48	-14.08*
29	Other Female Genital	2.82	9.29	-88.20*
30	Disorders of Menstruation	0.94	1.12	-5.03*
31	Complications of Pregnancy & Puerperium	3.04	1.41	28.69*
32	Abortion	0.88	0.66	6.97*
33	Normal Delivery	8.14	4.26	42.13*
34	Delivery Complications	0.84	0.96	-3.32*
35	Skin Disease	1.98	2.34	-7.00*
36	Orthopaedic	3.57	5.34	-25.37*
37	Congenital Malformation	0.99	1.02	-0.81
38	Perinatal	0.41	0.10	14.99*
39	Immaturity	0.26	0.10	9.59*
40	Symptoms, ill-defined	7.20	6.30	9.89*
41	Long Stay, ill-defined	0.80	1.00	-6.31*

Table 8.3 (cont.)

No.	Diagnostic Category	Public Hospitals (%)	Private Hospitals (%)	t-value
42	Other Fractures (excl. Femur Neck)	3.97	1.80	33.34*
43	Fracture of Neck of Femur	0.40	0.17	10.98*
44	Dislocations	0.58	0.38	7.77*
45	Internal Injury	2.62	0.34	45.11*
46	External Injury	2.89	1.21	30.19*
47	Poisoning	2.49	1.03	28.24*
	Total Cases	318,869	104,393	

Notes: *   Significant at 0.5% level.
             ** Significant at 1% level.
Source: Hospital Morbidity Data.

Delivery account for 11.5 per cent, and the five categories together for 21 per cent, of public hospital case load.

Further evidence on differences in case mix composition with respect to the additional case mix dimensions is presented in Table 8.4. A significantly higher proportion of public hospital patients are male. There is also a dramatic difference in the proportion of patients who had surgery, with the private hospital proportion being over 1.6 times as large as that for public hospitals. The differences in payment status are to be expected, although it is interesting to note that nearly 25 per cent of patients in public hospitals are not public patients in terms of payment status.[10] With regard to separation status, a higher proportion of public hospital patients are transferred or die. Private hospitals treat significantly higher proportions of patients aged 41-64 and 65+. However, the age proportions are very sensitive to the inclusion of two repatriation hospitals. If these two hospitals are excluded, public hospitals treat significantly higher proportions of cases in the 0-4 and 65+ age brackets and lower proportions of the remainder.

The findings reported in this section, where comparable, accord with those of the Commission of Inquiry into the Efficiency and Administration of Hospitals (1981). This Inquiry also investigated in more detail the

---

10   There is evidence of a significant difference in the diagnostic composition of public and non-public patients in public hospitals (see Queensland Department of Health 1982). This aspect will not be pursued here, however, as it is not possible to allocate a public hospital's costs between the different payment classes in any economically meaningful way.

differences in types of operations performed in public and private hospitals, finding that " ... routine and non-urgent surgery dominates the work of most private hospitals" (Commission of Inquiry into the Efficiency and Administration of Hospitals 1981, Vol.2, p.269). There is, therefore, strong evidence that there are substantial and significant differences in the composition of output of public and private hospitals.

Table 8.4. Proportionate Case Mix Composition in Public and Private Hospitals, Additional Case Mix Dimensions, Queensland, 1977-78

Case Mix Category	Public Hospitals (%)	Private Hospitals (%)	t-value*
Male discharges	47.44	39.31	45.81
Surgery performed	37.48	60.86	-132.33
Payment status			
- public	75.42	2.22	415.06
- intermediate	21.82	32.83	-71.76
- private	2.76	64.94	-451.97
Separation status			
- discharged	95.75	96.89	-16.35
- transferred	2.31	1.73	11.11
- died	1.94	1.38	11.83
Age bracket			
- 0-4	9.52	6.06	34.50
- 5-14	9.07	8.59	4.76
- 15-40	39.91	39.08	4.79
- 41-64	25.31	28.72	-21.78
- 65+	16.19	17.56	-10.33

Note: *   All significant at the 0.5% level.
Source: Queensland Hospital Morbidity Data.

8.4   Empirical Analysis of Cost Differences

The question remains as to how much of the difference in average cost per case between public and private hospitals is explicable by the differences in output composition just discussed. This section attempts to provide some evidence on this question by estimating a series of average cost equations relating average cost per case to case mix composition, scale and utilisation using pooled public and private hospital data (n=125). The predicted values of average cost per case for each of the four private hospital observations are then obtained from these equations. Taking the ratio of actual to predicted average cost per case gives a costliness ratio which indicates the extent to which the private hospitals are more or less costly than predicted *after* taking into account their case mix, scale and utilisation.

8.4.1   Specification

The following five specifications of the average cost function were adopted:

$$ACC = a_0 + \sum_{i=1}^{46} a_i p_i \qquad \text{... (8.1)}$$

$$ACC = b_0 + \sum_{j=1}^{56} b_j h_j \qquad \text{... (8.2)}$$

$$ACC = b_0 + \sum_{j=1}^{56} b_j h_j + r_1 CFR + r_2 CFR^2 + r_3 B + r_4 B^2 \qquad \text{... (8.3)}$$

$$ACC = b_0 + \sum_{j=1}^{56} b_j h_j + r_1 ALS + r_2 OCC + r_3 B + r_4 B^2 \qquad \text{... (8.4)}$$

$$ACC = b_0 + \sum_{j=1}^{56} b_j h_j + r_1 ALS + r_2 (365 / CFR) + r_3 (365 RBD / CFR)$$
$$+ r_4 B + r_5 B^2 \qquad \text{... (8.5)}$$

The first of these includes only the proportion of cases in each of the 47 diagnostic categories (the p_i) as explanatory variables (actually 46 plus a constant term a_0). Equation (8.2) includes the 47 diagnostic categories plus the additional case mix dimensions. The remaining three equations incorporate linear and quadratic terms in size (B and B^2) along with various specifications of the utilisation terms—average length of stay (*ALS*), occupancy rate (*OCC*) and case flow rate (*CFR*). Each of these specifications has been discussed earlier in this book.

8.4.2   Results with Public Hospital Medical Salaries and Private Hospital Outpatient Costs Included

The five equations just discussed were then estimated using multiple regression analysis applied to the data on public and private hospitals in

Queensland for 1977-78. Initially, medical salaries were included in public hospital cost per case, while no adjustment was made to private hospital costs to take account of outpatient services. On this basis, the results for equation (8.1) indicate that 42 per cent of the variation in average cost per case between hospitals in the sample is explicable by differences in the diagnostic mix of cases, after adjustment for degrees of freedom (adjusted $R^2 = 0.42$). The overall relationship is significant at the 0.5 per cent level (F = 2.92), but the individual parameter estimates (not included here) generally have implausible values and very high standard errors.

The addition of the extra case mix dimensions in equation (8.2) increased the amount of explained variation in average cost per case to 54 per cent (adjusted $R^2 = 0.54$), again significant at the 0.5 per cent level (F = 3.58).[11] Again, the parameter estimates generally have implausible values and high standard errors, and have not been included here. This problem with the parameter estimates was dealt with in more detail in Chapter 5 and will not be discussed again here. It should be noted that the additional case mix dimensions include patient payment status. Equation (8.2), along with equations (8.3) to (8.5), thus allow for the fact that public hospitals treat intermediate and private patients. Hence the predicted cost per case obtained from any equation allows for any independent influence of patient payment status.

The parameter estimates for the scale and utilisation variables in equations (8.3) to (8.5) are presented in Table 8.5. The addition of the case flow rate terms in equation (8.3) adds significantly to the amount of explained variation in average cost per case, with the coefficient implying that cost per case falls with increases in case flow up to 53.7 cases per bed per year. The alternative specification in equation (8.4) with linear terms in average length of stay and occupancy implies that a higher average length of stay will increase cost per case while higher occupancy will reduce cost per case. Equation (8.5) includes significant scale terms in beds, with the hospital size which minimises cost per case depending upon the case flow rate.[12] With a case flow rate of 23.61 cases per bed (the unweighted mean of the entire sample), cost per case is minimised at a size of 283 beds.

A predicted cost per case can now be obtained for each private hospital from each estimated equation. These predicted values, together with actual cost per case and the ratios of actual to predicted values, are given in Table

---

[11]   An incremental F test indicated that the increase in explanatory power arising from the addition of the other case mix dimensions was also significant at the 0.5 per cent level.

[12]   See Chapter 6 for a discussion of the interaction between size and the case flow rate in this specification.

Table 8.5. Parameter Estimates for Scale and Utilisation Variables, Pooled Public and Private Hospital Sample, Public Hospital Medical Salaries and Private Hospital Outpatient Costs Included, Queensland, 1977-78[a]

	Equation (8.3)	Equation (8.4)	Equation (8.5)
ALS		41.114 (6.26*)	13.655 (1.85)
OCC		-706.53 (-5.22*)	
CFR	-28.958 (-6.73*)		
CFR^2	0.26977 (4.93*)		
$\frac{365}{CFR}$			4.4285 (3.85*)
$\frac{365RBD}{CFR}$			.000252 (2.63**)
Beds			-1.7208 (-2.46**)
$Beds^2$			.000533 (1.63)
$\bar{R}^2$	.75	.74	.76
SEE	126.86	129.76	124.60
F	7.47*	7.09*	7.45*

Note: *   Significant at 0.5% level.
        **   Significant at 5% level.
       (a) t-values in parentheses. Parameter estimates for 47 diagnostic categories and additional case mix dimensions not included here.
Source: Regression results.

8.6. The first point to note about these data concerns the *actual* cost per case of the private hospitals relative to the weighted State mean cost per case in public and private hospitals of $613.17. This ratio is shown under each hospital's actual cost per case in Table 8.6 and is less than unity for three of the four observations with private hospital B having a cost per case nearly half that of the weighted State mean. These comparisons are, however, not very meaningful because the cost data have not been adjusted to exclude medical salaries in public hospitals or outpatient costs in private hospitals, and because no account has been taken of differences in output mix.

Table 8.6. Actual and Predicted Cost Per Case and Costliness Ratios for Private Hospitals Unadjusted for Public Hospital Medical Salaries and Private Hospital Outpatient Costs, Queensland, 1977-78

Hospital	Actual Cost per Case[a]	Predicted Cost per Case[b]				
		Eqn (8.1)	Eqn (8.2)	Eqn (8.3)	Eqn (8.4)	Eqn (8.5)
Aggregate Private Hospitals	423.36 0.69	544.04 0.78	553.19 0.77	516.51 0.82	501.89 0.84	548.27 0.77
A	498.22 0.81	511.33 0.97	562.51 0.89	506.94 0.98	494.46 1.01	507.99 0.98
B	334.35 0.55	331.38 1.01	311.74 1.07	250.77 1.33	267.93 1.24	235.52 1.42
C	1607.47 2.62	1406.94 1.14	1510.30 1.06	1505.07 1.07	1495.09 1.08	1497.70 1.07

Notes: (a) Figure under each cost per case is the ratio of actual to weighted state mean cost per case ($613.17).
(b) Figure under each predicted cost per case is the ratio of actual to predicted cost per case (the costliness ratio).
Source: Regression results.

This latter limitation is overcome by comparing each private hospital's actual cost per case with its predicted value from each cost equation rather than with the State mean. The costliness ratios (actual/predicted average cost per case) are given under each predicted cost per case figure in Table 8.6. The aggregate private hospital observation indicates that, in each of the five specifications investigated, actual cost per case is below that predicted. The predicted values, however, are all below the State mean, with the result that the costliness ratios all exceed the relative cost ratio (actual/State mean average cost per case). The superior cost performance of the aggregate private hospitals is reduced after differences in case mix and other factors are taken into account, but average cost per case is still less than expected.

Looking at the individual private hospitals, for private hospital A the same behaviour is demonstrated, although in this case the superior cost performance is virtually eliminated after adjusting for case mix and other factors. The performance of private hospital B is interesting. Although its actual cost per case is almost half the State mean, this difference is entirely eliminated and its position reversed after output and other relevant differences are adjusted for. This hospital's actual cost per case is seen to be up to 42 per cent above that expected, given its case mix, average length of stay, occupancy and size. Private hospital C is seen to have a cost per case over 2.5 times greater than the State mean, virtually all of which can be attributed to its case mix, average length of stay, occupancy and size.

8.4.3   Results with Public Hospital Medical Salaries and Private Hospital Outpatient Costs Excluded

The foregoing results are based on cost data which include medical salaries in public hospitals (but not private hospitals) and outpatient costs in private hospitals (but not public hospitals). Data on medical salaries and payments to visiting medical staff were available for each public hospital in the sample and were deducted from total cost. On average, such costs amount to $52.41 per case. No data are available, however, on outpatient costs in private hospitals, so it was decided to convert outpatient visits to equivalent inpatient days at the rate of 5:1, a ratio previously (but no longer) employed by the ABS in Queensland to estimate outpatient costs. With outpatient costs calculated in this fashion deducted from private hospital costs, and medical salaries deducted from public hospital costs, the five equations were re-estimated. Parameter estimates for the scale and utilisation terms in equations (8.3) to (8.5) from the re-estimated equations are presented in Table 8.7.[13]

Overall, the parameter estimates are similar to their counterparts in Table 8.5 with the same signs and approximately the same values and levels of significance. Equation (8.3) implies minimum average cost per case is achieved at a case flow rate of 53.9 (compared with 53.7 from equation (8.3) in Table 8.5), while equation (8.5) indicates economies of scale are exhausted at 279 beds (compared with 283 from equation (8.5) in Table 8.5).[14]

---

[13] Again the parameter estimates for the case mix categories are not included here for any specifications.

[14] Optimal size is again evaluated at a case flow rate of 23.61.

Table 8.7. Parameter Estimates for Scale and Utilisation Variables, Pooled Public and Private Hospital Sample, Public Hospital Medical Salaries and Private Hospital Outpatient Costs Excluded, Queensland, 1977-78[a]

	Equation (8.3)	Equation (8.4)	Equation (8.5)
ALS		40.347 (6.58*)	13.80 (2.00**)
OCC		-685.95 (-5.42*)	
CFR	-28.097 (-6.97*)		
CFR^2	0.26065 (5.09*)		
$\dfrac{365}{CFR}$			4.1818 (3.87*)
$\dfrac{365RBD}{CFR}$			.000247 (2.76**)
Beds			-1.6723 (-2.55**)
Beds^2			.000496 (1.62)
$\bar{R}^2$	.76	.75	.77
SEE	118.74	121.24	116.78
F	7.79*	7.42*	7.74*

Note: *   Significant at 0.5% level.
        **   Significant at 5% level.
        (a) t-values in parentheses. Parameter estimates for 47 diagnostic categories and additional case mix dimensions not included here.
Source: Regression results.

The actual and predicted cost per case and costliness ratios for each private hospital from these re-estimated equations are presented in Table 8.8. It can be seen that the actual cost figures are lower than in Table 8.5, the difference reflecting the exclusion of estimated outpatient costs. The reduction in the private hospitals' average cost per case on this account is considerably smaller than the reduction in the public hospitals' cost per case because of the exclusion of medical salaries which, as has already been noted, reduces mean cost per case in public hospitals by $52.41 per case. As a result, the overall mean cost per case for all hospitals in the sample falls by a much greater proportion than the private hospitals' average cost per case. Actual average cost per case in private hospitals is now higher relative to the State mean, as can be seen from the relative cost ratios in the actual cost per case column in Table 8.8 compared with those of Table 8.6. Hence, in terms of the comparisons of actual cost per case and the State mean, the removal of public hospital medical salaries and private hospital outpatient costs reduces the superior cost performance of private hospitals with average cost per case below the State mean, and increases the inferior cost performance of private hospitals with average cost per case above the State mean.

Table 8.8. Actual and Predicted Cost Per Case and Costliness Ratios for Private Hospitals Adjusted for Public Hospital Medical Salaries and Private Hospital Outpatient Costs, Queensland, 1977-78

Hospital	Actual Cost per Case[a]	Predicted Cost per Case[b]				
		Eqn (8.1)	Eqn (8.2)	Eqn (8.3)	Eqn (8.4)	Eqn (8.5)
Aggregate Private Hospitals	418.72 0.73	509.59 0.82	542.96 0.77	506.97 0.83	492.96 0.85	536.33 0.78
A	496.48 0.87	504.34 0.98	568.88 0.87	515.17 0.96	502.49 0.99	514.44 0.97
B	334.35[c] 0.58	332.31 1.01	315.51 1.06	256.21 1.30	273.60 1.22	239.50 1.40
C	1564.30 2.74	1350.36 1.16	1473.13 1.06	1468.03 1.07	1458.01 1.07	1460.66 1.07

Notes: (a) Figure under each cost per case is the ratio of actual to weighted state mean cost per case excluding public hospital medical salaries and private hospital outpatient costs ($571.76).
(b) Figure under each predicted cost per case is the ratio of actual to predicted cost per case (the costliness ratio).
(c) This figure is the same as in Table 8.6 because this hospital had no outpatient clinic.

Source: Regression results.

The effect of taking into account differences in case mix, average length of stay, occupancy and size is virtually the same in the re-estimated equations as in the original equations. For the aggregated private hospitals and private hospital A, predicted cost per case is less than the State mean, so that their superior cost performance is reduced after adjustment for output composition and the other factors, although they are still cheaper than predicted. Private hospital B again suffers a reversal of its position, while private hospital C's inferior performance with respect to the State average is almost entirely explained by the variables in equations (8.3) to (8.5).

8.5   Summary and Conclusions

This chapter has been concerned with the relative productive efficiency of public and private hospitals. The property rights and public choice literature in economics both lead to an expectation that private enterprises will be more efficient than their public counterparts, but the theory of regulation suggests that, if the private firms are highly regulated, they may well be as inefficient as public firms.

A major problem encountered in examining this issue was the paucity of cost data for private hospitals. Such data are not generally available and individual requests to private hospitals for such data elicited a poor response. Consequently an aggregate private hospital observation had to be employed, an unfortunate situation because a few of these hospitals, *viz.* repatriation hospitals, are private not in ownership but in that they cater for a restricted clientele. In any event, the ownership issue may not be of overriding importance because of the highly regulated environment within which private hospitals operate.

The empirical investigation found statistically significant differences between the mix of patients treated in public and private hospitals with respect to both diagnostic and other case classification criteria. Average cost per case was also found to be substantially lower in private hospitals. An attempt was then made to estimate the extent to which differences in case mix, along with differences in scale and utilisation, explain the superior cost performance of private hospitals.

The approach taken here was to estimate a number of average cost equations and obtain from such equations predicted values of average cost per case for each of the private hospital observations (four in total). The actual average cost per case in each of these hospitals was then compared with these predictions, the expectation being that if case mix, scale and utilisation fully explained the superior cost performance of private hospitals then the actual and predicted values would be at least equal.

The results indicated that while case mix, scale and utilisation did explain some of the superior cost performance of the private hospitals compared with the overall State mean, the aggregated private hospitals were still less costly than predicted. This was the case even after the public hospital cost data had been purged of medical salaries (which do not appear in the private hospital cost data) and the private hospital cost data had been purged of outpatient costs (which are not included in the public hospital cost data). This adjustment narrowed the difference in average cost per case between the two types of hospital but the aggregated private hospitals continued to have an actual average cost per case which was less than predicted.

This result was not replicated for the three individual private hospitals in the sample. For one of these, the superior cost performance virtually disappeared after adjustment for case mix, scale and utilisation. For another, an actual average cost per case of nearly half the State mean was actually 40 per cent higher than predicted based on that hospital's case mix, scale and utilisation. The third private hospital's actual average cost per case was substantially in excess of the State mean but was nearly equal to its predicted value.

Clearly the evidence from the four observations is not uniform, but if one placed more weight on the aggregated private hospital as being representative of the private hospital sector, the evidence tends to support superior cost performance by such hospitals even after allowance for the effects of case mix, scale and utilisation. This conclusion is advanced cautiously, however, and must be treated as tentative because of the lack of individual private hospital cost data. The availability of such data would enable a more accurate distinction to be drawn between private hospitals based on ownership, and hence would allow a more thorough investigation than that undertaken here of the hypotheses discussed at the beginning of this chapter.

9

A COMPARISON OF PUBLIC HOSPITAL COSTS

IN QUEENSLAND AND NEW SOUTH WALES

9.1   Introduction

This chapter addresses the perplexing question of the reasons for interstate differences in public hospital costs between two States in Australia. At the outset, one may well question the wisdom of such a venture. To say that the Commonwealth Grants Commission (CGC)—a body vitally concerned with interstate comparisons—has found this area bothersome would be an understatement. In both the Report on State Tax Sharing Entitlements 1981 (CGC 1981) and the Report on State Tax Sharing and Health Grants 1982 (CGC 1982), the Commission was forced to exercise "broad judgment" as a supplement to the meagre amount of information and analysis available on the causes of interstate variations in per capita expenditures in the General Medical Services category (of which expenditure on hospital-type services accounted for about 76 per cent—CGC 1981, Vol.I, p.181). The inadequacy of currently available data was mentioned several times in the latter Report (see CGC 1982, Vol.I, pp.9,114,115), leading the CGC to assert that "if any future inquiry into tax sharing relativities on hospital costs is to be undertaken by the Commission, it would regard it as essential to develop appropriate procedures and institute suitable inquiries to overcome the basic data deficiencies ... " (CGC 1982, Vol.I, p.9).

In the mid-1980s, the Grants Commission again undertook a review of State tax-sharing relativities (CGC 1985). At the conclusion of this inquiry, which was completed within twelve months, the Commission again lamented the absence of any arrangements which provide for effective data collection in the absence of a specific reference for a further inquiry. Accordingly it favoured "a system of continuing data collection and investigations independent of actual references ... " (CGC 1985, Vol.I, p.89).

Apart from problems of data, some may query the need to undertake an exercise of this nature. A major justification undoubtedly arises from the fact that in the foreseeable future the Grants Commission will continue to require answers to this type of question in providing recommendations on grants to the States. This argument neither endorses nor rejects horizontal fiscal equalisation (the objective of the Grants Commission) as an objective of public policy but accepts it as a constraint.[1] Nor does it endorse or reject the arguments of those such as Wallace (1983) that the need for an answer to this question would disappear if a large part of the provision of hospital services was transferred to the private sector. Such issues are undoubtedly worthy of debate but lie outside the scope of this study.

Apart from the issues connected with the Grants Commission, explaining interstate differences in hospital costs is important for health policy at the State level. Knowledge of the reasons for interstate differences may suggest organisational and administrative reforms which could reduce hospital costs, or may indicate that such matters are irrelevant.

This chapter contains two main empirical sections. The first of these contains some descriptive statistics on differences between the two States (Section 9.3). The second presents some results on the extent to which the observed differences in hospital costs are attributable to differences in case mix, scale and utilisation (Section 9.4). This will help to clarify whether and to what extent the interstate differences are due to differences in policy or to relative efficiency. Before proceeding with the empirical results, however, some background discussion on the Grants Commission and its procedures is necessary to set the stage for these results.

---

[1]   The efficiency and equity effects of fiscal equalisation have been thoroughly debated in economics. For an overview of these arguments see Oates (1972) and references cited therein. In the Australian context, see Mathews (1979), Brennan (1979) and Walsh (1989).

9.2 The Grants Commission Procedures

From its inception in 1933 until 1978, the Commonwealth Grants Commission was charged with the responsibility of providing recommendations to the Commonwealth Government on special grants for claimant States. The rationale for such grants was the existence of horizontal fiscal imbalance between the States. Such imbalance can arise on either the revenue or expenditure sides of the budget or both. On the revenue-raising side, fiscally poorer States which have lower values of one or more tax bases will have to impose higher tax rates than their fiscally richer neighbours in order to raise an equivalent amount of revenue. On the expenditure side, some States may incur higher costs of providing equivalent services than other States because of factors such as differences in the composition and geographical dispersion of their populations. "The simplest way of correcting for horizontal fiscal imbalance, and the one which has been used in Australia, is for the central government to make grants to the fiscally poorer States to enable them to attain the same average fiscal standard as the richest State" (Lane 1974, p.141).

It must be emphasised that the Grants Commission has never simply used a comparison of actual budget results between the States as a basis for recommending special grants. Clearly the unadjusted budget results also reflect policy differences between the States in addition to differences in revenue-raising capacity and the costs of providing equivalent services. For example, a State may levy a higher tax rate on a particular tax base because of a conscious policy decision to raise more revenue and not just to compensate for a lower value of its tax base. The Grants Commission has always attempted to make modifications and adjustments to State budgets so as to exclude the effects of policy differences between the States.

The terms of reference of the Grants Commission were considerably broadened in 1978 when it was asked to undertake an inquiry into the relative positions of all six States following an agreement between the Commonwealth and the States regarding new arrangements for the sharing of personal income tax revenue.[2] In the submissions and hearings leading up to the Commission's recommendations, the General Medical Services category of State expenditures (the bulk of which constituted expenditure on

---

2   A discussion of the events leading up to this request can be found in CGC (1983, Ch.7) and CGC (1981, Vol.I, Ch.1). The former also contains a detailed history of the Commission since its inception.

hospitals) proved to be controversial.[3] This was also the case for the second State relativities review (CGC 1982). An important part of this controversy revolved around the problem of determining to what extent interstate differences in expenditure on General Medical Services reflected policy decisions by the States as opposed to non-policy related differences in costs.[4]

The Grants Commission had insufficient data at its disposal to investigate the possible effects of interstate differences in case mix on interstate differences in hospital costs. This chapter explores this issue for two States in an attempt to ascertain whether the higher costs incurred in one State (New South Wales) can be attributed to the treatment of a more costly case load by hospitals in that State. The influences of scale and utilisation are also investigated.

In undertaking this analysis, the treated case, as opposed to the occupied bed day, is again adopted as the conceptually preferred measure of output. As such, the interstate comparisons presented here are in terms of average cost per case. The possibly misleading nature of occupied bed day cost comparisons was discussed earlier (see Chapter 3, Section 3.3.2) where it was pointed out that, because of the length of stay/cost per day trade-off faced by hospitals, a relatively high average cost per day does not necessarily indicate a relatively high average cost per case.

It appears, however, that the evidence which the Grants Commission collected on hospital costs was expressed in terms of occupied bed day costs. For example, "a scale-related dispersion index was calculated by applying to the size distribution of urban centres the levels of bed provision recommended by the Sax Report on Hospitals in Australia, adjusted by the higher numbers of occupied beds per capita provided to non-metropolitan populations and the *higher occupied bed day cost* of those beds provided to the populations residing in centres of less than 5,000 persons" (CGC 1981, Vol.I, p.183, emphasis added). Also, the expenditure weights applied to each component of General Medical Services were based on relative bed day costs (CGC 1982, Vol.I, p.125).[5]

---

[3] On the composition of the General Medical Services category, see footnote 12 in Chapter 4.

[4] The relevant sections which discuss the assessment of expenditure needs for General Medical Services in the two Reports are CGC (1981, Vol.I, pp.178-83) and CGC (1982, Vol.I, pp.112-38).

[5] See also CGC (1983, p.29). Interstate comparisons using bed day costs have also been presented by Sanderson (1983). For interstate comparisons based on average cost per

A further point to be noted about the Grants Commission interstate comparisons is that they are generally expressed in per capita terms. With regard to hospitals, such a comparison reflects not only differences in the cost of treating cases admitted to hospitals but also differences in admission rates. Consider the following relationship:

$$\frac{\text{Total Hospital Costs}}{\text{Total Population}} = \frac{\text{Total Hospital Costs}}{\text{Number of Cases}} \times \frac{\text{Number of Cases}}{\text{Total Population}}$$

This can be expressed as follows:

$$\text{Hospital Costs Per Capita} = ACC \times \text{Admission Rate}$$

Hence interstate differences in per capita hospital costs may reflect differing average costs per case (ACC) or differing admission rates or both. For example, the hospitals in two States may have exactly the same average cost per case but one State may have per capita hospital costs which are greater than the other because the admission rate is higher. In this case, the search for causes of interstate differences in per capita hospital costs should focus on the reasons for interstate differences in admission rates. This study avoids any interstate comparisons of admission rates by concentrating on average cost per case.

9.3 Descriptive Statistics

9.3.1 The Data

This study employs the data on 121 Queensland public hospitals used elsewhere in this study together with data on 222 New South Wales public hospitals for the financial year 1979-80. For this particular year, the Health Commission of New South Wales counted 241 Second and Third Schedule Medical, Surgical and Obstetrics hospitals in that State. Some hospitals have been deleted in each State for one or more a number of reasons—no inpatients were treated in the year; hospital morbidity data were unavailable; the proportion of days attributable to long stay patients was so high that the institution appeared to be more like a nursing home; the hospital did not

---

case which also take into account the cost per case/cost per day/length of stay relationship, see Marshall and Robb (1984).

operate for the full year; or the hospital finance and hospital morbidity data could not be reconciled.

In obtaining estimates of hospital inpatient costs the problem of outpatient costs arises again. Recall that, in Queensland, each hospital produces estimates of the costs of providing outpatient services, and these (along with the costs of dental clinics and ambulance services where relevant) have been deducted from maintenance expenditures to arrive at inpatient costs. In New South Wales, no such estimates are produced by hospitals. The Health Commission, for 1979-80, made an adjustment for outpatient services by equating 700 outpatient visits with an average daily census of unity (or 365 occupied bed days). This adjustment was applied to each hospital to produce adjusted numbers of cases and days which were then used to calculate average cost per case and average cost per day. No capital charges are included in the cost data of either State.

9.3.2   Cost/Volume Characteristics

The weighted mean cost per case, cost per day and length of stay for Queensland and New South Wales are presented in Table 9.1 and illustrated diagrammatically in Figure 9.1. Average cost per case in New South Wales is over $200 greater than in Queensland, and this is reflected in both a higher mean cost per day and a higher mean length of stay. These mean cost per case figures conceal a wide range of values of average cost per case for hospitals in each State. This can be seen in the relative frequency distribution of hospitals by cost per case for the two States in Figure 9.2. Both distributions are skewed to the left with each State having a relatively small number of high cost hospitals.

Table 9.1. Weighted Mean Cost Per Case, Cost Per Day, and Length of Stay, Queensland and New South Wales Public Hospitals, 1979-80

	ACC	ACD	ALS
Queensland	$719.16	$103.65	6.94
New South Wales	$926.11	$127.04	7.29

Source: Hospital Morbidity Data and Hospital Finance Data supplied by Queensland and New South Wales.

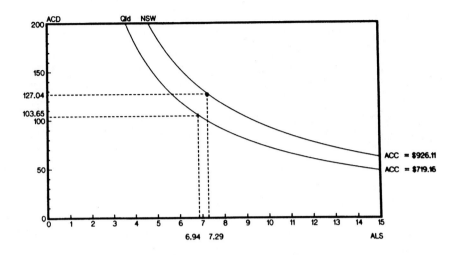

Figure 9.1. Weighted Mean Cost per Case, Cost per Day and Length of Stay,
Queensland and New South Wales, 1979-80

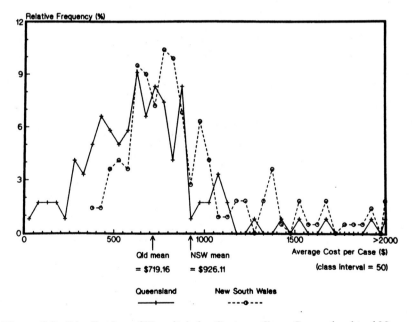

Figure 9.2. Distribution of Hospitals by Cost per Case, Queensland and New
South Wales, 1979-80 (with outpatient adjustment)

Some additional indicators of variation in the cost/volume characteristics of hospitals within and between the two State systems are provided in Table 9.2. The means in this Table are unweighted means, i.e. they are calculated as the sum of the particular value for each hospital divided by the number of hospitals. On every characteristic listed, Queensland has a higher degree of dispersion than New South Wales as indicated by the higher coefficients of variation. It is interesting to note that New South Wales hospitals, on average, have a higher case flow rate and higher occupancy than Queensland hospitals although the average size of hospitals in New South Wales (in terms of beds) is not substantially greater. These differences are reflected in the higher average number of patients treated in New South Wales hospitals compared with Queensland.

Table 9.2. Selected Characteristics of Queensland and New South Wales Public Hospital Systems, 1979-80

	Queensland			New South Wales		
	Mean	SD	CV	Mean	SD	CV
ACC ($)	690.27	495.57	0.72	903.20	396.11	0.44
ACD ($)	109.10	106.20	0.97	101.57	35.38	0.35
ALS	7.98	11.43	1.43	9.69	6.04	0.62
Case Flow Rate	24.67	15.88	0.64	29.82	12.97	0.44
Occupancy	0.43	0.20	0.47	0.65	0.15	0.23
Beds	99	182	1.84	115	168	1.46
Inpatients	2991	6474	2.16	4098	6501	1.59

Notes: SD = standard deviation.
CV = coefficient of variation.
Means are unweighted means where applicable.
Source: Table 5.6 and Hospital Morbidity and Hospital Finance Data supplied by New South Wales.

9.3.3   Case Mix Differences

The final comparison in this section concerns the case mix of the hospitals in the two States. Using the 47 diagnostic category classification, the weighted mean proportion of cases treated in each diagnostic category in each State was calculated. These proportions are presented in Table 9.3. The difference in proportions in each category was tested for statistical significance, giving the t-values shown in the Table. In only eight diagnostic categories was the difference *not* significant at the one per cent level. The categories where Queensland's proportions are most significantly *greater* than New South Wales are: 41 Long Stay, ill-defined; 33 Normal Delivery; 3 Enteritis, Diarrhoeal Disease; 26 Nephritis and Nephrosis; and 8 Psychiatric. The categories where Queensland's proportions are most significantly *less* than New South Wales are: 34 Delivery Complications; 45 Internal Injury; 38 Perinatal; and 30 Disorders of Menstruation.

It might be argued that these differences are a reflection of different coding practices of physicians which may appear at this level of disaggregation. As a check on this, the proportions were recalculated using the 18 diagnostic category classification scheme and the differences again checked for statistical significance. It seems reasonable to expect that any differences in coding practices would have little or no effect at this level of aggregation. The results of this exercise are presented in Table 9.4. The difference between the proportions in each category is significant at the one per cent level for all categories except category 3 Endocrine, Nutritional and Metabolic.

Further evidence of differences in case mix composition is presented in Table 9.5. With the exception of the proportion of patients discharged, there are significant differences between the States along all of these additional dimensions. This is particularly so with respect to the proportion of cases which receive surgery (lower in Queensland), the public/intermediate-private mix of patients (Queensland has a much higher proportion of public patients) and the proportions of patients who are transferred and who die (respectively higher and lower in Queensland).

9.4   Empirical Results on the Causes of Interstate Cost Differences

The question arises as to what extent the difference in average cost per case between Queensland and New South Wales documented in the previous section is explicable by differences in case mix, scale and utilisation rates and size between the States. The influence of these factors must be estimated if the effect of organisational differences between the States is to be explored. As was pointed out in Chapter 4, the Queensland hospital system developed along quite different lines to the hospital systems in the other States, in particular adopting a higher degree of centralised control over its hospitals. It was also pointed out in that chapter that Queensland has had the lowest hospital costs, per case or per capita, for some decades. The idea that Queensland had lower hospital costs than other States *because* of its more centralised control over hospitals has a number of adherents.

Table 9.3. Public Hospital Case Mix Composition, 47 Diagnostic Categories, Queensland and New South Wales, 1979-80[a]

No.	Diagnostic Category	Qld (%)	NSW (%)	t-value
1	Factors Influencing Health States	6.06	5.62	9.62
2	Infectious & Parasitic	1.44	1.41	1.29*
3	Enteritis, Diarrhoeal Disease	1.02	0.29	52.78
4	Malignant Neoplasms	3.54	4.24	-18.09
5	Benign Neoplasms	0.88	1.56	-29.80
6	Endocrine & Metabolic	1.31	1.32	-0.45*
7	Blood	0.59	0.69	-6.28
8	Psychiatric	3.84	2.40	44.34
9	Other CNS & Nerves	2.18	1.90	10.23
10	Eye & Ear	2.47	2.65	-5.76
11	Other Heart, Hypertension	2.34	2.91	-17.74
12	Acute Myocardial Infarction	1.07	1.20	-6.17
13	Symptomatic Heart Disease	1.52	1.51	0.42*
14	Cerebrovascular Disease	1.26	1.36	-4.44
15	Circulation	1.69	2.05	-13.26
16	Upper Respiratory	1.96	1.79	6.44
17	Pneumonia	1.14	0.88	13.61
18	Bronchitis, Emphysema, Asthma	3.57	2.65	27.84
19	Tonsils & Adenoids	0.98	1.10	-5.95
20	Other Respiratory	1.52	1.50	0.84*
21	Dental	0.58	0.79	-12.55
22	Upper Gastrointestinal	1.33	2.04	-26.90
23	Appendicitis	1.10	1.40	-13.40
24	Hernia	1.29	1.31	-0.90*
25	Other Gastrointestinal	3.84	4.59	-18.66
26	Nephritis & Nephrosis	4.42	2.85	44.74
27	Other Urinary	1.73	2.20	-16.81
28	Male Genital	0.92	1.06	-7.09
29	Other Female Genital	3.00	3.74	-20.41
30	Disorders of Menstruation	0.75	1.54	-35.29
31	Complications of Pregnancy & Puerperium	2.42	2.43	-0.33*
32	Abortion	0.89	1.66	-32.88
33	Normal Delivery	6.09	3.68	60.01
34	Delivery Complications	2.55	4.54	-51.84
35	Skin Disease	1.93	2.14	-7.49
36	Orthopaedic	4.26	4.81	-13.29
37	Congenital Malformation	0.85	1.30	-21.28
38	Perinatal	0.27	0.99	-41.51
39	Immaturity	0.11	0.30	-19.52
40	Symptoms, ill-defined	7.15	6.00	24.04
41	Long Stay, ill-defined	1.70	0.14	104.18
42	Other Fractures (excl. Femur)	3.40	3.48	-2.33*

Table 9.3 (cont.)

No.	Diagnostic Category	Qld (%)	NSW (%)	t-value
43	Fracture of Neck of Femur	0.35	0.41	-4.88
44	Dislocations	0.54	0.78	-14.53
45	Internal Injury	2.58	1.41	-45.49
46	External Injury	3.26	3.26	0.00*
47	Poisoning	2.30	2.11	7.77

Notes: *   *Not* significant at 1% level.
      (a)   Case mix proportions are weighted means.
Source: Hospital Morbidity Data, Queensland and New South Wales.

Table 9.4. Public Hospital Case Mix Composition, 18 Diagnostic Categories, Queensland and New South Wales, 1979-80[a]

No.	Diagnostic Category	Qld (%)	NSW (%)	t-value
1	Infectious & Parasitic Diseases	2.46	1.70	28.21
2	Neoplasms	4.42	5.80	-31.05
3	Endocrine, Nutritional & Metabolic	1.31	1.32	-0.45*
4	Blood	0.59	0.69	-6.28
5	Mental Disorders	3.84	2.40	44.34
6	Nervous System	4.66	4.55	2.68
7	Circulatory System	7.88	9.03	-20.76
8	Respiratory System	9.18	7.93	23.07
9	Digestive System	8.14	10.12	-34.27
10	Genito-Urinary System	10.82	11.40	-9.35
11	Complications of Pregnancy, Childbirth & Puerperium	11.95	12.30	-5.44
12	Skin & Subcutaneous Tissue	1.93	2.14	-7.49
13	Musculoskeletal System	4.26	4.81	-13.29
14	Congenital Anomalies	0.85	1.30	-21.28
15	Causes of Perinatal Morbidity & Mortality	0.38	1.29	-45.84
16	Symptoms & ill-defined	8.85	6.13	54.59
17	Accidents, Poisonings & Violence	12.43	11.45	15.50
18	Supplementary Classifications	6.06	5.62	9.62

Notes: *   *Not* significant at 1% level.
      (a)   Case mix proportions are weighted means.
Source: As for Table 9.3.

Table 9.5. Additional Public Hospital Case Mix Dimensions, Queensland and New South Wales, 1979-80[a]

Case Mix Category	Qld (%)	NSW (%)	t-value
Male discharges	46.60	44.43	22.19
Surgery performed	32.95	54.54	-219.83
Payment status			
- public	77.81	39.88	386.04
- intermediate and private	22.19	60.12	-386.04
Separation status			
- discharged	93.06	92.93	2.59*
- transferred	3.28	0.88	98.45
- died	3.66	6.20	-56.80
Age bracket			
- 0-4	9.75	9.25	8.72
- 5-14	9.19	7.99	22.10
- 15-40	39.35	40.05	-7.28
- 41-64	24.85	25.01	-1.88
- 65+	16.86	17.70	-11.26

Note: * *Not* significant at 1% level.
(a) Case mix proportions are weighted means.
Source: As for Table 9.3.

Hielscher (1983) has expounded this view, and the Grants Commission" concluded that Queensland's management policy ... was a major cause of Queensland's relatively low hospital costs." (CGC 1982, Vol.I, p.134).

The current state of knowledge in this area suggests that this position must still be taken as an hypothesis. What is required is systematic, empirical estimation of the factors likely to influence the interstate differentials in hospital costs within a theoretical framework which takes cognisance of the fact that the hospital is a multiproduct firm. A step in this direction has been taken by Marshall and Robb (1984) using CAPAS data, but information on case mix was unavailable. The aim of this chapter is to extend our knowledge in this direction.

9.4.1   Separate State Estimates

As a first step, the amount of variation in cost per case *within* each State explained by case mix (using the 47 diagnostic category proportions and other case mix dimensions), scale and utilisation has been estimated. This was done by estimating a series of five average cost equations, the specifications of which are identical to the five equations used in the previous chapter on public and private hospitals (see Section 8.4.1). These equations are as follows:

$$ACC = a_0 + \sum_{i=1}^{46} a_i p_i \qquad \text{... (9.1)}$$

$$ACC = b_0 + \sum_{j=1}^{56} b_j h_j \qquad \text{... (9.2)}$$

$$ACC = b_0 + \sum_{j=1}^{56} b_j h_j + r_1 CFR + r_2 CFR^2 + r_3 B + r_4 B^2 \qquad \text{... (9.3)}$$

$$ACC = b_0 + \sum_{j=1}^{56} b_j h_j + r_1 ALS + r_2 OCC + r_3 B + r_4 B^2 \qquad \text{... (9.4)}$$

$$ACC = b_0 + \sum_{j=1}^{56} b_j h_j + r_1 ALS + r_2 (365 / CFR) + r_3 (365 RBD / CFR)$$

$$+ r_4 B + r_5 B^2 \qquad \text{... (9.5)}$$

It might seem that the estimated equations for any particular specification for each State could be used to indicate whether the *between* State variation in average cost per case has been reduced. Could not the average *predicted* cost per case be calculated for each State to see if this difference is less than the actual difference after allowing for the factors included in the equation? The answer is no, because of a well-known property of ordinary least squares regression that the mean of estimated values of the dependent variable is equal to the mean of the actual values of that variable (Koutsoyiannis 1977, p.67). Consequently, the mean predicted cost per case for Queensland and New South Wales from any of the above specifications will be equal to their respective actual (unweighted) means in Table 9.2.

The results, however, may still bring some evidence to bear on the hypothesis that the higher degree of centralised control of hospitals in Queensland has led to its superior cost performance. If this hypothesis is true, then it might also seem reasonable to expect that a larger proportion of the *within* State variation in cost per case in Queensland is explicable by the factors included in the cost equations. Since (at least until the late 1980s) "planning, administration, standards of care and efficiency, staffing,

purchasing, pharmaceutical manufacturing and budgetary policy generally
are centralised in and strictly supervised by the Department of Health in
Queensland" (Hielscher 1983, p.77), there would seem to be less scope for
individual hospital variation in quality of care, staffing and X-inefficiency
than in a less centralised system. On the basis of this argument, one would
expect that the estimated equations would explain a larger amount of cost
per case variation in Queensland than in New South Wales.

While the results lend some support to this argument, the evidence is not
conclusive. The summary statistics presented in Table 9.6 show that, for the
first specification equation (9.1), 58 per cent of the variation in average cost
per case in Queensland is explained by the diagnostic mix of patients
compared with 47 per cent in New South Wales. When the additional
dimensions of case mix are added (equation (9.2)), the proportion of the
variation so explained increases to 59 per cent for Queensland and 57 per
cent for New South Wales. Of the three remaining specifications, equation
(9.3) has greater explanatory power for New South Wales while equations
(9.4) and (9.5) have slightly less. The standard error of estimate (the
standard deviation of predicted cost per case) is less for New South Wales in
every equation.

Table 9.6. Summary Statistics for Estimated Cost Functions, Queensland and New
South Wales Public Hospitals, 1979-80

Specification		Queensland			New South Wales		
		$\bar{R}^2$	F*	SEE	$\bar{R}^2$	F*	SEE
Equation	(9.1)	.58	4.62	320.83	.47	5.25	288.47
	(9.2)	.59	4.10	318.36	.57	6.17	260.66
	(9.3)	.72	5.86	264.46	.77	14.01	188.55
	(9.4)	.89	16.12	166.93	.85	22.09	154.96
	(9.5)	.92	24.12	139.83	.90	33.48	125.48

Notes: *   All significant at 1% level.
                   SEE = standard error of estimate.
Source: Tables 5.7, 5.10, 6.4 and 6.5 (Queensland) and regression results.

Turning to individual parameter estimates, attention is concentrated on
equation (9.5). The estimated coefficients for the terms in average length of
stay, case flow rate and size for Queensland and New South Wales from this

specification are presented in Table 9.7.[6] As was reported in Chapter 6, the signs on the coefficients for Queensland correspond with those found using 1977-78 data, but the 'pure' scale terms and the scale/case flow interaction term lack statistical significance. The 'pure' scale terms were insignificant in the New South Wales equation also and had the wrong sign, so both equations were re-estimated excluding these two terms. The parameter estimates for the remaining scale and utilisation terms are also presented in Table 9.7. All these terms are statistically significant in the equations for both States with the scale/case flow interaction term indicating mild diseconomies of scale which are smaller the larger is the case flow rate.[7]

Table 9.7. Scale and Utilisation Parameter Estimates using Separate State and Pooled Data, Queensland Public Hospitals, 1979-80[a]

	$\dfrac{365}{CFR}$	$\dfrac{365 RBD}{CFR}$	ALS	B	B^2	$\bar{R}^2$	F	d.f.
Qld	9.32 (6.3*)	0.00005 (0.35)	35.71 (8.4*)	-0.1465 (-0.16)	0.00042 (0.99)	.92	24.1*	59
	8.41 (6.5*)	0.00010 (2.2**)	34.69 (10.4*)			.92	24.7*	61
NSW	11.58 (8.7*)	0.00011 (2.0**)	36.03 (11.9*)	0.066 (0.2)	-0.00004 (-0.2)	.90	33.5*	160
	11.49 (9.2*)	0.00012 (6.7*)	36.00 (12.3*)			.90	35.0*	162
Pooled	8.46 (10.0*)	0.00011 (1.9)	29.85 (13.6*)	0.006 (0.001)	-0.00001 (-0.03)	.86	35.0*	281
	8.46 (10.7*)	0.00011 (5.7*)	29.86 (15.6*)			.86	36.4*	283

Notes: *   Significant at 1% level.
          **   Significant at 5% level.
          d.f. = degrees of freedom.
Source: Table 6.4, and NSW and pooled regression results.

---

6   The parameter estimates for the case mix classification variables in each of the separate State equations again have generally implausible values with high standard errors and are not included here.

7   For example, in the Queensland equation, with a case flow rate of 20, an additional bed would add $0.67 to average cost per case.

The parameter estimates presented in Table 9.7 permit an examination of the relationship between cost per case and the case flow rate in each State. These estimated relationships are depicted in Figure 9.3. For each State the unweighted mean case mix proportions, average length of stay and size have been inserted in the truncated version of equation (9.5), i.e. equation (9.5) with the 'pure' scale terms excluded, giving the relationship shown. The two State mean case flow rates are also shown, indicating that the lower mean in Queensland increases its cost per case by about $31 over what it would have been if it had the New South Wales mean case flow rate. If, however, Queensland had the higher mean New South Wales average length of stay in addition to the higher case flow rate, its predicted mean cost per case would be $718.76, about $28 over the actual mean. This is indicated by the dashed line in Figure 9.3 which shows the relationship which would apply to Queensland if it had the New South Wales mean length of stay.

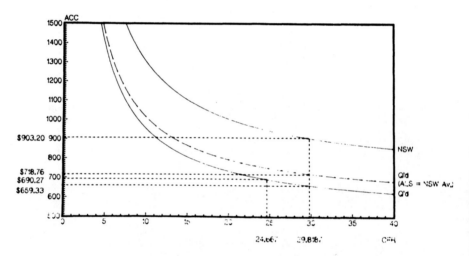

Figure 9.3. Relationship between Cost per Case and Case Flow Rate, Queensland and New South Wales, 1979-80

9.4.2   Pooled Results

From the foregoing discussion and the graphs in Figure 9.3 it is apparent that, even though the variation in average cost per case *within* each State is explicable to the same extent by the same factors, the variation *between* the two States remains to be explained. To provide some insight into this, the data from each State were pooled (giving 343 observations) and the five cost equations re-estimated. Table 9.8 provides the summary statistics from these estimations. For comparative purposes, the adjusted R^2 values for the separate State results from Table 9.6 are also included in Table 9.8.

Table 9.8. Summary Statistics from Estimated Average Cost Equations using Pooled Data, Queensland and New South Wales Public Hospitals, 1979-80

Specification		Qld	NSW	Pooled Results				
		$\overline{R}^2$	$\overline{R}^2$	$\overline{R}^2$	F*	SEE	Chow's F*	d.f.
Equation	(9.1)	.58	.47	.39	5.77	347.20	3.23	296
	(9.2)	.59	.57	.44	5.85	332.15	3.10	286
	(9.3)	.71	.77	.62	10.42	276.04	4.16	284
	(9.4)	.87	.85	.80	24.42	199.53	3.53	284
	(9.5)	.92	.90	.86	34.96	167.48	4.01	281

Note: *   All significant at 1% level.
         SEE = standard error of estimate.
         d.f. = degrees of freedom.
Source: Regression results.

It is immediately evident that estimating combined cost relationships for the two States reduces the amount of variation in average cost per case explained by case mix, length of stay, case flow rate and size. The adjusted R^2 values are lower for the pooled results compared with the separate State results for every specification. Now if the two underlying populations differ in some respects not taken into account in the cost equation, this result is not unexpected. Taking a different example, suppose one were estimating a relationship between income and consumption expenditure for India and Australia. If there is some factor other than income which affects consumption and varies systematically between the two countries, one would expect a pooled estimate of the consumption function to give poorer results. Of course, if the factor which varies systematically is known and can be incorporated in the equation, this could be expected to improve the pooled result.

Returning to our results, the reduction in adjusted R^2 for the pooled results indicates the effect of one or more factors which differ between the States *other than* case mix, length of stay, case flow rate and size and which influence average cost per case. There is a statistical test which can be applied to indicate whether the reduction in explained variation is significant. Chow's F statistic, when compared with the appropriate critical value of F, indicates whether the reduced explanatory power of the pooled equation is significant.[8] As indicated by these statistics in Table 9.8 the reduction in explained variation is statistically significant at the one per cent level for every specification. That is, there is a structural difference in the cost equations for the two States, a difference which is attributable to some factor which differs between the States other than case mix, length of stay, case flow rate and size. The possibility that this other factor is a difference in the degree of centralised control over hospitals in the two States cannot be dismissed.

Turning again to the individual parameter estimates, Table 9.7 contains such estimates for the scale and utilisation terms in equation (9.5) arising from the use of the pooled data. The linear and quadratic terms in beds are insignificant here as they were in the separate State equations, indicating again an absence of any 'pure' scale effects. The utilisation terms were again highly significant, with the scale/case flow interaction term indicating only mild diseconomies of scale.

With regard to the parameter estimates for the case mix categories, it was mentioned in Chapter 5 (see Section 5.5.2) that increasing the number of observations was one means of attacking the multicollinearity problem. It was suggested that pooling data for two or more years, or two or more States, might improve the precision of the case mix category coefficient estimates and render them positive. This has not eventuated here despite an increase in the number of degrees of freedom from 121 (the Queensland sample size) to 343 (the pooled sample size). In each of the five equations, such estimates generally have implausible signs and magnitudes and are insignificant. These estimates are not reproduced here.

The effect of pooling is illustrated in Figure 9.4. This diagram contains a scattergram of hospitals on the basis of average cost per case and case flow rate with differentiated markers for the two States. Superimposed on this scatter is the estimated pooled relationship between average cost per case and the case flow rate from equation (9.5) evaluated at the pooled mean case mix proportions and average length of stay (the full line in the diagram). The corresponding separate State relationships as presented in Figure 9.3 are also included for comparative purposes (the dashed lines).[9] As stated above, the Chow test indicates that the reduction in explanatory power with the

---

[8]   For a discussion of the Chow test, see Koutsoyiannis (1977, pp.164-8).

[9]   In plotting the estimated pooled relationship, the terms in beds and beds-squared have been dropped to ensure comparability with the separate State relationships. Recall that these terms were insignificant in both of the separate State equations and the pooled equation (see Table 9.7).

pooled equation is statistically significant and is indicative of a structural difference between the two States.

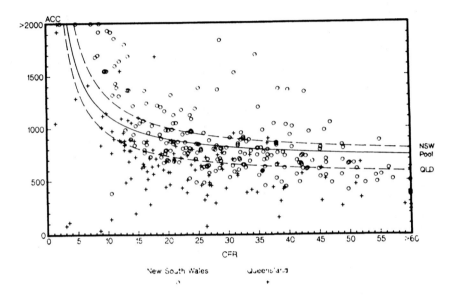

Figure 9.4 Scattergram of Cost per Case and Case Flow Rates by State with Separate State and Pooled Equations

To obtain further evidence on this matter the five average cost equations were re-estimated using the pooled data but this time including a dummy variable as a State identifier (0 = Queensland, 1 = New South Wales). The resulting dummy variable coefficient estimates are presented in column (1) in Table 9.9. For every specification the estimate is positive and significant at the five per cent level—holding all other factors in any equation constant, a New South Wales hospital would have a significantly higher average cost per case than its Queensland counterpart. This conclusion is particularly significant for equations (9.3) to (9.5) which include the effects of differences in scale and utilisation. Equation (9.5), for instance, predicts a New South Wales hospital to have a cost per case $187.20 higher than a Queensland hospital with the same case mix, average length of stay, case flow rate and size. Again, the possibility that this difference is attributable to organisational differences in the hospital systems of the two States cannot be dismissed.

Table 9.9. Estimated Coefficients for State Identifier Dummy Variables, Queensland and New South Wales Public Hospitals, 1979-80[a]

Specification	Original Results	NSW Outpatient Adjustment applied to Queensland	Using Net Operating Payments in NSW and deducting Outpatient Costs only from Total Costs in Qld
	(1)	(2)	(3)
Equation (9.1)	260.27 (3.90*)	488.80 (7.57*)	199.34 (3.01*)
(9.2)	258.83 (2.00**)	541.32 (4.48*)	214.17 (1.71)
(9.3)	403.31 (3.78*)	639.71 (6.39*)	321.44 (3.21*)
(9.4)	195.01 (2.51**)	484.27 (7.77*)	169.17 (2.17**)
(9.5)	187.20 (2.86*)	477.53 (8.03*)	169.87 (2.55**)

Note: *   Significant at 1% level.
        **   Significant at 5% level.
        (a) t-values in parentheses.
Source: Regression results.

9.4.3   Effects of Other Adjustments

It is possible that the above results may be due to the different ways in which the cost data have been adjusted for outpatient costs in Queensland and New South Wales, or due to the use of 'gross' rather than 'net' operating payments as the basis for calculating average cost per case in New South Wales public hospitals.[10] Each of these possibilities was subsequently investigated and will be discussed in turn.

Recall that, in Queensland, each public hospital provides its own estimate of outpatient costs. These estimates, along with the estimated costs of dental and ambulance clinics and the costs of services provided to other hospitals where relevant, were deducted from a hospital's maintenance

---

10   I am indebted to Jo Martins of the New South Wales Department of Health for these perceptive suggestions (see Martins 1985).

expenditure to give total inpatient costs. For New South Wales no such estimates were provided, so the adjustment used by the Health Commission of New South Wales was employed. This involved converting outpatient visits into an equivalent number of cases treated, with 700 outpatient visits being equated to an average daily census of unity (or 365 occupied bed days), and the resulting number of equivalent bed days being divided by the hospital's average length of stay to produce the equivalent number of cases. This number was then added to the number of cases actually treated, producing an adjusted number of cases which was subsequently used to calculate average cost per case.

To see if these different methods of adjusting for outpatient costs in the two States affected the results, average cost per case for each hospital in Queensland was recalculated using the outpatient adjustment formula adopted for New South Wales. That is to say, *total* maintenance expenditure was divided by an adjusted number of cases where the adjustment for outpatient visits was the same as that used in New South Wales.[11]

Applying the New South Wales outpatient adjustment to Queensland hospitals made a massive difference to the interstate differential in average cost per case—it *widened* it in excess of another $250. The New South Wales outpatient adjustment resulted in a much greater outpatient cost allocation than the Queensland hospitals themselves estimated, with the result that average cost per case in Queensland fell dramatically when the New South Wales adjustment was applied—from an unweighted mean of $690.27 per case to $429.78 per case. With the New South Wales unweighted mean cost per case at $903.20 (see Table 9.2), the gap between the two States widened to over $470 per case.

Using these adjusted Queensland figures, the five average cost equations were re-estimated using the pooled data set and including a State identifier dummy variable. The estimated coefficients for the dummy variables can be found in column (2) of Table 9.9. As can be expected given the substantial increase in the difference between the two States, the magnitude and significance of each coefficient is greater than the corresponding figure in column (1). Again, there is a significant difference in average cost per case between the two States not accounted for by case mix, scale and utilisation. Clearly, using Queensland hospitals' estimates of outpatient costs rather than the New South Wales adjustment has not biased the results in favour of Queensland.

---

11 Total maintenance expenditure includes dental and ambulance clinic expenditures and the costs of services to other hospitals. However, it was decided *not* to deduct these so the total cost figure for each Queensland hospital would be a maximal one.

The second possible problem, and one which does operate against New South Wales in the comparisons, relates to the use of 'gross' rather than 'net' operating payments as a measure of total expenditure in New South Wales public hospitals. To quote Martins (1985, p.262),

> ... there are major problems in the use of gross operating payments for those hospitals which have a high degree of over-estimation and double-counting. Included in the gross operating payments of hospitals in New South Wales are employee contributions for superannuation which is not a hospital expenditure but part of 'recoveries'. This is an unfortunate accounting practice adopted by New South Wales authorities. It is about the same as including the employee's PAYE tax in hospital payments and then treating it as a recovery. This practice leads to an over-statement of the recorded payments and consequently to higher average costs for New South Wales hospitals.

Using net operating payments (gross operating payments minus recoveries) to calculate average cost per case in New South Wales public hospitals reduces the unweighted State mean cost per case from $903.20 to $880.96 per case, or by nearly $23 per case. In order to produce a maximal estimate of average cost per case in Queensland public hospitals, ambulance and dental clinic costs and the costs of services to other hospitals were added to estimated total inpatient costs, i.e. only the outpatient cost estimates were deducted from total maintenance costs. This increased the unweighted State mean cost per case in Queensland from $690.27 to $722.39 per case, or by just over $30. Consequently this adjustment, together with the use of net operating payments for New South Wales public hospitals, has reduced the difference between the unweighted State means by over $50 per case.

Again the five average cost equations were re-estimated using the pooled data set and including a State identifier dummy variable. The resulting parameter estimates for the dummy variable in each equation, in column (3) of Table 9.9, are now smaller in magnitude than those obtained originally in column (1), but are still significant in four of the five equations. The unexplained difference between the two States is still evident even in these results.

In concluding this section, two possible sources of the interstate difference in average cost per case which have not been addressed so far must be mentioned. *First*, nowhere in this study has any attempt been made to adjust for differences in the quality of hospital care between the two

States. How one might adjust for such differences is a most complex issue which will not be addressed here. However, the point must be made that if quality is defined in terms of *inputs* rather than *outputs*, one gets the tautological conclusion that Queensland's quality of care must be lower. This follows from the fact that Queensland devotes less inputs to each case treated and hence has lower costs per case. This highlights the necessity for adopting measures of quality which are output related.

Second, interstate variations in input prices have not been considered. In fact, there is some evidence that Queensland does have lower award rates in some hospital staffing categories, as can be seen from Table 9.10. However the differences, at least in the staffing categories covered in the Table, are not substantial and do not always favour Queensland. Hence they are unlikely to account for more than a small proportion of the interstate difference in average cost per case.

Table 9.10. Capital City Award Wage Relativities for Selected Hospital Employees, Queensland and New South Wales Public Hospitals, 1976 to 1980[a]

	Ratio of Award Rate (Qld) to Award Rate (NSW)			
	Hospital Cook (Adult Male)	Hospital Orderly (Adult Male)	Nurse, 1st yr, Qualified (Adult Female)	Nursing Aide (Adult Female)
1976	0.98	0.96	0.98	1.07
1977	0.98	0.96	0.99	1.04
1978	0.98	0.96	0.99	1.04
1979	0.97	0.93	0.99	0.87
1980	0.91	0.92	1.02	0.90

Note: (a) Based on Award Rates in force as at 31 December each year.
Source: Information supplied by the Commonwealth Grants Commission.

9.5   Summary and Conclusions

This chapter has sought to explain the interstate differential in average cost per case that exists between Queensland and New South Wales public hospitals. Viewing the hospital as a multiproduct firm, differences in the composition of output, or case mix, between hospitals may explain some of the observed variation in cost per case. After demonstrating significant differences in hospital case mix between the two States, a set of case mix proportions along with average length of stay, case flow rate, occupancy and size were incorporated into various specifications of an average cost function to analyse within and between State variation in average cost per case.

In estimating the effects of the above factors on within State variation in average cost per case, a tentative hypothesis was advanced that if, as has been suggested by some, organisational differences between the States as manifested in differing degrees of centralised control over hospitals are important in explaining the interstate differential, then the amount of within State variation explicable by these factors may be less in the State with less centralised control. This hypothesis was not strongly supported by the results. The amount of variation in average cost per case within each State explicable by case mix, scale and utilisation is approximately the same.

However, this can hardly be taken as disproving the argument that organisational differences are important, because this result is consistent with the existence of an interstate differential in average cost per case. Indeed, all hospitals within each of two States may have the same cost per case yet the cost per case may differ widely between the States. Consequently, the Queensland and New South Wales data were pooled and the cost equations re-estimated. The pooled results demonstrated a statistically significant reduction in the amount of explained variation in average cost per case, indicating a structural difference in the cost relationships between the two States attributable to one or more factors other than case mix, scale and utilisation.

This evidence was reinforced by that which resulted from the inclusion of a State identification dummy variable in the analysis. In every specification the dummy variable was positive and significant, indicating that a New South Wales hospital would have a *higher* cost per case than a Queensland hospital with the *same* case mix, length of stay, case flow rate and size.

Is the reason for this unexplained difference the greater degree of centralised control which Queensland exercised over its hospitals? The results of this chapter support an affirmative answer to this question. However, further research to ascertain whether these results are robust is necessary. In particular, a replication of this study for other years for these two States would provide evidence on the consistency of the results. An extension to include comparisons with other States would also be appropriate.

PART C

HOSPITAL COST ANALYSIS AND

HOSPITAL PAYMENT SCHEMES

10

A Hospital Performance Appraisal

and Payment Scheme Based on

Estimated Cost Functions

10.1   Introduction

This and the following chapter are concerned generally with demonstrating the relevance of hospital cost analysis to appraising hospital performance and determining hospital payments. The present chapter shows how an econometric approach to these problems might be adopted using estimated cost equations and the cost per case/cost per day/length of stay relationship. Chapter 11 is concerned with a payment scheme already in use in the United States for a number of years.

This chapter has three major sections. Section 10.2 outlines the theoretical framework of an econometric scheme, explaining prediction intervals and costliness ratios and their use in the context of the cost per case/cost per day/length of stay relationship. The role of average cost per case data disaggregated by input category is also incorporated. Section 10.3 demonstrates an empirical application of the scheme using data on

Queensland public hospitals for 1977-78, while Section 10.4 addresses two major problems which arise with this kind of scheme because of multicollinearity. A summary and conclusions are presented in Section 10.5.

10.2   Theoretical Considerations

10.2.1   Cost per Case Predictions, Prediction Intervals and Costliness Ratios

A hospital performance appraisal and payment scheme based upon estimated cost functions requires predicted values of average cost per unit of output—average cost per case—for each hospital from these estimated functions. Two issues immediately arise. *First*, how accurate are such predictions? *Second*, what independent variables should be incorporated into the prediction equation? Each of these issues will be discussed in turn.

A predicted value of average cost per case for a hospital is obtained by substituting into the estimated equation that hospital's values of whatever independent variables are included in the equation. Such a prediction or conditional forecast is, of course, a statistical estimate and as such is prone to error. Reflecting this, it is possible to construct a prediction interval around the predicted value, analogous to a confidence interval constructed for a parameter estimate.

How the prediction is constructed depends upon which of two kinds of prediction is made. The first kind of prediction involves interpreting the predicted value as the conditional *mean* value of average cost per case for a given set of values of the independent variables. That is, it makes a prediction about the average value of the dependent variable for all observations which have the particular values of the independent variables.[1] The second kind of prediction "involves predicting an individual, as opposed to a conditional mean, value" of the dependent variable (Dillon and Goldstein 1984, p.227). With this kind of prediction, the resulting predicted value for average cost per case would be interpreted as the prediction for one individual hospital which has the values of the independent variables used in obtaining the prediction.

---

[1]   For example, if we have an estimated equation which expresses weight as a function of height for all Australian males, a conditional mean prediction of weight would indicate the average weight of Australian males with a particular height. See Pfaffenberger and Patterson (1977, pp.537-41) for a discussion of this kind of prediction and a numerical example. See also Intriligator (1978, pp.109-12) and Johnston (1972, pp.38-43, 152-5).

For a given set of values of the independent variables, the predicted value is the same for the two types of prediction but the prediction *intervals* differ. For a conditional mean value prediction, the prediction interval is given by

$$A\hat{C}C \pm t_{\alpha/2;n-K}\, s \sqrt{\mathbf{X}_0(\mathbf{X}'\mathbf{X})^{-1}\mathbf{X}_0'} \qquad \dots (10.1)$$

where $A\hat{C}C$ is predicted average cost per case, $t_{\alpha/2;n-K}$ is the critical t-value for a $100(1-\alpha)$ per cent confidence interval with $(n-K)$ degrees of freedom, s is the estimated standard deviation of the error term or the standard error of estimate, $\mathbf{X}_0$ is a $(1 \times K)$ row vector of values of the independent variables from which the predicted average cost per case is being obtained, and $\mathbf{X}$ is the $(n \times K)$ data matrix. The expression by which the critical t-value is multiplied is the standard error of prediction.

If predicting an individual value, the prediction interval is given by

$$A\hat{C}C \pm t_{\alpha/2;n-K}\, s \sqrt{1 + \mathbf{X}_0(\mathbf{X}'\mathbf{X})^{-1}\mathbf{X}_0'} \qquad \dots (10.2)$$

The important difference between this and the preceding expression is that unity has been added to the expression inside the brackets, so increasing the standard error of prediction. This gives rise to a wider prediction interval, *ceteris paribus*, "reflecting the fact that it is much more difficult to estimate (predict) a single value than the mean of a set of values" (Pfaffenberger and Patterson 1977, p.542).[2]

The second major issue which must be confronted in obtaining a prediction of average cost per case for a hospital concerns the independent variables to be included in the estimated equation. Since the purpose of the independent variables in the equation is to 'explain' the variation in average cost per case, this amounts to deciding what are 'allowable' sources of variation. Strictly speaking, if the cost function is to be the dual of the underlying production technology, only output levels and input prices enter

---

[2]   It should be noted that both of the formulae for the standard errors of prediction given here are based on the assumption that the values of the independent variables used to obtain the prediction are known constants. If this is not the case then the formulae for the standard errors of prediction need to be modified to take account of the fact that the predicted values of the independent variables themselves are subject to error. This consideration has been addressed by Feldstein (1971). See also Fomby, Hill and Johnson (1984, Ch.23, esp. pp.522-4).

the cost function, at least in the long run (see Chapter 2, Section 2.3)—no other sources of variation are 'allowable'. In this context, the distinction between inputs and outputs is again critical, for if inputs are entered into a cost function which is then used as the basis of a payment scheme, hospitals can increase their revenue simply by increasing input usage.

A further point here relates to the use of a single-equation model of hospital cost behaviour to predict average cost per case. Use of such a model presupposes that all the independent variables are exogenous to the hospital. If this is not the case, then a multi-equation model may be more appropriate. A problematic variable in this regard, already discussed in Chapter 6 (see Section 6.3), is average length of stay. This problem led Leiken and Dusansky (1983) to develop a simultaneous equation model of hospital costs with average cost per case and average length of stay as the dependent variables in a two-equation system.

This problem is not confined to scale and utilisation variables. It is debatable whether surgery is an exogenously determined characteristic of a case or an endogenous characteristic of the treatment. Pauly (1978, p.80) argues this as follows:

> ... whether or not a patient is surgically treated, given some diagnosis, might be interpreted as an exogenous indicator of his type of condition, whether the condition requires surgery or not. It could also be interpreted as just a more direct measure of the way in which a medical staff of a certain character (e.g., one with more general surgeons) chooses to treat a given diagnosis.

While this is an important problem it is not critical that it be resolved in this chapter, the purpose of which is to develop and demonstrate a framework for a hospital performance appraisal and payment scheme using estimated cost functions. Consequently it was decided to finesse the problem here by employing five different average cost per case equations as used earlier in this study. These five equations are as follows:

$$ACC = a_0 + \sum_{i=1}^{46} a_i p_i \qquad \text{... (10.3)}$$

$$ACC = b_0 + \sum_{j=1}^{56} b_j h_j \qquad \text{... (10.4)}$$

$$ACC = b_0 + \sum_{j=1}^{56} b_j h_j + r_1 CFR + r_2 CFR^2 + r_3 B + r_4 B^2 \qquad \ldots (10.5)$$

$$ACC = b_0 + \sum_{j=1}^{56} b_j h_j + r_1 ALS + r_2 OCC + r_3 B + r_4 B^2 \qquad \ldots (10.6)$$

$$ACC = b_0 + \sum_{j=1}^{56} b_j h_j + r_1 ALS + r_2 (365 / CFR) + r_3 (365 RBD / CFR)$$

$$+ r_4 B + r_5 B^2 \qquad \ldots (10.7)$$

The first of these equations includes only the 47 diagnostic category proportions as independent variables (actually 46 plus a constant) while equation (10.4) adds the additional case mix dimensions to these. Equations (10.5) to (10.7) add scale and utilisation variables in various ways, all of which were discussed in Chapter 6. Equations (10.5) and (10.6) do not contain any 'pure' scale terms because of their insignificance as reported in earlier chapters.

Each of the above equations can be used to obtain a predicted value of average cost per case for each hospital in the sample. Further, for each prediction the associated prediction interval could be calculated. As will be explained later in this chapter, a prediction interval was calculated for equation (10.7) only, but was also calculated for average cost per case disaggregated into ten input components. Equation (10.2) pertaining to individual predictions was used to calculate prediction intervals since the predictions are for individual hospitals.

Using the data from which the average cost relationships were estimated, a predicted value of average cost per case can be used, together with the corresponding actual value, to construct a costliness ratio. This is a term coined by Feldstein (1967) to describe the ratio of actual to predicted average cost per case. These ratios, which were used in Chapter 7 in the discussion of public and private hospitals, indicate whether a hospital's average cost per case exceeds or falls short of that predicted according to whether the ratio is greater or less than unity respectively.

The prediction interval can then be used to assess whether the costliness ratio is statistically significantly different from unity. The costliness ratio prediction interval for a given confidence level has an upper bound equal to $A\hat{C}C_u / A\hat{C}C$ where the subscript 'u' indicates the upper bound of the ACC prediction interval obtained from equation (10.2). Similarly, the lower bound of the costliness ratio prediction interval can be calculated as $A\hat{C}C_{\ell} / A\hat{C}C$ where 'ℓ' indicates the lower bound of the ACC prediction interval. If a hospital's costliness ratio $ACC / A\hat{C}C$ lies outside the costliness ratio prediction interval, it can be concluded that the ratio is statistically significantly different from unity at the relevant level of statistical significance.

10.2.2   The Cost per Case/Cost per Day/Length of Stay Relationship

This relationship was discussed in detail in Chapter 3 where it was argued that average cost per day and average length of stay are *input* related concepts and that the 'case' is the conceptually preferred unit of output. This being so, of what relevance are average cost per day and average length of stay to the scheme being outlined here? The implication is that they are not relevant. Certainly the Diagnosis Related Group (DRG) payment scheme to be discussed in the next chapter does not consider average cost per day or average length of stay (except for 'outliers') in determining a hospital's payment. In the DRG scheme, only the number of cases discharged in each DRG is relevant. So why consider cost per day and length of stay?

The answer is that while they may not directly determine the payment a hospital receives, they can be used in a performance appraisal context to indicate possible causes of a hospital's discrepancy between actual and predicted average cost per case. Given the relationship $ACC = ACD \times ALS$, if predictions can be obtained for average cost per day and average length of stay, then any deviation of actual from predicted average cost per case should be reflected in a deviation of the actual from the predicted values of average cost per day and/or average length of stay.

To illustrate this, consider the following hypothetical data:

	ACC	ACD	ALS
Actual	600	100	6.00
Predicted	560	70	8.00
Actual/Predicted	1.07	1.43	0.75

The actual cost per unit of output in this hospital (actual *ACC*) is in excess of that predicted. The additional information on cost per day and length of stay indicates that this is not due to excessive length of stay. On the contrary, this hospital's predicted average length of stay is less then its actual value. The data suggest that this hospital's excessive costliness is rather due to treating patients too intensively on each day of stay—average cost per day is well in excess of that predicted.

How then can average cost per day and average length of stay predictions be obtained?

10.2.3   Cost per Day Predictions

Recall that, for given input prices and assuming non-jointness and overall constant returns to scale, the total cost function can be written as

$$C = \sum_i a_i y_i$$

where y_i is the number of cases treated in the ith case mix category and a_i is the average and marginal cost of treating a case of the ith type. Now total cost can also be expressed as a function of the number of days care provided to each case type category (d_i),

$$C = \sum_i b_i d_i \qquad \qquad \text{... (10.8)}$$

where b_i is the average and marginal cost per day for the ith case mix category. Dividing through equation (10.8) by the total number of days care provided (d) gives

$$\frac{C}{d} = ACD = \sum_i b_i p_i^d \qquad \qquad \text{... (10.9)}$$

where $p_i^d = d_i / d$ is the proportion of total days of care provided to cases of the ith type and C/d is average cost per day. With C/d and the p_i^d known, equation (10.9) can be estimated using multivariate techniques, and the resulting estimated equation used to obtain a prediction of average cost per day.

The two issues which arose in the context of cost per case predictions arise again here, *viz.* the accuracy of the forecast and the independent variables to be included. In assessing the accuracy of the forecasts, prediction intervals can again be constructed using equation (10.2) with the relevant standard errors of estimate, row vectors of observations of the independent variables on the basis of which the prediction is sought, and data matrices.

In considering what independent variables to include in the average cost per day equation, the same issues which arose in the context of the average cost per case equations are relevant here. Again the problem was finessed by estimating five different average cost per day equations, each of which 'corresponds' to one of the average cost per case equations specified in Section 10.2.1. The actual specifications adopted and the results obtained are discussed later in this chapter (see Section 10.3.1).

A predicted value for average cost per day for each hospital can then be obtained from each of these equations and prediction intervals calculated. In the same way that costliness per case ratios were formed using actual and predicted average cost per case, so too a set of costliness per day ratios can be formed. The costliness per day ratio is given as actual/predicted average cost per day. Costliness ratio prediction intervals can also be calculated as the ratio of the upper and lower bounds of the average cost per day prediction interval to predicted average cost per day. A decision can then be made as to whether the costliness per day ratio is statistically significantly different from unity at the specified level of significance.

10.2.4   Length of Stay Predictions

The total number of days care provided in the jth hospital (d_j) can be expressed as

$$d_j = \sum_i ALS_{ij} y_{ij}$$

where ALS_{ij} is the average length of stay in the ith diagnostic category in the jth hospital and y_{ij} is the number of cases treated in the ith diagnostic category in the jth hospital. Dividing through by y_j (the total number of cases treated in the jth hospital) gives

$$ALS_j = \sum_i ALS_{ij} p_{ij} \qquad\qquad \text{... (10.10)}$$

If ALS_j and the p_{ij} only were known, the ALS_{ij} could be estimated using multivariate techniques and a prediction obtained for ALS_j. This is unnecessary, however, as all terms in this expression are known. Consequently, a predicted average length of stay for the jth hospital can be obtained by calculating the State mean length of stay for each case type (ALS_i) and substituting this into equation (10.10) giving

$$A\hat{L}S_j = \sum_i ALS_i p_{ij} \qquad \qquad \text{... (10.11)}$$

This indicates the average length of stay the jth hospital would have had if it had the State mean length of stay in each case mix category.

This kind of calculation is employed in constructing what is known as the Relative Stay Index (RSI), "a number which states the percentage by which a group of hospital patients stay a longer or shorter time in hospital than would be expected" (Ontario Hospital Services Commission 1972b, p.1). The index is calculated as follows:

$$\text{RSI} = 100(\text{Actual } ALS/\text{Expected } ALS) - 100 \qquad \text{... (10.12)}$$

where the expected *ALS* is computed using the general kind of calculation given in equation (10.11).[3] In calculating expected average length of stay, cases are disaggregated by age, sex and the presence or absence of surgery, in addition to diagnosis. As such, it indicates what a hospital's average length of stay would have been if it had the State mean length of stay for its particular age/sex/surgical/diagnostic mix of patients.

In Queensland, a Relative Stay Index is routinely constructed for all hospitals. Only live discharges are included in the calculations and hospitals are grouped as follows: teaching hospitals; non-teaching hospitals with more than 5,000 separations annually; non-teaching hospitals with less than 5,000 separations annually but more than 50 registered beds; and non-teaching hospitals with less than 50 registered beds (Queensland Department of Health 1980, para.33). Hence the expected average length of stay for a hospital is calculated by reference only to the other hospitals in the same group.

For the purposes of this chapter, the RSI is not presented in the form given by equation (10.12) but is expressed as the ratio of actual/expected average length of stay. This gives a ratio analogous in interpretation to the costliness ratios for cost per case and cost per day. A value of this ratio in excess of unity indicates that actual exceeds expected average length of stay and conversely for a ratio less than unity.

---

[3] A thorough discussion of the construction of the index can be found in Ontario Hospital Services Commission (1972a, 1972b). See also Leigh and McBride (1974) and Queensland Department of Health (1980).

10.2.5   Disaggregating Cost per Case by Input Components

A hospital faced with a situation where its actual average cost per case is not equal to its predicted average cost per case obtains no information from this prediction alone as to the *causes* of this deviation. Such a prediction does not indicate to the hospital the case types (or output categories) on which it is 'overspending', and nor does it indicate what inputs are being excessively or insufficiently used.

It is possible to disaggregate average cost per case by expenditure on inputs. Medical salaries cost per case, nursing salaries cost per case and so on can be calculated. These input component costs per case can be used as the dependent variable in the cost per case equations (10.3) to (10.7) and a predicted value obtained for each hospital. Prediction intervals can be calculated and costliness ratios produced by input component, indicating on which particular inputs a hospital's actual expenditure per case exceeds or falls short of that predicted. Further, it can be shown that, because the sum of the *actual* input component costs per case equals actual average cost per case, then the sum of the *predicted* input component costs per case will equal predicted average cost per case.[4]

As with the cost per day and length of stay predictions, these predictions of input component costs per case are not germane to the hospital payment scheme so much as performance appraisal. They enable a hospital to ascertain the input categories in which actual expenditure per case is not in line with that predicted and so suggest areas where the hospital might look to cutting or increasing expenditure so as to move into line with the overall predicted value of average cost per case.

10.3   Empirical Analysis

The purpose of this section is to demonstrate the application of the foregoing theoretical framework. This is done with reference to the 121 Queensland public hospitals using data for the 1977-78 financial year. The estimated average cost per case equations have been reported in detail elsewhere in this study. It is, however, necessary to present the results for the average cost per day equations and this is done in Section 10.3.1. Following this, the costliness per case and costliness per day ratios and the Relative Stay Index are discussed (Section 10.3.2) after which prediction

---

4   A proof of this proposition is given in Appendix 10.I.

intervals and costliness ratios disaggregated by input component are presented for one particular specification of the average cost equations.

10.3.1   The Estimated Cost per Day Equations

The first average cost per day equation to be estimated contained only the proportions of days in each of the 47 diagnostic categories, i.e. the specification given by equation (10.9). The diagnostic mix of days alone explained 31 per cent of the interhospital variation in average cost per day after adjusting for degrees of freedom (adjusted $R^2 = 0.31$; d.f. $= 74$). The overall relationship was significant at the one per cent level (F $= 2.15$).[5]

The individual parameter estimates from this equation (which was actually estimated using 46 proportions and a constant term) are presented in Table 10.1. As with the parameter estimates in the equivalent cost per case equation, the sum of the constant term and each parameter estimate provides the estimated value of average and marginal cost per day in each diagnostic category. These values are also tabulated in Table 10.1. The problems of statistical insignificance and implausible signs and magnitudes are evident here as they were in the equivalent cost per case equation, despite the overall significance of the relationship. Multicollinearity is again suspected, but this will not be explored in detail here. The implications of multicollinearity for the performance appraisal and payment scheme outlined in this chapter will be discussed in Section 10.4.

The second average cost per day equation initially contained the proportions of days in each of 46 diagnostic categories as above plus the proportions of days in each of the additional case mix classification categories (sex, surgery performed, patient payment status, patient separation status and age). Statistical insignificance and implausible signs and magnitudes of the coefficients continued to plague the estimates. It was also found, by using incremental F-tests on the sub-groups within these additional classification variables, that only the set of age categories increased significantly the explanatory power of the equation. Consequently, for the purposes of this chapter, only the age categories were added to the diagnostic categories in the second equation. On this basis, the amount of

---

5   It should be noted that this result is not directly comparable with those obtained by Feldstein (1967) and Lee and Wallace (1973) who used the proportions of *cases* in each diagnostic category as the independent variables in their average cost per day equations.

Table 10.1. Parameter Estimates, Average Cost per Day Equation Using
47 Diagnostic Categories, Queensland Public Hospitals, 1977-78

No.	Diagnostic Category	Estimated Coefficient	t-value*	Implied Average & Marginal Cost per Case ($)
	Constant[a]	103.46		103.46
2	Infectious & Parasitic	454.57	1.11	558.03
3	Enteritis, Diarrhoeal Disease	87.50	0.21	190.96
4	Malignant Neoplasms	146.97	0.38	250.43
5	Benign Neoplasms	-152.89	-0.10	-49.43
6	Endocrine & Metabolic	-187.75	-0.41	-84.29
7	Blood	-600.88	-1.02	-497.42
8	Psychiatric	-102.24	-0.28	1.22
9	Other CNS & Nerves	-30.17	-0.78	73.29
10	Eye & Ear	-409.03	-0.95	-305.57
11	Other Heart, Hypertension	72.06	0.18	175.52
12	Acute Myocardial Infarction	232.30	0.52	335.76
13	Symptomatic Heart Disease	11.04	0.03	114.50
14	Cerebrovascular Disease	-188.39	-0.51	-84.93
15	Circulation	19.19	0.05	122.65
16	Upper Respiratory	-309.15	-0.89	-205.69
17	Pneumonia	-66.96	-0.18	36.50
18	Bronchitis, Emphysema, Asthma	138.78	0.35	242.24
19	Tonsils & Adenoids	-354.98	-0.48	-251.52
20	Other Respiratory	-100.27	-0.26	3.19
21	Dental	-1602.01	-1.09	-1498.55
22	Upper Gastrointestinal	-417.00	-0.87	-313.54
23	Appendicitis	46.36	0.09	149.82
24	Hernia	-133.10	-0.18	-29.64
25	Other Gastrointestinal	-449.54	-0.94	-346.08
26	Nephritis & Nephrosis	800.36	1.05	903.82
27	Other Urinary	-157.44	-0.38	-53.98
28	Male Genital	-831.51	-1.28	-728.05
29	Other Female Genital	477.84	0.75	518.30
30	Disorders of Menstruation	234.96	0.18	338.42
31	Complications of Pregnancy & Puerperium	-679.75	-1.56	-576.29
32	Abortion	-482.34	-0.44	-378.88
33	Normal Delivery	57.09	0.15	160.55
34	Delivery Complications	541.23	1.07	644.69
35	Skin Disease	-263.80	-0.61	-160.34
36	Orthopaedic	-186.03	-0.48	-82.57
37	Congenital Malformation	245.26	0.55	348.72
38	Perinatal	-590.67	-0.79	-487.21
39	Immaturity	686.71	1.28	790.17

Table 10.1 (cont.)

No.	Diagnostic Category	Estimated Coefficient	t-value	Implied Average & Marginal Cost per Case ($)
40	Symptoms, ill-defined	18.27	0.05	121.73
41	Long Stay, ill-defined	-50.49	-0.14	52.97
42	Other Fractures (excl. Femur)	185.36	0.47	288.82
43	Fracture of Neck of Femur	135.13	0.32	238.59
44	Dislocations	781.97	1.23	885.43
45	Internal Injury	687.48	1.41	790.94
46	External Injury	271.63	0.65	375.09
47	Poisoning	202.78	0.41	306.24

Notes: * All insignificant at 5% level.
(a) Suppressed category is Investigations, Procedures, Healthy.
Source: Regression results.

explained variation increased to 43 per cent (adjusted $R^2 = 0.43$; d.f. = 70) with the overall relationship significant at the one per cent level (F = 2.80).[6]

The remaining three average cost per day equations each incorporate scale and/or utilisation terms in various ways. The relevant parameter estimates are presented in Table 10.2. Equation I includes linear and quadratic terms in the case flow rate, both of which are significant at the one per cent level. Average cost per day is predicted to decline with increases in case flow up to 41.1 cases per bed per year, and increase thereafter. This indicates that the decrease in average cost per case as *case* flow increases, as discussed in Chapter 6, is also reflected in a decrease in average cost per day at least up to a case flow rate of 41.1.

Equation II in Table 10.2 includes linear terms in average length of stay and occupancy. Both of these have negative signs but only the occupancy term is statistically significant. It indicates that increasing occupancy (which increases the case flow rate, *ceteris paribus*) reduces average cost per day, consistent with the behaviour indicated by equation I for case flow rates up to 41.1 cases per bed per year.

Equation III in Table 10.2 includes inverted terms in average length of stay and occupancy, and linear and quadratic terms in beds. There is also an interactive term between scale and occupancy (*RBD/OCC*). Only the inverse

---

6   The individual case mix parameter estimates for this and the remaining average cost per day equations are not included here.

average length of stay term is significant. It indicates a non-linear inverse relationship between average cost per day and average length of stay. If average length of stay were increased by one day from its State mean value in 1977-78 of 7.44 days (see Table 5.6), this equation predicts average cost per day would fall by about $2. A reduction of this magnitude would clearly be insufficient to outweigh the cost-increasing effect of the longer stay and is consistent with the estimated increase in average cost per case of $52.77 arising from the same increase in average length of stay (see Section 6.5.1).

Table 10.2. Scale and Utilisation Parameter Estimates using Alternative Specifications of Average Cost per Day Equation with 47 Diagnostic Categories and Five Age Categories, Queensland Public Hospitals, 1977-78[a]

Equation	CFR	CFR²	ALS	OCC	$\bar{R}^2$	F	d.f.
I	-2.468 (-3.20*)	0.03004 (2.87*)			.49	3.21*	68
II			-1.9406 (-1.51)	-89.088 (-4.24*)	.57	4.06*	68

Equation	$\frac{1}{ALS}$	$\frac{1}{OCC}$	$\frac{RBD}{OCC}$	B	B²	$\bar{R}^2$	F
III (d.f.=64)	125.101 (2.62**)	-0.68585 (-0.97)	0.00021 (1.53)	-0.1671 (-1.44)	0.00005 (0.96)	.55	3.59*

Notes: *   Significant at 1% level.
         **   Significant at 5% level.
         (a) t-values in parentheses.
         d.f. = degrees of freedom.
Source: Regression results.

In all three equations the addition of scale and/or utilisation terms increases significantly the explanatory power of the equation, but such explanatory power is always less than that of the corresponding average cost per case equation (see Chapters 5 and 6). However, this is not unexpected. Two hospitals with the same case mix, scale, utilisation and average cost per case may still achieve this with differing combinations of average cost per day and average length of stay, so it is quite conceivable that there would be less systematic variation between case mix, scale and utilisation, and average cost per day.

These five equations can then be used to obtain predicted values of average cost per day and costliness per day ratios for each hospital. The use of these results together with the costliness per case ratios and the Relative Stay Index will now be demonstrated.

10.3.2   Costliness Ratios and the Relative Stay Index

Using the estimated cost equations for 1977-78 for predictive purposes yields five costliness per case ratios and five costliness per day ratios for each hospital for that year. Even though the case mix category coefficients have generally implausible values, the predicted values of average cost per case and average cost per day for each hospital are, with only a few exceptions, all positive. In the average cost per case predictions two hospitals had one or more negative predicted values, while in the average cost per day predictions one hospital had a negative predicted value from one of the equations. The two hospitals with negative predicted values of average cost per case had relatively low actual average costs per case ($34.71 and $132.50) and similarly for the hospital with a negative predicted average cost per day (actual value $34.80).

The costliness ratios for ten hospitals from the sample are presented in Table 10.3. In addition, this Table contains the relative cost per case and relative cost per day ratios, defined as the ratio of the relevant average magnitude to the unweighted State mean. Finally, the Table contains two measures of relative length of stay. The first of these is based on the Relative Stay Index for the financial year 1977-78 and gives the ratio of actual/expected average length of stay. The second measure is obtained as the ratio of costliness per case to costliness per day using the fifth specification of each average cost equation (see column headed RLS).[7] The fifth specifications were used for these calculations because they incorporate both scale and utilisation effects, and the RSI is calculated for hospital groups categorised according to the criteria noted earlier in this chapter.

The first point to note about these data is the substantial difference between relative cost and costliness for most hospitals, indicating that comparing a hospital's average cost (per case or per day) with the State

---

7   Recall that costliness per case is given by $(ACC / A\hat{C}C)$ where the numerator and denominator are actual and predicted average cost per case respectively, and analogously for costliness per day. The ratio of costliness per case to costliness per day then gives $(ACC / ACD)/(A\hat{C}C / A\hat{C}D)$, or the ratio of actual average length of stay to predicted average length of stay where the prediction is obtained as the ratio of the predicted values of average cost per case and average cost per day.

Table 10.3. Relative Cost, Costliness and Relative Stay Indices for Ten Queensland Public Hospitals, 1977-78(a)

No.	Relative Cost per Case	Costliness per Case					Relative Cost per Day	Costliness per Day					RSI 1977-78	RLS
		1	2	3	4	5		1	2	3	4	5		
1	0.42	4.47	1.48	1.43	1.43	1.41	0.40	1.31	1.08	1.13	1.13	1.25	1.10	1.13
2	0.52	0.48	0.81	0.84	0.75	0.84	0.77	0.70	0.82	0.78	0.69	0.71	1.07	1.18
3	0.60	0.79	1.01	1.28	1.16	1.02	1.11	1.02	1.14	1.19	1.23	1.23	0.80	0.83
4	0.79	0.91	0.71	0.85	0.78	0.80	0.92	1.05	1.23	1.63	1.17	0.98	1.17	0.82
5	0.99	0.85	1.01	1.04	1.18	1.09	0.81	1.18	1.90	1.98	1.50	1.38	1.07	0.79
6	1.09	1.01	0.86	0.85	0.95	0.94	0.58	0.62	0.66	0.64	0.70	0.79	1.85	1.19
7	1.19	1.00	0.94	1.04	1.04	1.13	1.03	0.93	0.91	0.95	0.93	1.02	1.08	1.11
8	1.41	0.91	0.92	0.95	0.93	0.91	1.25	1.06	0.95	0.99	1.02	0.92	0.83	0.99
9	1.74	1.43	1.17	1.25	1.23	1.19	1.91	1.69	1.74	1.55	1.65	1.59	0.56	0.75
10	2.49	1.13	1.15	1.10	1.08	1.05	1.26	0.89	0.79	0.79	0.94	0.96	1.81	1.09

Note: (a)   Relative cost = actual cost/State mean cost; Costliness = actual cost/predicted cost; RSI = relative stay index; RLS = relative length of stay = costliness per case/costliness per day.

Sources: Costliness ratios from regression results. Relative cost ratios from Hospital Finance Data. RSI figures from Queensland Department of Health RSI Tables (unpublished).

mean is not an accurate indicator of its productive efficiency. Consider hospital number 1, for example. While its actual average cost per case is *less than* half the State mean, it is 40-50 per cent *greater than* predicted (given its case mix, scale and utilisation) in four of the five predictions. Hospital number 10 illustrates a situation where an actual average cost per case nearly one and a half times the State mean is only about 5 to 15 per cent greater than predicted after adjustment for case mix and other factors. Similar relationships (or lack thereof) are evident between relative cost and costliness per day.

The second main feature of the data in Table 10.3 is that they enable the 'cause' of a particular hospital's costliness per case rating to be expressed in terms of performance with respect to costliness per day and relative length of stay. For example, hospital number 1 has an actual average cost per case 41 per cent greater than that predicted by the fifth equation. The costliness per day and RSI figures indicate that this is partly due to excessive average cost per day (25 per cent greater than predicted) and partly due to excessive average length of stay (10 per cent greater than predicted). In other words, for this hospital the excessive costliness per case is attributable to both excessive intensity of treatment per day of stay and excessive length of stay.

A different situation emerges for hospital number 9 which has an actual average cost per case 19 per cent greater than predicted by the fifth equation. While this hospital has a much shorter length of stay than predicted (RSI = 0.56), its actual average cost per day exceeds the prediction by 59 per cent. This indicates that, for this hospital, the intensity/length of stay trade-off has been taken to the point where reductions in length of stay are being more than offset by increases in average cost per day.

Because the costliness ratios are based on econometric estimation, it is to be expected that such ratios will not always be 'consistent' with the RSI figure. The extent of the inconsistency is indicated by comparing the RSI figures with the RLS figures, the latter being the relative length of stay figures obtained by dividing the costliness per case ratios by the costliness per day ratios. 'Consistency' here means that the costliness per case ratio is equal to the product of the costliness per day and length of stay indexes. Hence the RLS figures guarantee consistency in this sense.

While the RSI and RLS figures generally point in the same direction, there is sometimes a large difference in their magnitude (e.g. hospital number 6) and sometimes a difference in their direction (e.g. hospital numbers 4 and 5). These latter differences are the more serious because they have opposite policy implications. An RSI or RLS value greater than unity indicates excessive average length of stay while such a value less than unity indicates too low an average length of stay.

The data in Table 10.3 relate to only ten of the 121 hospitals in the sample. A broader picture of the relationships between the various costliness and relative length of stay measures can be gained by considering the correlation coefficients between them (see Table 10.4). Relative cost per case is not highly correlated with any of the costliness per case or costliness per day measures and the same applies to relative cost per day. This implies a substantial difference between a hospital's unadjusted and adjusted costs and emphasises the importance of accounting for case mix differences between hospitals.

A second feature of these correlation coefficients is the relatively low correlation between most of the costliness per case indices, with some coefficients actually being negative. This indicates substantial differences in the predicted values of average cost per case for any hospital from each of the equations, emphasising the importance of the specification issue in deciding on the equation to be used. There is generally stronger correlation between the various costliness per day indices.[8]

Finally, there is only very low correlation between any particular costliness per case measure and the corresponding costliness per day measure and RSI value. This indicates a lack of systematic variation between high costliness per case values and costliness per day or RSI values. Hospitals which are relatively inefficient do not consistently tend to treat patients too intensively or to have relatively high lengths of stay. This reinforces one of the basic arguments of this study—that high costliness per unit of *output* need not necessarily be systematically related to either of the two *input* related indices—costliness per day and relative length of stay. That is, either high costliness per day or high relative length of stay on their own do not necessarily imply high costliness per case.

The data on costliness ratios for each hospital, a sample of which has been presented in Table 10.3, do not indicate whether such ratios are statistically significantly different from unity. As discussed earlier in this chapter, such a judgement requires the construction of prediction intervals. The calculation of such intervals, together with the results of disaggregating cost per case by input component, will now be discussed.

---

[8]   Feldstein and Schuttinga (1977) found substantially higher correlations than have been found here among their various costliness measures, but it could be argued that the alternative specifications explored in our study differ more substantially between one another than did the specifications of Feldstein and Schuttinga.

Table 10.4. Correlation Coefficients Between Relative Cost, Costliness and Relative Stay Indices, Queensland Public Hospitals, 1977-78

	Relative Cost per Case	Costliness per Case					Relative Cost per Day	Costliness per Day					RSI 1977-78
		1	2	3	4	5		1	2	3	4	5	
Relative Cost per Case	1.00	0.17	0.37	-0.14	0.22	0.23	0.35	0.31	0.33	0.16	0.04	0.34	0.45
Costliness per Case 1		1.00					0.12	0.20	0.18	0.07	-0.02	0.22	0.07
2		-0.10	1.00				0.14	0.12	0.18	0.15	0.02	0.26	0.28
3		0.43	-0.24	1.00			-0.06	0.01	-0.01	0.02	-0.03	0.01	-0.18
4		0.06	0.18	-0.38	1.00		0.26	0.18	0.20	0.15	0.06	0.18	0.07
5		-0.03	0.40	-0.40	0.60	1.00	0.28	0.20	0.19	0.20	0.07	0.28	0.14
Relative Cost per Day							1.00	0.36	0.38	0.32	0.20	0.30	-0.26
Costliness per Day 1								1.00					-0.09
2								0.88	1.00				-0.07
3								0.65	0.83	1.00			-0.08
4								0.21	0.25	0.22	1.00		-0.28
5								0.78	0.84	0.74	0.12	1.00	0.01
RSI 1977-78													1.00

Source: Regression results.

10.3.3   Prediction Intervals and Costliness Ratios for Input Components

Considering first average cost per case by input component, Table 10.5 presents some descriptive statistics on the ten input components into which average cost per case was dissected. Salaries account for 78 per cent of average cost per case, and when this category is further dissected into medical, nursing and other salaries, nursing salaries emerge as the largest single salaries item. It is interesting to note that medical salaries account for only four per cent of overall average cost per case.[9]

Table 10.5. Descriptive Statistics, Input Component Average Costs per Case, Queensland Public Hospitals, 1977-78

Input Component	Mean*	SD	CV	Range Min.	Max.
Salaries - Total	426.55	191.00	0.45	28.48	1113.44
- Medical	23.63	22.48	0.95	0.0	125.34
- Nursing	227.35	103.77	0.46	13.71	700.74
- Other	175.57	84.45	0.48	12.18	418.91
Provisions	21.68	10.80	0.50	0.0	52.08
Medicaments and Appliances	23.83	18.11	0.76	2.48	153.03
Domestic	9.30	7.51	0.81	0.38	63.36
Upkeep and Repairs	25.40	28.64	1.13	1.24	244.03
Fuel, Light and Power	15.61	9.78	0.63	0.33	62.56
Establishment and Management	24.46	16.55	0.68	1.07	75.13
Total	546.83	238.90	0.44	34.71	1361.16

Notes: *   Means are unweighted means.
Source: Hospital Finance Data, Queensland Department of Health.

---

[9]   The large percentage of average cost per case accounted for by salaries reflects to some (unknown) extent the fact that the cost data employed in this study exclude all capital charges.

Each input component average cost per case was then used as the dependent variable in the fifth specification of the average cost per case equation given by equation (10.7). The summary statistics of the resulting ten estimated equations are presented in Table 10.6. As can be expected, the cost per case of some input components is more sensitive to case mix, scale and utilisation than others. For Upkeep and Repairs, Fuel Light and Power, and Establishment and Management, such factors explain only 39 per cent of interhospital variation in cost per case. This compares with an explained variation of 77 per cent for Salaries and 75 per cent for Provisions. As discussed earlier in Chapter 6, this specification of the average cost function explained 77 per cent of the variation in overall average cost per case.

Table 10.6. Summary Statistics for Estimated Input Component Average Cost per Case Equations, Queensland Public Hospitals, 1977-78[a]

Input Component	$\bar{R}^2$	F*	SEE
Salaries - Total	.77	7.67	91.16
- Medical	.74	6.46	11.57
- Nursing	.76	7.13	51.16
- Other	.72	6.01	44.83
Provisions	.75	6.78	5.44
Medicaments and Appliances	.72	6.16	9.51
Domestic	.57	.61	4.92
Upkeep and Repairs	.39	2.24	22.44
Fuel, Light and Power	.39	2.26	7.64
Establishment and Management	.39	2.26	12.91
Average Cost per Case	.77	7.49	115.23

Notes: *   All significant at 1% level.
          (a) All equations are estimated with 59 degrees of freedom.
Sources: Regression results and Table 6.4.

Since our primary concern in this chapter is with prediction, the individual parameter estimates from each of the input component cost per case equations will not be presented here. It should be noted, however, that if the sum of the predicted values of each input component cost per case is to be equal to predicted average cost per case, the input component cost equations must contain the same explanatory variables as the average cost equation (see Appendix 10.I). If any such variables are deleted, for example, on the grounds of statistical insignificance, then this property is destroyed.[10]

Prediction intervals were then calculated for average cost per case and each input component average cost per case using the formula given in equation (10.2). Only the fifth specification of the average cost per case equation—equation (10.7)—was used for this exercise. A prediction interval for average cost per day was also calculated using the fifth specification of the average cost per day equation—equation III in Table 10.2. The costliness ratios and prediction intervals, together with the RSI value, were then tabulated for each hospital. The values for one particular hospital (hospital number 9 in Table 10.2) are given in Table 10.7.

It is apparent from the formula for the prediction interval that a confidence level must be specified for the t-value to be ascertained. The lower the confidence level, the lower the t-value and consequently the narrower the prediction interval. The null hypothesis is that the costliness ratio equals unity, i.e. H_0: $CR = 1$. The alternative hypothesis is that the costliness ratio does not equal unity, i.e. H_1: $CR \neq 1$. The higher the confidence interval which is specified, the lower is the probability of committing a Type I error—rejecting H_0 when it is in fact true. This probability is actually the level of significance (Daniel and Terrell 1975, p.153), so that a 95 per cent confidence level gives a probability of committing a Type I error of 0.05.

With reference to Table 10.7, the 95 per cent costliness ratio prediction interval then means that, with repeated sampling, 95 per cent of the costliness ratios obtained would fall in this interval. If the costliness ratio obtained actually falls in this interval, the null hypothesis is then accepted. The Table also provides costliness ratio prediction intervals for two other confidence levels—80 per cent and 60 per cent. At the 60 per cent confidence level, the probability of committing a Type I error is 0.4—in four cases out of ten it will be wrongfully concluded that a hospital's costliness ratio is *not* equal to unity when in fact it is. For the hospital in

---

10   Another point to note about the scale and utilisation parameter estimates in these equations is that such estimates will be biased if there is any systematic relationship between input substitution and scale or utilisation. Such a relationship would mean that the error term would no longer be independent of the explanatory variables, a property required for unbiased parameter estimates. Note that it is not input substitution *per se* which gives rise to bias, but a systematic relationship between such substitution and scale or utilisation. A discussion of this point can be found in Feldstein (1967, pp.81-3).

Table 10.7, one could conclude that actual average cost per case is statistically significantly different from that predicted only at the 60 per cent confidence level.

Table 10.7. Costliness Ratios and Prediction Intervals by Input Component for One Queensland Public Hospital, 1977-78

	ACC	ACD	ALS
Actual	951.79	152.90	4.9
Predicted	798.76	96.11	8.8
Actual/Predicted	1.19	1.59	0.56
Prediction Interval			
95%	0.62-1.38	0.38-1.62	
80%	0.76-1.24	0.60-1.40*	
60%	0.84-1.16*	0.73-1.27*	

ACC BY INPUT COMPONENT

	Total Salaries	Medical Salaries	Nursing Salaries	Other Salaries	Provisions
Actual	751.72	82.91	413.53	255.28	24.32
Predicted	602.70	58.89	307.78	236.03	26.70
Actual/Predicted	1.25	1.41	1.34	1.08	0.91
Prediction Interval					
95%	0.60-1.40	0.49-1.51	0.57-1.43	0.50-1.50	0.47-1.53
80%	0.74-1.26	0.67-1.33*	0.72-1.28*	0.68-1.32	0.65-1.35
60%	0.83-1.17*	0.78-1.22*	0.81-1.19*	0.79-1.21	0.77-1.23

	Medic. & Appl's	Domestic	Upkeep & Repairs	Fuel, Light & Power	Estab. & Man
Actual	26.84	30.99	49.11	24.90	43.92
Predicted	21.17	26.41	57.54	22.95	41.30
Actual/Predicted	1.27	1.17	0.85	1.08	1.06
Prediction Interval					
95%	-0.18-2.18	0.51-1.49	-0.02-2.02	0.13-1.87	0.18-1.82
80%	0.24-1.76	0.68-1.32	0.34-1.66	0.44-1.56	0.47-1.53
60%	0.50-1.50	0.79-1.21	0.57-1.43	0.63-1.37	0.65-1.35

Note: * Costliness ratio lies outside this prediction interval.
Source: Regression results.

The reason why a higher probability of a Type I error might be tolerated is that it gives rise to a concomitant reduction in the probability of a Type II error—accepting the null hypothesis when it is in fact false. Hence there is a trade-off, and "the choice of a criterion of significance depends largely upon the relative seriousness of Type I and Type II errors" (Croxton 1953, p.223).[11] The kind of information provided in Table 10.7 can assist decision-makers in appraising this trade-off.

Returning to the data contained in Table 10.7, the costliness per day ratio can be deemed statistically significantly different from unity at a confidence level in excess of 80 per cent. Turning to the input component costliness per case ratios, it seems that relatively high medical salaries and nursing salaries cost per case are the most likely cause of this hospital's costliness per case ratio of 1.19. The costliness per case ratios for these two input components are statistically significantly different from unity at a confidence level in excess of 80 per cent.

A more general picture of the number of hospitals in the sample which had costliness ratios statistically significantly different from unity is provided by the data in Table 10.8. This Table reports the numbers of hospitals out of the sample of 121 which had significantly high and low costliness per case and costliness per day ratios at various confidence levels. At the 95 per cent confidence level, no hospital had a costliness ratio significantly greater or less than unity. As can be expected, the numbers of hospitals falling outside the prediction intervals increase as the confidence level falls.

Table 10.8. Numbers of Hospitals with Costliness Ratios Statistically Significantly Different from Unity at Various Confidence Levels, Queensland Public Hospitals, 1977-78

Confidence Level	Costliness per Case Ratio		Costliness per Day Ratio	
	High	Low	High	Low
95%	0	0	0	0
80%	2	3	5	0
60%	9	9	11	8
50%	10	14	15	16

Source: Regression results and prediction intervals.

---

[11] On the selection of confidence intervals, see also Daniel and Terrell (1975, pp.153-4) and references cited therein.

The above results lead to the conclusion that, at the conventional 95 per cent confidence level, no hospital was significantly 'efficient' or significantly 'inefficient'. If the probability of committing a Type I error is not to rise above 0.05, then this implies that in 1977-78 there would have been no case on statistical grounds for paying any hospital an amount per case different to what was actually spent. Hospitals could be deemed to be highly 'efficient' or 'inefficient' only at a lower confidence level.

This completes the outline of a performance appraisal and payment scheme based on estimated cost equations. Before concluding this chapter, though, some problems with such a scheme arising from the existence of multicollinearity, and from replicating the results using different methods of estimation, will be briefly considered.

10.4   Some Problems

10.4.1   Multicollinearity and Implausible Parameter Estimates

The equations used for predicting average cost per case contain as explanatory variables case mix proportions and scale and utilisation terms. The problem of implausible parameter estimates for the case mix terms was discussed in Chapter 5 where it was found that a number of the estimates implied negative average and marginal costs for individual case types. Evidence was produced which suggested that multicollinearity was the underlying cause of this problem.

The first point to note is that, even though the parameter estimates are implausible and have high variances, the *predictive accuracy* of the equation is not necessarily impaired. In particular, "if one is willing to assume that the structure (the relationship among the explanatory variables) will remain unchanged, it is well known that collinearity does not impair the prediction of [the dependent variable]" (Newhouse 1971, p.5). This point will be taken up in Section 10.4.2.

If the relationship between the explanatory variables is unchanged so prediction is unimpaired, why are implausible parameter estimates with large variances a problem? Perhaps the most important reason in the context of a hospital payment scheme is that they would inspire little faith in the forecasts amongst the users of the scheme. Hospital administrators are unlikely to take seriously a scheme which embodies an average cost of, for example, a normal delivery of –$1,000, despite the overall accuracy of the prediction of average cost per case for the hospital. Assurances that the estimators are statistically unbiased despite the presence of strong multicollinearity are unlikely to allay the suspicion with which such predictions would be viewed.

The problem could be overcome by using the case mix category parameter estimates implied by the information theory index. It was seen in Chapter 5 that the use of this index gave rise to positive and plausible values of average and marginal cost per case (see Tables 5.20 and 5.21). A discussion of the use of the information theory index for hospital reimbursement can be found in Hardwick (1986).

10.4.2   Multicollinearity and Prediction

As pointed out in the foregoing discussion, predictive accuracy in the presence of multicollinearity requires that the underlying relationship between the explanatory variables remains unchanged over the forecast period. The importance of this condition should not be underestimated.

> Even for forecasting purposes the econometrician whose data are multicollinear is in an extremely exposed position. Successful forecasts with multicollinear variables require not only the perpetuation of a stable dependency relationship between y and X, but also the perpetuation of stable interdependency relationships within X. *Both conditions are met, unfortunately, only in a context in which the forecasting problem is all but trivial.* (Farrar and Glauber 1967, p.95, emphasis in original).

So far in this chapter the predictions used have been obtained using the values of the variables employed in estimating the original equations, i.e. the predicted values of average cost per case and average cost per day for 1977-78 were obtained from the estimated equations for 1977-78. It is, then, not surprising that sensible forecasts are obtained, because the values of the predictor variables used in obtaining the forecasts were the very values used to estimate the relationships in the first place. This guarantees that the two conditions stated by Farrar and Glauber will be fulfilled but also makes the forecasting exercise "all but trivial". What is more important, particularly if the equations are to be used as a basis for prospectively paying hospitals, is that the 1977-78 equations give accurate predictions for 1978-79 or subsequent years. It is here that difficulties arise with the two conditions quoted above.

The case mix category parameter estimates in this study not only suffered from implausible magnitudes and high variances but also varied substantially from one year to the next. While the predictions obtained for subsequent years using that particular year's estimated equation were all plausible, the large variability in the parameter estimates from one year to the next virtually guarantees that *future* period predictions using any particular year's equation will be seriously inaccurate. This capricious variation in parameter estimates indicates a fundamental flaw in the use of estimated cost equations for prospective hospital reimbursement purposes.[12]

Additional evidence in support of the view that the underlying pattern of multicollinearity in the data varies through time can be obtained by examining the stability of hospital case mix through time. The erratic changes in the case mix parameter estimates from one year to the next suggest intertemporal variation in case mix proportions. To gain some insight into this, the intertemporal variation in a subset of diagnostic categories was examined. The results of this exercise are discussed in more detail in the next chapter (see Section 11.4), but generally support the view that hospital case mix is subject to change through time, often quite substantially from one year to the next. Again, it seems highly unlikely that the conditions stated in the above quote from Farrar and Glauber would be fulfilled.

10.4.3   Replication with other Methods of Estimation

Apart from problems associated with multicollinearity, if an econometric approach is to adopted to performance appraisal and payment of hospitals, confidence in such an approach would be enhanced if alternative methods of estimation produced consistent results with respect to a hospital's relative efficiency. If one method of estimation showed a hospital to be highly efficient while another showed the opposite, it would be difficult to conclude one way or another whether the hospital was actually relatively efficient.

A study aimed at investigating this issue has been undertaken by Wagstaff (1989). Using data on 49 Spanish public hospitals, he employed three different statistical models to estimate frontier cost functions for these hospitals, along with a non-frontier model based on Feldstein (1967). The three frontier models were the deterministic cost frontier, a cross-section stochastic cost frontier and a panel data stochastic cost frontier. The

---

12 An interesting avenue for future research would be to see whether the case type cost estimates obtained from the information theory index are stable through time. Barer (1982), using pooled time series/cross section data on 87 British Columbia acute care hospitals, has found that "Case complexities based on information theory were found to be extremely stable over the eight years" (p.77).

deterministic cost frontier returned similar results to the Feldstein model with respect to hospital inefficiency. The costliness indexes (analogous to the costliness ratios used in this chapter) from the these two approaches had a simple correlation coefficient of 0.90 and a Spearman rank correlation coefficient of 0.82, both of which were significantly different from zero.[13]

The two stochastic cost frontiers, however, returned results which differed both from the deterministic/Feldstein models and from each other. In fact, the cross-section stochastic cost frontier suggested that there was no cross-sample variation in hospital efficiency, while the panel data stochastic cost frontier suggested greater mean inefficiency than the deterministic cost frontier. The rank correlation coefficient between the costliness indexes from the deterministic cost frontier and the panel data cost frontier was only 0.53, and between the latter and the Feldstein costliness index was only 0.28.

Wagstaff concluded that the substantially different efficiency rankings of hospitals from the different models was "really rather worrying", and that "government officials and others ought to be wary about accepting at face value the results of efficiency analyses that are based on only one estimation method" (Wagstaff 1989, p.671).

10.5   Summary and Conclusions

The performance appraisal and payment scheme outlined in this chapter is based on the use of estimated average cost per case and average cost per day equations and the Relative Stay Index. As has been argued earlier in this study, average cost per case is the conceptually preferred measure of cost per unit of *output*, with average cost per day and average length of stay being *input* related measures. Using the property that the latter two measures when multiplied together give average cost per case, a hospital's values of these measures can be compared to a set of predicted values and a conclusion drawn about its performance. The ratio of actual/predicted average cost per case is termed the costliness per case ratio. It is this index which indicates a hospital's relative performance in terms of productive efficiency. The costliness per day ratio and the Relative Stay Index, also being obtained as 'actual/predicted' ratios, then indicate the 'source' of the particular hospital's performance in terms of the cost per day/length of stay

---

[13]   The close correlation between these results is not surprising, given that the deterministic cost frontier is obtained as a vertical displacement of the ordinary least squares cost function so as to move the estimated function from a 'mean' position to a frontier position.

trade-off. Predicted values for cost per case and cost per day are obtained from the relevant average cost equations.

Two embellishments of this scheme were also explored. The first involved constructing prediction intervals to enable a statistical inference to be drawn about the significance of the deviation of a hospital's costliness ratios from unity. The second entailed disaggregating average cost per case by input component and obtaining predicted values for each component from a set of input component average cost per case equations. Hence, in terms of performance appraisal, the scheme would allow hospitals to ascertain in which direction their actual intensity/length of stay position deviates from that which would give a costliness per case ratio of unity, and indicates the particular input categories which may account for the hospital's level of productive efficiency.

The hospital payment aspects of this scheme suffer from a serious problem arising out of the presence of multicollinearity. While predictions for any particular year obtained using the estimated equation *for that year* may be plausible, the use of any year's equation to predict average cost in *future* years can give spurious results unless the underlying pattern of multicollinearity in the data is maintained in future periods. This condition is unlikely to be fulfilled, with the result that a prospective payment scheme based on estimated equations would be unworkable. Further, evidence produced in another study suggests that the efficiency rankings of hospitals may vary considerably when different econometric approaches are employed in estimating the cost function or cost frontier.

It is concluded that the potential usefulness of the scheme outlined in this chapter is limited to its performance appraisal aspects. Even confined to this role, however, implausible values and large variances of case mix parameter estimates make the scheme unattractive. Even though this may not mar the current period predictive accuracy of the cost equations and performance indicators, a scheme based on nonsensical individual case type cost estimates would have little superficial appeal to those involved in hospital financing decisions.

This chapter has been concerned with outlining how a hospital performance appraisal and payment scheme might work using estimated cost equations. The following chapter discusses hospital cost analysis in the context of a payment scheme which has actually been implemented in the US and in one State in Australia.

Appendix 10.I

Proof that the Sum of Predicted Input Component Costs per Case Equals Predicted Average Cost per Case

Begin with the classical linear regression model

$$\mathbf{y} = \mathbf{XB} + \mathbf{e} \qquad \dots (1)$$

where $\mathbf{y}$ is a ($T \times 1$) vector of observations of the dependent variable average cost per case, $\mathbf{X}$ is a ($T \times K$) matrix of T observations on each of K independent variables and $\mathbf{B}$ is a ($K \times 1$) vector of unknown regression coefficients. The 'least squares' estimates of $\mathbf{B}$ are given by

$$\hat{\mathbf{B}} = (\mathbf{X'X})^{-1}\mathbf{X'y} \qquad \dots (2)$$

The ($T \times 1$) vector of predicted values of average cost per case $\hat{\mathbf{y}}$ is given by

$$\begin{aligned}\hat{\mathbf{y}} &= \mathbf{X\hat{B}} \\ &= \mathbf{X}(\mathbf{X'X})^{-1}\mathbf{X'y}\end{aligned} \qquad \dots (3)$$

Now suppose that $\mathbf{y}$ is disaggregated into m input component costs per case so that

$$\mathbf{y} = \sum_{i=1}^{m} \mathbf{y}_i$$

i.e. actual average cost per case equals the sum of input component costs per case. Using the input component costs per case as dependent variables in the linear regression model produces the least squares estimates of $\mathbf{B}_i$ given by

$$\hat{\mathbf{B}}_i = (\mathbf{X'X})^{-1}\mathbf{X'y}_i \qquad \dots (4)$$

Predicted values of the input component costs per case are then obtained using the least squares parameter estimates:

$$\hat{\mathbf{y}}_i = \mathbf{X}\hat{\mathbf{B}}_i = \mathbf{X}(\mathbf{X}'\mathbf{X})^{-1}\mathbf{X}'\mathbf{y}_i \qquad \text{... (5)}$$

It remains to be shown that $\hat{\mathbf{y}} = \sum_{i=1}^{m}\hat{\mathbf{y}}_i$. From equation (5) this summation can be written as

$$\sum_{i=1}^{m}\hat{\mathbf{y}}_i = \sum_{i=1}^{m}\mathbf{X}(\mathbf{X}'\mathbf{X})^{-1}\mathbf{X}'\mathbf{y}_i$$

By the distributive law of matrix multiplication, this can be written as

$$\sum_{i=1}^{m}\hat{\mathbf{y}}_i = \mathbf{X}(\mathbf{X}'\mathbf{X})^{-1}\mathbf{X}'\sum_{i=1}^{m}\mathbf{y}_i \qquad \text{... (6)}$$
$$= \mathbf{X}(\mathbf{X}'\mathbf{X})^{-1}\mathbf{X}'\mathbf{y}$$

because $\mathbf{y} = \sum_{i=1}^{m}\mathbf{y}_i$

(actual average cost per case equals the sum of actual input component costs per case). Now the right-hand side of equation (6) is identical to the right-hand side of equation (3) which gives predicted average cost per case. Therefore, the sum of the *predicted* input component costs per case equals *predicted* average cost per case.

11

THE DRG HOSPITAL PAYMENT SCHEME:

SOME ECONOMIC ASPECTS

11.1   Introduction

The purpose of this chapter is to discuss some economic aspects of a
particular payment scheme for hospitals introduced in the US in the 1980s
and in Victoria, Australia, in the 1990s, *viz.* the payment scheme based upon
Diagnosis Related Groups (DRGs). The definition of output embodied in a
payment scheme is a matter of fundamental importance. The problems of
defining, measuring and classifying hospital output have been dealt with in
detail in Chapter 3, where it was argued that the 'case' was the conceptually
preferred unit of output appropriately classified to take account of the
heterogeneous types of cases treated by a hospital. DRGs as a case mix
classification scheme were discussed in that chapter also (see Section 3.4.1).
The revised version of these DRGs has been adopted as the output
taxonomy in a payment scheme for hospitals in the US.

Commencing on 1 October 1983, the US central government
implemented a radical change to the method of paying hospitals for patients

treated under the Medicare program for the aged.[1] The new scheme differed from the old in three important respects (Pointer and Ross 1984). *First*, the unit of payment has changed from 'services provided' to 'cases discharged', classified by DRG. *Second*, the payment is no longer made on the basis of costs incurred but is an established payment rate for each discharge taking account of the patient's DRG classification. *Third*, payments will be made prospectively (before the care is given) rather than retrospectively.

This new system of hospital financing has been described by one author as the "most significant transformation in almost two decades" (Vladeck 1984, p.576). Given the arguments presented in this study, it is not difficult to see why. In essence, the new scheme involved a change from an input-based payment scheme to an output-based payment scheme. Hospitals are no longer simply reimbursed for what they spend on inputs but receive a certain sum (or payment rate) per unit of output. The scheme enshrines the treated case as the unit of output, with appropriate adjustment for the multiproduct nature of hospital output by the use of the DRG case mix classification system. A consequent increase in productive efficiency is to be expected,[2] and there is some evidence available to support this expectation (Hsiao and Dunn 1987; Sloan, Morrisey and Valvona 1988).[3]

However, while this new scheme is defensible on these grounds, it will be argued in Section 11.3 of this chapter that the scheme as implemented fails to take into account some possibly important characteristics of hospital cost functions. As a result, hospitals may have an incentive to increase the treatment of some case types and reduce that of others, or they may find 'profits' being made or 'losses' being incurred on some case types simply because of the nature of the underlying cost function. Before elaborating upon this argument though, it is necessary to outline briefly the DRG payment scheme. This task is undertaken in Section 11.2. Then, following the appraisal of the scheme in terms of hospital cost analysis, Section 11.4 addresses a problem faced by all prospective hospital payment schemes—

---

[1]   Medicare patients give rise to about 40 per cent of total hospital revenue in the US (Vladeck 1984, p.576).

[2]   A theoretical analysis of reimbursement schemes based on units of service compared with schemes based on types of case can be found in Worthington (1977). See also Grimaldi (1978) and Worthington (1978).

[3]   For a discussion of the effects of the DRG payment scheme in the US, see Feldstein (1993, pp.291-3) and Folland, Goodman and Stano (1993, pp.616-19). The introduction of case mix funding of hospitals in Victoria, Australia, has occurred only recently so there is no evidence as yet on its effects in that State.

that of predicting hospital case mix. Even if one has a set of 'prices' by DRG, forecasts of volume by DRG are necessary if hospitals are to be paid on an ex-ante basis. This section presents some evidence concerning the effects of different levels of case mix aggregation on forecasting accuracy. Section 11.5 contains a summary and conclusions.

11.2   The DRG Hospital Payment Scheme

Under the DRG payment scheme, a hospital's total revenue is given by the sum of the number of cases discharged in each DRG multiplied by the payment rate for the relevant DRG. This can be expressed as follows:

$$TR_j = \sum_i n_{ij} r_i \qquad \qquad \text{... (11.1)}$$

where TR_j = total revenue for the jth hospital,
$\quad\quad\;\; n_{ij}$ = number of cases in the ith DRG in the jth hospital, and
$\quad\quad\;\; r_i$ = payment rate for the ith DRG.

Since the DRGs are mutually exclusive and exhaustive, this payment formula can also be written as

$$TR_j = \sum_i n_j p_{ij} r_i \qquad \qquad \text{... (11.2)}$$

where p_{ij} = proportion of cases in the ith DRG in the jth hospital, and
$\quad\quad\;\; n_j$ = total number of cases in the jth hospital.

For any given year, n_j is constant so equation (11.2) can be written as

$$TR_j = n_j \sum_i p_{ij} r_i \qquad \qquad \text{... (11.3)}$$

Rearranging (11.3) gives average revenue as the weighted mean of the reimbursement rates in each DRG with the weights being the proportions of cases in each DRG, as follows:

$$AR_j = \frac{TR_j}{n_j} = \sum_i p_{ij} r_i \qquad \qquad \text{... (11.4)}$$

From equation (11.4) it is evident that a change in the hospital's average revenue per case from one time period to the next will arise from either a change in the case mix proportions (the p_{ij}) or a change in the payment rate for one or more DRGs (the r_i). The payment rates in turn may all vary by a uniform percentage if relativities are maintained, or the relativities may be altered. To separate out these influences, (11.4) may be rewritten as follows:

$$AR_j = \sum_i p_{ij} w_i \bar{r} = \bar{r} \sum_i p_{ij} w_i \qquad\qquad \dots (11.5)$$

where $\bar{r}$ = mean reimbursement rate for all DRGs, and

$w_i = \dfrac{r_i}{\bar{r}}$ = reimbursement rate for the ith DRG relative to the mean.

An equal proportionate change in all the reimbursement rates would change $\bar{r}$ in the same proportion, leaving the relativities (or the w_i) unchanged, while a change in the relativities would affect the values of the w_i.

The extent to which such a scheme results in hospitals receiving revenues equal to the costs of providing treatment depends on how accurately changes in average revenue in equation (11.4) reflect changes in average costs. Suppose, for example, that in the first year of the scheme, a hospital receives average revenue equal to average cost. In the second year the hospital's case mix changes so that average revenue changes. Leaving aside adjustments for inflation, and assuming relative payment rates remain unchanged, will the average revenue in the second year then be equal to average cost? This depends on the extent to which the payment rates (the r_i) are an accurate reflection of the average cost within each DRG.

In the US system, payment rates within each DRG are constant and independent of the volume of cases treated.[4] The total amount received by a hospital under this system is designed to cover the total costs expected to be incurred by that hospital in treating its particular mix of Medicare cases with five exceptions: payments for outliers;[5] capital costs; direct medical education; patients transferred to other hospitals; and costs associated with kidney transplantation for approved transplantation centres. It is interesting

---

[4]   The rates may vary between hospitals depending on location (urban/rural) and regional variations in wage rates (see Vladeck 1984, pp.581-2).

[5]   Outliers are cases involving an unusually long length of stay or are unusually costly. Note that this is the only respect in which length of stay has an influence on a hospital's total payment. In terms of the discussion in Chapter 10, the five exceptions listed here are the only 'allowable' sources of variation in hospital costs other than case mix itself.

to note that scale and utilisation factors are not taken into account in determining a hospital's payment.

What assumptions does such a system imply about the underlying cost function of a hospital? This question is addressed in the following section.

11.3 Hospital Costs and the DRG Payment Scheme

To understand the model of hospital costs implied by the DRG payment scheme, it is necessary to employ some cost concepts which arise in the context of the multiproduct firm. As such, this section comprises two parts. First, the relevant cost concepts already discussed in detail in Chapter 2 will be briefly reviewed. Second, the DRG payment scheme is examined with reference to these concepts.

11.3.1 Cost Concepts for the Multiproduct Firm— Theoretical Review

Consider a firm producing two outputs y_1 and y_2 with a given quantity of inputs and state of technology.[6] As shown in Figure 11.1, this firm could produce OA units of output y_1 if all resources were devoted to the production of y_1 and OB of y_2 if all resources were used in the production of y_2. If the firm produced at either of these extremes, it would actually be a single product firm and the total cost of the resources could be unambiguously assigned to the relevant output.

Now suppose that the production processes for y_1 and y_2 are constrained to be completely separate and distinct, in that neither process has any shared or common inputs with the other. Put another way, suppose the two processes are constrained to be 'stand alone' processes which are completely self contained. The solid line between A and B in Figure 11.1 shows the combinations of y_1 and y_2 which could be produced under these circumstances by transferring resources from the production of one output to the other. Point C, for example, shows that Oy_1^0 and Oy_2^0 of y_1 and y_2 respectively can be produced with the given quantity of resources. Given that the production processes are completely separable, the total costs of producing y_1 and y_2 can again be unambiguously determined since *all* costs can be attributed to the production of the output for which they were

---

6   In the current context, this firm would be a hospital and y_1 and y_2 would be two DRGs.

incurred. The average and marginal cost of producing y_1 and y_2 can consequently be calculated.

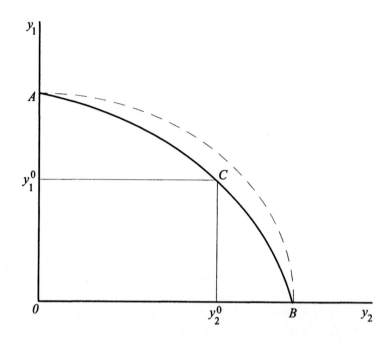

Figure 11.1. Production Possibility Frontier Under Joint and Non-Joint Production

The situation just discussed portrays the multiproduct firm simply as a collection of single product firms. More generally, firms produce several products because it is economically advantageous to do so. In terms of Figure 11.1, a firm which chooses to produce both y_1 and y_2 may find that the locus of production possibilities which it faces is given by the dashed line between A and B. If this is so, the production process is characterised by joint production because more of either or both outputs can be obtained if the products are produced together rather than each being produced from a separate production process. If this is not so, that is, if the firm finds it cannot produce more of either or both outputs by producing them together, then the locus of production possibilities which it faces will be ACB and the firm is nothing more than a collection of single product firms.

What can be said about the costs of producing y_1 and y_2 in the presence of joint production? If joint production is possible then the firm's cost function will exhibit economies of scope, that is, the firm can take advantage of cost savings which result "from simultaneous production of several different outputs in a single enterprise, as contrasted with their production in isolation, each by its own specialised firm" (Baumol, Panzar and Willig 1982, p.71). Generally, economies of scope arise because it is possible to share at least some inputs between the production of two or more commodities, i.e. some inputs may be used in common in the production of several outputs. Such inputs give rise to common costs, costs which are incurred in common in the production of the various outputs.[7] It is impossible to allocate these common costs between the jointly produced outputs in any economically meaningful way, and consequently the average cost of any one of the outputs cannot be calculated. This important point is made by Stigler in the following quotation concerning joint production:

> There is no ... possibility of calculating the average cost of one of several products. It is worth noticing that even though impossible, it is done every day. The costs which are common to several products—a machine or raw material used in producing both, an executive who manages the production of both—are often divided among the products in proportion to their separable variable costs, or in proportion to their sales. Such an allocation must be arbitrary, for there is no basis of allocation that is more persuasive than others. (Stigler 1966, p.165).

What can be calculated for jointly produced products, however, is average *separable* cost and marginal cost. As their name implies, separable costs are the costs of production which can be separately attributed to one particular product.[8] The decision as to whether to produce more or less of a particular product is made by comparing marginal revenue and marginal cost, while the overall contribution of a product line to the firm's common costs is given by the difference between total revenue and total separable cost. If average revenue is just equal to average separable cost for all outputs, the firm's total costs will not be recouped.

Finally, the concepts of economies of scale and product-specific economies of scale must be mentioned. For a multiproduct firm, economies of scale arise if, when *all* outputs are increased by some particular proportion, total costs increase by a smaller proportion. Economies of scale

---

7   In the extreme case where the various outputs are produced in fixed proportions, the common costs are referred to as joint costs.

8   Such costs are sometimes referred to as incremental costs.

are thus measured with reference to a particular output mix, with all outputs varying in the same proportion. On the other hand, product-specific economies of scale refer to the behaviour of the average separable costs of one product as its quantity varies, the quantities of all other products remaining unchanged. Product-specific economies of scale arise if average separable cost falls as the output of a particular product increases.[9]

11.3.2   Application to the DRG Payment Scheme

In the context of the DRG payment scheme, it is evident from the foregoing discussion that, unless hospital production processes are characterised by non-joint production of all outputs, it will be impossible to allocate all inpatient costs to the particular DRGs responsible for their incurrence. Unless a hospital is simply a collection of single product firms, so that it makes no difference to total costs whether two (or more) case types are treated in one hospital or two (or more) separate hospitals, the average cost per case within a DRG cannot be meaningfully calculated. Whether hospital production processes are actually characterised by joint production is an empirical question requiring further research, but it seems unlikely that this would be the case. With 467 different DRGs it would be expected that economies of scope would exist over some range of case types, implying that any attempt to allocate inpatient costs completely to DRGs is not economically sound.

As pointed out earlier, however, the DRG payment rates are designed to cover *all* the costs of treating cases within a DRG subject to certain exceptions, and are constant and independent of the volume of cases treated. This implies the following assumptions about hospital costs. *First*, the scheme presumes that all costs are separable, i.e. all costs are capable of being assigned to the cases responsible for their incurrence. As such it makes no allowance for the existence of joint costs and implies that production is non-joint. Economies or diseconomies of scope are precluded by this assumption. *Second*, within each DRG, the scheme presumes that all costs are variable and that average and marginal costs are equal and constant. These two assumptions taken together imply that the production process exhibits overall constant returns to scale.

To the extent that hospitals' production processes give rise to common costs, the DRG payment rates must then involve some arbitrary assignment of these costs to the various DRGs. This problem is evident in the cost

---

9   For a theoretical treatment of product-specific economies of scale, see Baumol, Panzar and Willig (1982, pp.251-7).

allocation system proposed by Thompson, Averill and Fetter (1979) which apparently forms the basis of the DRG reimbursement rates. In this system, 31 final cost centres are identified into which costs are allocated. Overhead accounts are divided into 'patient care related' and 'nonpatient care related', all of which are allocated into the final cost centres for the purpose of comparisons of DRG costs. The resulting figures in 21 of the final cost centres are then allocated to DRGs on the basis of the departmental cost-to-charges ratio. Of the remaining 10 final cost centres, one was specifically for outpatients and the remaining nine were allocated to DRGs using various other criteria.

The two main questions concerning this method of cost allocation are first, whether costs which, in principle, are unallocable to particular DRGs have been so allocated and secondly, whether the allocation criteria accurately ascribe the separable costs to the DRGs. On the first point, there is no apparent justification for attempting to allocate nonpatient care related overheads to DRGs, and at least a portion of the patient care related overheads are likely to be common costs as well. Even with respect to departmental costs, it is not necessarily the case that all such costs will be separable.

On the second point, the accuracy with which separable costs can be ascribed to particular cases is heavily dependent on the data available on resource utilisation by individual patients or patient classes. With respect to the final cost centres allocated on the basis of the departmental cost-to-charge ratio, the rationale for this is "the practice of the hospital measuring and charging for minutes of OR [operating room] time, relative laboratory units consumed, relative radiology units, and the like all based on standard measures of differential resources required" (Fetter, Mills, Riedel and Thompson 1977, p.142). For these costs, there is then some empirical basis for connecting resources used with the patients responsible although, as will be seen shortly, even with the allocation of these costs, serious inaccuracies may occur. Other final cost centres are generally allocated using a rule of thumb which is about as accurate as one could attain with the existing data.

The inaccuracies which may arise using the DRG cost allocation techniques outlined above have been evidenced in a study by Williams, Finkler, Murphy and Eisenberg (1982). Selecting two DRGs which had a primary diagnosis of inguinal hernia, a detailed study was made of two methods of allocating operating room, radiology and clinical laboratory costs to 106 patients treated in these categories. One method, termed the traditional method, was based on the departmental ratio of costs to charges as used in the DRG allocations discussed above. The other, termed the direct method, first divided departmental costs into overheads and direct costs, each of which was then assigned to inguinal hernia patients as accurately as was possible. It was found that, for both DRGs, the cost per case of these three departments was significantly lower (about one-third lower) using the direct method rather than the traditional DRG method. It is important to note that this result does *not* reflect different distinctions being drawn between common costs and separable costs in the two methods. The difference arises purely from the different methods used for allocating given volumes of departmental costs. Consequently, if these departmental costs had been allocated to all relevant DRGs, there would be some groups with higher cost allocations than those which would result from the traditional method.

The authors of this study concede that "theoretically one should not be concerned with assigning shared costs to any particular DRG. The cost would be incurred even if the DRG were not offered." However, they go on to argue that "all costs must be assigned to DRGs or the hospital will not be able to recover all of its costs" (Williams, *et al.* 1982, p.456). This argument does not counter the case for more accurate and theoretically defensible cost allocation procedures. The complications arising from cost analysis in the presence of joint production could be reflected in a reimbursement scheme more elaborate than that based on a flat rate per case treated. For example, Berki suggests that "the existence of such joint production efficiencies would indicate the desirability of adjusting the payment rates for interrelated specific case types by a factor reflecting the volume of related cases" (Berki 1983, p.8).

Turning now to the question posed in Section 11.2 about the effects of a change in case mix on a hospital's payment, if either or both of the assumptions about hospital cost behaviour implied by the DRG scheme break down, intertemporal variation in a hospital's case mix may lead to a discrepancy between total revenue from the payment scheme and total costs. Further, this discrepancy may not be a reflection of either a highly efficient or inefficient process but arises simply because of the behaviour of the actual cost function.

The incentive effects of a scheme based on payment rates which do not reflect actual cost conditions can be illustrated in terms of these two assumptions. Consider first Figure 11.2(a) which pertains to the case where not all costs are separable, i.e. there is joint production. The horizontal line *PR* represents the payment rate for this particular case type, a rate which is constant and independent of the volume of cases treated. Since this rate is based on the presumption that all costs are separable, the presence of common costs means that the actual average separable cost (*ASC*) will be less than the payment rate. Consequently, the hospital is in a situation where it will receive an amount per case treated, *PR*, which exceeds the marginal

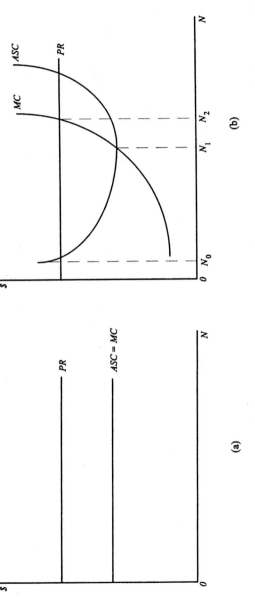

Figure 11.2. DRG Payment Rates in the Presence of Common Costs and Non-Constant Product-Specific Returns to Scale

cost of treating the case. This provides an incentive to expand the number of cases treated since each additional case contributes to the hospital's 'profit'. The excess of revenue over separable cost per case would be used as an offset against the hospital's common costs, but by increasing volume sufficiently the hospital may be able to cover more than its common costs. One possible alternative scheme under these cost conditions would be to give hospitals a lump sum grant approximating the common costs and a payment rate equal to average separable cost and marginal cost per unit, i.e. a two part tariff. This would eliminate any financial incentive to increase the volume of cases treated.

Figure 11.2(b) depicts a situation where average separable cost falls as the number of cases treated increases up to ON_1, i.e. there are product-specific economies of scale up to ON_1 cases treated per time period. Hospitals now have an incentive to increase volume up to the point where $PR = MC$ at output level ON_2, or to reduce output to this level if the volume of cases treated exceeded this amount. Hospitals which treated a relatively small number of cases in this DRG, e.g. ON_0, may find that average separable cost exceeds the payment rate PR and so incur losses. If, as some authors have asserted, fixed costs are generally relatively high (Berki 1983, p.8; Pointer and Ross 1984, p.110), product-specific economies of scale may well be significant. Hospitals may then find that they are earning 'profits' or incurring 'losses' on particular case types simply because of the behaviour of the underlying cost function, a cost function which, for given input prices, is technologically determined.[10]

This discussion has shown that, for a constant rate of payment per case within a DRG to be an accurate reflection of a hospital's cost structure, the hospital's costs would have to be completely separable with no economies of scope arising from joint production, and per unit costs would have to be independent of the volume of cases treated. Whether these conditions are fulfilled or not is an empirical question.

A fundamental problem confronting empirical analysis in this area is the dilemma discussed in Chapter 2 concerning parameter parsimony and the large number of hospital output categories required if anything like homogeneity within case mix categories is to be approximated. Indeed the cost function specifications employed in this study are based on the same two assumptions indicated above as underlying the DRG payment scheme. In fact, if the two assumptions are satisfied, the average cost function

---

10   The incentive effects just discussed do not explicitly consider physician behaviour. For an analysis of hospital and physician behaviour under prospective reimbursement, see Ellis and McGuire (1986).

becomes a linear weighted sum of case mix proportions with the weights being constant average and marginal costs per case. Now average revenue under the DRG scheme is also a linear weighted sum of case mix proportions where the weights are the reimbursement rates—the r_i in equation (11.4). Hence if the cost function specifications employed in this study are empirically supported, the constant payment rates within each DRG may adequately reflect the underlying hospital cost function.

A potentially serious criticism of the foregoing analysis must now be addressed.[11] It can be argued that the DRG payment rates are, in effect, a set of prices and are not designed to reflect the average cost of production at all output levels. This argument sees the DRG payment scheme as simulating a market outcome with hospitals reacting to the payment rates in the same way as competitive firms react to exogenously determined prices. Indeed, Figure 11.2(b) in particular bears a close resemblance to textbook diagrams of a perfectly competitive firm. As drawn, there is a range of output levels over which this hospital is capable of earning 'super-normal profits' from the treatment of this particular case type and, if making a loss, will adjust its output level accordingly. Hence, according to this argument, the payment authorities need not concern themselves with how well the payment rates accurately map the underlying cost function of hospitals. The payment rates are prices, and it is up to individual hospitals to react in response to these 'price signals' so as to avoid losses on the treatment of particular case types.

The crucial proposition underlying this argument is that the output level, or the number of cases treated, in each diagnostic category for any particular hospital is an endogenous variable, i.e. hospitals have complete control over the volume and composition of cases which they treat. Under this proposition the competitive analogy applies. Hospitals are no different in kind from retail stores which can add and delete product lines at will and determine the volume of each product line to be offered for sale.

The position adopted in this chapter is that this proposition is unrealistic at a positive level and unacceptable at a normative level. It implies that hospitals can, and should, be allowed to admit patients selectively, rejecting those which are seen to be 'unprofitable' and encouraging the admission of those which are 'profitable'. In Australian public hospitals at least, case mix is for the most part a variable exogenous to the hospital. Selective admission of cases on the basis of diagnosis is not standard practice and, it could be argued on ethical grounds, it should not be.

---

11   I am indebted to George Palmer of the University of New South Wales for bringing this criticism to my attention.

Consequently, the problem of hospitals experiencing 'profits' or 'losses' on particular case types because of the exogenous nature of the volume and composition of their output is seen as being a real one. If hospitals are required to treat all cases which present themselves for treatment, then it is important that the payment scheme take into account the behaviour of the underlying cost function. Failure to do so will result in the stochastic nature of hospital case mix being reflected in the financial performance of hospitals.

But just how stochastic is hospital case mix? Does it vary significantly through time? These questions will be addressed in the following discussion of case mix prediction.

11.4   Predicting Hospital Case Mix

A prospective reimbursement scheme is one where a hospital is paid a sum of money prior to its provision of treatments to patients. Since, under the DRG system, this payment is case-based, it is then necessary to have a forecast of the numbers of cases a hospital is expected to treat in each DRG. These volume forecasts can then be applied to the payment rate for each DRG to determine the hospital's budget. In the words of Fetter, *et al.* (1979, p.137): "From a forecast of patient load by class, budgets can be computed from the cost profiles and revenues determined from the charging profiles."

Under the original DRG classification scheme, all diagnosis codes were initially divided into 83 mutually exclusive and exhaustive disease areas known as Major Diagnostic Categories (MDCs). The DRG algorithm was then applied to each MDC, generating a total of 383 DRGs. The subsequent classification system was based on an initial set of 23 MDCs defined primarily in terms of major organ systems. Application of the algorithm resulted in the 467 DRGs originally employed in the Medicare reimbursement scheme in the US.[12]

The DRG classification scheme thus involves a considerable degree of disaggregation. For example, under the original classification DRG 343 contained cases with the following description: "Fracture (Lower Jaw, Upper Arm, Ankle) with Surgical Procedure (Closed Reduction, Open Reduction of Face) without Secondary Diagnosis" (Fetter *et al.* 1980, p.51). An important issue which arises here is the extent to which the level of

---

[12]   An Australian version of the DRGs—The Australian National DRGs (AN-DRGs)—is currently under development, sponsored by the Commonwealth Casemix Development Program.

disaggregation of case types is correlated with increased difficulty of forecasting case mix. For instance, as an initial hypothesis it could be argued that a higher level of disaggregation would make forecasting more difficult because of the smaller cell size.

To exemplify this argument, some data have been gathered on the behaviour of case mix at various levels of aggregation for two Queensland public hospitals. The finest level of disaggregation employed in this exercise is the Major Diagnostic Category of the original DRG classification. In particular, the eleven MDCs which encompass neoplasms were selected. A description of these categories together with their corresponding ICDA-8 codes is provided in Table 11.1. These MDCs, when further subdivided using the DRG algorithm, gave rise to 68 separate DRGs.

Table 11.1. Major Diagnostic Categories relating to Neoplasms

MDC No.	Description	ICDA-8 Codes
2	Malignant Neoplasm of Digestive System	140-1590
3	Malignant Neoplasm of Respiratory System	160-1639
4	Malignant Neoplasm of Skin	172-1739
5	Malignant Neoplasm of Breast	174-1740
6	Malignant Neoplasm of Female Genital Organ	180-1849 2340,6211 6291
7	Malignant Neoplasm of Male Genital Organ	185-1879
8	Malignant Neoplasm of Urinary System	188-1899
9	Malignant Neoplasm of Other and Unspecified Sites	170-1719 190-1991
10	Neoplasm of Lymphatic and Hemopoietic Tissue	200-2090
11	Benign Neoplasm of Female Genital Organ	218-2219
12	Benign Neoplasm of Other Sites	210-2169 222-2330 2341-2399 2552,7434 7571

Source: Fetter, *et al.* (1980, Table 1).

The number of discharges in each of the eleven MDCs was extracted from Queensland Hospital Morbidity Data for two hospitals—a large metropolitan hospital with about 39,000 discharges in 1978 and a country hospital with nearly 5,000 discharges in 1978. Annual data were obtained for each of the eight calendar years 1971 to 1978. Moving up one level of aggregation, the discharges in MDCs 2-10 were summed for each hospital to give a figure for total malignant neoplasms. MDCs 11-12 were then added in also to give a figure for total neoplasms. Finally, for comparative purposes, total discharges for each year for each hospital were obtained.

The advantage of dealing with a large metropolitan hospital is that, as expected, it discharged several hundred patients in each MDC for each of the eight years so that problems of small cell size did not arise. For this hospital, total discharges, total neoplasms, total malignant neoplasms, and discharges in MDCs 2, 4 and 8 are plotted in Figures 11.3 to 11.8 respectively.

In order to gain some idea of the relative stability of the various series and to illustrate the forecasting problem, a curve which represents a constant growth rate was fitted to each of the series.[13] These estimated curves are plotted on Figures 11.3 to 11.8 also, generating a prediction for each year. The actual and predicted values for each of the graphed series are tabulated in Table 11.2. The column labelled 'z' in this Table contains the standardised residual, that is, the actual minus the predicted figure divided by the standard error of the estimate.[14] This z-score can be used as a measure of success of the prediction and is comparable across all the series.

Taking first of all total discharges, the fitted curve has performed rather poorly in predicting the behaviour of this series with seven of the eight z-scores being in excess of two. The degree of volatility exhibited by this series was unexpected as it encompasses all discharges and represents a large volume of cases. The data for 'All Neoplasms' and 'All Malignant Neoplasms' present a somewhat more stable picture, particularly in the years 1975-78, and this is reflected in the relatively lower z-scores. MDC 2 (Digestive System) was selected for presentation as it appeared to be the most stable of the eleven MDCs selected, while MDC 4 (Skin) was rather unstable and produced a fitted curve showing negative growth. MDC 5 (Urinary System) was also rather unstable and produced an estimated curve with a zero growth rate. Overall, the two series representing total neoplasms

---

[13]   The estimated equation is of the form

$$y = e^{a} + bt$$

where y = annual discharges in the relevant category, e = the exponential, $t = 1, ..., n$ for n time periods, and a, b are the parameters to be estimated. If b is not significantly different from zero, a curve with zero growth, i.e. a horizontal line, is the curve of best fit.

[14]   The standardised residual is an approximate z-score, approximate because the estimation procedure has been based on the assumption that the data are Poisson distributed.

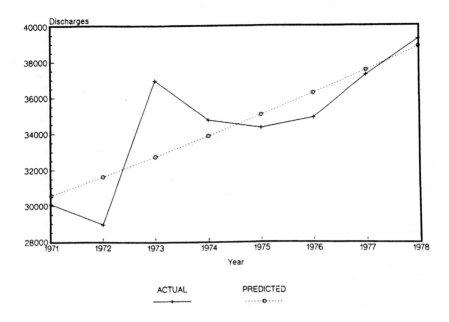

Figure 11.3. All Discharges, Sample Hospital, 1971 to 1978

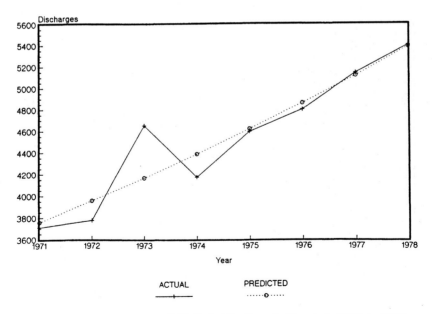

Figure 11.4. All Neoplasms (MDCs 2-12), Sample Hospital, 1971 to 1978

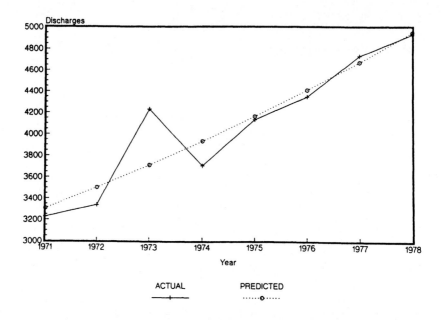

Figure 11.5. All Malignant Neoplasms (MDCs 2-10), Sample Hospital,
1971 to 1978

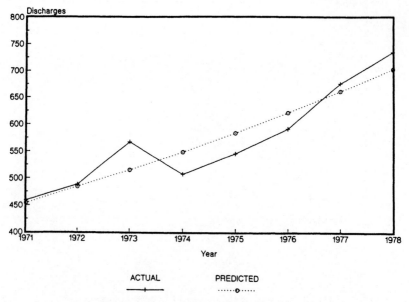

Figure 11.6. Malignant Neoplasms, Digestive System (MDC 2), Sample Hospital,
1971 to 1978

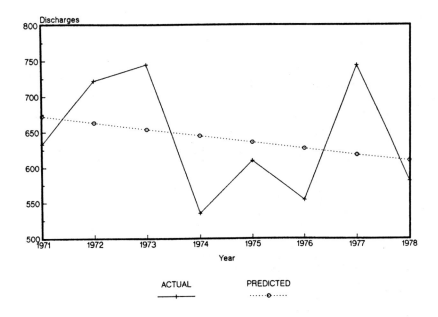

Figure 11.7. Malignant Neoplasms, Skin (MDC 4), Sample Hospital, 1971 to 1978

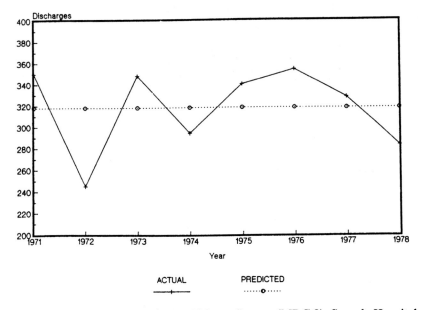

Figure 11.8. Malignant Neoplasms, Urinary System (MDC 8), Sample Hospital, 1971 to 1978

Table 11.2. Actual and Predicted Separations and Standardised Residuals, All Separations, All Neoplasms, All Malignant Neoplasms and Selected Malignant Neoplasms, Sample Hospital, 1971 to 1978

Year	All Separations			All Neoplasms			All Malignant Neoplasms		
	Actual	Predicted	z	Actual	Predicted	z	Actual	Predicted	z
1971	30,083	30,560	-2.7	3,711	3,758	-0.8	3,227	3,306	-1.4
1972	28,940	31,620	-15.1	3,777	3,957	-2.9	3,338	3,502	-2.8
1973	36,946	32,720	23.4	4,652	4,165	7.5	4,231	3,710	8.6
1974	34,732	33,860	4.7	4,172	4,385	-3.2	3,703	3,930	-3.6
1975	34,315	35,040	-3.9	4,591	4,617	-0.4	4,133	4,164	-0.5
1976	34,886	36,260	-7.2	4,799	4,860	-0.9	4,348	4,411	-0.9
1977	37,262	37,530	-1.4	5,143	5,117	0.4	4,734	4,673	0.9
1978	39,269	38,840	2.2	5,401	5,387	0.2	4,932	4,950	-0.3

Year	MDC 2—Digestive			MDC 4—Skin			MDC 8—Urinary		
	Actual	Predicted	z	Actual	Predicted	z	Actual	Predicted	z
1971	459	454	-1.4	633	672	-1.5	350	318	1.8
1972	488	484	0.2	722	663	2.3	245	318	-4.1
1973	567	515	2.3	745	654	3.6	348	318	1.7
1974	507	548	-1.7	535	645	-4.3	294	318	-1.3
1975	545	583	-1.6	610	636	-1.0	340	318	1.2
1976	591	621	-1.2	554	627	-2.9	354	318	2.0
1977	676	661	0.6	744	618	5.1	328	318	0.6
1978	735	703	1.2	581	610	-1.2	283	318	-1.9

Source: Queensland Hospital Morbidity Data and projections.

and total malignant neoplasms seem to be more stable than the more disaggregated series based on individual MDCs, although the most highly aggregated series exhibited the worst performance of all series.

This exercise has been undertaken for illustrative purposes and is not designed to provide definitive answers. Clearly, data from one hospital for eleven out of 83 MDCs can hardly be claimed to be representative. It does, however, suggest avenues for further inquiry. Would other forecasting techniques produce better results? Should quarterly or monthly data be employed? How sensitive will hospital reimbursement be to incorrect forecasts? How rapidly could hospital morbidity data be produced to update forecasts? This last question suggests that the consequences of inaccurate forecasts may not be so serious if they are made for short periods, e.g. quarterly, and actual data is available without lengthy lags, e.g. within one quarter. Alternatively, if reimbursement is based on annual case mix forecasts and actual data are not available until one year later, hospitals may end up being flush with funds or going bankrupt if their actual case mix deviates widely from the forecast.

The data also suggest another aspect of DRG reimbursement which requires further research in an Australian context. As mentioned previously, the eleven MDCs selected for this exercise split up into 68 separate DRGs. Even for the sample hospital, one of the largest hospitals in Queensland, some of the DRGs may contain only a few, if any, separations. With about 5,000 separations for all neoplasms in a year, the average number of separations per DRG is about 74. The data extracted for the country hospital, which is slightly above Queensland average size with about 110 beds, highlights this problem. Over the eight year period, the largest number of separations for 'All Neoplasms' was 178, an average of less than three separations per DRG. The largest number of cases in any MDC was 48 in MDC 2 in 1978. This hospital also had above average total separations—the Queensland average for the financial year 1979-80, for example, was 2,840 discharges per hospital.

In this context, it is interesting to consider the following comment on the US Commission on Professional and Hospital Activities (CPHA) classification which ran to nearly 7,000 patient classes. Averill (1984, p.8) says of this classification, "The large number of patient classes presented operational problems since for a typical hospital most of the classes were empty or had just a few patients." And on DRGs:

> Limiting the number of DRGs to manageable numbers ... insures that for most of the DRGs, a typical hospital will have enough experience to allow meaningful comparative analysis to be performed. If there were only a few patients in each DRG, then

it would be difficult to detect patterns in case mix complexity
and cost performance and to communicate the results to the
physician staff.

The problem which Averill has identified with respect to the CPHA
classification in the US may also be applicable to DRGs in Australia. Some
evidence on this is provided by the Relative Stay Index (RSI) in
Queensland. As explained in Chapter 10, this index is constructed on the
basis of 47 diagnostic categories, adjusted for age, sex and surgery.
Hospitals are also grouped on the basis of teaching/non-teaching, size and
annual separations. For a large number of diagnostic categories in a number
of hospitals, there are insufficient cases to make any statistical judgement on
the significance of the difference between actual and expected length of
stay. This small cell size problem consequently suggests there may be
difficulties in forecasting the case mix of particular hospitals.

11.5   Summary and Conclusions

The DRG payment scheme for Medicare patients in US hospitals represents
a significant change in the way hospitals are to be paid for what they
produce. In paying hospitals on the basis of the number of cases treated,
appropriately adjusted for case mix, the scheme represents a move away
from an input-based payment scheme to one based on a conceptually
defensible and empirically workable definition of output. Hospitals will no
longer be paid on the basis of 'services provided' but will receive a fixed
amount per case treated which depends on the case mix classification of the
patient. There are strong grounds for arguing that this will lead to an
increase in productive efficiency.

There is a problem, however, with the incentives which this scheme
provides for hospitals. Since it is unlikely that a flat rate per case treated will
accurately reflect the cost conditions of providing treatment, hospitals may
have an incentive to treat larger numbers of some case types which increase
'profits' and treat a smaller number of other case types which incur 'losses'.
Allowing hospitals to behave in this manner means that they can be
selective in deciding on the volume and types of cases to treat, i.e. the
volume and composition of hospital output become endogenous to the
hospital. In an Australian context, this would represent a radical change
from current practice, a change which can be subject to argument on
normative grounds.

A second issue concerning the DRG payment scheme is the problem of intertemporal variation in, and forecasting of, case mix by DRG. The level of disaggregation embodied in the DRGs employed in the US may give rise to difficulties in forecasting case mix, and these could be compounded by problems of small cell size in the Australian context. In considering the use of DRGs in Australia, both of these issues have important implications for the implementation of the concept and its use in hospital financing, and consequently warrant further research efforts.

12

CONCLUSIONS

Economists interested in empirically estimating hospital cost functions face a dilemma. Flexible functional form multiproduct cost functions which allow non-jointness, input/output separability, and overall and product-specific economies and diseconomies of scale to be incorporated as testable rather than maintained hypotheses entail an exponential increase in the number of parameters to be estimated as the number of output categories increases. For hospitals, the number of output categories required to achieve approximate homogeneity within each category is quite large. Consequently, the use of flexible functional forms generally requires *ad hoc* aggregation to collapse hospital outputs into a smaller number of categories in order to achieve parameter parsimony. The alternative is to adopt a more restricted functional form which incorporates the above possible multiproduct cost function characteristics as maintained hypotheses but which then allows the use of a more disaggregated output classification scheme. This alternative has been chosen in the empirical work presented in this book.

In discussing the concept of hospital output, two main schools of thought were distinguished. The first adopts a 'health status' conception of hospital output—that the output of a hospital is an improvement in the health status of its patients. The second adopts a 'treatment' conception of hospital output —that hospitals produce treatments which may or may not improve a patient's health status. It has been argued by some that, while the first position is conceptually preferred, the second position underlies most empirical work for pragmatic reasons—health status changes are difficult to measure, and the marginal contributions of the multifarious factors which influence health status are difficult to disentangle.

This study has adopted a stronger position on this matter, arguing that the 'treatment' conception of hospital output is defensible on conceptual grounds also. This argument is based upon the uncertain impact of treatment on health status and the consequential scope for the provision of insurance cover against unsuccessful treatment. If improvements in health status were what hospitals offered for sale in the market, patients would pay only for successful treatments, i.e. treatments which improved their health. It can then be argued that hospitals would be producing two outputs—treatment, and insurance against the possibility of unsuccessful treatment. Even in these circumstances then, it can be argued that the output of a hospital is not a change in health status.

It has also been argued that the 'case' rather than the 'day' should be taken as the unit of output measurement. While it has often been argued that these are alternative units of output measurement, the position taken in this study is that, for acute inpatient hospital care, the 'day' is an input related measure connected to the time dimension over which a unit of output (a treated case) is produced. Interhospital comparisons of average cost per patient day can be quite misleading because of the confounding influence of variations in average length of stay. Given these arguments, average cost per case becomes the measure of average cost per unit of output.

The empirical part of this book has presented estimates of hospital cost functions using, for the most part, data on 121 public hospitals in Queensland, Australia. Hospital discharges were classified initially into 18 diagnostic categories (the chapter headings of the International Classification of Diseases), and then further subdivided into 47 diagnostic categories (as used in the Relative Stay Index in Queensland). Cases were also classified on the basis of several additional case mix dimensions—sex; surgery performed; patient payment status; separation status; and age. The use of this number of output categories still left a respectable number of degrees of freedom for estimation purposes because of the decision made to adopt a restricted functional form. Use of a more flexible functional form would entail working at a higher level of case mix aggregation.

This is not to pretend that the case mix classification scheme employed in this study achieves within-group homogeneity of case types. Even the Diagnosis Related Group (DRG) classification scheme—perhaps the most sophisticated scheme yet produced—with its 467 categories has been criticised on the grounds of within-group heterogeneity. Nevertheless, the case mix classifications used here would suffer less from this problem than, say, a four group classification based solely on sex and the presence or absence of surgery.

Case mix was found to exert a statistically significant influence on interhospital variation in average cost per case. Further, the influence became stronger when the more disaggregated diagnostic classification scheme was used and the additional case mix dimensions were added. A scalar case mix index—a single valued measure of case complexity—was found to have the least explanatory power. This suggests that more finely disaggregated case mix classification schemes do more effectively capture the multiproduct nature of hospital output and do reduce the amount of within-group heterogeneity.

The ordinary least squares case mix parameter estimates, however, are plagued by insignificance and incorrect signs implying negative values for average and marginal cost by case type. The overall significance of the estimated relationships, coupled with insignificant coefficient estimates, suggested that collinearity between the case mix proportions was a problem. This was also suggested by other evidence including selectivity bias, a correlation matrix determinant approaching zero, and inequality in the characteristic roots derived from the correlation matrix. Use of the *ad hoc* data reduction technique of principal components analysis failed to improve the credibility of the parameter estimates (although the variances of many were reduced), indicating that the attainment of positive, plausible, significant estimates via this procedure would be fortuitous. Case mix parameter estimates obtained from pooled Queensland and New South Wales data, which increased the sample size considerably, were equally unsatisfactory. The scalar case mix index was found to imply a set of positive, plausible case type cost estimates. However, these were produced for only one year. Further research is needed to determine the stability of these estimates through time.

Noting that the cost data contain no capital charges, the effects of scale, utilisation and input prices on average cost per case were also investigated. Short run and long run aspects of cost behaviour were considered, where the former refers to the effects of changes in the utilisation of any given level of capacity and the latter refers to changes in the level of capacity or scale of plant. Several alternative specifications of the scale and utilisation terms were used, and results were produced for several financial years. For short run cost behaviour, the evidence that increasing capacity utilisation will reduce average cost per case was overwhelming, arising in every specification in every year. Increasing a hospital's case flow rate, whether by increasing occupancy or reducing average length of stay, was always found to reduce average cost per case. The evidence on long run cost behaviour—economies of scale—was much weaker. While a U-shaped average cost curve with significant scale/case flow interaction was found in one year, the patterns of long run cost behaviour were neither consistent nor significant across different specifications or different years. With regard to input prices as a source of cost variation, such prices were found to vary only slightly across the sample and so were assumed constant.

The remaining empirical work involved comparing groups of hospitals dichotomised successively on the basis of three criteria—teaching/non-teaching, public/private, and Queensland/New South Wales. The first of these criteria split the sample of 121 Queensland public hospitals into teaching and non-teaching groups using three definitions of a teaching hospital—medical school affiliation, the presence of a General Nurse (3 year) program, and the presence of an Enrolled Nurse—General (1 year) program. For the public/private groups, the original sample was supplemented by the inclusion of private hospitals.

In exploring the influence of teaching on public hospital costs, all three teaching programs (the presence or absence of which were indicated by dummy variables) were found to be associated positively with the proportions of cases treated in various diagnostic categories. Further, these categories tended to rank high in a complexity ordering based on an information theory complexity measure, i.e. teaching hospitals tend to treat more complex cases. Teaching status was also found to be positively associated with other case mix dimensions, particularly the proportion of cases which involved surgery. Size, too, was positively associated with all three teaching variables.

It was, then, not surprising to find that after taking into account the effects of case mix, scale and utilisation, there was only limited evidence that the presence of any kind of teaching program affects average cost per case. What evidence there was suggested that medical school affiliation has a positive effect, and General Nurse training a negative effect, on average cost per case. This evidence, however, arose mostly in equations where an aggregated scalar case mix index was used in place of a disaggregated set of case mix categories. While this suggested that teaching may serve as a proxy for case mix, it was found to be a poor proxy since the cost equations in which teaching status appeared as the only case mix indicator, along with scale and utilisation, had substantially inferior explanatory power compared with those equations which incorporated more detailed case mix measures. Consequently, the scanty evidence of any independent influence of teaching status on average cost per case indicates that most of the costs involved in teaching are common costs and that the separable costs of teaching are quite small.

The public/private hospital cost comparisons were hampered by the dearth of private hospital cost data. Without adjusting for case mix, scale or utilisation, average cost per case in private hospitals was found to be substantially lower than in public hospitals. Significant differences between the two types of hospital were also found in case mix, scale and utilisation. The technique used to gauge the impact of these differences in explaining the cost differential involved first of all estimating the cost functions including the private hospitals in the sample (for which there were only four observations—three individual hospitals and an aggregated observation for all the the remaining private hospitals). Predicted values of average cost per case were then obtained for each of the private hospital observations and compared with the actual values, the objective being to see whether the private hospitals were less costly than predicted after adjustment for case mix, scale and utilisation. This turned out to be the case for the aggregated observation, but was not replicated for all three individual hospitals in the sample. In view of the meagre amount of financial data available for private hospitals, any conclusions here must be treated with caution but there was some indication of a superior cost performance by private hospitals even after allowing for case mix, scale and utilisation differences.

The Queensland/New South Wales public hospital cost comparisons found that Queensland's lower average cost per case was not explicable by case mix, scale and utilisation differences between the States. Using pooled data from the two States and including a State identifier dummy variable in the equation, the estimated coefficient on the latter indicated that a New South Wales hospital would have a higher average cost per case than a Queensland hospital with the same case mix, length of stay, case flow rate and size. These results lend support to the argument that Queensland's superior cost performance can be attributed to organisational factors manifested in a higher degree of centralised control over its hospitals.

The third major part of this study was concerned with the relevance of hospital cost analysis to hospital payment schemes. This relevance was demonstrated first of all by elaborating a possible performance appraisal and payment scheme using estimated cost functions. The average cost per case equations can be used to obtain a predicted value of average cost per case for each hospital, and a prediction interval can be constructed around each such prediction. Average cost per case can also be disaggregated by input category to indicate the inputs on which a hospital might be 'overspending' or 'underspending'. Using the multiplicative relationship between average cost per day and average length of stay which yields average cost per case, predictions for the two former input related concepts can also be used to indicate how a particular hospital's cost performance is 'explained' in terms of this intensity/length of stay trade-off. This hypothetical scheme was illustrated using Queensland public hospital data, but it was concluded that it suffers from two serious drawbacks stemming from the multicollinearity problem. The first of these is the credibility problem associated with implausible values of average and marginal cost by case type. The second is the problem of forecasting for future periods with parameter estimates affected by a pattern of multicollinearity which is unlikely to remain stable over time. In addition, a study comparing measures of hospital efficiency obtained from four different statistical models (including three cost frontier models) applied to a common data set has found that the ranking of hospitals on the basis of relative efficiency differed markedly across a number of the models. It is therefore concluded that the econometric approach to hospital performance appraisal and payment has a number of serious limitations which militate against its adoption.

The second application of hospital cost analysis to a hospital payment scheme dealt with a payment scheme already in use in the US and in one State in Australia—the DRG payment scheme. This payment scheme can be expected to give rise to an increase in productive efficiency (and there is evidence emerging to support this expectation) because it represents a change to an output-based scheme paying a fixed 'price' per case discharged where the 'prices' vary according to the DRG classification of the patient. This avoids the open-ended nature of an input-based payment scheme such as one which pays a 'price' per day of care. It was argued, however, that if the volume and composition of hospital output are exogenous, then hospitals may experience 'profits' or 'losses' on particular case types unless the average and marginal cost of treatment are equal and constant, and equal to the DRG payment rate. Under these circumstances, the DRG payment scheme implies that hospital cost functions are characterised by non-jointness and an absence of overall or product-specific returns to scale. The problems of intertemporal variation in, and predictability of, a hospital's case mix were also addressed because of their importance to prospective payment schemes in general and the DRG payment scheme in particular. Some limited evidence was produced which suggested that, at least in an Australian context, intertemporal variation coupled with small cell size might be serious problems to be confronted by a case-based payment scheme.

In concluding, a few brief thoughts will be offered on some agenda items for future research. Perhaps the most serious and intractable problem is the dilemma discussed in Part A of this book—the trade-off between flexibility in functional form and disaggregation of hospital output categories. Future work must be directed towards a solution to this problem so that non-jointness and product-specific economies and diseconomies of scale can be incorporated as testable hypotheses in a cost function which also allows for a sufficiently large number of output categories to capture the multiproduct nature of hospital output. According to Cowing, Holtmann and Powers (1983, p.269), "The real trick lies in strategic aggregation or grouping: that is, grouping services for which the necessary aggregation conditions are likely to be reasonably well satisfied and not forcing aggregation where it is unwarranted." This is so, but it remains a difficult task to ascertain when the necessary aggregation conditions are satisfied.

Data collection activities are another area where fruitful gains could be made. At present, hospital accounting systems generally either are input oriented or employ 'step down' algorithms which allocate *all* costs to specific case types. The result is that the separable costs of producing particular case types are not known. The limitations of input-oriented cost data are well known:

> Hospitals collect cost information based on services such as surgery or radiology rather than product lines. This would be analogous to an auto manufacturer's knowing the total cost and average cost of bumpers for all car models combined, but not knowing the bumper costs associated with any particular model. (Finkler 1979, p.286).

This has important implications for the estimation of hospital cost functions.

> Econometric techniques are unable to distinguish between diseconomies due to size and those due to inefficient production of specific products. This is a result of the type of cost data available. Such data are highly aggregate in nature at the level of the firm. As a result, inefficiencies in the production of specific products are hidden, and study results may lead to potentially incorrect policy recommendations about appropriate hospital size. (Finkler 1979, p.287).

One may well speculate at this point whether there would be greater returns from the production of more relevant data than from the application of more econometrics to existing types of data.

It is perhaps fitting to end with a cautionary note. It is not being suggested here that an 'accounting' solution can replace an 'econometric' solution. Rather it is suggested that more refined cost data of an output oriented kind may enable a more penetrating analysis of hospital cost functions. The accounting systems must, of course, be designed to produce economically meaningful cost estimates. Capital charges, for example, must reflect opportunity costs and not historic costs. In particular, *ad hoc* allocations of joint or common costs to particular case types must be avoided. While such allocations may well produce positive and plausible estimates of average cost by case type, they may well be as meaningless as some of the case type cost estimates produced in this study using multivariate techniques. To the extent that a particular set of cost allocations has no theoretical basis, it should have no more claim to our attention than any other set of such allocations or estimates.

REFERENCES

Aigner, D.J. (1971) *Basic Econometrics*, Prentice-Hall, New Jersey.

Alchian, A.A. (1959) "Costs and Outputs" in M. Abramovitz (ed.), *The Allocation of Economic Resources*, Stanford University Press, Stanford, pp.23-40.

Alchian, A. and Demsetz, H. (1972) "Production, Information Costs and Economic Organization", *American Economic Review*, Vol.62 No.5, December, pp.777-95.

Andrew, R.R. (1976) "Hospital Staffing and Hospital Costs", *Medical Journal of Australia*, Vol.2, 7 August, pp.222-5.

Andrew, R.R. and Nehrmann, M.H.P. (1977) "Hospital Costs—The Medical Student Component", *Medical Journal of Australia*, Vol.1, 28 May, pp.823-6.

Arrow, K.J. (1963) "Uncertainty and the Welfare Economics of Medical Care", *American Economic Review*, Vol.53 No.5, December, pp.941-73.

Arrow, K.J. (1974) *Essays in the Theory of Risk-Bearing*, North-Holland, Amsterdam.

Auster, R.D. and Gordon, J.G. (1978) "Individual Responsibility Incentives for the Health Sector" in G. Tullock and R.E. Wagner (eds), *Policy Analysis and Deductive Reasoning*, D.C. Heath and Company, Massachusetts, pp.47-59.

Australian Bureau of Statistics (1981) *Health and Welfare Establishments 1977-78*, Cat. No. 4302.3, Australian Bureau of Statistics, Brisbane.

Australian Bureau of Statistics (1993) *1991-92 Private Hospitals, Australia*, Cat. No. 4390.0, Australian Bureau of Statistics, Canberra.

Averill, R.F. (1984) "The Design and Development of the Diagnosis Related Groups" in Health Systems International, *The Revised ICD-9-CM Diagnosis Related Groups*, Health Systems International, New Haven, Connecticut.

Babson, J.H. (1973) *Disease Costing*, The University Press, Manchester.

Bailey, N.T.J. (1956) "Statistics in Hospital Planning and Design", *Applied Statistics*, Vol.5, pp.146-57.

Baker, S.P., O'Neill, B., Haddon, W. and Long, W. (1974) "The Injury Severity Score: A Method for Describing Patients with Multiple Injuries and Evaluating Emergency Care", *Journal of Trauma*, Vol.14, March, pp.187-96.

Banker, R.D., Conrad, R.F. and Strauss, R.P. (1986) "A Comparative Application of DEA and Translog Methods: An Illustrative Study of Hospital Production", *Management Science*, Vol.32, pp.30-44.

Barer, M.L. (1982) "Case Mix Adjustment in Hospital Cost Analysis: Information Theory Revisited", *Journal of Health Economics*, Vol.1 No.1, May, pp.53-80.

Barone, E. (1955) "Related Costs in the Economics of Transport", *International Economic Papers*, No.5, pp.134-44.

Baumol, W.J. (1977) *Economic Theory and Operations Analysis*, 4th edn, Prentice-Hall, New Jersey.

Baumol, W.J., Panzar, J.C. and Willig, R.D. (1982) *Contestable Markets and the Theory of Industry Structure*, Harcourt Brace Jovanovich, New York.

Bays, C.W. (1977) "Case-Mix Differences between Nonprofit and For-Profit Hospitals", *Inquiry*, Vol.14 No.1, March, pp.17-21.

Bays, C.W. (1979) "Cost Comparisons of Forprofit and Nonprofit Hospitals", *Social Science and Medicine*, Vol.13C No.4, December, pp.219-25.

Bays, C.W. (1980) "Specification Error in the Estimation of Hospital Cost Functions", *Review of Economics and Statistics*, Vol.62 No.2, May, pp.302-5.

Bays, C.W. (1986) "The Determinants of Hospital Size: A Survivor Analysis", *Applied Economics*, Vol.18, pp.359-77.

Becker, E.R. and Steinwald, B. (1981) "Determinants of Hospital Casemix Complexity", *Health Services Research*, Vol.16 No.4, Winter, pp.439-58.

Bell, J. (1968) "Queensland's Public Hospital System: Some Aspects of Finance and Control", *Public Administration* (Sydney), Vol.27 No.1, March, pp.39-49.

Belsley, D., Kuh, E. and Welsh, R. (1980) *Regression Diagnostics*, Wiley, New York.

Beresford, J.C. (1972) "Use of Hospital Costs in Planning" in M.M. Hauser (ed.), *The Economics of Medical Care*, George Allen & Unwin, London, pp.165-76.

Berki, S.E. (1972) *Hospital Economics*, Lexington Books, Massachusetts.

Berki, S.E. (1983) "The Design of Case-Based Hospital Payment Systems", *Medical Care*, Vol.21 No.1, January, pp.1-13.

Berki, S.E., Ashcraft, M.L.F. and Newbrander, W.C. (1984) "Length-of-Stay Variations Within ICDA-8 Diagnosis-Related Groups", *Medical Care*, Vol.22 No.2, February, pp.126-42.

Berry, R. (1967) "Returns to Scale in the Production of Hospital Services", *Health Services Research*, Vol.2, Summer, pp.123-39.

Blackorby, C., Primont, D. and Russell, R.R. (1978) *Duality, Separability and Functional Structure: Theory and Economic Applications*, North-Holland, Amsterdam.

Blair, R.D. and Vogel, R.J. (1978) "A Survivor Analysis of Commercial Health Insurers", *Journal of Business*, Vol.51 No.3, July, pp.521-9.

Blaug, M. (1968) *Economic Theory in Retrospect*, Heinemann, London.

Blaug, M. (1978) *Economics of Education: A Selected Annotated Bibliography*, 3rd edn, Pergamon Press, Oxford.

Blumberg, M.S. (1961) ""DPF Concept" Helps Predict Bed Needs", *The Modern Hospital*, Vol.97 No.6, December, pp.75 et seq.

Borts, G.H. (1960) "The Estimation of Rail Cost Functions", *Econometrica*, Vol.28 No.1, January, pp.108-31.

Braeutigam, R. (1981) "Comment" in G. Fromm (ed.), *Studies in Public Regulation*, MIT Press, Cambridge, pp.314-20.

Brennan, G. (1979) "Commentary on Paper by Russell Mathews on Regional Disparities and Fiscal Equalisation in Australia" in *Proceedings of the International Seminar in Public Economics on Regional Aspects of Fiscal Policies*, reprinted in A.N.U. Centre for Research on Federal Financial Relations Reprint Series, No.30.

Breyer, F. (1987) "The Specification of a Hospital Cost Function: A Comment on the Recent Literature", *Journal of Health Economics*, Vol.6 No.2, June, pp.147-57.

Brown, M.C. (1980) "Production and Cost Relations of Newfoundland's Cottage Hospitals", *Inquiry*, Vol.17 No.3, Fall, pp.268-77.

Brown, R.S., Caves, D.W. and Christensen, L.R. (1979) "Modelling the Structure of Cost and Production for Multiproduct Firms", *Southern Economic Journal*, Vol.46 No.1, July, pp.256-73.

Bruggink, T.H. (1982) "Public versus Private Enterprise in the Municipal Water Industry: A Comparison of Operating Costs", *Quarterly Review of Economics and Business*, Vol.22 No.1, Spring, pp.111-25.

Burgess, D.F. (1974) "A Cost Minimization Approach to Import Demand Equations", *Review of Economics and Statistics*, Vol.56 No.2, May, pp.225-34.

Burgess, D.F. (1975) "Duality Theory and Pitfalls in the Specification of Technologies", *Journal of Econometrics*, Vol.3, pp.105-21.

Burgess, D.F. (1976) "Tariffs and Income Distribution: Some Empirical Evidence for the United States", *Journal of Political Economy*, Vol.84 No.1, February, pp.17-45.

Burmeister, E. and Turnovsky, S.J. (1971) "The Degree of Joint Production", *International Economic Review*, Vol.12 No.1, February, pp.99-105.

Busby, D.D., Leming, J.C. and Olson, M.I. (1972) "Unidentified Educational Costs in a University Teaching Hospital: An Initial Study", *Journal of Medical Education*, Vol.47 No.4, April, pp.243-53.

Butler, J.R.G. (1988a) "The Effect of Teaching on Public Hospital Costs: Evidence from Queensland" in J.R.G. Butler and D.P. Doessel (eds), *Economics and Health: 1987 Proceedings of the Ninth Australian Conference of Health Economists*, Australian Studies in Health Service Administration No.63, School of Health Administration, University of New South Wales, Sydney, pp.38-75.

Butler, J.R.G. (1988b) "Hospital Costs and Information Theory Case Mix Indexes: Results for Queensland", *Prometheus*, Vol.6 No.2, December 1988, pp.327-50.

Butler, J.R.G. (1992) "Specific Purpose Payments and the Commonwealth Grants Commission", *Economic Record*, Vol.68 No.201, June 1992, pp.165-79.

Byrnes, P., Grosskopf, S. and Hayes, K. (1986) "Efficiency and Ownership: Further Evidence", *Review of Economics and Statistics*, Vol.68 No.2, May, pp.337-41.

Cameron, J.M. (1985) "The Indirect Costs of Graduate Medical Education", *New England Journal of Medicine*, Vol.312 No.19, 9 May, pp.1233-8.

Carey, J. (1985) "Litigants The Third Class", *The Proctor*, Newsletter of the Queensland Law Society, May, Special Litigation Issue, pp.3-4.

Carlson, S. (1956) *A Study in the Pure Theory of Production*, Basil Blackwell, Oxford.

Carr, W.J. and Feldstein, P.J. (1967) "The Relationship of Cost to Hospital Size", *Inquiry*, Vol.4 No.2, June, pp.45-65.

Caves, D.W., Christensen, L.R. and Tretheway, M.W. (1980) "Flexible Cost Functions for Multiproduct Firms", *Review of Economics and Statistics*, Vol.62 No.3, August, pp.477-81.

Chambers, R.G. (1988) *Applied Production Analysis: A Dual Approach*, Cambridge University Press, Cambridge.

Chant, D. (1986) "The Allocation of Hospital Costs to Type of Case" in J.R.G. Butler and D.P. Doessel (eds), *Economics and Health 1985: Proceedings of the Seventh Australian Conference of Health Economists*, Australian Studies in Health Service Administration No.56, School of Health Administration, University of New South Wales, Sydney, pp.188-209.

Chatterjee, S. and Price, B. (1977) *Regression Analysis by Example*, Wiley, New York.

Cheng, D.C. and Iglarsh, H.J. (1976) "Principal Component Estimators in Regression Analysis", *Review of Economics and Statistics*, Vol.58 No.2, May, pp.229-34.

Chiang, A.C. (1984) *Fundamental Methods of Mathematical Economics*, 3rd edn, McGraw-Hill, Tokyo.

Christensen, L.R. and Greene, W.H. (1976) "Economies of Scale in U.S. Electric Power Generation", *Journal of Political Economy*, Vol.84 No.4 Part 1, August, pp.655-76.

Clark, Colin (1940) *The Conditions of Economic Progress*, Macmillan, London.

Clarkson, K.W. (1972) "Some Implications of Property Rights in Hospital Management", *Journal of Law and Economics*, Vol.15 No.2, October, pp.363-84.

Cohen, H.A. (1963) "Variations in Cost among Hospitals of Different Sizes", *Southern Economic Journal*, Vol.33, pp.355-66.

Cohen, H.A. (1970) "Hospital Cost Curves with Emphasis on Measuring Patient Care Output" in H.E. Klarman (ed.), *Empirical Studies in Health Economics*, Johns Hopkins Press, Baltimore, pp.279-93.

Cohn, E. (1979) *The Economics of Education*, Ballinger Publishing Company, Massachusetts.

Commission of Inquiry into the Efficiency and Administration of Hospitals (Mr. J.H. Jamison, Chairman) (1981) *Report*, 3 Vols, Australian Government Publishing Service, Canberra.

Committee of Inquiry into Rights of Private Practice in Public Hospitals (Professor D.G. Penington, Chairman) (1984) *Final Report*, Australian Government Publishing Service, Canberra.

Committee on Medical Schools (Professor P.H. Karmel, Chairman) (1973) *Expansion of Medical Education: Report to the Australian Universities Commission*, Australian Government Publishing Service, Canberra.

Commonwealth Committee of Enquiry into Health Insurance (The Hon. Mr Justice J.A. Nimmo, Chairman) (1969) *Report*, Commonwealth Government Printing Office, Canberra.

Commonwealth Grants Commission (1981) *Report on State Tax Sharing Entitlements 1981*, 3 Vols, Australian Government Publishing Service, Canberra.

Commonwealth Grants Commission (1982) *Report on State Tax Sharing and Health Grants 1982*, 2 Vols, Australian Government Publishing Service, Canberra.

Commonwealth Grants Commission (1983) *Equality in Diversity: Fifty Years of the Commonwealth Grants Commission*, Australian Government Publishing Service, Canberra.

Commonwealth Grants Commission (1985) *Report on Tax Sharing Relativities 1985*, 2 Vols, Australian Government Publishing Service, Canberra.

Commonwealth Grants Commission (1988) *Report on General Revenue Grant Relativities 1988*, 2 Vols, Australian Government Publishing Service, Canberra.

Commonwealth Grants Commission (1993) *Report on General Revenue Grant Relativities 1993*, 2 Vols, Australian Government Publishing Service, Canberra.

Conrad, R.F. and Strauss, R.P. (1983) "A Multiple-Output Multiple-Input Model of the Hospital Industry in North Carolina", *Applied Economics*, Vol.15 No.3, June, pp.341-52.

Cooper, M.H. and Culyer, A.J. (eds) (1973) *Health Economics*, Penguin, Harmondsworth.

Cornes, R. (1992) *Duality and Modern Economics*, Cambridge University Press, Cambridge.

Cowing, T.G. and Holtmann, A.G. (1983) "Multiproduct Short-Run Hospital Cost Functions: Empirical Evidence and Policy Implications from Cross-Section Data", *Southern Economic Journal*, Vol.49 No.3, January, pp.637-53.

Cowing, T.G., Holtmann, A.G. and Powers, S. (1983) "Hospital Cost Analysis: A Survey and Evaluation of Recent Studies" in R.M. Scheffler and L.F. Rossiter (eds), *Advances in Health Economics and Health Services Research*, Volume 4, JAI Press, Connecticut, pp.257-303.

Crain, W.M. and Zardkoohi, A. (1978) "A Test of the Property Rights Theory of the Firm: Water Utilities in the U.S.", *Journal of Law and Economics*, Vol.21 No.2, October, pp.395-408.

Croxton, F.E. (1953) *Elementary Statistics with Applications in Medicine and the Biological Sciences*, Dover Publications Inc., New York.

Crum, W.L. (1926) "The Statistical Allocation of Joint Costs", *Journal of the American Statistical Association*, Vol.21 (New Series) No.153, March, pp.9-24.

Cullis, J.G. and West, P.A. (1979) *The Economics of Health*, Martin Robertson, London.

Culyer, A.J. (1978) "Needs, Values and Health Status Measurement" in A.J. Culyer and K.G. Wright (eds), *Economic Aspects of Health Services*, Martin Robertson, London, pp.9-31.

Culyer, A.J. (1980) *The Political Economy of Social Policy*, Martin Robertson, Oxford.

Culyer, A.J. (1990) "Cost Containment in Europe" in Organisation for Economic Co-operation and Development (OECD), *Health Care Systems in Transition: The Search for Efficiency*, OECD Social Policy Studies No.7, OECD, Paris, pp.29-40.

Culyer, A.J. and Drummond, M.F. (1978) "Financing Medical Education—Interrelationships Between Medical School and Teaching Hospital Expenditure" in A.J. Culyer and K.G. Wright (eds), *Economic Aspects of Health Services*, Martin Robertson, London, pp.123-40.

Culyer, A.J., Lavers, R.J. and Williams, A. (1972) "Health Indicators" in A. Schonfield and S. Shaw (eds), *Social Indicators and Social Policy*, Heinemann Educational Books, London, pp.94-118.

Culyer, A.J., Wiseman, J., Drummond, M.F. and West, P.A. (1978) "What Accounts for the Higher Costs of Teaching Hospitals?", *Social and Economic Administration*, Vol.12 No.1, Spring, pp.20-30.

Daniel, W.W. and Terrell, J.C. (1975) *Business Statistics*, Houghton Mifflin Company, Boston.

Davies, D.G. (1971) "The Efficiency of Public versus Private Firms: The Case of Australia's Two Airlines", *Journal of Law and Economics*, Vol.14 No.1, April, pp.149-65.

Davies, D.G. (1977) "Property Rights and Economic Efficiency—The Australian Airlines Revisited", *Journal of Law and Economics*, Vol.20 No.1, April, pp.223-6.

Davies, D.G. (1980) "Property Rights and Efficiency in a Regulated Environment: Reply", *Economic Record*, Vol.56 No.153, June, pp.186-9.

Deeble, J.S. (1965) "An Economic Analysis of Hospital Costs", *Medical Care*, Vol.3 No.3, July-September, pp.138-46.

Deeble, J.S. (1980) "Hospital Costs and Reimbursement Formulae" in P.M. Tatchell (ed.), *Economics and health: Proceedings of the first Australian Conference of Health Economists*, Technical Paper No.3, Health Research Project, Australian National University, Canberra, pp.31-59.

Deeble, J.S. (1983) "Discussion" in P.M. Tatchell (ed.), *Economics and health: 1982 Proceedings of the fourth Australian Conference of Health Economists*, Technical Paper No.7, Health Economics Research Unit, Australian National University, Canberra, pp.320-2.

Denny, M. and Pinto, C. (1978) "An Aggregate Model with Multi-Product Technologies" in M. Fuss and D. McFadden (eds), *Production Economics: A Dual Approach to Theory and Applications*, Volume 2, North-Holland, Amsterdam, pp.249-67.

Dewald, W.G., Thursby, J.G. and Anderson, R.G. (1986) "Replication in Empirical Economics: The Journal of Money, Credit and Banking Project", *American Economic Review*, Vol.76 No.4, September, pp.587-603.

Diewert, W.E. (1971) "An Application of the Shephard Duality Theorem: A Generalised Leontief Production Function", *Journal of Political Economy*, Vol.79 No.3, May/June, pp.481-507.

Diewert, W.E. (1973) "Functional Forms for Profit and Transformation Functions", *Journal of Economic Theory*, Vol.6 No.3, June, pp.284-316.

Diewert, W.E. (1974) "Applications of Duality Theory" in M.D. Intriligator and D.A. Kendrick (eds), *Frontiers of Quantitative Economics*, Volume II, North-Holland, Amsterdam, pp.106-71.

Diewert, W.E. (1982) "Duality Approaches to Microeconomic Theory" in K.J. Arrow and M.D. Intriligator (eds), *Handbook of Mathematical Economics*, Volume II, North-Holland, Amsterdam, pp.535-99.

Dillon, W.R. and Goldstein, M. (1984) *Multivariate Analysis*, Wiley, New York.

Dixon, B.L., Batte, M.T. and Sonka, S.T. (1984) "Random Coefficients Estimation of Average Total Product Costs for Multiproduct Firms", *Journal of Business and Economic Statistics*, Vol.2 No.4, October, pp.360-6.

Doessel, D.P. and Marshall, J.V. (1982) Quality Assessment of Health Care: An Economic Conception, paper presented to the Australian and New Zealand Society for Epidemiology and Research into Community Health/Australian Public Health Association Conference, Christchurch, New Zealand, May.

Doessel, D.P. and Marshall, J.V. (1985) "A Rehabilitation of Health Outcome in Quality Assessment", *Social Science and Medicine*, Vol.21 No.12, pp.1319-28.

Dogramaci, A. and Färe, R. (eds) (1988) *Applications of Modern Production Theory: Efficiency and Productivity*, Kluwer Academic Publishers, Boston.

Donabedian, A. (1969) *A Guide to Medical Care Administration, Volume II: Medical Care Appraisal—Quality and Utilization*, American Public Health Association, Washington D.C.

Dowling, E.T. (1980) *Mathematics for Economists*, Schaum's Outline Series, McGraw-Hill, New York.

Dusansky, R. and Kalman, P.J. (1974) "Toward an Economic Model of the Teaching Hospital", *Journal of Economic Theory*, Vol.7, pp.210-23.

Dutta, M. (1975) *Econometric Methods*, South-Western Publishing Co., Cincinnati.

Ekelund, R.B. and Hulett, J.R. (1973) "Joint Supply, the Taussig-Pigou Controversy and the Competitive Provision of Public Goods", *Journal of Law and Economics*, Vol.16 No.2, October, pp.369-87.

Ellis, R.P. and McGuire, T.G. (1986) "Provider Behavior under Prospective Reimbursement: Cost Sharing and Supply", *Journal of Health Economics*, Vol.5, pp.129-51.

Evans, R.G. (1971) ""Behavioural" Cost Functions for Hospitals", *Canadian Journal Of Economics*, Vol.4 No.2, May, pp.198-215.

Evans, R.G. (1981) "Incomplete Vertical Integration: The Distinctive Structure of the Health-Care Industry" in J. van der Gaag and M. Perlman (eds), *Health, Economics, and Health Economics*, North-Holland, Amsterdam, pp.329-54.

Evans, R.G. and Walker, H.D. (1972) "Information Theory and the Analysis of Hospital Cost Structure", *Canadian Journal of Economics*, Vol.5 No.3, August, pp.398-418.

Färe, R. and Lovell, C.A.K. (1985) *The Measurement of Efficiency of Production*, Kluwer Academic Publishers, Boston.

Farrar, D.E. and Glauber, R.R. (1967) "Multicollinearity in Regression Analysis: The Problem Revisited", *Review of Economics and Statistics*, Vol.49 No.1, February, pp.92-107.

Farrell, M.J. (1957) "The Measurement of Productive Efficiency", *Journal of the Royal Statistical Society*, Series A, Vol.120, pp.253-81.

Feigenbaum, S. and Teeples, R. (1983) "Public versus Private Water Delivery: A Hedonic Cost Approach", *Review of Economics and Statistics*, Vol.65 No.4, November, pp.672-8.

Feldstein, M.S. (1967) *Economic Analysis for Health Service Efficiency*, North-Holland, Amsterdam.

Feldstein, M.S. (1969) "Discussion" in V.R. Fuchs (ed.), *Production and Productivity in the Service Industries*, National Bureau of Economic Research, New York, pp.139-46.

Feldstein, M. (1971) "The Error of Forecast in Econometric Models when the Forecast Period Exogenous Variables are Stochastic", *Econometrica*, Vol.39, pp.55-60.

Feldstein, M.S. and Schuttinga, J. (1977) "Hospital Costs in Massachusetts: A Methodological Study", *Inquiry*, Vol.14 No.1, March, pp.22-31.

Feldstein, P.J. (1983) *Health Care Economics*, 2nd edn, Wiley, New York.

Feldstein, P.J. (1993), *Health Care Economics*, 4th edn, Delmar, New York.

Fetter, R.B., Mills, R.E., Riedel, D.C. and Thompson, J.D. (1977) "The Application of Diagnostic Specific Cost Profiles to Cost and Reimbursement Control in Hospitals", *Journal of Medical Systems*, Vol.1 No.2, pp.137-49.

Fetter, R.B., Riedel, D.C., Thompson, J.D., Mills, R.E., Mross, C.D., Averill, R.F. and Shin, Y. (1979) "Diagnostic-Specific Cost Profiles for Hospital Cost and Reimbursement Control" in G.K. Chacko (ed.), *Health Handbook*, North-Holland, Amsterdam, pp.993-1014.

Fetter, R.B., Shin, Y., Freeman, J.L., Averill, R.F. and Thompson, J.D. (1980) "Case Mix Definition by Diagnosis-Related Groups", *Medical Care*, Vol.18 No.2, February, Supplement.

Finkler, S.A. (1979) "On the Shape of the Hospital Industry Long-Run Average Cost Curve", *Health Services Research*, Vol.14 No.4, Winter, pp.281-9.

Folland, S., Goodman, A.C. and Stano, M. (1993) *The Economics of Health and Health Care*, Macmillan, New York.

Fomby, T.B., Hill, R.C. and Johnson, S.R. (1984) *Advanced Econometric Methods*, Springer-Verlag, New York.

Forsyth, P.J. and Hocking, R.D. (1980) "Property Rights and Efficiency in a Regulated Environment: The Case of Australian Airlines", *Economic Record*, Vol.56 No.153, June, pp.182-5.

Francisco, E.W. (1970) "Analysis of Cost Variations among Short-Term General Hospitals" in H.E. Klarman (ed.), *Empirical Studies in Health Economics*, Johns Hopkins Press, Baltimore, pp.321-32.

Frech, H.E. III and Ginsburg, P.B. (1974) "Optimal Scale in Medical Practice: A Survivor Analysis", *Journal of Business*, Vol.47 No.1, January, pp.23-36.

Frech, H.E. III (1976) "The Property Rights Theory of the Firm: Empirical Results from a Natural Experiment", *Journal of Political Economy*, Vol.84 No.1, February, pp.143-52.

Frick, A.P., Martin, S.G. and Shwartz, M. (1985) "Case-mix and Cost Differences Between Teaching and Nonteaching Hospitals", *Medical Care*, Vol.23 No.4, April, pp.283-95.

Friedman, B. and Pauly, M. (1981) "Cost Functions for a Service Firm with Variable Quality and Stochastic Demand: The Case of Hospitals", *Review of Economics and Statistics*, Vol.63 No.4, November, pp.620-4.

Friedman, B. and Pauly, M. (1983) "A New Approach to Hospital Cost Functions and Some Issues in Revenue Regulation", *Health Care Financing Review*, Vol.4 No.3, March, pp.105-14.

Friedman, M. (1955) "Discussion" in National Bureau of Economic Research, *Business Concentration and Price Policy*, Princeton University Press, Princeton, pp.230-8.

Fuchs, V.R. (1969) "Introduction and Summary" in V.R. Fuchs (ed.), *Production and Productivity in the Service Industries*, National Bureau of Economic Research, New York, pp.1-13.

Fuchs, V.R. (1972) "The Contribution of Health Services to the American Economy" in V.R. Fuchs (ed.), *Essays in the Economics of Health and Medical Care*, National Bureau of Economic Research, New York, pp.3-38.

Fuchs, V.R. (1974) *Who Shall Live?*, Basic Books, New York.

Fuss, M., McFadden, D. and Mundlak, Y. (1978) "A Survey of Functional Forms in the Economic Analysis of Production" in M. Fuss and D. McFadden (eds), *Production Economics: A Dual Approach to Theory and Applications*, Volume 1, North-Holland, Amsterdam, pp.219-68.

Fuss, M. and Waverman, L. (1981) "Regulation and the Multiproduct Firm: The Case of Telecommunications in Canada" in G. Fromm (ed.), *Studies in Public Regulation*, MIT Press, Cambridge, pp.277-313.

Garber, A.M., Fuchs, V.R. and Silverman, J.F. (1984) "Case Mix, Costs, and Outcomes: Differences Between Faculty and Community Services in a University Hospital", *New England Journal of Medicine*, Vol.310, pp.1231-7.

Geary, R.C. and Leser, C.E.V. (1968) "Significance Tests in Multiple Regression", *The American Statistician*, Vol.22, February, pp.20-1.

Glaister, S. (1978) *Mathematical Methods for Economists*, Revised edn, Basil Blackwell, Oxford.

Gold, B. (1981) "Changing Perspectives on Size, Scale, and Returns: An Interpretive Survey", *Journal of Economic Literature*, Vol.19 No.1, March, pp.5-33.

Grannemann, T.W., Brown, R.S. and Pauly, M.V. (1986) "Estimating Hospital Costs: A Multiple-Output Analysis", *Journal of Health Economics*, Vol.5, pp.107-27.

Gravelle, H. and Rees, R. (1992) *Microeconomics*, 2nd edn, Longman, London.

Green, H.A.J. (1964) *Aggregation in Economic Analysis*, Princeton University Press, New Jersey.

Greenberg, E. and Webster, C.E. (1983) *Advanced Econometrics*, Wiley, New York.

Grimaldi, P.L. (1978) "Prospective Reimbursement Rates for Hospitals: Comment", *Quarterly Review of Economics and Business*, Vol.18 No.4, Winter, pp.94-7.

Grimaldi, P.L. and Micheletti, J.A. (1982) "Homogeneity Revisited: the new DRGs", *Journal of American Medical Record Association*, Vol.53 No.4, April, pp.56-70.

Grosskopf, S. and Valdmanis, V. (1987) "Measuring Hospital Performance: A Non-Parametric Approach", *Journal of Health Economics*, Vol.6 No.2, June, pp.89-107.

Hadley, J. (1974) "Research on Health Manpower Productivity: A General Overview" in J. Rafferty (ed.), *Health Manpower and Productivity*, Lexington Books, Massachusetts, pp.143-203.

Hadley, J. (1983) "Teaching and Hospital Costs", *Journal of Health Economics*, Vol.2 No.1, March, pp.75-9.

Haitovsky, Y. (1969) "Multicollinearity in Regression Analysis: Comment", *Review of Economics and Statistics*, Vol.51, November, pp.486-9.

Hall, R.E. (1973) "The Specification of Technology with Several Kinds of Output", *Journal of Political Economy*, Vol.81 No.4, July/August, pp.878-92.

Hanoch, G. (1970) "Homotheticity in Joint Production", *Journal of Economic Theory*, Vol.2 No.4, December, pp.423-6.

Hanoch, G. (1975) "The Elasticity of Scale and the Shape of Average Costs", *American Economic Review*, Vol.65 No.3, June, pp.492-7.

Harbeson, R.W. (1953) "Cost-Finding in Rail Transportation: Some Lessons from American Experience", *The Transport and Communication Review*, Vol.6 No.4, October/December, pp.25-33.

Hardwick, J. (1986) "Hospital Case Mix Standardisation: A Comparison of the Resource Need Index and Information Theory Measures" in J.R.G. Butler and D.P. Doessel (eds), *Economics and Health 1985: Proceedings of the Seventh Australian Conference of Health Economists*, Australian Studies in Health Service Administration No.56, School of Health Administration, University of New South Wales, Sydney, pp.36-63.

Hartunian, N.S., Smart, C.N. and Thompson, M.S. (1981) *The Incidence and Economic Costs of Major Health Impairments*, Lexington Books, Massachusetts.

Hasenkamp, G. (1976a) *Specification and Estimation of Multiple-Output Production Functions*, Springer-Verlag, Berlin.

Hasenkamp, G. (1976b) "A Study of Multiple-Output Production Functions: Klein's Railroad Study Revisited", *Journal of Econometrics*, Vol.4, pp.253-62.

Health Commission of New South Wales (1978) A Regression Model to Predict Hospital Maintenance Expenditure, Report No.78/11, Division of Health Services Research, Health Commission of New South Wales, Sydney, September.

Health Systems International (1984) *The Revised ICD-9-CM Diagnosis Related Groups*, Health Systems International, New Haven.

Hefty, T.R. (1969) "Returns to Scale in Hospitals: A Critical Review of Recent Research", *Health Services Research*, Vol.4 No.4, Winter, pp.267-80.

Henderson, J.M. and Quandt, R.E. (1958) *Microeconomic Theory*, McGraw-Hill, New York.

Hibdon, J.E. (1969) *Price and Welfare Theory*, McGraw-Hill, New York.

Hielscher, L.A. (1983) "Cost Control in Queensland Hospitals" in R.L. Mathews (ed.), *Hospital Funding*, Centre for Research on Federal Financial Relations, Australian National University, Canberra, pp.75-81.

Higham, W.J. and Robb, W.F. (1977) Cost Differences in Queensland Country Hospitals, Health Services Planning and Development Unit, Queensland Department of Health, Brisbane, November.

Hirota, M. and Kuga, K. (1971) "On an Intrinsic Joint Production", *International Economic Review*, Vol.12 No.1, February, pp.87-98.

Hirshleifer, J. (1962) "The Firm's Cost Function: A Successful Reconstruction?", *Journal of Business*, Vol.35 No.3, July, pp.235-55.

Horn, S. (1983) "Measuring Severity of Illness: Comparisons Across Institutions", *American Journal of Public Health*, Vol.73, pp.25-31.

Horn, S.D. and Schumacher, D.N. (1979) "An Analysis of Case Mix Complexity Using Information Theory and Diagnostic Related Grouping", *Medical Care*, Vol.17 No.4, April, pp.382-9.

Horn, S.D. and Sharkey, P.D. (1983) "Measuring Severity of Illness to Predict Patient Resource Use With DRGs", *Inquiry*, Vol.20 No.4, Winter, pp.314-21.

Horn, S.D., Sharkey, P.D. and Bertram, D. (1983) "Measuring Severity of Illness: Homogeneous Case Mix Groups", *Medical Care*, Vol.21 No.1, January, pp.14-25.

Hornbrook, M.C. (1982a) "Hospital Case Mix: Its Definition, Measurement and Use: Part I. The Conceptual Framework", *Medical Care Review*, Vol.39 No.1, Spring, pp.1-43.

Hornbrook, M.C. (1982b) "Hospital Case Mix: Its Definition, Measurement and Use: Part II. Review of Alternative Measures", *Medical Care Review*, Vol.39 No.2, Summer, pp.73-123.

Hornbrook, M.C. and Monheit, A.C. (1985) "The Contribution of Case-Mix Severity to the Hospital Cost-Output Relation", *Inquiry*, Vol.22 No.3, Fall, pp.259-71.

Hosek, J.R. and Palmer, A.R. (1983) "Teaching and Hospital Costs", *Journal of Health Economics*, Vol.2 No.1, March, pp.29-46.

Hospitals and Health Services Commission (1974) *A Report on Hospitals in Australia*, Australian Government Publishing Service, Canberra.

Hsiao, W.C. and Dunn, D.L. (1987) "The Impact of DRG Payment on New Jersey Hospitals", *Inquiry*, Vol.24 No.3, Fall, pp.212-20.

Illich, I. (1975) *Medical Nemesis*, Marion Boyars, London.

Ingbar, M.L. and Taylor, L.D. (1968) *Hospital Costs in Massachusetts*, Harvard University Press, Cambridge.

Intriligator, M.D. (1978) *Econometric Models, Techniques and Applications*, North-Holland, Amsterdam.

Ironmonger, D.S. (1972) *New Commodities and Consumer Behaviour*, Cambridge University Press, Cambridge.

Jenkins, A.W. (1977) A Policy-Oriented Analysis of Hospital Costs, unpublished PhD thesis, University of Western Ontario, Ontario.

Jenkins, A.W. (1980) "Multi-Product Cost Analysis: Service and Case-Type Cost Equations for Ontario Hospitals", *Applied Economics*, Vol.12 No.1, March, pp.103-13.

Johnson, S.C. and Lahiri, K. (1992) "A Panel Data Analysis of Productive Efficiency in Freestanding Health Clinics", *Empirical Economics*, Vol.17 No.1, pp.141-51.

Johnston, J. (1958) "Statistical Cost Functions: A Reappraisal", *Review of Economics and Statistics*, Vol.40, November, pp.339-50.

Johnston, J. (1972) *Econometric Methods*, 2nd edn, McGraw-Hill, London.

Johnston, J. (1984) *Econometric Methods*, 3rd edn, McGraw-Hill, New York.

Jones, K.R. (1985) "Predicting Hospital Charge and Stay Variation", *Medical Care*, Vol.23 No.3, March, pp.220-35.

Joskow, P.L. (1980) "The Effects of Competition and Regulation on Hospital Bed Supply and the Reservation Quality of the Hospital", *Bell Journal of Economics*, Vol.11 No.2, Autumn, pp.421-47.

Judge, K. (1986) "Value for Money in the British Residential Care Industry" in A.J. Culyer and B. Jönsson (eds), *Public and Private Health Services*, Blackwell, Oxford, pp.200-18.

Judge, G.G., Griffiths, W.E., Hill, R.C. and Lee, T. (1980) *The Theory and Practice of Econometrics*, Wiley, New York.

Judge, G.G., Hill, R.C., Griffiths, W.E., Lütkepohl, H. and Lee, T. (1982) *Introduction to the Theory and Practice of Econometrics*, Wiley, New York.

Just, R.E., Zilberman, D. and Hochman, E. (1983) "Estimation of Multicrop Production Functions", *American Journal of Agricultural Economics*, Vol.65 No.4, November, pp.770-80.

Kane, E.J. (1984) "Why Journal Editors Should Encourage the Replication of Applied Econometric Research", *Quarterly Journal of Business and Economics*, Vol.23 No.1, Winter, pp.3-8.

Kaufman, S.L. and Shepard, D.S. (1982) "Costs of Neonatal Intensive Care by Day of Stay", *Inquiry*, Vol.19 No.2, Summer, pp.167-78.

Kay, J.A. and Thompson, D.J. (1986) "Privatisation: A Policy in Search of a Rationale", *Economic Journal*, Vol.96 No.381, March, pp.18-32.

Kennedy, P. (1992) *A Guide to Econometrics*, 3rd edn, The MIT Press, Cambridge..

Kershaw, J.A. (1969) "Productivity in American Schools and Colleges" in M. Blaug (ed.), *Economics of Education 2*, Penguin, Harmondsworth, pp.305-12.

Klarman, H.E. (1965) "Syphilis Control Programs" in R. Dorfman (ed.), *Measuring Benefits of Government Investments*, The Brookings Institution, Washington D.C., pp.367-414.

Klarman, H.E. (1969) "Discussion" in V.R. Fuchs (ed.), *Production and Productivity in the Service Industries*, National Bureau of Economic Research, New York, pp.132-9.

Klastorin, T.D. and Watts, C.A. (1980) "On the Measurement of Hospital Case Mix", *Medical Care*, Vol.18 No.6, June, pp.675-85.

Klein, L.R. (1953) *A Textbook of Econometrics*, Row, Peterson and Company, Illinois.

Klein, L.R. (1962) *An Introduction to Econometrics*, Prentice-Hall, Englewood Cliffs.

Kleinbaum, D.G. and Kupper, L.L. (1978) *Applied Regression Analysis and Other Multivariable Methods*, Duxbury Press, Massachusetts.

Knapp, M. (1986) "The Relative Cost-Effectiveness of Public, Voluntary and Private Providers of Residential Child Care" in A.J. Culyer and B. Jönsson (eds), *Public and Private Health Services*, Blackwell, Oxford, pp.171-99.

Kohli, U. (1983) "Non-joint Technologies", *Review of Economic Studies*, Vol.50 No.1, January, pp.209-19.

Kolsen, H.M. (1966) "The Economics of Electricity Pricing in New South Wales", *Economic Record*, Vol.42 No.100, reprinted in J. Dixon (ed.), *The Public Sector*, Penguin, Harmondsworth, 1972, pp.94-114.

Kolsen, H.M. (1968) *The Economics and Control of Road-Rail Competition*, Sydney University Press, Sydney.

Kolsen, H.M. (1986) "That Privatisation of Public Authority Business Undertakings should be a Policy Objective: The Negative Case" in J.R.G. Butler (ed.), *Current Economic Issues 1986*, Brisbane College of Advanced Education, Brisbane, pp.117-22.

Koutsoyiannis, A. (1977) *Theory of Econometrics*, 2nd edn, Macmillan, London.

Krischer, J.P. (1976) "Indexes of Severity: Underlying Concepts", *Health Services Research*, Vol.11 No.2, Summer, pp.143-57.

Krischer, J.P. (1979) "Indexes of Severity: Conceptual Development", *Health Services Research*, Vol.14 No.1, Spring, pp.56-67.

Laitinen, K. (1980) *A Theory of the Multiproduct Firm*, North-Holland, Amsterdam.

Lancaster, K.J. (1966a) "A New Approach to Consumer Theory", *Journal of Political Economy*, Vol.74 No.2, April, pp.132-57.

Lancaster, K.J. (1966b) "Change and Innovation in the Technology of Consumption", *American Economic Review*, Vol.56 No.2, May, pp.14-23.

Lane, W.R. (1974) "Direct Taxes in Relation to the Division of Fiscal Powers" in R.L. Mathews (ed.), *Intergovernmental Relations in Australia*, Angus and Robertson, Sydney, pp.132-58.

Lau, L.J. (1972) "Profit Functions of Technologies with Multiple Inputs and Outputs", *Review of Economics and Statistics*, Vol.54 No.3, August, pp.281-9.

Lau, L.J. (1978) "Applications of Profit Functions" in M. Fuss and D. McFadden (eds), *Production Economics: A Dual Approach to Theory and Applications*, Volume 1, North-Holland, Amsterdam, pp.133-216.

Lave, J.R. and Lave, L.B. (1970a) "Hospital Cost Functions", *American Economic Review*, Vol.60 No.3, June, pp.379-95.

Lave, J.R. and Lave, L.B. (1970b) "Economic Analysis for Health Service Efficiency: A Review Article", *Applied Economics*, Vol.1 No.4, December, pp.293-305.

Lave, J.R. and Lave, L.B. (1979) "Empirical Studies of Hospital Cost Functions: A Review" in G.K. Chacko (ed.), *Health Handbook*, North-Holland, Amsterdam, pp.957-73.

Lave, J.R., Lave, L.B. and Silverman, L.P. (1972) "Hospital Cost Estimation Controlling for Case-Mix", *Applied Economics*, Vol.4 No.3, September, pp.165-80.

Leamer, E.E. (1983) "Let's Take the Con out of Econometrics", *American Economic Review*, Vol.73 No.1, March, pp.31-43.

Leamer, E.E. (1985) "Sensitivity Analyses Would Help", *American Economic Review*, Vol.75 No.3, June, pp.308-13.

Lee, M.L. and Wallace, R.L. (1973) "Problems in Estimating Multiproduct Cost Functions: An Application to Hospitals", *Western Economic Journal*, Vol.11, September, pp.350-63.

Leigh, J. and McBride, A.J. (1974) "Computing an Index of Relative Hospital Performance from an Inpatient Reporting System" in *Proceedings of the 6th Australian Computer Conference*, pp.119-30.

Leiken, A.M. and Dusansky, R. (1983) "The Impact of Health Insurance on Hospital Costs: A Multi-Equation Econometric Approach", *Atlantic Economic Journal*, Vol.11 No.3, September, pp.79-85.

Lerner, M. (1977) "The Non-Health Services Determinants of Health Levels: Conceptualisation and Public Policy Recommendations", *Medical Care*, Vol.15 No.5, May, Supplement, pp.74-83.

Lipscomb, J., Raskin, I.E. and Eichenholz, J. (1978) "The Use of Marginal Cost Estimates in Hospital Cost Containment Policy" in M. Zubkoff, I.E. Raskin and R.S. Hanft (eds), *Hospital Cost Containment*, Prodist, New York, pp.514-37.

Long, M.F. (1964) "Efficient Use of Hospitals" in S.J. Axelrod (ed.), *The Economics of Health and Medical Care*, University of Michigan, Ann Arbor, pp.211-26.

Long, M.F. and Feldstein, P.J. (1967) "Economics of Hospital Systems: Peak Loads and Regional Coordination", *American Economic Review*, Vol.57 No.2, May, pp.119-29.

Long, M.J., Ament, R.P., Dreachslin, J.L. and Kobrinski, E.J. (1985) "A Reconsideration of Economies of Scale in the Health Care Field", *Health Policy*, Vol.5, pp.25-44.

Lorenz, M.O. (1926) "Discussion", *Journal of the American Statistical Association*, Vol.21 (New Series) No.153, March, pp.25-6.

Mackay, K.R. (1979) "A Comparison of the Relative Efficiency of Australian Domestic Airlines and Foreign Airlines" in Department of Transport, *Domestic Air Transport Policy Review, Volume II: Appendices*, Parliamentary Paper No.148, Australian Government Publishing Service, Canberra, pp.1-62.

Maddala, G.S. (1977) *Econometrics*, McGraw-Hill, Tokyo.

Mann, J.K. and Yett, D.E. (1968) "The Analysis of Hospital Costs: A Review Article", *Journal of Business*, Vol.41 No.2, April, pp.191-202.

Marder, W.D. and Zuckerman, S. (1985) "Competition and Medical Groups: A Survivor Analysis", *Journal of Health Economics*, Vol.4 No.2, June, pp.167-76.

Marshall, A. (1923) *Industry and Trade*, 4th edn, Macmillan, London.

Marshall, J.V. and Mason, C.A. (1984) Financing Health Care and the Australian Health Insurance Experiment, Health Planning Studies No.19, Planning and Development Unit, Department of Health, Queensland, October.

Marshall, J.V. and Robb, W.F. (1984) Inter-State Comparison of Public Hospital Efficiency: Australia 1977/78, Health Planning Studies No.18, Planning and Development Unit, Department of Health, Queensland, June.

Martins, J. (1985) "Discussion" in P.M. Tatchell (ed.), *Economics and Health: 1984 Proceedings of the sixth Australian Conference of Health Economists*, Health Economics Research Unit, Australian National University, Canberra, pp.257-62.

Martz, E. and Ptakowski, R. (1978) "Educational Costs to Hospitalized Patients", *Journal of Medical Education*, Vol.53 No.5, May, pp.383-6.

Massy, W.F. (1965) "Principal Components Regression in Exploratory Statistical Research", *Journal of the American Statistical Association*, Vol.60, March, pp.234-56.

Mathews, R.L. (1979) "Regional Disparities and Fiscal Equalisation in Australia" in *Proceedings of the International Seminar in Public Economics on Regional Aspects of Fiscal Policies*, reprinted in A.N.U. Centre for Research on Federal Financial Relations Reprint Series, No.30.

McAleer, M., Pagan, A.R. and Volker, P.A. (1985) "What Will Take the Con Out of Econometrics?", *American Economic Review*, Vol.75 No.3, June, pp.293-307.

McCallum, B.T. (1970) "Artificial Orthogonalization in Regression Analysis", *Review of Economics and Statistics*, Vol.52 No.1, February, pp.110-13.

McGuire, A. (1985a) "The Theory of the Hospital: A Review of the Models", *Social Science and Medicine*, Vol.20 No.11, pp.1177-84.

McGuire, A. (1985b) Methodological Considerations of Hospital Production and Cost Functions: Relationships to Efficiency, Discussion Paper No.08/85, Health Economics Research Unit, University of Aberdeen.

Meyer, J.R. and Kraft, G. (1961) "The Evaluation of Statistical Costing Techniques as Applied in the Transportation Industry", *American Economic Review*, Vol.51 No.2, May, pp.313-34.

Mill, J.S. (1909) *Principles of Political Economy*, Longmans, Green and Company, London.

Mills, R., Fetter, R.B., Riedel, D.C. and Averill, R. (1976) "AUTOGRP: An Interactive Computer System for the Analysis of Health Care Data", *Medical Care*, Vol.14 No.7, July, pp.603-15.

Mittelstaedt, R.A. and Zorn, T.S. (1984) "Econometric Replication: Lessons from the Experimental Sciences", *Quarterly Journal of Business and Economics*, Vol.23 No.1, Winter, pp.9-15.

Morrison, D.F. (1976) *Multivariate Statistical Methods*, 2nd edn, McGraw-Hill, Tokyo.

Morrison, D.G. (1969) "On the Interpretation of Discriminant Analysis", *Journal of Marketing Research*, Vol.6 No.2, May, pp.156-63.

Mueller, D.C. (1989) *Public Choice II*, Cambridge University Press, Cambridge.

Mundlak, Y. (1963) "Specification and Estimation of Multiproduct Production Functions", *Journal of Farm Economics*, Vol.45 No.2, May, pp.433-43.

Mundlak, Y. and Razin, A. (1971) "On Multistage Multiproduct Production Functions", *American Journal of Agricultural Economics*, Vol.53 No.3, August, pp.491-9.

Needham, D. (1978) *The Economics of Industrial Structure Conduct and Performance*, Holt, Rinehart and Winston, London.

Nerlove, M. (1965) *Estimation and Identification of Cobb-Douglas Production Functions*, Rand McNally, Chicago.

Newhouse, J.P. (1971) Is Collinearity a Problem?, P-4588, The Rand Corporation, Santa Monica, March.

Nicholson, C.L. (1983) "Measurement of Hospital Costliness" in P.M. Tatchell (ed.), *Economics and health: 1982 Proceedings of the fourth Australian Conference of Health Economists*, Technical Paper No.7, Health Economics Research Unit, Australian National University, Canberra, pp.234-76.

Nicholson, W. (1985) *Microeconomic Theory*, The Dryden Press, Chicago.

Niskanen, W.A. (1971) *Bureaucracy and Representative Government*, Aldine-Atherton, Chicago.

O'Neill, B., Zador, P. and Baker, S.P. (1979) "Indexes of Severity: Underlying Concepts—A Reply", *Health Services Research*, Vol.14 No.1, Spring, pp.68-76.

Oates, W.E. (1972) *Fiscal Federalism*, Harcourt Brace Jovanovich, New York.

Ontario Hospital Services Commission (1972a) Ontario Length of Stay Tables 1969-1971, Ontario Hospital Services Commission, Toronto, January.

Ontario Hospital Services Commission (1972b) The Relative Stay Index Report, 1971 Edition, Ontario Hospital Services Commission, Toronto, February.

Organisation for Economic Co-operation and Development (OECD) (1993) *OECD Health Data: A Software Package for the International Comparison of Health Care Systems*, Version 1.5, OECD, Paris.

Oster, G., Colditz, G.A. and Kelly, N.L. (1984) *The Economic Costs of Smoking and the Benefits of Quitting*, Lexington Books, Massachusetts.

Palmer, G.R. and Short, S.D. (1994) *Health Care and Public Policy: An Australian Analysis*, 2nd edn, Macmillan, Melbourne.

Palmer, G.R. (1986) "The Economics and Financing of Hospitals in Australia", paper presented to the Eighth Australian Conference of Health Economists, Australian National University, Canberra, September.

Palmer, G. and Wood, T. (1984) "Diagnosis Related Groups: Recent Developments and their Adaptation and Application in Australia", *Australian Health Review*, Vol.7 No.2, pp.67-80.

Panzar, J.C. and Willig, R.D. (1981) "Economies of Scope", *American Economic Review*, Vol.71 No.2, May, pp.268-72.

Pauly, M.V. (1968) "The Economics of Moral Hazard: Comment", *American Economic Review*, Vol.58 No.3, June, pp.531-7.

Pauly, M.V. (1978) "Medical Staff Characteristics and Hospital Costs", *Journal of Human Resources*, Vol.13, Supplement, pp.77-111.

Pauly, M. (1983) "More on Moral Hazard", *Journal of Health Economics*, Vol.2 No.1, March, pp.81-5.

Pfaffenberger, R.C. and Patterson, J.H. (1977) *Statistical Methods for Business and Economics*, Irwin, Illinois.

Pointer, D.D. and Ross, M.B. (1984) "DRGs kick off a whole new game: hospitals need new tactics to win", *Modern Healthcare*, 15 February, pp.109-12.

Queensland Department of Health (1980) The Relative Stay Index: Queensland, Planning and Development Unit, Division of Research and Planning, Queensland Department of Health, Brisbane, August.

Queensland Department of Health (1982) Submission to Senate Select Committee on Private Hospitals and Nursing Homes in Australia, Queensland Department of Health, Brisbane, April.

Reder, M.W. (1965) "Some Problems in the Economics of Hospitals", *American Economic Review*, Vol.55 No.2, May, pp.472-80.

Reder, M.W. (1969) "Some Problems in the Measurement of Productivity in the Medical Care Industry" in V.R. Fuchs (ed.), *Production and Productivity in the Service Industries*, National Bureau of Economic Research, New York, pp.95-131.

Renn, S.C., Schramm, C.J., Watt, J.M. and Derzon, R.A. (1985) "The Effects of Ownership and System Affiliation on the Economic Performance of Hospitals", *Inquiry*, Vol.22 No.3, Fall, pp.219-36.

Richardson, J. and Wallace, R. (1983) "Health Economics" in F.H. Gruen (ed.), *Surveys of Australian Economics*, Volume 3, George Allen & Unwin, Sydney, pp.124-86.

Ro, K. (1969) "Patient Characteristics, Hospital Characteristics, and Hospital Use", *Medical Care*, Vol.7, July-August, pp.295-312.

Ro, K. and Auster, R. (1969) "An Output Approach to Incentive Reimbursement for Hospitals", *Health Services Research*, Vol.4 No.3, Fall, pp.177-87.

Robinson, J.C. and Luft, H.S. (1985) "The Impact of Hospital Market Structure on Patient Volume, Average Length of Stay, and the Cost of Care", *Journal of Health Economics*, Vol.4, pp.333-56.

Russell, L.B. (1979) *Technology in Hospitals*, The Brookings Institution, Washington.

Russell, L.B. and Burke, C.S. (1975) *Technological Diffusion in the Hospital Sector*, National Planning Association, Chicago.

Samuelson, P.A. (1966) "The Fundamental Singularity Theorem for Non-Joint Production", *International Economic Review*, Vol.7 No.1, January, pp.34-41.

Sanderson, K.G. (1983) "Hospital Cost Problems in Western Australia" in R.L. Mathews (ed.), *Hospital Funding*, Centre for Research on Federal Financial Relations, Australian National University, Canberra, pp.82-105.

Savas, E.S. (1980) "Comparative Costs of Public and Private Enterprise in a Municipal Service" in W.J. Baumol (ed.), *Public and Private Enterprise in a Mixed Economy*, Macmillan, London, pp.253-69.

Schapper, P.R. (1984) An Economic Analysis of Hospital and Medical Services, unpublished PhD thesis, University of Western Australia, Western Australia.

Schmidt, P. (1986) "Frontier Production Functions", *Econometric Reviews*, Vol.4 No.2, pp.289-328.

Schroeder, S.A. and O'Leary, D.S. (1977) "Differences in Laboratory Use and Length of Stay between University and Community Hospitals", *Journal of Medical Education*, Vol.52 No.5, May, pp.418-20.

Schuerman, J.R. (1983) *Multivariate Analysis in the Human Services*, Kluwer-Nijhoff Publishing, Boston.

Schuttinga, J.A. (1976) Three Empirical Essays on the Economics of Hospital Care, unpublished PhD thesis, Massachusetts Institute of Technology, Massachusetts.

Scitovsky, A.A. (1964) "An Index of the Cost of Medical Care—A Proposed New Approach" in S.J. Axelrod (ed.), *The Economics of Health and Medical Care*, University of Michigan Press, Michigan, pp.128-47.

Scitovsky, A.A. (1967) "Changes in the Costs of Treatment of Selected Illnesses, 1951-1965", *American Economic Review*, Vol.57 No.5, December, pp.1182-95.

Scitovsky, A.A. (1985) "Changes in the Costs of Treatment of Selected Illnesses, 1971-1981", *Medical Care*, Vol.23 No.12, December, pp.1345-57.

Scotton, R.B. (1974) *Medical Care in Australia: An Economic Diagnosis*, Sun Books, Melbourne.

Seiford, L.M. and Thrall, R.M. (1990) "Recent Developments in DEA: The Mathematical Programming Approach to Frontier Analysis", *Journal of Econometrics*, Vol.46, pp.7-38.

Senate Select Committee on Medical and Hospital Costs (Senator Dame Ivy Wedgwood, Chairman) (1969) *Report*, Commonwealth Government Printing Office, Canberra.

Senate Select Committee on Medical and Hospital Costs (Senator Dame Ivy Wedgwood, Chairman) (1970) *Part 1. Report*, Commonwealth Government Printing Office, Canberra.

Sharkey, W.W. (1982) *The Theory of Natural Monopoly*, Cambridge University Press, Massachusetts.

Shephard, R.W. (1970) *Theory of Cost and Production Functions*, Princeton University Press, New Jersey.

Shepherd, W.G. (1967) "What does the Survivor Technique show about Economies of Scale?", *Southern Economic Journal*, Vol.34 No.1, July, pp.113-22.

Shepherd, W.G. (1979) *The Economics of Industrial Organization*, Prentice-Hall, New Jersey.

Sloan, F.A., Morrisey, M.A. and Valvona, J. (1988) "Effects of the Medicare Prospective Payment System on Hospital Cost Containment: An Early Appraisal", *Milbank Memorial Fund Quarterly*, Vol.66 No.2, pp.191-220.

Sloan, F.A. and Becker, E.R. (1981) "Internal Organization of Hospitals and Hospital Costs", *Inquiry*, Vol.18 No.3, Fall, pp.224-39.

Sloan, F.A., Feldman, R.D. and Steinwald, A.B. (1983) "Effects of Teaching on Hospital Costs", *Journal of Health Economics*, Vol.2 No.1, March, pp.1-28.

Sloan, F.A. and Steinwald, B. (1980) *Insurance Regulation and Hospital Costs*, D.C. Heath and Co., Massachusetts.

Smith, C.A. (1955) "Survey of the Empirical Evidence on Economies of Scale" in National Bureau of Economic Research, *Business Concentration and Price Policy*, Princeton University Press, Princeton, pp.213-30.

Solberg, E.J. (1982) *Intermediate Microeconomics*, Business Publications Inc., Texas.

Spann, R.M. (1977) "Public versus Private Provision of Governmental Services" in T.E. Borcherding (ed.), *Budgets and Bureaucrats: The Sources of Government Growth*, Duke University Press, North Carolina, pp.71-89.

Srivastava, M.S. and Carter, E.M. (1983) *An Introduction to Applied Multivariate Statistics*, North-Holland, Amsterdam.

Steinwald, B. and Neuhauser, D. (1970) "The Role of the Proprietary Hospital", *Law and Contemporary Problems*, Vol.35 No.4, Autumn, pp.817-38.

Stewart, J. (1976) *Understanding Econometrics*, Hutchinson, London.

Stigler, G.J. (1958) "The Economies of Scale", *Journal of Law and Economics*, Vol.1, October, pp.54-71.

Stigler, G.J. (1966) *The Theory of Price*, 3rd edn, Macmillan, London.

Stopher, P.R. and Meyburg, A.H. (1979) *Survey Sampling and Multivariate Analysis for Social Scientists and Engineers*, D.C. Heath and Co., Massachusetts.

Tatchell, P.M. (1977) An Economic Analysis of Hospital Costs in New Zealand, unpublished PhD thesis, University of Waikato, New Zealand.

Tatchell, P.M. (1980) *Measuring Hospital Output: A Review*, Technical Paper No.2, Health Research Project, Australian National University, Canberra.

Tatchell P.M. (1983) "Measuring Hospital Output: A Review of the Service Mix and Case Mix Approaches", *Social Science and Medicine*, Vol.17 No.13, pp.871-83.

Theil, H. (1967) *Economics and Information Theory*, North-Holland, Amsterdam.

Theil, H. (1971) *Principles of Econometrics*, Wiley, New York.

Thompson, J.D., Averill, R.F. and Fetter, R.B. (1979) "Planning, Budgeting, and Controlling —One Look at the Future: Case-Mix Cost Accounting", *Health Services Research*, Vol.14 No.2, Summer, pp.111-25.

Thompson, J.D., Fetter, R.B., McIntosh, C.S. and Pelletier, R.J. (1963) "Predicting Requirements for Maternity Facilities", Hospitals: *Journal of the American Hospital Association*, Vol.37, 16 February, pp.45-9,132.

Tucker, K.A. (1977) "The Nature and Size of the Service Sector" in K.A. Tucker (ed.), *Economics of the Australian Service Sector*, Croom Helm, London, pp.13-52.

Vladeck, B.C. (1984) "Medicare Hospital Payment by Diagnosis Related Groups", *Annals of Internal Medicine*, Vol.100 No.4, April, pp.576-91.

Wagstaff, A. (1989) "Estimating Efficiency in the Hospital Sector: A Comparison of Three Statistical Cost Frontier Models", *Applied Economics*, Vol.21, pp.659-72.

Wallace, R.H. (1983) "God, Man and the Universe: A Brief Note" in R.L. Mathews (ed.), *Hospital Funding*, Centre for Research on Federal Financial Relations, Australian National University, Canberra, pp.124-30.

Walsh, C. (1989) "Fiscal Equalisation and Allocative Efficiency" in C. Walsh (ed.) *Fiscal Equalisation, Allocative Efficiency and State Business Undertakings: The Commonwealth Grants Commission 1988 Report on Relativities*, Centre for Research on Federal Financial Relations, Australian National University, Canberra, pp.1-11.

Walters, A.A. (1960), "Expectations and the Regression Fallacy in Estimating Cost Functions", *Review of Economics and Statistics*, Vol.42, pp.210-15.

Walters, A.A. (1963) "Production and Cost Functions: An Econometric Survey", *Econometrica*, Vol.31 No.1-2, January-April, pp.1-66.

Watts, C.A. and Klastorin, T.D. (1980) "The Impact of Case-Mix on Hospital Cost: A Comparative Analysis", *Inquiry*, Vol.17 No.4, Winter, pp.357-67.

Weisbrod, B.A. (1965) "Some Problems of Pricing and Resource Allocation in a Non-Profit Industry—The Hospitals", *Journal of Business*, Vol.38 No.1, January, pp.18-28.

Weiss, L.W. (1971) "Quantitative Studies of Industrial Organization" in M.D. Intriligator (ed.), *Frontiers of Quantitative Economics*, North-Holland, Amsterdam, pp.362-403.

Wiles, P.J.D. (1961) *Price, Cost and Output*, Basil Blackwell, Oxford.

Willan, A.R. and Watts, D.G. (1978) "Meaningful Multicollinearity Measures", *Technometrics*, Vol.20 No.4, November, pp.407-12.

Williams, S.V., Finkler, S.A., Murphy, C.M. and Eisenberg, J.M. (1982) "Improved Cost Allocation in Case-Mix Accounting", *Medical Care*, Vol.20 No.5, May, pp.450-9.

Winch, D.M. (1971) *Analytical Welfare Economics*, Penguin, Harmondsworth.

World Health Organization (1967) *Manual of the International Statistical Classification of Diseases, Injuries, and Causes of Death*, Eighth Revision, 2 Vols, World Health Organization, Geneva.

World Health Organization (1977) *Manual of the International Statistical Classification of Diseases, Injuries, and Causes of Death*, Ninth Revision, 2 Vols, HMSO, London.

Worthington, P.N. (1977) "Prospective Reimbursement Rates for Hospitals—by Unit of Services Versus Type of Case", *Quarterly Review of Economics and Business*, Vol.17 No.3, Autumn, pp.65-72.

Worthington, P.N. (1978) "Prospective Reimbursement Rates for Hospitals: Rejoinder", *Quarterly Review of Economics and Business*, Vol.18 No.4, Winter, pp.97-8.

Wright, K.G. (1978) "Output Measurement in Practice" in A.J. Culyer and K.G. Wright (eds), *Economic Aspects of Health Services*, Martin Robertson, London, pp.46-64.

Young, H.P. (ed.) (1985) *Cost Allocation: Methods, Principles, Applications*, North-Holland, Amsterdam.

INDEX OF NAMES

INDEX OF SUBJECTS

Printed in the United States
29011LVS00002B/6